■ *God of Many Names*

For Gerald, in friendship,
for — children

Athens, Oct 30, 1994

GOD OF MANY NAMES

Play, Poetry, and Power in Hellenic Thought from Homer

to Aristotle ■ *Mihai I. Spariosu*

DUKE UNIVERSITY PRESS ■ *Durham and London*

© 1991 Duke University Press. All rights reserved.
Printed in the United States of America on acid-free paper ∞
Library of Congress Cataloging-in-Publication Data appear
on the last page of this book.

For my parents, Ana and Cornel, in memoriam.

■ Contents

■ Preface

■ This work is primarily addressed to contemporary theorists, historians of ideas, aestheticians, philosophers, literary critics, and play researchers. Although my study draws liberally on past and recent classical scholarship, it deals with questions that go beyond the field of classics, directly concerning and affecting the humanities in general. What is the relationship between poetry, ethics, and politics? What is the nature of the interplay between art, culture, and power? Why has literary or fictional discourse been so often marginalized in the history of Western thought? How can literature contribute to the creation of new ethical and cultural values? These are some of the crucial issues in contemporary literary theory and criticism that I attempt to reexamine here by retracing their beginnings in Hellenic culture.

Like other students of modern thought, I had to wrestle with countless Protean notions inherited from our near and distant past, such as nature, culture, reason, irrationality, Being, Becoming, reality, illusion, play, imitation, power, competition, necessity, chance, and even philosophy, religion, poetry, drama, literature, aesthetics, ethics, and more. At first sight these notions, so worn with use, seemed within easy grasp, but then kept slipping through the fingers. If caught at last, they would instantly turn into a tangled mess, especially upon attempts to weave them into a historical fabric. Perhaps I could manage after all, I felt, if I first unraveled their threads all the way to Greek Antiquity. That so many before me seemed to have lost their bearings only made the journey more pressing. I was first led, of course, to Plato and Aristotle, but there I found matters no less slippery and tangled, for these philosophers required some unraveling of their own. I was led further back, to the oracular Presocratics and the no less enigmatic tragic and comic poets, to playful Homer and serious Hesiod, and then to the fabulous beginnings of the Hellenic world, where I plunged into shrouded depths of silence, only to come up again for fear of monsters. Back to the present, and perhaps a little more enlightened than at the outset, I found that I had never left in the first place (which was, I suppose, part of my enlightenment). In reading ancient texts from a modern perspective I simply followed an age-old hermeneutical principle, consciously or unconsciously adopted by classical scholars as well, and perceptively summed up by Friedrich Schlegel: "Jeder hat noch in den Alten gefunden, was er brauchte und wünschte; vorzüglich sich selbst" ("Each man has found already in the ancients what he needed and desired, especially himself").

I hope, however, that my account à rebours of this journey into classics will be of some use not only to the nonspecialists but also to the specialists, without whom my travels would have been impossible. The winds of change are beginning to sweep through the classical field, where new methodologies are heatedly debated and old issues, newly reopened.[1] Perhaps I have in some measure helped, if not to put these issues to rest, at least to give them a different orientation.

Given its modern viewpoint, this book can best be read in conjunction with Dionysus Reborn: Play and the Aesthetic Dimension in Modern Philosophical and Scientific Discourse (Ithaca, N.Y., 1989); the book is part of a larger cultural historical project that attempts to define the relationship of literature to other modes of discourse in Western thought by focusing on the notions of play, mimesis, and power, which have, ever since Antiquity, occupied a central place for Western thinkers. In Dionysus Reborn I start from the premise that Western communities, modern and ancient, largely share a mentality of power that, for descriptive purposes, can be divided into prerational and rational. This division, for me, signifies neither an evolutionary movement nor a hidden value judgment; rather, it describes the various immediate or mediated, concrete or abstract, physical or metaphysical forms that a Nietzschean will to power has assumed in the process of shaping the Western world.[2] In the present book, my basic

1. For a short but illuminating review of the impact of contemporary theory on the Anglo-American classical field, see George Kennedy, "Brief Mention," AJP 116 (1989): 492–98.

2. For a full discussion of Nietzsche's concept of Wille zur Macht, see Mihai I. Spariosu, Dionysus Reborn (Ithaca, N.Y., 1989), 68–99. For an elaboration on Nietzsche's idea of power as becoming increasingly mediated, representational, or symbolic in the course of the development of a human community, see Helmuth Plessner, Gesammelte Schriften, 10 vols. (Frankfurt, 1980–85), esp. vol. 5, Macht und menschliche Natur; and André Leroi-Gourhan, Le geste et la parole, 2 vols. (Paris, 1964–65). I question Nietzsche's notion of

premise remains the same, but I have modified my terms in order to take into account the linguistic and cultural context that is specifically Hellenic. I have divided the Hellenic mentality of power into "archaic" and "median," thus both acknowledging and revising the traditional distinction between archaic and classical Greece. As far as Hellenic thought is concerned, I have distinguished it from modern rational thought by calling it *logo-rational*, and from modern prerational thought by calling it *proto-logo-rational*. I apply the second term mostly to some of the Presocratics in order to distinguish their particular brand of archaic thought from the Homeric or heroic one, in which the word *logos* is absent (see chapter 2). My assumption has been that in archaic Greece, a proto-logo-rational mode of thought has its origin in an aristocratic, warlike mentality that transpires especially in the Homeric epic, but that, later on, can in principle be adopted by any individual or social group in a given community. In turn, a logo-rational mode of thought betokens a median mentality that finds initial expression in traditional gnomic poetry, for example in Hesiod and some of the Seven Sages (but also in Homer), as well as in such Delphic injunctions as "nothing in excess," "measure is best," and "know thy limits"; this mode of thought and behavior later becomes associated mainly with what we moderns call the "middle class," but can equally be adopted by other individuals or social groups, including the aristocracy. Both archaic and median values appear on record in Greece from the earliest historical times, and therefore the question of a shift from one kind of mentality to another is not an evolutionary one, but one of cultural emphasis. Although the archaic mentality seems to dominate the beginnings of a certain community, settlement, or city, it gradually recedes into the background and allows its counterpart to become more visible. For example, the doctrine of the so-called golden mean can be traced back directly to the attempts of a logo-rational thought to temper the violent excesses of a warlike, archaic mentality. Hellenic logo-rationality, then, should not be confused with modern rationalism (and even less with modern logocentrism) as developed by Bacon, Descartes, Newton, Leibniz, Kant, and others. The latter kind of rationality can itself become extreme or unreasonable, for instance in some dogmatic forms of Cartesianism and scientific positivism in the modern age.

The five chapters of my book investigate the interplay of the archaic and the median mentalities in several key Hellenic texts, including the *Iliad*, the *Odyssey*, Hesiod's *Theogony* and *Works and Days*, some Presocratic

power as an existential first principle in "Nietzsche's *Genealogy of Morals: A Reassessment*," in *The Wreath of Wild Olive: Essays on Play, Literature, and Culture* (forthcoming).

fragments, Euripides' *Bacchae* and Aristophanes' *The Frogs*, Plato's *Republic* and *Laws*, and Aristotle's *Poetics* and *Politics*. A warlike mode of thought and behavior seems to loom large in the Homeric and Hesiodic worlds, but the compositions that bring these worlds into being appear, in turn, to promote a median mentality. The Homeric and Hesiodic texts can thus be seen as the product of a partial shift in emphasis from archaic to median values, a shift that also seems to leave abundant traces in the Presocratic fragments and Greek drama. It is only through such philosophers as Xenophanes, Parmenides, Plato, and Aristotle that a median mentality, accompanied by a logo-rational mode of thought, gains a strong foothold in Hellenic letters (but not necessarily in most Hellenic communities) and the foundations are laid for "modern" ethics and metaphysics.

Yet my study also shows that the shift from an archaic to a median mentality in Hellenic thought (or in the Hellenic world in general, notorious for its unwieldy heterogeneity) is by no means complete or irreversible. Even when archaic values and beliefs become submerged, they can easily resurface, especially during massive migrations, invasions, wars, revolutions, and other kinds of social and cultural upheaval. The relation between the archaic and the median mentalities can be understood in terms of Freud's theory of the coexistence of two stages in what he calls "mental evolution." According to Freud, "every earlier stage of [mental] development persists alongside the later stage which has developed from it. . . . The earlier stage may not have manifested itself for years, but nonetheless it is so far present that it may at any time again become the mode of expression of the forces in the mind, and that exclusively, as though all later developments had been annulled, undone."[3] Unlike Freud's, however, my model is explicitly nonevolutionary, and its reversible nature derives from the fact that both of the mentalities it describes are power-oriented. Indeed, once these mentalities come into being, they wage a constant battle, and it is largely this battle that accounts for both the general orientation of a specific cultural paradigm and the mechanism of change from one cultural paradigm to another.

Play, which along with power is a main theme in this book, may well be one of those phenomena that ultimately elude power and point to an anarchical, nonviolent kind of mentality which, from the perspective of Western history, seems to be on the order of Utopia. But play in this sense appears to have had a rather limited place in the Hellenic (and the

3. Sigmund Freud, "Reflections upon War and Death," in Ph. Rieff, ed., *Character and Culture* (New York, 1963), 118–19. For a detailed discussion of Freud's cultural theory and its relation to play, see Spariosu, *Dionysus Reborn*, 176–85.

Western) world, and the history which I have attempted to trace here is that of play as an instrument of power. Moreover, even the most cursory look at the history of play in Hellenic thought will show that this thought operates not with one but with several ludic notions, which in turn seem to be direct products of either an archaic or a median mentality. The first two chapters, "The Hawk and the Nightingale: Play, Power, and Poetry in Homer and Hesiod" and "*Agōnes Logōn*: Power and Play in Presocratic Thought," examine, on the one hand, the shifting relation between play and power in archaic and classical thought and, on the other hand, the genealogy and interrelation of several archaic and median notions of play, such as agon, chance, necessity, play as freedom, mimicry, and simulation (in the sense of pretense, role-playing, and an *as if* cognitive approach). Some of these notions are not commonly perceived as ludic, and it has been my task here, as in *Dionysus Reborn*, to show in what sense and to what extent they belong in that category.

The problem is compounded by the fact that there is no single Greek word which covers all the aspects of the ludic activity in the Hellenic world, and the conceptualization of this activity most likely took place, as in the case of many other Greek abstract notions, some time during the fifth century B.C., with the development of a logo-rational, philosophical vocabulary.[4] Yet it would be unsafe to conclude that certain activities are not present in a culture just because apparently there are no words that fully describe them or because these activities are not conceptualized. Indeed, attempts at conceptualization appear precisely at the moment when implicit governing cultural assumptions become problematic, that is, when they are no longer automatically accepted and require (re)definition. In studying the Hellenic notions of play, therefore, one needs to look beyond such obvious words as *paidia* and *paignion* and take into consideration terms like *agōn*, *athlos*, *eris*, *tuchē*, *anankē*, *charmē*, *scholē*, *diagōgē*, and *paideia*. Finally, *mimēsis* should be accorded a central place in any examination of play in Hellenic culture, and I have attempted, in the first two

4. For relevant discussions of the semantic shift from concrete to abstract language in ancient Greece, see, among many others, Bruno Snell, *The Discovery of the Mind: The Greek Origins of European Thought*, English trans. (Cambridge, Mass., 1950); Kurt von Fritz, "*Nous, Noein*, and Their Derivatives in Presocratic Philosophy" (1945–46), rptd. in A. P. D. Mourelatos, ed., *The Pre-Socratics* (New York, 1974); and Richard B. Onians, *The Origins of European Thought: About the Body, the Mind, the Soul, the World, Time, and Fate* (Cambridge, 1951), hereafter cited as Onians, *OET*. A recent phenomenological analysis of the concrete, performative character of archaic language can be found in Raymond A. Prier, *Thauma Idesthai: The Phenomenology of Sight and Appearance in Archaic Greek* (Tallahassee, Fla., 1989).

chapters as well as throughout the book, to trace the intricate relationship between play, power, and mimesis, showing that this latter notion acquires such great importance in the classical period precisely because it hides beneath it an archaic, Dionysian experience of play and power. Here, as in my previous book, the ludic figure of Dionysus or Sophocles' "god of many names" looms large (see especially chapter 3) and stands for the conflictive, double nature of Western humans and their play: gentle, reasonable, and peace-loving on the one hand, and competitive, intractable, and warmongering on the other.

A third theme of my study concerns poetry as a major form of play (and mimesis), viewed in relation to other cultural phenomena. The shift in emphasis from an archaic to a median mentality seems also to bring about the split of the holistic, mythopoeic language of archaic Greece (still traceable in epic and lyrical poetry, in some Presocratic fragments, and in the choral parts of tragedy) into several autonomous discursive stretches. These stretches later develop into fields and disciplines, including what we moderns call philosophy, science, literature, theology, jurisprudence, history, rhetoric, and so forth. From the outset, these fields or disciplines (in all the senses of that term) engage in a contest for cultural authority, and the contest that interests us most in the present context is that between philosophy and poetry. The temporary victory of the median values in Hellenic thought also means the temporary victory of the philosophical-scientific discourse over poetry and myth, which still appear to promote archaic, warlike values because these values are woven into their very fabric. Philosophers such as Plato and Aristotle not only convert the violent and arbitrary play of Becoming into the rational and orderly play of Being, but also turn heroic and tragic poetry into a nonserious, simulative, and mendacious discourse, subordinating it to the serious, truthful, and moral discourse of philosophy. The last two chapters, "Plato and the Birth of Philosophy from the Spirit of Poetry" and "Aristotle: Poetics, Politics, and Play," in addition to further examining the transformations that a median mentality brings to the relationship between play, mimesis, and power, focus largely on philosophy's quarrel with poetry and the cultural stakes that this quarrel involves. On the other hand, chapter 3, "Masks of Dionysus: The *Bacchae* and *The Frogs*," which occupies the middle position in the book, attempts to show how poetry as play, specifically Greek drama at the end of its development, begins the process of turning away from an agonistic mentality by situating itself in a no man's land and questioning both the archaic and the median values of Hellenic culture.

Finally, a word about method might be necessary in a book that makes such broad claims as mine does. As in *Dionysus Reborn*, I attempt to support these claims with close readings of some of the most influential works in Western culture, combining cultural historical considerations with relatively extensive textual analysis. Nevertheless I am fully aware that the historical record upon which I have based my generalizations is often scant and ambiguous and, therefore, can equally well substantiate other views. But even though my understanding of the ancients must at best remain tentative and partial, I hope that it will be perceived as generally empathic, and often sympathetic. This understanding is inevitably shaped by present-day intellectual and ethical concerns, and therefore I cannot avoid the hermeneutical circle any more than any of my contemporaries can: we all find in the ancients what we need and desire, mostly ourselves.

A methodological question related to that of historical interpretation is the question of the anthropological status of literature. Many of the texts upon which I have based my cultural historical considerations are of a literary nature (including Plato's dialogues), and thus the question arises as to the relation between human history and human imagination. Not only the thinkers who affirm, but also those who deny the factual basis of literary texts start from a rationalist concept of literature as imitation or representation of (historical) reality. They operate, moreover, with a positivistic notion of reality that favors pure facticity. But the notion of reality can comprise many nonfactual elements, including the imaginary or possible worlds projected by, say, literary works. My study therefore assumes that literary works rarely imitate but often respond to and modify, or even produce, reality. Granted that it is often impossible to sort out fact from fiction in dealing with a literary work, this sorting operation is of only secondary importance to my historical interpretive method, because for me fictional and real objects constitute equally significant anthropological evidence. The main questions I wish to address are: What kinds of mentality are present in a given culture, whether in factual form (archaeological finds, stone inscriptions, written documents, and so on) or imaginary form (oral traditions, art works, and so forth)? What are the individual features of these mentalities? And what are the conditions under which a certain mentality can change? My basic assumption is that whatever appears in the human imagination *can* become reality, even though only certain historical avenues (or modes of thought and behavior) are at any given moment accessible to certain communities, depending on their imaginative choices. This does not mean, of course, that a certain community cannot eventually change its historical path, if it so chooses.

It is in this imaginative spirit that one should also understand my division of the Hellenic mentality into archaic and median, a heuristic model that admittedly runs counter to the positivistic historical method. But one should consider what this model can do, rather than what it cannot. It allows us, for example, to restore a certain balance between those thinkers who, like Nietzsche, emphasize the Dionysian element in Hellenic culture and those who, like many contemporary Anglo-American classicists, emphasize its so-called Apolline element (although not in a Nietzschean but in a rationalist sense). My model thus bears a certain family resemblance to Nietzsche's dichotomy of Dionysian and Apolline, but it also attempts to go beyond this dichotomy. As I have already pointed out, my concern, like Nietzsche's, is with the various cultural transformations of power in the Western world. What Nietzsche calls "Dionysian" and "Apolline" and I call "archaic" and "median" are two faces of the same mentality of power, with one engaging the other in a ceaseless contest. For me, however, power does not have the ontological primacy or supreme existential value that it has for Nietzsche, nor do I long for a return to an archaic or Dionysian dispensation, as Nietzsche does. Power, for me, is a man-made, historical principle rather than an inevitable, "natural" phenomenon. Unlike Nietzsche and his heirs (such as Freud, Heidegger, Fink, Plessner, Foucault, Deleuze, and others), I believe that power is only one of the ways, and not necessarily the best way, in which human beings can construct their world or relate to it.

My model can also be seen as a useful addition to, and possible revision of, the various models of orality versus literacy that are beginning to gain significant momentum in contemporary cultural studies.[5] Although my model acknowledges the important distinction between an oral and a

5. See, for example, the work of Eric A. Havelock, including *Preface to Plato* (Oxford, 1961) and *The Muse Learns to Write: Reflections on Orality and Literacy from Antiquity to the Present* (New Haven, 1986); Marshall McLuhan, *The Gutenberg Galaxy: The Making of Typographic Man* (Toronto, 1962); Jack Goody, ed., *Literacy in Traditional Societies* (Cambridge, 1968) and *The Interface Between the Written and the Oral* (Cambridge, 1987); Elizabeth Eisenstein, *The Printing Press As an Agent of Change: Communications and Transformations in Early Modern Europe*, 2 vols. (New York, 1979); M. T. Clanchy, *From Memory to Written Record: England, 1066–1307* (New York, 1979); Walter Ong, *Orality and Literacy: The Technologizing of the Word* (London, 1982); and Brian Stock, *The Implications of Literacy: Written Language and Models of Interpretation in the Eleventh and Twelfth Century* (Toronto, 1983). A historicist critique of some of these models can be found in William K. Harris, *Ancient Literacy* (Cambridge, Mass., 1989).

literate culture or frame of mind, it allows for the kind of flexibility in dealing with cultural reversibility that the models of orality versus literacy have so far been unable to provide. Furthermore, whereas these models start from the scientistic notion of technology as a fundamental factor in cultural change (often regarded as irreversible progress), my model treats technology as an effective, but not always and necessarily primary, form of power.

Finally, my model can affirm the essential unity of the Western mentality without either idealizing or denigrating it, as certain contemporary moralists, including Alasdair MacIntyre, tend to do. Like Freud, MacIntyre is fully aware of our common ethical heritage when he observes: "We are, whether we acknowledge it or not, what the past has made us and we cannot eradicate from ourselves, even in America, those parts of ourselves which are formed by our relationship to each formative stage in our history. If this is so, then even heroic society is still inescapably part of us all, and we are narrating a history that is peculiarly *our own history* when we recount its past in the formation of our moral culture."[6] But I narrate a different version of our moral history and draw different conclusions from it than MacIntyre does. Like any critic of modernity, MacIntyre inevitably tends to idealize the past, occasionally turning it into a golden age, against which he contrasts the evils of the present. He believes that our moral troubles are the result of an irreconcilable conflict between modern, "emotivist" individualism and the social responsibility fostered by a tightly knit traditional community, including the heroic one. In MacIntyre's historical drama, Nietzsche is largely the villain (because he misinterprets heroic competitive values as "emotivist" individualism) and Aristotle largely the hero (because he advocates the traditional, median virtues of individual responsibility and communal cooperation). To translate his argument into my own terms, MacIntyre favors median values over archaic ones, without considering their intricate complicity as two faces of the same mentality of power. By contrast, there are no heroes and no villains in my story, my narrative method being descriptive rather than proscriptive, diagnostic rather than critical. And if a cure be needed for our current ethical distress (which, *mutatis mutandis*, is not all that different from the moral dilemmas of the Homeric epic or Hellenic tragedy), then this cure should begin not by choosing Aristotle over Nietzsche, but by turning away from both. My model thus opens the possibility (at least in the imagination) of going not only beyond the dichotomy of archaic

6. Alasdair MacIntyre, *After Virtue* (Notre Dame, Ind., 1981), 122, MacIntyre's emphasis.

and median, but also beyond all the other instruments of an agonistic mode of thought. In turn, this path would involve moving away from our mentality of power as a whole, a step that, at least so far, very few Western thinkers, ancient and modern, have seemed prepared to take.

My intellectual debts are many and it would be impossible to list them all here. The classicists and nonclassicists alike will undoubtedly notice my tacit staging of a philosophical banquet with such convivial figures as Giambattista Vico, Jacob Burckhardt, Friedrich Nietzsche, Sigmund Freud, Johan Huizinga, Georg Simmel, Max Weber, Helmuth Plessner, Martin Heidegger, Hans-Georg Gadamer, Claude Lévi-Strauss, Gilles Deleuze, Michel Foucault, René Girard, André Leroi-Gourhan, and others. The classicists in particular will notice my dependence on, but also, I hope, fruitful dialogue with, such fine scholars as Gilbert Murray, M. P. Nilsson, Francis Cornford, Bruno Snell, Harold Cherniss, E. R. Dodds, Victor Ehrenberg, Werner Jaeger, Gregory Vlastos, Moses I. Finley, G. S. Kirk, W. K. C. Guthrie, Gerald Else, Eric Havelock, Arthur W. Adkins, Hugh Lloyd-Jones, Jean-Pierre Vernant, Marcel Detienne, Bernard Knox, Walter Burkert, James Redfield, Charles Kahn, Gregory Nagy, Helen North, and Charles Segal, to mention only a few.

Because this book was written during approximately the same period that *Dionysus Reborn* was, I am grateful to some of the same institutions and individuals that assisted me with the previous project: the Andrew W. Mellon Postdoctoral Fellowship Program at Cornell University and its director Anna Geske, as well as Professors W. Wolfgang Holdheim and William Kennedy of the Comparative Literature Department at Cornell; the Alexander von Humboldt Stiftung and Professor Wolfgang Iser of the University of Konstanz; and Dr. Michael Moriarty, Associate Vice President for Research at the University of Georgia.

I am equally grateful to Bernard Knox, who in his capacity as director of the Center of Hellenic Studies in Washington D.C., allowed me to carry out research at the library and invited me to participate in the intellectual life of the center during the fall quarter of 1984 and the winter quarter of 1985; to Rosemary Sheldon, the secretary of the center, who was equally helpful with my research there; Michael Poliakoff of Hillsdale College, Michigan, Nancy Rubin and Ronald Bogue of the University of Georgia, at Athens, and Mihai Nasta of the University of Padova, who read and commented on an early version of the manuscript; to Matei Calinescu of Indiana University, Virgil Nemoianu of Catholic University, and Thomas Pavel of Princeton University for their substantial suggestions to later versions; to Stanley Corngold, Lionel Gossman,

Robert Fagles, Charles Segal, and Claudia Brodsky of Princeton University, and Thomas Cole, Louis Dupré, Cyrus Hamlin, Giuseppe Mazzotta, and Heinrich von Staden of Yale University, with whom I have debated, with much profit, some of the intellectual and ethical issues involved in this project during my tenure as a Fellow in Comparative Literature at Princeton (Fall 1988) and Yale (Fall 1989); to Raymond A. Prier who has generously and gallantly supported the book in its final stages, commenting extensively on and providing crucial editorial help with the manuscript. I should finally like to thank Pam Morrison and Tom Campbell for expert assistance with the copyediting and, above all, Reynolds Smith of Duke University Press for his unflagging faith in and loyal support of this book.

■ *Abbreviations*

I have used the following abbreviations for the principal Anglo-American classical journals cited in the footnotes:

AJP   *American Journal of Philology*

CP   *Classical Philology*

CQ   *Classical Quarterly*

CR   *Classical Review*

CW   *Classical World*

HSCP   *Harvard Studies in Classical Philology*

JHS   *Journal of Hellenic Studies*

TAPA   *Transactions of the American Philological Association*

YCS   *Yale Classical Studies*

1 ■ The Hawk and the Nightingale: Play, Power, and Poetry in Homer and Hesiod ■

■ In his *Works and Days*, Hesiod recounts an ancient fable. A hawk is carrying away a nightingale in his claws, and when the latter cries, "Pity me!," the proud predator replies: "Foolish thing, why are you shrieking? Your captor is much stronger than you./ There shall you go wherever I take you though you are a singer,/ and, as I wish, I shall eat you for dinner or let you go free./ Foolish the man who wishes to fight against those who are stronger;/ he loses the victory and suffers pain in addition to disgrace [*l'aischea*]."[1]

This fable perfectly illustrates the relationship between archaic power and play that I wish to examine in this chapter. On the one hand, there is the perspective of the hawk, for whom might makes right and for whom power is unashamedly playful, arbitrary, and violent. The hawk experiences power as freedom of action: he can let the nightingale go or eat it as he pleases, that is, he can play with it, the way a cat plays with a mouse. The hawk cannot identify with the shrieks of his toy object any more than the nightingale could identify with the wriggling worm he might have caught earlier that morning. The hawk thus asks the nightingale to accept a "natural" state of affairs in which the strong and the weak continually switch places, each having his play before they both perish without a trace in the cosmic hecatomb. In other words, the hawk asks the nightingale to accept living *dangerously*.

1. Hesiod, *Works and Days*, in *The Poems of Hesiod*, trans. R. M. Frazer (Norman, Okla., 1983), lines 207–11. Subsequent English citations from Hesiod refer to this edition, although I have occasionally modified Frazer's translations, to convey my own sense of the Greek passage in question. Greek and line citations are from Hesiod, *Theogonia, Opera et Dies, Scutum, Fragmenta Selecta*, eds. F. Solmsen, R. Merkelbach, and M. L. West (Oxford, 1970).

On the other hand, there is the perspective of the victim, the nightingale or the worm that can no longer experience power as joyous, free play but as painful constraint. Once the aggressor finds himself in a weak position, he cries foul play and sets about changing the rules of the power game. This shift of perspective from aggressor to victim, I shall argue, ultimately accounts for a change in emphasis from archaic to median values in Hellenic thought.

Hesiod's use of the fable also points to the problematic relation between poetry and archaic power. Because the poet addresses his fable to "lords who understand," he obviously alludes to the might-makes-right mentality of his archaic community, a mentality of which he apparently disapproves. He seems to identify with the nightingale (who is, like the poet, a singer, *aoidos*), and thus implicitly to distance himself from the world of the hawk, which is also the heroic world of the epic. By attempting a critical use of this fable, the poet seems to shift from the point of view of the hawk to that of the nightingale, emphasizing median values over archaic or aristocratic ones. Hence he problematizes both the prevalent warlike mentality and the role of the poet in his archaic community.[2] I shall first turn to the hawk's world as it appears in the Homeric epic, and then I shall look at this world as both Homer and Hesiod seem to do, through the eyes of the nightingale. I shall focus especially on the shifting relationship between power and play in the Homeric and Hesiodic texts, arguing that this shift is central to understanding the conflicting worldviews embedded in these texts.

■ Aien Aristeuein: *The World of the Hawk*

The Homeric heroic world, as it comes across in the *Iliad* and the *Odyssey*, is a predominantly aristocratic, warrior-culture whose mentality is largely governed by power in its naked, immediate form.[3] *Aretē*, a key

2. Here I do not mean, however, to imply either a temporal or a social *décalage* between Homer and Hesiod. It is not entirely implausible to regard the Homeric and the Hesiodic works as more or less coeval (even though Homer uses more traditional epic material than Hesiod does), a view that seems to be gaining authority among modern scholars. In this sense, both Homer and Hesiod are in all likelihood removed from the heroic world presented in their compositions, looking back to it at times nostalgically and at other times disapprovingly. I shall return to this question, as well as to Hesiod's fable, in the section "The Nightingale and the Hawk."

3. No scholar writing about Homer can avoid the Homeric Question, although the issue of Homer's historical existence is of minor consequence for the present discussion. In regard to this question, my position is that the name "Homer" (whether there actually

word in understanding the Homeric hero's behavior, points to the ethical ideals of the *aristoi* (noblemen, aristocrats)—significantly, the two words seem to have a common etymological root—and it emphasizes the agonistic nature of their values. Although it is usually translated as "virtue" or "excellence," *aretē* in Homer can more accurately be rendered as "prowess in battle" and is geared toward those qualities that are most needed in a warlike society, such as physical strength, valor, endurance,

---

existed a singer of tales called by that name or not) grants authority to a number of collective productions and to a number of traditional singers of tales (the Homeridae). The *Iliad* and the *Odyssey* are probably traditional books (in Gilbert Murray's sense) that reach their final authoritative form only during the Hellenistic period. Although the residual oral nature of their composition cannot be denied, the Homeric epics bear the unmistakable imprint of an increasingly influential median mentality, which has, through the ages, adapted and transformed them according to its own needs and goals. I start from the premise, therefore, that the Homeric epics probably began their life around the late ninth or the early eighth century B.C. and reached a relatively stable, written form in sixth-century Athens. They thus parallel a long period of transition in Hellenic culture, during which archaic values gradually give way to their median counterparts. Given these assumptions, my discussion will necessarily refer, on the one hand, to the Homeric or heroic world as it appears in the poems and, on the other, to direct or indirect comments on this world by Homer or the poetic persona of the epics. No matter how self-effacing this persona appears to be, its point of view is often obvious, betraying a nightingale's perspective, especially in the passages that refer to the warriors' violent excesses. This is not to say, however, that these are the only places where median values come through, or that we can ascertain with precision, on that basis, what is "old" and what is "new" in the poems. Rather, median values are superimposed upon and infuse the whole composition, creating a divided or tragic perspective.

For an account of the present state of the Homeric Question one can consult, among many others, G. F. Else, "Homer and the Homeric Problem," in *University of Cincinnati Classical Studies* (Semple Lectures) 1 (1967): 315–65; Adam Parry, ed., *The Making of Homeric Verse: The Collected Papers of Milman Parry* (Oxford, 1971); Alfred Heubeck, *Die Homerische Frage, ein Bericht über die Forschung der letzten Jahrzehnte* (Darmstadt, 1974); Michael Nagler, *Spontaneity and Tradition: A Study in the Oral Art of Homer* (Berkeley and London, 1974); G. Broccia, *La questione omerica* (Florence, 1979); Hugh Lloyd-Jones, "Remarks on the Homeric Question," in H. Lloyd-Jones, ed., *History and the Imagination: Essays in Honour of H. R. Trevor-Roper* (New York, 1982), 15–29; D. G. Miller, *Improvisation, Typology, Culture, and "the New Orthodoxy": How "Oral" Is Homer?* (Washington, D.C., 1982); David M. Shive, *Naming Achilles* (Oxford, 1987); as well as two collective volumes, B. Fenik, ed., *Homer: Tradition and Invention* (Leiden, 1978) and J. Latacz, ed., *Homer: Tradition und Neuerung* (Darmstadt, 1979). The general reader can find useful background on both the Homeric world and Homeric composition in A. J. B. Wace and F. H. Stubbings, eds., *A Companion to Homer* (New York, 1963). The most important studies of the heroic world include M. C. Bowra's *Heroic Poetry* (London, 1952), and Gregory Nagy's *Best of the Acheans: Concepts of the Hero in Archaic Greek Poetry* (Baltimore, 1979), hereafter cited as Nagy, *BTA*.

and so on. Homeric *aretē* also has a second meaning, describing intellectual rather than physical abilities, but again in a competitive context: for
example, Odysseus is praised as being *aristos* in counsel, that is, because of
his ability to bring about, through skillful manipulation or cunning (*mētis*),
his own party's success in war or peace. In the Homeric world, therefore,
power presents itself as agon or competitive play. This means not only
that contest has an important function in Homeric society, but also that
the hero sees his relationship to other humans and to the divinities, as
well as to existence at large, in terms of a universal game of power.
Hippolochus' valedictory words to his son Glaukos, "*Aien aristeuein kai
hupeirochon emmenai allon*" ("always be best and excel others," *Il.* 6.208),
repeated by Nestor, who this time puts them in the mouth of Peleus as the
latter sends his son Achilles off to the Trojan War (*Il.* 11.784), aptly
express the Hellenic aristocratic ideal of life, based on play as contest.[4]

Before examining the various forms of agonistic play in the Homeric
epic, it would be useful to recall briefly the semantic history of words
such as *agōn* and *aethlos*. In Homer, *agōn* designates "an assembly with
games or contests," "the place where the games are held," and the
"competitors or the potential competitors" themselves (any member of

---

4. It is through agon that modern scholarship has implicitly recognized the importance
of play in Hellenic thought. The ubiquity of agon in Hellenic culture has led such
influential scholars as Ernst Curtius and Jacob Burckhardt to qualify this culture as
specifically agonistic, but without seeing it necessarily as playful (see, for example, Ernst
Curtius, "Der Wettkampf," in *Altertum und Gegenwart. Gesammelte Rede und Vorträge*
[Berlin, 1877]; and Jacob Burckhardt, "Der koloniale und agonale Mensch," in *Griechische Kulturgeschichte* [Stuttgart, 1941], vol. 3). With Friedrich Nietzsche and Johan
Huizinga, on the other hand, the link between play and agon becomes explicit and the
way is opened to a full understanding of play as an all-pervasive cultural phenomenon
(see Friedrich Nietzsche, *Philosophy in the Tragic Age of the Greeks*, trans. M. Cowan
[Chicago, 1962], esp. 53–55, and *The Will to Power*, trans. W. Kaufmann and R. J.
Hollingdale (New York, 1968), esp. Aphorisms 1066 and 1067, 549–50.; and Johan
Huizinga, *Homo ludens: A Study of the Play Element in Culture* (Boston, 1950), esp. chap. 3,
"Play and Contest as Civilizing Functions" and chap. 5, "Play and War." The concept of
power as agon, however, is not a distinctive mark of ancient Greece, as Curtius,
Burckhardt, Nietzsche, and a host of lesser known cultural historians have suggested.
(Burckhardt, moreover, draws a distinction between *der heroische* and *der agonale Mensch*
even as he cites *Il.* 11.784 to describe the former.) Nor is it, for that matter, limited to
Western culture in general, being found, for example, in ancient Egypt, China, India, and
in medieval Japan. For a detailed discussion of *Il.* 11.784 see Ingomar Weiler, "*Aien
aristeyein*. Ideologiekritische Bemerkungen zu einem vielzitierten Homerwort," *Stadion* 1,
no. 2 (1975): 199–227.

the assembly may join in the competition).[5] Some dictionaries list "place of assembly" as the original meaning of *agōn* and "assembly to witness games" as a secondary meaning.[6] A closer look at the *Iliad* and the *Odyssey*, however, shows that the *agōn* semantic group is almost always used in connection with games or contests. Out of the twenty-three lines where *agōn* appears in the *Iliad*, sixteen relate to the funeral games held in Patroclus' honor (book 23), whereas in the *Odyssey* all six lines where the word appears are in some way associated with games.[7] G. G. P. Autenrieth lists the Homeric meanings of *agōn* in the correct order: (1) assembly, especially to witness games; contest, games; (2) assemblage or place of assemblage of the ships; (3) place of combat, arena, including the space occupied by the spectators.[8] At the outset, therefore, the word *agōn* clearly holds a central position in the Hellenic vocabulary of play. In post-Homeric times, *agōn* becomes increasingly abstract, designating only the game or the contest itself. It gradually transcends the sphere of athletic games, extending to such abstract contexts as law, politics, warfare, eros, rhetoric, history, philosophy, and literary criticism; even in these contexts, however, its connection with the notion of play remains firm.

In turn, Homeric *aethlos* (Att. *athlos*) specifically signifies "prize-contest," but it can also mean "combat in war" as well as "toil" and "hardship," such as Euristheus imposes on Heracles (*Il.* 8.363). Like *agōn*, *athlos* turns increasingly abstract and in the classical period the two terms become interchangeable: both of them can denote "athletic contest,"

5. See James D. Ellsworth, *Agon: Studies in the Use of a Word*, Ph.D. diss., University of California at Berkeley, 1971 (University Microfilms, Ann Arbor, Mich., 1972).
6. See L. Doederlein, *Homerisches Glossarium* (Wiesbaden, 1967) and R. J. Cunliffe, *A Lexicon of the Homeric Dialect* (Oklahoma City, 1963).
7. See Ingomar Weiler, *Der Agon im Mythos: Zur Einstellung der Griechen zum Wettkampf* (Darmstadt, 1974), 25–27.
8. G. G. P. Autenrieth, *A Homeric Dictionary*, 7th ed. (Norman, Okla., 1979). For a detailed examination of *agōn* in Homer and later authors see, in addition to Ellsworth and Weiler, Thomas F. Scanlon, "The Vocabulary of Competition: *Agōn* and *Aethlos*, Greek Terms for Contest," *Arete: The Journal of Sport Literature* 1, no. 1 (Fall 1983): 147–62. Scanlon also discusses the semantic parallels of *agōn* in several Indo-European languages, suggesting that the common root of the word may have been connected with aggression or domination, a sense which then may have been "carried over to related words applied to peaceful athletic competition in *agōn*" (148). He concludes that "from the lexical evidence of Greek, Sanskrit, and Irish, it appears that there was an Indo-European noun for both military and athletic competition whose common root is seen in the element *ag-*, "to drive, to lead" (149).

such as the great Panhellenic festivals.[9] At the same time *agōn* undergoes an ethical polarization, acquiring negative meanings; like *athlos*, it can signify "hardship" or "toil," for example, in *agōnia*. This polarization appears approximately at the moment when, in certain Sophists and in Plato, *paidia* comes to denote not only "children's play" but also "play" in general. It is the moment when philosophy separates play from *agōn*, that is, from violent contest and power—a separation that took place especially in the context of the Platonic theory of education (*paideia*) and that was adopted and perpetuated by subsequent classical scholarship. It can be concluded, then, that the semantic development of *agōn* and *aethlos* equally reflects the shift in emphasis from an archaic to a median mentality in Hellenic thought, where the aristocratic notion of contest undergoes a process of ethical polarization, acquiring an increasingly ambivalent emotional value.

In the Homeric epic, play as *agōn* governs the transactions among heroes, among gods, between men and gods, and between mortals and Moira. Heroes relate to other heroes in terms of a competitive game, the goal of which is to establish a relative hierarchy (*primus inter pares*) within the aristocratic group. This hierarchy, however, remains highly unstable. The hero ceaselessly worries about his order of rank in relation to his peers and about "what people will say," because success is labile by nature. He constantly has to prove his *aretē* in battle and in the assembly, constantly has to remain in the public eye. For instance, after his quarrel with Agamemnon, Achilles cannot afford to stay away from the battlefield for too long lest he should be forgotten, a fate worse than death for the Homeric hero. He has no moral scruples in enlisting the help of his mother, Thetis (even if this means bringing almost total disaster upon the Greek camp), in order to make sure that his comrades need his services. Moral scruples (in the modern sense, arising from the notion of ethical responsibility toward fellow humans at large) are irrelevant in a heroic society, where intentions count less than performance, and where performance is judged largely in terms of success and failure.[10] Achilles is less

9. See Scanlon, "The Vocabulary of Competition," 154–59.
10. For a detailed discussion of the Homeric moral code, which operates with explicit values different from those of modern (Christian) ethics, see especially Arthur W. H. Adkins, *Merit and Responsibility: A Study in Greek Values* (Oxford, 1960), hereafter cited as Adkins, *MR*. Although he never states it quite explicitly, Adkins' thesis seems to be that Hellenic society attempts, with only partial success, to pass from a system of predominantly competitive values to one of predominantly cooperative or "quiet" values, in which social responsibility prevails over individual merit. This thesis has come under heavy attack, notably through Hugh Lloyd-Jones' *Justice of Zeus* (Berkeley, 1971), which

concerned with the common good than with his own *timē* (fame, reputation, but also sphere of influence), which depends only indirectly upon
this common good. (Actually, the welfare of the Greek camp can only be,
and should have been, Agamemnon's concern, being part of his *timē* as the
commander-in-chief of the army.)

---

attempts to show that cooperative or quiet values are already present in the archaic
period, where they are at least as common as their competitive counterparts. These two
theses are ultimately not as widely apart as they might appear, because both scholars
seem to share a (Kantian) notion of moral responsibilty as an implicit ideal of human
conduct. The question for them seems largely to determine at what point this ideal
becomes at least partial reality in Hellenic culture. For example, Adkins explicitly
distances himself from the notion of might makes right in discussing the archaic Greek
world as a "results culture" and prefers an (unspecified) form of social Darwinism to
account for its values. For him, the competitive activities are "needed" more than the
cooperative ones in the struggle for survival of an archaic community (see Adkins, *Moral
Values and Political Behavior in Ancient Greece. From Homer to the End of the Fifth Century*
[London, 1972], 13–15). Adkins is not concerned with the question of power-oriented
mentalities and the kind of values they create, choosing instead to see them as inevitable
(being demanded by the struggle for existence). From the perspective of this book, the
theses of both Adkins and Lloyd-Jones are helpful as long as they are applied to the right
social group (warriors, political rulers, shaman-priests, commoners, and so forth). One
should also draw a distinction between the relations among groups and those within the
same group. For example, what may appear as "quiet" and "cooperative" within the
same social group (such as loyalty, friendship, pity, protecting a guest—see Lloyd-Jones,
The Justice of Zeus) may not apply to relationships between groups (for instance, between
aristocrats and farmers) and may be the result of a temporary balance among equal
forces or among allies, rather than an expression of an inner sense of moral responsibility. In other words, one should distinguish between two kinds of cooperation:
"horizontal" (among equals) and "vertical" (from subordinate to master). This distinction is helpful, for example, in determining whether a certain community is eunomic or
isonomic: *eunomia* (good rule) is characteristic of aristocratic communities and largely
emphasizes vertical cooperation, whereas *isonomia* (equality before the law) is characteristic of democratic communities and mostly emphasizes horizontal cooperation,
among equals. But even during periods of high democracy (in fifth-century Athens, for
example), Hellenic cooperative values retain their double nature (vertical and horizontal) because the distinction between citizens and noncitizens, freemen and slaves remains
in place throughout the history of the Greek *polis*. Finally, one should also distinguish
between archaic and median kinds of cooperation because they play substantially
different social roles: in an archaic world such as the Homeric one, cooperative values
are directly subordinated to the aristocratic contest, supporting the formation and
temporary observance of heroic hierarchies, whereas in a predominantly median world
they aim primarily at tempering, without ever completely arresting, various forms of
social competition. Yet even those median values that, through their "quiet" appearance,
seem to come closest to our modern, rational ones remain subordinated to a mentality of
power, and are easily replaced by their rivals in times of sociocultural crisis. Conse-

Like any game, including games of power, heroic agon has rules, but these rules seem to have little to do with moral responsibility in the modern sense of the word. Rather, they are based on mutual agreement, which remains in force only as long as it is perceived as being advantageous to all parties involved. Neither is playing by the rules, or "fair play," a moral exigency; it is merely the result of cooperation among almost equally powerful contestants, guaranteeing the continuation of the game.[11] Competitors are "fair" not because of inner, but because of exterior compulsion, which comes from the other contestants (in this regard, archaic cooperation appears more openly—and unashamedly—based on self-interest than its median counterpart). When Agamemnon finally acknowledges his mistake, which he predictably seeks to explain through $at\bar{e}$ (blindness sent by the gods), it turns out that he regards it less as moral error than as miscalculation.[12] To him, his action against Achilles does not seem unfair or morally objectionable per se; it proves to be so only in hindsight, after its consequences become known and he is in

---

quently, throughout this book I shall use adjectives such as "quiet" and "peaceful" to describe median values, with the understanding that these values, no less than their archaic counterparts, can be both cooperative and competitive. As far as the Homeric or heroic ethical code is concerned, it seems to be a predominantly aristocratic or archaic one; this does not mean, however, that the Homeric epic is not infused with median values, as I have already suggested. For the beginning of the Adkins controversy, see A. A. Long, "Morals and Values in Homer," *JHS* 90 (1970): 121–39, as well as Adkins' reply, "Homeric Values and Homeric Society," *JHS* 91 (1972): 1–14 and "Homeric Gods and the Values of Homeric Society," *JHS* 92 (1972): 1–19. For a detailed treatment of the notions of *eunomia* and *isonomia*, see, for instance, Martin Ostwald, *Nomos and the Beginnings of the Athenian Democracy* (Oxford, 1969). Compare also my discussion of *isonomia* and *isomoiria* in chapter 2.

11. Modern theorists of play such as Johan Huizinga and Roger Caillois and classicist cultural historians such as Hartvig Frisch (for example, in *Might and Right in Antiquity* [Copenhagen, 1949; trans. C. C. Martindale; rpt. New York, 1976]) seem to me inconsistent when they accuse certain European nations before World War II of lacking a sense of fair play. These scholars are in the ironical position of Odysseus, who marauds the coast of the Cicones but then complains about Zeus' sending him a foul share (*moira*) in the form of the avengers of his victims (*Od.* 9). Fair play is also invoked by some recent scholars in combating Adkins' notion of archaic individual merit (see, for example, Matthew W. Dickie, "Fair and Foul Play in the Funeral Games in the *Iliad*," *Journal of Sport History* 2, no. 2 [Summer 1984]: 8–17; and Erich Segal, " 'To Win or Die': A Taxonomy of Sporting Attitudes," in the same issue, 25–31). But "fair play" implies the kind of modern, rational cooperative (*and* competitive) values that seem foreign to a warlike, heroic mentality.

12. For a perceptive description of Agamemnon's archaic mentality in general, see E. R. Dodds, *The Greeks and the Irrational* (Berkeley, 1951), chap. 1, "Agamemnon's Apology."

danger of bringing *ta aischea*, disgrace, upon himself through the defeat of the Greek army. Agamemnon's "flaw," then, is not so much that he is morally in the wrong, but that he lacks cunning or the intellectual ability to gauge the political consequences of his actions accurately. By contrast, someone like Odysseus is often presented as a model of heroic and political conduct: he combines physical force with *mētis*, the kind of agonistic intelligence that is most valued by an archaic mentality (Zeus himself, as the embodiment of supreme power, could not have maintained his position without cunning, so he swallowed his own daughter Metis, after she had helped him defeat Cronus, in order to become invincible).[13]

Whereas cunning is the main agonistic virtue needed in the assembly, physical prowess is the main *aretē* needed on the battlefield, and *aristeia* is the most important means by which the hero can display this *aretē*. Being etymologically related to *aristos* and *aretē*, *aristeia* is a hero's single-handed tour de force whereby he proudly displays his fighting skills over the entire battlefield.[14] Although *aristeia* is undoubtedly an important form of combat, it seldom decisively affects the outcome of a battle; it is first and foremost a highly ritualized agonistic game, designed partly as a display of power for its own sake and partly as a means of establishing fighting hierarchies among heroes.

A hero about to engage in *aristeia* does not randomly take on just any opponent, but wanders around the field in search of a worthy match. Once he spots his man, he does not immediately proceed to fight him, but pauses to find out his identity and fighting record. Both combatants may deliver a vow or boast (*euchē*), which is itself a sort of verbal contest. They may also decide not to fight, but rather to exchange courtesies and gifts, as in the case of Diomedes and Glaucus (*Il.* 6.119–236). Even in this case, however, the contest is carried on beyond physical prowess, in terms of *mētis*, because the poet comments at the end of the episode: "But Zeus the son of Kronos stole away the wits of Glaukos/who exchanged with Diomedes the son of Tydeus armour/of gold for bronze, for nine oxen's worth the worth of a hundred."[15] If the fighting does take place, it is

---

13. On *mētis* see, for example, M. Detienne and J. P. Vernant, *Les ruses de l'intelligence: La metis chez les grecs* (Paris, 1974).

14. For discussions of *aristeia*, see, among many others, Ulrich von Wilamowitz-Moellendorff, *Die Ilias und Homer* (Berlin, 1916); and Karl Reinhardt, *Die Ilias und ihr Dichter* (Göttingen, 1961).

15. *Il.* 6.234–36. Unless otherwise specified, all English translations from the *Iliad* are those of Richmond Lattimore, *The Iliad of Homer* (Chicago and London, 1951). For the *Odyssey* I have generally used Robert Fitzgerald's English version (New York, 1961).

highly ritualized, rather like the single combat between knights in the Middle Ages or like the modern duel. The encounter does not end with the death (or the ransom) of the defeated, but with additional parting words from both sides. The slaying of the vanquished is moreover to be followed by the victor's no less ritualized despoiling of the corpse, over which renewed fighting may break out.[16]

During his *aristeia*, the hero is possessed by *charmē* (battle-lust), which renders combat "sweeter" than going home (*Il.* 2.453–54). Hector, for example, is forever "avid of battle" (*Il.* 13.80), while the two Aiantes are "joyful in the delight of battle the god had put in their spirits" (*Il.* 13.81– 82). The warrior joyfully "sweeps over the field with instincts and energies free, [experiencing] the supreme realization of the pride of power."[17] Carried away by this pride of power, he can even attack and temporarily defeat gods, as in the case of Diomedes. For the hero, *aristeia* is the delightful and exhilarating activity that modern theorists usually associate with physical play. He experiences power both as pleasure (it is in this sense, and only in this sense, that aristeia can be said to be a display of power for its own sake) and as desire.[18] This desire can, however, become insatiable and the hero can go, beyond *aristeia*, on a killing spree that betrays an obsession with death ultimately leading to insanity—this is the case of Achilles after the death of Patroclus, or the case of Telamonian Ajax after his contest of *mētis* with Odysseus (see Sophocles' *Ajax*). Power as contest can easily degenerate into wrath or "irrational"

Greek and line citations are from Homer, *Opera*, 5 vols., eds. D. B. Monroe and T. W. Allen (Oxford, 1902, 1908, 1912).

16. Very few bodies are actually despoiled in the *Iliad*, largely due to the valor of a fallen warrior's comrades. For a discussion of this topic, see S. Bassett, "Achilles's Treatment of Hektor's Body," *TAPA* 64 (1933): 41–58.

17. See Onians, *OET*, 20. Onians points out that the original association of battle and joy in Homeric Greek finds a striking parallel in Sanskrit where "raña has a basic meaning 'joy, delight' but in many contexts means 'battle'" (22). He also notes that in the German word *Lust* "desire and delight are still combined," as they were in the Anglo-Saxon *lust* (21 n.3). Along the same lines, we have seen that the Greek word *agōn*, which originally meant "contest," having both positive and negative emotional connotations, ends up meaning "toil, pain," a meaning that has been preserved to this day in *agony*. (The original meaning survives only as a technical term in Greek drama.) These examples and many others seem to indicate a direct connection, in any power-oriented mentality, between power and the sensations of pleasure and pain, between well-being and discomfort.

18. Compare Onians, *OET*, 21–22.

violence, always oscillating between what Freud calls a pleasure-principle and a death-wish.[19] It is precisely this "dynamic" pleasure-desire (the German *Lust*), derived from power in its violent, unmediated form that later thinkers distrust and attempt to replace by the "static" pleasure of philosophical contemplation (for example, Plato, in the wake of the Pythagoreans, distrusts the realm of the senses not so much because of their epistemological unreliability as because of their explicit connection with violent power).

In addition to *aristeia* (a war-game in which the hero literally gambles for life or death), there are other heroic games that can be called "peaceful"—not because they are not equally agonistic, but because they normally take place either during the temporary cessation of hostilities in war or during periods of relative peace. The stakes of the peaceful games may often be less dangerous but no less serious. These games can be divided into ritual and leisure games. The ritual games can in turn be connected with the funeral of a warrior who dies in combat (and here ritual games bespeak their violent, sacrificial origin) or with a public occasion.[20]

19. See Sigmund Freud, *Beyond the Pleasure Principle*, trans. J. Strachey (New York, 1961). What has been translated into English as the "pleasure-principle" significantly appears in German as the *Lustprinzip*. For a discussion of the Freudian notions of power, pleasure, and the death-wish (which are also present in Nietzsche), see Spariosu, *Dionysus Reborn*, pt. 1, sec. 2.1 and pt. 2, sec. 1.2. For an intriguing Freudian interpretation of the *Iliad*, including a psychoanalysis of the heroic mentality in general (with Achilles as a case study), see W. Thomas MacCary, *Childlike Achilles: Ontogeny and Philogeny in the Iliad* (New York, 1982). Although I am sympathetic to many of MacCary's insights, our basic premises are different. MacCary approaches the archaic world mainly through Freud and Hegel, I look at it mainly through that part of Freud's thought which owes most to Nietzsche and, consequently, is profoundly non-Hegelian. Thus I focus less on Freud's psychoanalytical views on narcissism, the Oedipus complex, and the like than on his *cultural* theory as developed, for example, in *Totem and Taboo*, *Civilization and Its Discontents*, and *Moses and Monotheism*.

20. Compare L. Malten, "Leichenspiel und Totenkult, *Mitteilungen des deutschen archae-ologischen Instituts (römische Abteilung)*, 38–39 (1932–34): 300–340, and K. Meuli, "Der Ursprung der olympischen Spiele," *Die Antike* (1941): 189–208. Both these scholars believe that combats at funeral games have a residual sacrificial character (propitiating the soul of the deceased) and, posssibly, are later replacements of real human sacrifices, preserved in gladiator fights. James Redfield shares their view in his discussion of the funeral games in *Nature and Culture in the Iliad: The Tragedy of Hector* (Chicago, 1975), chap. 5. The assumption behind this view is a rationalist one: the funeral games are not only largely nonviolent but also attempt to purge real-life violence by a symbolical reenactment of it. For example, Redfield, echoing Lévi-Strauss, observes: "Funeral

The games that are part of the funeral rites for Patroclus offer an excellent insight into the agonistic nature of play in Homeric society. They can be seen as serving several cultural functions. For example, they honor, bring delight to, and thereby propitiate the deceased hero: through the games both the participants and the dead hero accumulate *kleos* (fame), an important kind of immortality sought by heroic society. The funeral games also serve to reestablish and reconfirm hierarchies among the surviving heroes, thus guaranteeing the continuation of the heroic order even in the face of and beyond death. They may finally attempt to heal or, rather, dress up the wounds of warring contest (resulting almost invariably in violent death), within the relatively safe space of the athletic playground. In the funeral games, violent contest is downplayed and therefore appears only in its positive role as creator of cultural values. In this respect, the criteria of awarding prizes in a funeral game differ from those employed in public games: the contestant is first and foremost rewarded for his participation in or even for his mere presence at the games—for example, Nestor is

---

games are . . . midway between games and ritual; they are both *disjunctive* (generating a distinction between winners and losers) and *conjunctive* (constructing an organic unity among the players, between players and audience, and between the living, on the one hand, and, on the other hand, the dead warrior in whose honor honor is bestowed on the living)" (262 n.78). The standard rationalist view of the nonviolent character of Hellenic games in general is already present in Schiller (see Spariosu, *Dionysus Reborn*, pt. 1, sec. 1.2) and is largely based on the passage in *Il.* 23.820–23, where the fighting in armor between Telamonian Ajax and Diomedes is broken off by popular demand for fear that Ajax may get hurt (compare also earlier, *Il.* 23.735–37, where Achilles stops the wrestling match between Odysseus and Telamonian Ajax). Yet the stressful context of the event should be taken into account: all the participants will later be sorely needed on the battlefield. Hellenic competitive games, including funeral ones, can often display considerable violence even when they attempt to limit this violence to a simulative level.

As to the funeral games in the *Iliad*, they are not a playful imitation of real combat (as Redfield claims); on the contrary, real combat is itself a form of play, albeit with a different set of (archaic) rules. This is not to say that in time Hellenic games could not have become less violent under the pressure of median values, but even then they certainly preserved their agonistic character. For sport and violence in Hellenic culture see, for example, C. A. Forbes, "Accidents and Fatalities in Greek Athletics," *Classical Studies in Honor of William Abbott Oldfather* (Urbana, Ill., 1943), 50–59; and R. H. Brophy, "Deaths in the Panhellenic Games, Arrichion and Creugas," *AJP* 99 (1978): 363–90. For a full list of games and sports in Homer, as well as a brief discussion of the funeral games in *Iliad* 23, see Ingomar Weiler, *Der Sport bei den Völkern der alten Welt* (Darmstadt, 1981), chap. 4, esp. 78–88; and W. E. Sweet, *Sport and Recreation in Ancient Greece: A Sourcebook with Translations* (New York and Oxford, 1987), esp. chap. 2, "Athletics in Homer," with a careful prose translation of *Iliad* 23. I should also like to thank Robert Fagles for letting me consult his fine verse translation of *Iliad* 23 (forthcoming), and for discussing with me some important interpretive points in regard to book 23.

awarded fifth prize in the chariot race, *hors concours*, in token of his *aretē* as a horseman—and only secondarily for winning the event. Prizes can literally be given away, although the selection criteria are by no means arbitrary, being often based on past heroic accomplishments or on current heroic hierarchies.[21]

But it cannot be stressed enough that although the funeral games attempt to deal in a seemingly cooperative manner with the irrationality and arbitrariness of violence, and therefore do not appear to be explicitly agonistic, they serve to reaffirm under the guise of cooperation the agonistic foundation of heroic values, to revalidate the heroic way of life in general. As has often been remarked, the episode of the funeral games reflects the dramatic conflict of the epic as a whole, presenting heroic attitudes toward contest and *timē*, and suggesting ways in which the clash of interests that inevitably arises among heroes in pursuit of the same goals can peaceably be resolved. The funeral games cannot be taken out of their immediate context, however, without running the risk of consider- able distortion. In these games, the heroic community is restricted to the Greek military camp—to the exclusion of the Trojan enemy camp and of Hellenic society as a whole—and, therefore, involves transactions among equals and among allies (in other words, it involves horizontal rather than vertical cooperation). The games are also part of the customary mourning rites and, as such, require not only a period of truce in the war but also a temporary suspension of all ongoing, open hostility among participants— contestants and spectators alike. Achilles underscores this point when he sternly reminds the bickering Oilean Ajax and Idomeneus that they are

21. Classicists have generally chosen to concentrate on the relatively straightforward question of Hellenic games and sports, including those in *Iliad* 23. But this should not be done at the expense of the more complicated question of the Hellenic notion of play in general, which involves, but also goes beyond, games and sports. Obviously, it is the latter question that interests me here. Among the recent Anglo-American works on games and sports in the Hellenic world, in addition to Weiler's *Der Sport bei den Völkern der alten Welt* and Sweet's *Sport and Recreation in Ancient Greece*, the reader can consult: A. J. Butler, *Sport in Classic Times* (Los Altos, Calif., 1975); L. Drees, *Olympia: Gods, Artists, and Athletes* (New York, 1968); M. I. Finley and H. W. Pleket, *The Olympic Games: The First Thousand Years* (New York, 1976); H. A. Harris, *Sport in Greece and Rome* (Ithaca, N. Y., 1972); Michael Poliakoff, *Studies in the Terminology of the Greek Combat Sports* (Königstein, 1982); R. S. Robinson, *Sources for the History of Greek Athletics* (Urbana, Ill., 1955); D. C. Young, *The Myth of Greek Amateur Athletics* (Chicago, 1984). One can also consult the issue on "Athletics in Antiquity," *The Ancient World* 7, nos. 1–2 (March 1983); and the issue on "The Significance of Sport: Ancient Athletics and Ancient Society," ed. Michael Polia- koff, *Journal of Sport History* 2, no. 2 (Summer 1984). For a full bibliography, see Thomas F. Scanlon, *Greek and Roman Athletics: A Bibliography* (Chicago, 1984).

out of place (*Il.* 23.490–98). He also attempts to settle all the conflicting claims resulting from the athletic contests themselves in a peaceable, if not necessarily equitable, manner. Yet the very fact that such outbreaks and conflicts occur even within these highly restrictive, ritualistic circumstances betrays the deeply agonistic nature of a warlike community. The chariot race and the spear-throwing contest, which are usually offered as examples of the "rational," cooperative values of heroic society, are cases in point.[22]

Nestor's son Antilochus has been seen as a perpetrator of foul play, which is presumably decried not only by his community but also by his own father. Yet Antilochus fares quite well both during and in the aftermath of the two contests he enters. He displays a good deal of *mētis*, first by "taking advantage" (*Il.* 23.515) of Menelaus in the chariot race and, then, by sweet-talking the Spartan king out of the second prize and

22. See, for example, Dickie, "Fair and Foul Play." Dickie goes against the proposition that all that matters in Greek athletics is victory, which, he believes, is based on the more general assumption that "Greek society in the Archaic and Classical periods was a results culture," an assumption which he associates primarily with Adkins' work and which he does not share. In turn, Dickie suggests that archaic and classical Greek society essentially has the same attitudes toward competitiveness and victory that contemporary Western society does, and sets out to prove his thesis through the funeral games in the *Iliad*. One problem with his argument is that he ignores the immediate, ritualistic and agonistic context of these games and therefore the archaic nature of the cooperation between heroes. Another problem is that he does not take into account the fact that even in modern society certain social groups exhibit attitudes that can be associated with a "results culture"—witness, for instance, the "look-out-for-number-one" mentality of the so-called New Right in contemporary American politics. In other words, Dickie reads his own ideological interests into a past culture, a natural and probably unavoidable interpretive procedure. Similar discussions of the funeral games from a modern, rationalist standpoint can be found in F. M. Stawell, *Homer and the Iliad* (London, 1909), 84–90; C.W. Macleod, *Homer, Iliad Book XXIV* (Cambridge, 1982); and Jenny Strauss Clay, *The Wrath of Athena: Gods and Men in the Odyssey* (Princeton, N.J., 1983), 176–80. More balanced (if still essentially rationalist) analyses of these games can be found in M. M. Wilcock, "The Funeral Games of Patroclus," *Bulletin of the Institute of Classical Studies of the University of London* 20 (1973): 1–11, and Redfield, *Nature and Culture*, 204–10. For rationalist discussions of Hellenic competitiveness in general see, for example, Weiler, "*Aien aristeyein*," and E. Segal, "'To Win or Die,'" the second essay being, to a sizable extent, an (unacknowledged) rehearsal of the first. Brief but illuminating discussions of the games in the larger context of Homeric values are Moses I. Finley's in *The World of Odysseus*, 2d ed. (Harmondsworth, Middlesex, 1956), chap. 5, 108–10; and Marcel Detienne's in *Les maîtres de vérité dans la Grèce archaique* (Paris, 1967), chap. 5. For the relationship between funeral games and law, see Louis Gernet, "Jeux et droit (Remarques sur le XXIIIe chant de l'*Iliade*), in his *Droit et société dans la Grèce ancienne* (Paris, 1955), 2–18.

Achilles into creating another prize for Eumelus. The latter is allegedly the best charioteer in the race, who has nevertheless arrived last because of foul play on the part of Athena, in response to Apollo's own foul play on one of her favorites, Diomedes. Another instance of foul play comes to light after Achilles gives the fifth prize of the chariot race to Nestor in recognition of his past horsemanship. In return, the old sage offers him a story of his youthful exploits at a similar funeral game. Ironically, on that occasion Nestor won all contests except for the chariot race, where he lost as a result of foul play almost identical to that committed by his own son on Menelaus. Finally, Antilochus again displays morally dubious versatility, this time by flattering Achilles into doubling the value of the third prize, which he wins in the footrace (*Il.* 23. 785–97).

As this proliferation of mortal and divine foul playing indicates, the question is not that of abiding by the rules in the name of some transcendental sense of fair play, but that of whether one can get away with breaking them, when it is to one's advantage to do so, without paying too high a price. The "blameless" Antilochus (*Il.* 23.522) does get away with his ruses, thereby winning not only valuable prizes, but also the admiration of the Homeric audience, which undoubtedly looks upon him as a budding Odysseus *polumētis*, "versed in every advantage" (*Il.* 23.709).[23] What some critics interpret as his father's indirect rebuke can be interpreted, on the contrary, as implicit praise. Nestor underscores Antilochus' cunning intelligence, which is superior even to his own when he was his son's age. Nestor lost the first prize in the chariot race because he was unable to

23. Not all critics share Dickie's moral indignation at Antilochus' foul play. Witness Wilcock: "The impression given [by Antilochus] is of a personable and attractive young man, and this is supported by his second appearance in the Games: for he enters the foot race, comes in last, makes an amused comment to the spectators [about Odysseus, who comes in first], including a compliment to Achilles, who promptly doubles the value of the prize" ("The Funeral Games," 1–2). Dickie also unfairly accuses Antilochus of ignoring his father's good tips for the race and of treating his horses with uncommon cruelty. But the fledgeling hero does listen to his father's advice and skillfully negotiates the post: otherwise he would have ended up like Eumelus. By implication, Antilochus also proves to be pious when he ascribes Eumelus' failure to his not having "prayed to the immortal gods" (*Il.* 23.546–47). As to his horses, Antilochus treats them with the kind of abusive language that, together with coaxing and cajoling, is part of the normal repertory of any accomplished charioteer. The poet, for example, employs the same formula for both Antilochus and Menelaus: "For so he spoke and fearing the angry voice of their master [the horses] ran harder" (*Il.* 23.417–18 and, again, *Il.* 23.446–47). In other words, contrary to Dickie's argument, Antilochus never really transgresses the accepted norms of heroic behavior, his display of *mētis* being, as we have seen, an important part of this behavior.

uphold his claim, whereas his son successfully defends his, and this in the face of two of the greatest heroes of the Homeric world, Achilles and Menelaus.

As scholars have pointed out, Antilochus will, moreover, replace Patroclus in Achilles' affections (a fact of which the poet of the *Iliad* seems fully aware). Indeed, a good deal of the action of the *Iliad* is duplicated in another epic, the *Aethiopis*, where Antilochus is killed by Memnon, whom Achilles slays in turn in order to avenge his beloved companion.[24] That Achilles and Antilochus are "birds of a feather" seems to be implied, for instance, at the very end of the games, when Achilles possibly plays no less foul than Antilochus. Although Achilles has formally made up with Agamemnon, he never really forgives him, and their relationship remains strained to the end of the epic. Taking advantage of his role as master of ceremonies, Achilles effectively bars Agamemnon from winning the spear-throwing contest by canceling the event. He shrewdly justifies his action by claiming that Agamemnon's *aretē* as a spear-thrower is so great that it need not be put to the test, but then apparently awards him the second prize, a decorated cauldron, giving the first prize, a bronze spear, to Meriones.[25] On the other hand, Agamemnon's eagerness to compete

24. See, among many others, Wilamowitz-Moellendorff, *Die Ilias und Homer*; Reinhardt, *Die Ilias und ihr Dichter*; and W. Schadewaldt, *Von Homers Welt und Werk* (Leipzig, 1944).
25. This interpretation of the spear-throwing contest obviously goes against the commonly accepted view. But this view is really a prejudice, since nowhere does Homer state that Achilles gives Agamemnon the first prize, and his words remain (deliberately?) ambiguous. Besides, Achilles does not have a good reason to cancel the spear-throwing contest as he does in the case of, say, the fight in armor between Telamonian Ajax and Diomedes (in this last contest, incidentally, there is also some confusion about what the first prize is). Also, Achilles' exaggerated praise of Agamemnon is somewhat suspect and may give pause for thought. On the other hand, a case could be made for the spear being the first prize, since it is mentioned before the unfired cauldron (compare the horse race, where prizes are mentioned in the order of their importance and where a similar cauldron is laid down as a third prize, *Il.* 23.267). It may also be that Achilles, no less than Homer, deliberately sows confusion as to which the first prize actually is, once Agamemnon offers to compete. In this light, Homer's comment that Agamemnon "did not disobey" (*Il.* 23.895) Achilles' decision to cancel the contest and give him the cauldron while giving Meriones the spear may go beyond the purely formulaic meaning that the phrase usually has. It could be that Agamemnon is too confused to understand that he has been tricked (compare the contest of *mētis* between Diomedes and Glaucus in book 6). The irony of Achilles' distribution of prizes in the spear-throwing contest is further enhanced by the fact that cauldrons figure prominently among the gifts offered by Agamemnon as compensation to Achilles in book 9. (I owe this last observation to Robert Fagles, which does not necessarily mean that he subscribes to my overall interpretation of this passage.) In a manner of speaking, Achilles seems to pay Agamem-

and accumulate fame at the funeral of a man for whose death he is at least partly responsible does not show much (rationalist) good taste. The point is precisely that, given the heroic ethical code, it would never have occurred to him either to assume any responsibility for Patroclus' death or to pass up the opportunity of displaying his *aretē* on such an important communal occasion as a hero's funeral.[26]

Finally, the funeral games honoring Patroclus are doubly sacrificial. On the one hand, they are conflictive, enacting, through the athletic contests, the agon that has led to the death of the hero-victim; on the other hand, they are reconciliatory, effecting the bringing together of the heroic community over the dead body. This community, however, never questions the agonistic mentality which creates the need for a sacrificial mechanism in the first place, and the warriors will return to battle soon after the funeral. Any relief or "purification" remains temporary, and so does the feeling of "togetherness" that the funeral games may have served to bring about.[27]

---

non back for the way in which the latter has robbed him of his own prizes (and *timē*) at the beginning of the epic.

Finally, given the contestants' and the spectators' behavior during the games, one can hardly agree with Strauss Clay's rationalist view of these games. Commenting on the aftermath of the chariot race, Strauss Clay concludes: "This little drama, the sequel to the contest itself, reveals a purely human sense of generosity, fairplay, and gentlemanliness which tends to soften the harsh realities of victory and defeat. Under certain circumstances, the heroes, when left to themselves, can act with nobility, humanity, and kindness" (*The Wrath of Athena*, 180). As we have seen, in the course of the games the heroes are far from exhibiting the sense of generosity and fair play that is proper of English gentlemen in Victorian novels, and these are hardly the circumstances when, "left to themselves," they act with "nobility, humanity, and kindness."

26. On the issue of attributing anachronistic moral responsibility to the Homeric heroes' actions, compare, among others, Snell, *The Discovery of the Mind*, 160; and Finley, *The World of Odysseus*, 116–17 (however, for a reading different from Finley's regarding Achilles' scornful refusal of Agamemnon's gifts, see the end of this section). For this issue in fifth-century drama see Richard Garner, *Law and Society in Classical Athens* (London, 1987), 11–19. Garner's book also contains very useful sections on the competitive nature of the fifth- and fourth-century law courts and on the relationship between these courts and the theater. See also my remarks on the relationship between justice and strife in the next section as well as in chapter 2.

27. Many recent critics, including Redford (who nevertheless detects the "illusory" character of the funeral games as scapegoat ritual) believe that we get a glimpse of a new, nonheroic mentality, based on an ethics of pity, in the Priam-Achilles scene (*Iliad* 24). To me, however, this scene does not show Achilles' compassion for Priam, but temporary sadness for his own fate, which he does not intend to change, even though it lies within his power to do so. In other words, Achilles learns from his wrath nothing that he has not already known before, and grimly (or perhaps joyfully?) accepts its tragic conse-

Public games can also have a sizable role in Homeric society, as we can see, for example in *Odyssey* 8, where Alcinous entertains his guest, of whose identity he is as yet ignorant, with athletic events and songs of heroic deeds. Apart from their customary (practical) value of training and adjudication of prowess, the Phaeacian games serve the purpose of honoring a potentially illustrious guest and of showing the foreigner the polished manners of the island's *aristoi*; in other words, they can be seen as the ancient equivalent of a public-relations event.[28] At the same time, they are a convenient test for the foreigner's physical skills as well as for his sociocultural and ethnic background (the games are one way of distinguishing a Greek community from a barbarian one and, therefore, appeal to a common Hellenic heritage). Alcinous also employs the games for personal reasons, as a test for a potential son-in-law and powerful ally. By taking part in the games, Odysseus may become integrated into Phaeacian society (many a hero obtained a wife and a kingdom through participation in public games), and the discrete marriage proposal that the Phaeacian king has earlier extended to him on his daughter's behalf (*Od.* 7.310–17) must still be on Alcinous' mind.

When Odysseus responds with an appropriately heroic boast (*euchē*) to the uncouth challenge of one of the Phaeacian courtiers (although not without making his words good by throwing the discus farther than any Phaeacian athlete), Alcinous soothes ruffled tempers in a highly diplomatic speech:

> Friend, we take your challenge in good part,
> for this man angered and affronted you
> here at our *peaceful games*. You'd have us note
> the prowess that is in you, and so clearly,
> no man of sense would ever cry it down!

---

quences. For further elaboration of this view, see my concluding remarks in this section. For a full description of the double nature of the scapegoat ritual and of the *pharmakos* itself, see René Girard, *La violence et le sacré* (Paris, 1972) and *Le bouc émissaire* (Paris, 1982); for the sacrificial nature of funeral rites in particular, see Walter Burkert, *Homo Necans* (Berlin, 1972; trans. Berkeley, 1983), pt. 1, esp. chap. 6, "Funerary Ritual."

28. This propagandistic character was quite explicit in the Hellenic games, and has been preserved in the modern Olympics. Consider, for example, the Olympic games of 1936 in Nazi Germany, or the Olympic games of 1980 in Moscow and those of 1984 in Los Angeles. For a detailed comparison of the ancient and the modern games see, among many others, Finley and Pleket, *The Olympic Games*.

Come, turn your mind now on a thing to tell
among your peers when you are home again

> . . . .

I mean our prowess . . .
for we, too, have our skills . . .
not in the boxing ring nor the palestra
conspicuous, but in racing, land or sea;
and all our days we set great store by feasting,
harpers, and the grace of dancing choirs

> . . . .

O master dancers of the Phaiakians!
Perform now: let our guest on his return
tell his companions we excel the world
in dance and song, as in our ships and running.
(*Od.* 8.236–55, emphasis added)

But here Alcinous as master of ceremonies does more than simply placate Odysseus and settle peaceably a potentially violent conflict. He actually extends another challenge to the foreigner, who this time is expected to match the Phaeacian *aretē* in heroic song, or poetry reciting. Odysseus eventually complies by telling the story of his own adventures, and Alcinous is not sparing of praise for his performance.[29] Play as agon, then, can also include dancing, music, and verse making: as is well known, the Hellenic games connected with religious festivals or other public occasions often included not only athletic but also artistic events.[30]

29. Scholars (Strauss Clay, among many others) usually point out the difference between Odysseus' performance and that of a singer of tales. Odysseus is obviously not a professional minstrel any more than Achilles and Patroclus are, because he does not sing for a living. But the heroes are trained to sing as part of their education, and they may sing for pleasure or when challenged to a contest. Apollo himself can perform before the gods (soothing even Zeus' eagle into a peaceful slumber) or in competition, for example, in his music contest with Marsyas.

30. A detailed discussion of the Greek artistic performance as contest can be found, for example, in Weiler, *Der Agon im Mythos*, 37–122. Note that many of these contests, which can take place not only among mortals but also among the gods, as well as between mortals and gods, may result, no less than the athletic ones, in violence and destruction (witness the contest between Apollo and Marsyas, which ends with the flaying alive of the latter). For music, dancing, and poetry reciting, which as it becomes obvious in the Phaeacian episode are still integral parts of the same performance, see, among others, H. T. Wade-Gery, *The Poet of the Iliad* (Cambridge, 1952); Albert Lord, *A Singer of Tales* (Cambridge, Mass., 1960); and Max Wegner, *Musik und Tanz* (Göttingen, 1968).

Unlike public games, leisure games remain, as a rule, outside a ritualistic or an organized framework, although they can still constitute social occasions. As can be expected, they are predominantly agonistic, at least in the case of Homeric men. When Achilles stays away from the battlefield, his men amuse themselves on the beach "with discs and with light spears for throwing and bows" (*Il.* 2.773–75). Even such a seemingly harmless game as dice-throwing can become dangerous when engaged in by fledgeling heroes. Patroclus is a case in point, when he reminds Achilles that he was brought into the latter's house "by reason of a baneful manslaying"; Patroclus was only a child then and did not mean to kill Amphidamas' son, but "was angered over a dice-game" (*Il.* 23.86–87).

In the case of Homeric women and (unheroic) small children, leisure games are predictably quieter than those of men, because women and children are as a rule mere accessories to, rather than dynamic agents of, power (and when they are not, as in the case of Clytemnestra, Medea, and Hecuba, they are viewed with horror, as "unnatural" freaks). For example, Nausicaa plays ball with her companions on the shores of Scheria, while taking care of the palace laundry (*Od.* 6.85–109). Because of this association with the less powerful social elements in an archaic community, quiet, cooperative play is often regarded as inconsequential, as mere children's pastime. It is this relatively nonviolent, cooperative quality of women's and children's play, however, that was taken over and given speculative priority by such classical philosophers as Plato and Aristotle. (In this respect, it is highly significant that the word *paidia*, children's play, is absent from the Homeric text and becomes frequent only in fifth- and fourth-century works.)

In the Homeric world, artistic performance, such as dancing, singing, or poetry reciting, occupies an intermediary place between leisure and public games. It can be engaged in for leisure purposes, as in the case of Achilles, whom the heroes' embassy finds "delighting his heart in a lyre . . . and singing of men's fame" (*Il.* 9.186–89). Or it can be part of a festive occasion honoring a guest, a god, or an important event, and I have already mentioned the dancing and poetry reciting at the Phaeacian court in the *Odyssey*. Odysseus no less than Achilles is a consummate singer of tales, as skillful as Demodocus and Phemius, who are professional rhapsodes. In his case, private pleasure overlaps with both public entertainment and contest, as indeed it often happens not only in the Homeric world but also in Hellenic culture as a whole.[31]

31. For the relationship between art, contest, and political life in ancient Greece, see

Irrespective of the context in which it appears, however, Homeric artistic performance seems always to remain a form of power, through what I have elsewhere called "mimesis-play."[32] For example, in the *Odyssey*, the rhapsode's performance strongly affects his audience and can move it either to happiness or to grief. Odysseus finds "sweet pleasure" in Demodocus' sung tale of the adulterous relationship between Aphrodite and Ares, and of their punishment at the hands of the jealous husband, Hephaestus (*Od.* 8.368); he is also moved to tears when he hears Demodocus' account of the Trojan horse episode, in which the Ithacan hero himself has played a crucial role (*Od.* 8.521–35). Likewise, Odysseus cannot resist, except through one of his famous ruses, the bewitching chant of the Sirens (*Od.* 12.153–200), which can, like an *aristeia* gone out of control, cause pleasure-desire (the German *Lust*) to the point of madness and self-destruction (compare the powerful effect of Orpheus' legendary songs, as well as his own violent fate).

We have a partial glimpse into the nature of Homeric mimesis as play in Plato's account of the rhapsode's performance and its impact on the audience. In the *Ion*, for example, Socrates employs the analogy of the lodestone in order to describe the mimetic "frenzy" that spreads from the bard to the audience. The archaic audience totally identifies with the singer of tales through *methexis*, mimetic participation, or an ecstatic trance similar to that caused by Dionysian intoxication.[33] Such ecstatic trance often results in catharsis, a pleasurable relief of dammed-up emotional tension. In this regard, Eric Havelock observes:

Friedrich Nietzsche, "Homer's Contest," in *Complete Works*, 18 vols., ed. O. Levy, vol. 2, *Early Greek Philosophy and Other Essays*, trans. M. A. Mügge (London, 1911), 59–60.

32. See Spariosu, *Dionysus Reborn*, 16–20. There I suggest that one should draw a distinction between archaic and classical mimesis, based on the primarily performative nature of the first kind.

33. For a full discussion of archaic mimesis as play in the *Ion*, see Spariosu, "Plato's *Ion*: Mimesis, Poetry, and Power," in R. Bogue, ed., *Mimesis in Contemporary Theory*, vol. 2, *Mimesis, Semiosis, and Power* (Philadelphia and Amsterdam, 1990), 13–26. Compare also Nietzsche's description of Dionysiac intoxication (*Rausch*) as creating a heightened sense of reality: "Man now expresses himself through song and dance as the member of a higher community; he has forgotten how to walk, how to speak, and is on the brink of taking wing as he dances. Each of his gestures betokens enchantment; through him sounds a supernatural power, the same power which makes the animals speak and the earth render up milk and honey. He feels himself to be godlike and strides with the same elation and ecstacy as the gods he has seen in his dreams" (see, Nietzsche, *The Birth of Tragedy*, trans. F. Golffing [New York, 1956], 24). Nietzsche's evaluation of this mimetic frenzy is entirely positive, whereas that of Socrates is at best ambiguous, considering his discrepant accounts of poetic madness in the *Ion* and the *Phaedrus*.

The regularity of the performance had a certain effect of hypnosis which relaxed the body's physical tensions, the fears, anxieties, and uncertainties which are the normal lot of our mortal existence. Fatigue was temporarily forgotten and perhaps the erotic impulses, no longer blocked by anxiety, were stimulated. . . . It is therefore to be concluded that the recital of the tribal encyclopaedia, because of the technology of the recital, was also a tribal recreation. In more familiar terms, the Muse, the voice of instruction, was also the voice of pleasure.[34]

In the case of Odysseus at the Phaeacian court, the cathartic mechanism works only with the first song, because the second one is too close to home. Shrewd Alcinous soon notices that this song fails to fulfil its customary function (to relax and bring joy to all the guests at his feast) and immediately stops the performance (*Od.* 8.539–43). But Odysseus will achieve catharsis through his own performance, later on, when he tells of his adventures. The performer no less than the audience can obtain pleasurable relief from his song, as when Achilles is found by the Greek embassy "delighting his heart in a lyre" (undoubtedly a much-needed catharsis after his angry confrontation with Agamemnon and his decision to boycott the war).

The archaic bard's mimetic activity as described by Havelock and other classicists has been identified as play by many modern psychologists from Spencer to Groos to Freud.[35] Because archaic mimesis as play combines the auditory-visual with emotion-action and collective participation, it gives the bard considerable power over his audience, whom he can move at will to laughter or tears, to pleasurable composure or violent emotion. This power, which during the early archaic period probably remains unconscious (being attributed to the god and shared collectively), later comes to be used consciously and self-servingly by politicians, rhetoricians, priests, and teachers, as well as by the new breed of professional rhapsodes who are organized in guilds (such as the Homeridae) and who, like Ion, make a living out of performing at religious festivals.

Depending on the occasion, then, in Homer poetic performance as mimesis-play can have an agonistic, a peaceful, or a mixed nature at the

34. Havelock, *Preface to Plato,* 152.
35. We routinely refer to a performer as *playing* a musical piece, which shows that everyday language has preserved the archaic link between playing and performing. For a discussion of modern psychological concepts of play, including those of Spencer, Groos, and Freud, see Spariosu, *Dionysus Reborn,* pt. 2, sec. 1.

same time that its relation to immediate power remains firm. As in the case of women's and children's play, however, it is the quiet rather than the agonistic aspects of artistic play that will receive philosophical sanction in late classical Greece, when Plato and Aristotle attempt to separate it from immediate power and subordinate it to a median mentality. What makes these philosophers uneasy is precisely the archaic mimetic experience underlying both Dionysian ritual and artistic performance, and they seek to effect a divorce between the two by redefining *mimēsis* in logo-rational, philosophical terms.

In the Homeric world, agonistic play is a favored pursuit not only of men but also of the gods. In this respect, the Homeric divine world is an extension rather than a projection of the heroic world: gods differ from heroes, just as heroes differ from ordinary men, in the degree, not in the nature, of their power. Olympian society is as agonistic as the heroic one, having come into existence as a result of a power struggle with an older generation of gods and being organized hierarchically according to the power that each god possesses. This power needs to be constantly put to the test and acknowledged: gods are as jealous of other gods' *timē* and mindful of their own as heroes are. The supreme Olympian authority, Zeus, imposes his will on other gods solely by employing or threatening to employ physical force. The similes that he invokes in his heroic boasts are intended as a display of power and are openly agonistic, as when he effectively challenges the other gods to a "tug of war" in order to overrule any possible objection to his plans: "Come, you gods, make this endeavor, that you may all learn this./ Let down out of the sky a cord of gold; lay hold of it/ all you who are gods and all who are goddesses, yet not/ even so can you drag down Zeus from the sky to the ground. . . ./ So much stronger am I than the gods, and stronger than mortals" (*Il.* 8.18–27). This passage makes it obvious that even such a famous cultural topos as the Great Chain of Being originates in Homeric agonistic play.[36]

Like the *aristoi*, the gods spend a good deal of their time in pursuit of pleasure, which means indulging their feeling of power. Their most beloved games are played with human toys. As scholars have often pointed out, the whole plot of the *Iliad* is a war game among the Olympian gods, with Greeks and Trojans as their pawns. When the two camps wish to cease hostilities and seek resolution of the conflict through a single combat between Menelaus and Paris (that is, through a kind of divine lottery—see *Il.* 3.314–25), the gods have no moral scruples in playing

36. See Arthur O. Lovejoy, *The Great Chain of Being* (Cambridge, Mass., 1936).

foul in order to bring about the resumption of the war (*Il.* 4.1–126). In the *Odyssey*, the central hero is also a plaything of the gods, being tossed back and forth on the high seas for ten years before he is allowed to return home from the Trojan war. When the gods content themselves with remaining neutral, they become spectators, watching human war with great delight, much as human audiences watch athletic games, and death may often enhance rather than diminish their pleasure.[37] Zeus himself is delighted not only by human but also by divine fighting, for example in *Il.* 21.388–90, where he hears the cries of battle on the plains of Ilion, and is "amused in his deep/ heart for pleasure, as he watche[s] the gods' collision in conflict." (Compare also *Il.* 20.19–23, where Zeus prefers to stay on Mount Olympus and watch the human battle, to "pleasure [his] heart," but urges the other gods to go down among the mortals and "give help to either side, as your own pleasure directs you.")

The gods can equally engage in war with other gods and with mortals, experiencing *charmē*, battle-lust, as intensely as heroes do. Apollo's *aristeia*, for example, is explicitly described in terms of pleasurable play: "As when a little boy piles sand by the sea-shores/ when in his innocent play he makes sand towers to amuse him/ and then still playing, with hands and feet ruins them and wrecks them./ So you, lord Apollo, piled in confusion much hard work/ and painful done by the Argives and drove terror among them" (*Il.* 15.362–66).

The analogy of divine and child play in an agonistic context, then, appears for the first time in Homer, suggesting the innocence, spontaneity, and exuberance of unmediated power. This Homeric notion of play as arbitrary, free, and effortless movement analogous to a god's or a child's activity becomes a philosophical principle for the first time in Heraclitus, and will be taken over, in modern times, by Nietzsche and the twentieth-century "artist metaphysicians."[38] The Homeric simile also implicitly opposes the effortlessness and freedom of play with the painful constraints of work, an opposition to which play theorists will return again and again. Finally, Apollo's *aristeia* highlights the difference between archaic play and games of an orderly, median nature: a god, like a child, can invent games to amuse himself, and as such he can create an orderly, rule-governed world ("sand-towers"); as soon as he gets bored, however, still playing, he may destroy this world and start building a new one

---

37. Some readers will undoubtedly be reminded here of *King Lear*: "As flies to wanton boys, are we to the gods/ They kill us for their sport" (act 3, scene 4).
38. See Spariosu, *Dionysus Reborn*, pt. 1, secs. 2 and 3. For a discussion of Heraclitus' notion of power as play, see chapter 2.

according to different rules for no other reason than the sheer pleasure of the game.

The relation of gods to mortals can be not only one of player to plaything but also one of competition. Gods can engage in all kinds of contests with humans, including quarrels during feasts, fighting on the battlefield, athletic and artistic competitions, amorous agon, and so forth.[39] Occasionally they even have to suffer *elenchea* (reproaches or shame) that comes from defeat, at the mortals' hands, especially if the latter are helped by another god. When "sweet-laughing" Aphrodite is wounded by Diomedes, Dione (her mother) consoles her by drawing a list of gods that have had to suffer shameful defeat from men (*Il.* 5.381–404). The gods, however, have immortality on their side, which means that they are only occasionally subjected to disease, suffering, and hard labor (i.e., as long as they are in power—witness, for instance, the older generation of gods, defeated by the Olympians and thrown into Tartarus, whose life could not have been very pleasant). So Dione issues a warning to the mortals who dare compete with gods: "Poor fool, the heart of Tydeus' son knows nothing/ of how that man who fights the immortals lives for no long time,/ his children do not gather to his knees to welcome their father/ when he returns home after the fighting and the bitter warfare" (*Il.* 5.406–9).

Because immortality means relatively extensive freedom for the Homeric gods (limited only by their power), they do not act under the same constraints in relation to mortals that mortals do in relation to one another. For instance, they largely lack a sense of justice or fair play in the modern sense. Since gods are considerably more powerful than men and therefore are "above" them, they have no good reason to behave equitably toward them, although as a rule they are forced to behave equitably toward one another. At the same time, however, they can act as arbiters or even dispensers of human justice, and they do so not out of a sense of duty but simply for the pleasure they derive from the game (which

39. Competitive strife (*eris*) is also the cause of the rift between men and gods, explaining the current miserable human condition. The poet presents strife not only as beneficial but also as destructive: this, of course, is the main (median) theme of the *Iliad*, which shows the destructive consequences of the quarrels among *basileis*. Homer's division of *eris* into good and bad parallels Hesiod's. For a full discussion of strife as determinant of the human condition, see Nagy, *BTA*, 215–21 and 309–16. Nagy also draws useful distinctions between the various Greek words that point to a competitive mentality, such as *neikos* (quarrel, conflict, blame), *eris* (strife, conflict), and *agōn* (contest). All these concepts have a prominent place in the epic tradition and are later adopted by the Greek cosmologists.

enhances their feeling of power). It is for this reason that, from a human perspective, Homeric divine order often appears as a huge lottery in which misery and happiness are distributed according to pure chance rather than merit. Achilles, for instance, invokes this aleatory nature of divine dispensation with regard to humans when he attempts to console Priam: "There is not/ any advantage to be won from grim lamentation./ Such is the way the gods spun life for unfortunate mortals,/ that we live in unhappiness, but the gods themselves have no sorrows./ There are two urns that stand on the door-sill of Zeus. They are unlike/ for the gifts they bestow: an urn of evils, an urn of blessings./ If Zeus who delights in thunder mingles these and bestows them/ on man, he shifts, and moves now in evil, again in good fortune" (*Il.* 24.524–30). Likewise, when Nausicaa finds Odysseus stranded on the shores of Scheria, she consoles him, after his polished plea for hospitality convinces her of his aristocratic background: "Stranger, there is no quirk or evil in you/ that I can see. You know Zeus metes out fortune/ to good and bad men as it pleases him" (*Od.* 6.187–89). In other words, Zeus scatters good and bad fates or lots (*moirae*) among mankind not according to fair play, let alone (rational) divine justice, but according to his own whims.

But the view of the cosmos as a divine lottery is only a partial one, or a view from below (the Homeric gods can in turn have their share of sorrows, even though these are of little concern to mortals, who are rarely directly affected by them). By contrast, Zeus offers a view from above when he comments that mortals blame the gods for their woes (*kaka*) instead of blaming themselves. For example, the gods had warned Aegisthus that it was *huper moron* for him to murder Agamemnon, but he would not listen, acting wantonly or presumptuously (*atasthaliēisin . . . echousin, Od.* 1.34). This passage has been regarded as an example of a dawning sense of moral responsibility in Greek thought (by Adkins, Strauss Clay, and others), but an equally plausible explanation from the standpoint of the Homeric ethical code can be sought in the archaic notion of *atē*, blindness, lack of foresight, which leads to *hubris*, a false step in the cosmic power game. What Zeus omits mentioning is that Aegisthus, from his position below, could not know for certain whether he could get away with Agamemnon's murder or not; in other words, he could not know whether the gods were trying to help him or mislead him, and therefore had to find out for himself. Only after he fails does his action appear reprehensible (heroes frequently commit iniquitous acts and get away with them—witness, for instance, Theseus, Heracles, and Jason), bringing with it the explanation that he became intoxicated with power and went

beyond his share (*huper moron*).[40] Zeus himself seems somewhat to pre-
clude a moral interpretation of *atasthaliai* (wantonness) when he observes
that Aegisthus miscalculated his move, discounting not only several divine
warnings but also, more palpably, Orestes, who was bound to come and
avenge his father's murder (*Od.* 1.40).

From the point of view of the defeated, agon no longer looks like
unlimited freedom, but like shameful bondage, and power is no longer
experienced as ecstatic pleasure, but as unbearable pain. From below,
then, agon will often appear as a wheel of fortune that lifts some
contestants and sinks others. When the contestants are on top, as Simone
Weil points out, "their own destruction seems impossible to them. For
they do not see that the force in their possession is a limited quantity. . . .
And at this point they exceed the measure of the force that is actually at
their disposal. Inevitably they exceed it, since they are not aware that it is
limited. And now we see them committed irretrievably to chance; suddenly things cease to obey them. Sometimes chance is kind to them,
sometimes cruel. But in any case there they are exposed, open to
misfortune."[41]

Agon becomes an interminable "game (*jeu*) of seesaw" in which the
temporary victor "forgets to treat victory as a transitory thing."[42] It also
brings about a kind of negative justice whose logic demands that those
who live by the sword must also die by it: "The war god is impartial.
Before now he has killed the killer" (*Il.* 18.309).[43] Heraclitus formulates
the same principle later on, when he says, for example, that "war is
common and right is strife and . . . all things happen by strife and
necessity."[44] In this respect, note the close link between contest, justice,
and *moira* in archaic thought.

Moira (or *Aisa*) is commonly regarded as immutable Fate that binds man

40. Of course, the viewpoint of the poet, standing as he does outside the Homeric world,
is a view from above, coinciding with that of Zeus. From the poet's standpoint, both
Aegisthus and, say, the violators of hospitality in the *Odyssey* get their just deserts. We are
for the moment considering the Homeric world from within, not as the (median) poet
might see it, and the reader is urged to keep this double perspective in mind throughout
our discussion.
41. Simone Weil, *The Iliad or the Poem of Force*, trans. M. McCarthy (Wallingford, Pa.,
1956), 14–15.
42. Ibid., 14.
43. This is a judgment from below. Pallas-Athena, for instance, calls Ares a "thing of fury,
evil-wrought, that double-faced liar" (*Il.* 5.831).
44. Heraclitus, Diels-Kranz B 214, in G. S. Kirk and J. E. Raven, *The Presocratic
Philosophers: A Critical History with a Selection of Texts* (Cambridge, 1957), 195.

from his birth. But in the Homeric world it can also appear as the share of power that man competes for, with defeat or death circumscribing the limits of the game. As in the case of Aegisthus, the hero takes calculated risks against the celestial bank, and his *moira* (share, portion) becomes fate, in the modern sense, only after he loses and comes to grief. For an archaic mentality, misery and sorrow are not caused by power per se but, rather, by a lack of it.

The gods, who from below are always seen as gay, carefree, and "rejoicing in power," can change a mortal's share (and in a very few cases they do), but this would mean playing against their own rules. Their (largely self-assumed) role is that of celestial overseers, who guarantee the observance of the rules for men. When Zeus considers saving Hector's life, Athena objects: "Father of the shining bolt, dark misted, what is this you said?/ do you wish to bring back a man who is mortal, one long since/ doomed by his destiny [share], from ill-sounding death and release him?/ Do it then; but not all the rest of us gods shall approve you" (*Il.* 22.178–81).

Athena reminds Zeus that he ought to play by the gods' rules, which normally deny immortal shares to men (otherwise, the latter may get too powerful and attempt to unseat the gods—consider, for instance, the myth of the hermaphrodites in Plato's *Symposium*).[45] Should Zeus lift Hector *huper moron*, he would set a dangerous precedent for the other gods, thus disturbing the established Olympian order and ultimately leading to anarchy (a word with the strongest negative emotional coloration for a power-oriented system of values).

It seems, then, that in an archaic world of the Homeric type, agon creates *moira*, just as it creates and destroys all human and divine hierarchies. The gods themselves have their *moirae* or their shares of power; it is just that their shares both encompass and supersede those of the mortals. From below, the Homeric world order appears "not so much like a piece of clockwork as . . . like a game of celestial snakes and ladders." Whereas most moves are free, once one alights "at the foot of one's particular ladder, or at the head of one's particular snake, the next move is determined."[46]

45. Compare also the Mesopotamian myth, as it appears in the *Gilgamesh*, in which the gods steal immortality (a physical rather than a transcendental object) from men and hide it in a safe place.
46. Adkins, *MR*, 19. Archaic *moira* supposedly also meant "land" or "property share," and if this supposition is correct, then its archaic connection to power is again obvious. See George Thomson, *Aeschylus and Athens* (London, 1941), 37. I disagree, however, with Thomson's suggestion that the Greek notion of *moira* is a protocommunist one. For other

Moira can finally be seen as a way of turning competition into a median, logo-rational principle, of transforming the arbitrary, violent, and irrational play of power into a cultural game subjected to rules. In this sense, power can also assume the cultural guise of an interplay of necessity and chance, as Adkins' game metaphor of chutes and ladders suggests. The connection of necessity and chance to power as freedom (or as lack thereof) can equally be traced linguistically because both *anankē* and *tuchē* seem to be related to the notion of "binding." *Anankē* has been seen by some scholars (for example, by Onians) as an etymological relative of *anchein*, to strangle. Likewise, its Latin equivalent *necesse* is "almost naturally related to *necto, nexus*, with an original reference to binding or being bound."[47] *Anankē* is thus connected to the threads of the Moirae who spin their nets around mortals. *Tuchē*, chance, seems in turn to have been conceived as tying cords (*peismata*) around men which they can loosen after death.[48] In archaic thought, *anankē* and *tuchē* seem often to be used interchangeably and, from below, the Homeric cosmos appears as the play of chance-necessity. It is only in later classical thought (for example, in Plato, Aristotle, and the Stoics) that chance becomes separated from and subordinated to necessity, and *Anankē* becomes interchangeable with *Moira*, to denote pre-established Fate or Destiny.[49]

In Homer, moreover, *moira* and death are also often used interchangeably, so perhaps death itself can best be understood as a power concept: the *psuchē* or "shade" of the dead hero is *powerless*. Odysseus has to feed blood to the shades of the dead so that they can temporarily regain force (*Od.* 11.23–50). In its live form, Homeric *psuchē* can perhaps also be translated as "life-force," or that which actuates and moves the body.[50]

discussions of *moira*, see E. Ehnmark, *The Idea of God in Homer* (Uppsala, 1935); E. Leitzke, *Moira und Gottheit* (Göttingen, 1930); M. P. Nilsson, *Greek Piety*, trans. H. J. Rose (Oxford, 1951); Onians, *OET*; and B. C. Dietrich, *Death, Fate and the Gods: The Development of a Religious Idea in Greek Popular Belief and in Homer* (London, 1965).
47. See Onians, *OET*, 332–33. On *anchein* and *apanchein* in Homer, see Prier, *Thauma Idesthai*, 32 n.12. For a detailed examination of the historical development of *anankē*, see Wilhelm Gundel, *Beiträge zur Entwicklungsgeschichte von Anankē und Heimarmene* (Giessen, 1914) and, more recently, Heinz Schreckenberg, *Anankē: Untersuchungen zur Geschichte des Wortgebrauchs*, Zetemata 36 (Munich, 1964).
48. Onians, *OET*, 450. For further discussion of the relation between *anankē*, *moira*, and *tuchē*, see below, chapter 2.
49. Compare Schreckenberg, *Anankē*, 109–10 and 122–24.
50. This interpretation is admittedly conjectural, since all we know for certain about archaic *psuchē* in Homer is that it leaves the body upon swooning or death. For a full discussion of this question, see David B. Claus, *Toward the Soul: An Inquiry into the Meaning*

An archaic mentality, therefore, possibly sees not only death but also life in terms of power, and *bios* (life) and *bia* (force, violence) seem to bear a strong family resemblance.[51]

I have so far viewed Homeric epic from within, that is, from the standpoint of the heroic world. One can now change perspectives and look at this world from outside, from the poet's standpoint. From this standpoint, Homeric values based on unmediated, violent power, have lost their innocence and are experienced in the tragic guise that becomes the main concern of Hellenic drama.[52] The crisis of archaic values

of "Psyche" before Plato (New Haven, 1981). See also Nagy, who notes that in some contexts *anapsuchein* "overtly means not 'bring back to life' but 'bring back to vigor' " and argues that, judging from other contexts, the "*psuchē* that is lost in the process of swooning is surely the same *psuchē* that is regained in the process of reviving from a swoon" (Nagy, *BTA*, 168). Nagy thus seems to corroborate my view that at least in certain contexts *psuchē* can mean "force" or "vigor."

51. For an illuminating discussion of the vocabulary of power in the Homeric poems, see Nagy, *BTA*, esp. 69–93 and 317–46. In Homer words such as *menos* (might, rage), *sthenos* (strength), *biē* (physical might, violence), *is* (physical might, violence), *kratos* (superior or divine power), and *dunamis* (physical force) seem generally to denote concrete, physical, and often violent forms of power. One may add, on the other hand, that in Classical Greek (and especially in the philosophical vocabulary), these words tend to acquire increasingly abstract and metaphorical connotations until some of them come to designate impersonal symbols of force, such as *dunamis* and *energeia* in physics (we still preserve this power-oriented terminology in the modern sciences). Nagy's analysis also shows that the ethical polarization of power as good and bad is already present in archaic poetry. This polarization can equally be related to a shift in emphasis from archaic to median values.

52. It is also the self-conscious standpoint of the poet (and reader) that transcends the Homeric world and creates the intertextual play to which Pietro Pucci, among others, draws attention. In *Odysseus Polutropos* (Ithaca, N.Y., 1987), Pucci notes: "All the language in Homer is allusive: to different degrees, all the epic language plays constantly in a ludic display of intertextual noddings, winks, and gestures, and accordingly puts itself on stage and acts out its own idiosyncrasies and preferences in a sort of narcissistic extravaganza while it says what it says. This signifying level, that of the allusive sense, is unknown to the characters, may also fully or in part escape the intention of the poets, and constitutes an implicit addition for the reader to decode in order to interpret the text. What we call literature is nothing else but this" (240). It can be argued that, at the level of the poet, this self-conscious, intertextual play is a way of undermining traditional, heroic values, an argument that seems especially plausible in the case of the *Odyssey* (although even in the *Iliad* there is, as we have seen, a constant tension between the heroic and the poetic viewpoints). At the level of text-reader, on the other hand, even the median values that seem to be endorsed by the poet are open to question at least in two ways: either from an archaic standpoint or from a perspective other than power oriented. Although Pucci's arguments go beyond a modern ethical code, they seem to subscribe to a mentality of power, as indeed all deconstructive criticism does.

becomes also the crisis of the Homeric hero, who can be seen as the product of a transitional period. In historical terms, one can establish a parallel between the shift in emphasis from archaic to median values in the Homeric epic and the transition from the archaic *oikos* (aristocratic rural estate) to the classical *polis* (city-state) in the Hellenic world. As some archaic, rural communities based on strictly hierarchical, aristocratic power configurations move toward the median sociopolitical structures of the classical *polis*, they require fewer "heroes" and more responsible citizens. The historical counterpart of the Homeric hero slowly becomes useless, unless he can adapt himself to median power configurations that increasingly stress cooperation and persuasion over raw, physical contest.[53] Achilles and Odysseus, the two heroes at the center of the two epics, seem best to embody this shift in cultural emphasis, which has far-reaching consequences for the Homeric world.

The poet of the *Iliad* seems to present Achilles as an uncompromising hero who undergoes a personal crisis in terms of the changing values in

53. From this point of view, the problematic of the Homeric epic can roughly and *mutatis mutandis* be compared to that of the modern American western: in the latter, the gunfighter, who has always operated on the archaic principle of might makes right, must slowly integrate himself into or be expelled from a community that increasingly operates on a median principle of law and order. For historical background on the transition from the archaic community to the classical *polis*, the reader can consult, among many others, Finley, *The World of Odysseus*, and *Early Greece: The Bronze and Archaic Ages* (London, 1970); and Victor Ehrenberg, *The Greek State*, 2d ed. (Oxford, 1969) and *From Solon to Socrates: Greek History and Civilization during the Sixth and Fifth Centuries B.C.* (London, 1968). Here one may also wish to raise the question of the value of the Homeric epic as historical evidence. There are those who deny the existence of heroic societies outside the fictional worlds of the epic (both ancient and medieval) contending that these societies have left very few, if any, traces in the historical record. Other scholars reply that since these archaic societies are mostly oral, they can have left only indirect traces in some of the written documents (such as the recorded epic) that already belong to a nonheroic society. But whether heroic societies existed or not is of secondary importance to my analysis, since I am interested in describing a certain mentality, which can have both historical and imaginary features (compare my methodological remarks in the preface). Furthermore, a certain mentality can survive through many political, economical, and institutional changes, and consequently, its study is only secondarily dependent on an examination of the socioeconomic and political structures of specific communities such as ancient Athens or Sparta. It is this asynchronous relation between mentality and institution that a positivist historicism, including the orthodox Marxian kind, often ignores. Witness, for example, the modern communist regimes that, true to their Marxist-Leninist positivistic view of history, attempt to abolish median or "bourgeois" socioeconomic structures and institutions, allegedly in order to change the mentality of power that produced them, but invariably end up with unmediated, repressive, or absolutist forms of power.

his community, a change that in effect leads to the demise of the heroic way of life. When he rejects Agamemnon's embassy, Achilles does not do so out of willfulness or false pride, but because he has little choice.[54] In an impassioned speech, he points to the leveling of heroic values under the pressure of commercialism: "Fate [*moira*, share, lot, but also war booty] is the same for the man who holds back, the same if he fights hard/ We are held in a single honor, the brave with the weaklings./ Nothing is won for me, now that my heart has gone through its afflictions/ in forever setting my life on the hazard of battle" (*Il.* 9.318–21).

What Achilles deplores (at the very moment that he is offered ample compensation by Agamemnon) is that the war booty (*moira*) is no longer distributed according to the old standard of prowess in battle, but according to political and economic expediency. In the Homeric world *timē* and material possessions cannot be separated, and it is their alleged separation by Agamemnon that precipitates Achilles' crisis. In the latter's eyes, possessions seem no longer to bespeak *timē* but solely mercantile values. He opposes a heroic economy of exchange (a short, violent life in return for *timē* or immortality in song as communal memory) to a purely commercial economy of exchange based on material goods.[55] Achilles contends that Agamemnon replaces his prizes with wares, seeking to shortchange him again: "Of possessions/ cattle and fat sheep are things to be had for the lifting,/ and tripods can be won, and the tawny high heads of horses,/ but a man's life cannot come back again, it can not be lifted/ nor captured again by force, once it has crossed the teeth's barrier" (*Il.* 9.406–9).

Next Achilles appropriately invokes his mother's prophecy regarding his choice of *moirae*: if he stays and fights under the walls of Troy, his life

54. For a different view of Achilles and the embassy episode, see Finley, *The World of Odysseus*, 117–18, and Redfield, *Nature and Culture*, 15–17. My own interpretation of Achilles' situation, which I regard as *the* tragic paradigm, parallels Bernard Knox's view of Ajax's tragic situation as presented by Sophocles in his *Ajax*. See Knox, "The Ajax of Sophocles," *HSCP* 65 (1961): 1–37.

55. Of course, the heroic economy of exchange could be a pure invention of the poet, who through Achilles idealizes an archaic aristocratic mentality that gives no more transcendental value to material goods (except, perhaps, as symbols of power) than a median mentality does. Indeed, the aristocratic transcendentalization of material possessions probably takes place only after median values become dominant; it then begins to function as a mode of social differentiation between an impoverished aristocracy and an increasingly wealthy middle class. In sum, it must not be forgotten that the poem has a double perspective, that of the Homeric world and that of the poet, who looks back upon this world; as such, it remains an amalgam of aristocratic and median values.

will be short, but his fame everlasting; if he returns home, his glory will be gone, but he will enjoy a long life (*Il.* 9.410–16).[56] In effect, as Achilles well knows, he has no choice but to die in battle precisely because he cannot renounce heroic values. Given Achilles' decision, Agamemnon's compensation remains useless to him (despite Odysseus' shrewd argument to the contrary), and this is why later Achilles listlessly accepts it while impatiently urging return to the battlefield—the only place where he can accumulate fame. Significantly, it is again Odysseus who deters him with talk of food and rest (*Il.* 19.145–83). With the death of Achilles shortly following that of his main Trojan competitor, Hector, there dies a whole heroic age. In this sense, the poet's ending of the *Iliad* with Hector's funeral is doubly appropriate. The "tragedy of Hector" (in Redfield's sense) is no different from that of Achilles and both are seen, at the end of the epic, from the median perspective of the poet, who regards the values of the Homeric world as alien and yet feels their inescapable, nostalgic attraction. The poet of the *Iliad*, then, is in the position of Odysseus who, tied to the mast, listens to the heartbreaking song of the Sirens, but is finally forced to sail by, recognizing their seductive dangers.

Yet *quod non licet Jovi, licet bovi*: whereas Achilles' heroic portion is to die in battle, Odysseus' *moira* is to return home to a long, peaceful life, but not before he undergoes a ten-year period of partial transition from heroic to median values.[57] This transition begins with his sojourn on the island of

56. The very fact that Achilles has a choice seems to indicate that archaic *moira* is not predetermined, but is actively sought.

57. I am partly indebted for this discussion to Theodor W. Adorno and Max Horkheimer, *Dialektik der Aufklärung* (Amsterdam, 1944), trans. John Cumming (New York, 1972), esp. "Excursus I: Odysseus or Myth and Enlightenment." There is also a certain resemblance between Adorno and Horkheimer's dialectic of Myth and Enlightenment based on domination (*Herrschaft*) and my model of archaic and median mentality based on immediate and mediated power configurations. But our basic premises are different. For example, for Adorno and Horkheimer mimesis in its original form (before it becomes contaminated by domination and turns into imitation) is an authentic mode of Being, while for me it is already power in its innocent form of violent, archaic play. Consequently, Adorno and Horkheimer still employ the Vaihengerian fiction of the totality of Being, which is a philosophical product of the median nostalgia for immediate power, and which for them functions as a golden age. They also make an implicit distinction, characteristic of Marxist theory, between power and domination, which is of secondary importance for my argument: domination is the most naked and visible form of power, which is relatively easy to detect but which, by its very visibility, covers up other, more occult forms. The distinction between domination and power makes it possible, for example, to justify theoretically such "good" forms of power as the dictatorship of the proletariat. In this regard, Adorno and Horkheimer fail to see that power is neither good

Calypso, whose offer of immortality and unwedded love he rejects in favor of family and community. Having safely arrived in the civilized, Hellenic world, at the court of urbane Alcinous, who is "secure in power" (*Od.* 7.167), Odysseus can now leave behind not only the heroic world of the Trojan War (which is already rationalized into nostalgia, in the song of the Sirens), but also the mythical worlds of the Cyclops (a barbarian equivalent of the Homeric world in its unashamed, violent guise) and of the Lotus-eaters (a nonviolent, anarchical utopia based on drug-induced serenity and peaceful inactivity, which for a power-oriented mentality is as unacceptable as raw violence).

In his voyage to Hades, Odysseus also meets a changed Achilles, who would now gladly trade his fate of a famous but dead hero for that of an obscure but alive farmhand (*Od.* 11.488–91). The implication is that Achilles has also left behind the heroic ethical code for the median values of the "country gentleman" (in the modern sense), which favor a long, relatively peaceful existence over a short and violent one, no matter what the gains might be in terms of posthumous *timē*.[58]

Penelope's suitors behave very similarly to the heroes in the Trojan War, yet they incur the poet's disapproval, being sharply contrasted with such polished *aristoi* as Nestor and Menelaus, who have seemingly left violence behind them and have become "secure in power." Odysseus' homecoming is, moreover, contrasted to that of Agamemnon: whereas Odysseus still has the loyal support of his family, Agamemnon meets a violent death at the hands of his wife and her lover (it is Orestes' portion to effect the Atridae's transition to mediated power, for instance, in Aeschylus' trilogy).

Arbitrary, immediate power is now often disapproved of and repudiated as non-Hellenic or barbarian (as in the Cyclops episode), but the violent origin of median values becomes all too obvious in the episode of the slaying of the suitors (just as, in Aeschylus, Orestes has to kill his mother before Athena introduces a relatively quiet dispensation in the

---

nor evil but, rather, that it creates good and evil, as well as many other cultural dichotomies (including that between an archaic and a median mentality).

58. Achilles' words can also be interpreted in terms of an archaic mentality because his contemptuous references to the dead as "exhausted" and as "after-images of used-up men" are in line with an archaic definition of death as lack of power. In this sense, the last among human beings (a farmhand) would have more power (life-force) than the first among the dead (a hero-king). The poet's implicit comment still indicates a change in values, even though these values remain power oriented: a heroic life leads to an early death, and therefore to an early loss of power.

aftermath of the famous trial scene). In this episode, Odysseus temporarily reverts to a heroic mentality and reenacts the violence that lies at the foundation of any power-oriented culture. Once he reestablishes his authority, he can return to the quiet values that have been praised in his wife and son throughout the epic.

Teiresias' oracle, advising Odysseus to bury an oar in a place where it would be mistaken for a winnowing fan, is an apt symbol for the cultural transformation that takes place in the *Odyssey*. The oar stands for Poseidon in his violent guise, as the embodiment of the adventurous, dangerous, and uncontrollable world of the sea. When it is buried in the ground, it becomes a symbol of the peaceful world of agriculture but also of Odysseus' change of identity from warrior to country gentleman (it was not uncommon in ancient Greece to bury a person with the appurtenances of his profession). And so the world of the hawk recedes into the background, allowing the world of the nightingale to come to the fore.[59]

■ *The Nightingale and the Hawk*

The Homeric epic shows archaic values in transition, largely from the nostalgic perspective of a Golden Age, in which men were twice as strong

59. Here, again, I mean a shift in emphasis from one world to another, rather than the replacement of one world by the other. One should also not insist, as Marxist scholarship would, on the strict affiliation of the two worlds to specific social classes. Although archaic and median values can loosely be associated with various aristocratic and median groups, they are only partially dependent on these groups. Probably both sets of values originate with the archaic ruling elite, and it is only later on, in the classical period, that median values become primarily identified with nonaristocratic groups. At the same time, the warrior group itself tends to moderate its violent, agonistic values during relatively quiet moments in the history of its community or under the pressure of a central authority, such as a king or an emperor. In predominantly median communities, aristocratic values become idealized in the figure of the "gentleman," who plays by fair rules and exercises authority mostly through natural superiority of mind and demeanor rather than physical coercion (although the "gentleman" is mainly an Italian, French, and English invention of the late Middle Ages and early Renaissance, his type can already be discerned, as we have seen, in the *Odyssey*, in King Alcinous of Phaeacia, as well as in Odysseus, Menelaus, and Nestor, after these warriors return from the Trojan War and become "secure in power"). It is for these reasons that the aristocracy itself can often contribute to the creation and dissemination of median values. For instance, such aristocrats as Solon and some of the other Old Sages or, later, Plato play an important role in enhancing the authority of median values in Hellenic thought. Also Christianity, which as a cross-cultural movement was supported by both the aristocracy and the median groups, was instrumental in spreading a median mentality to most of Western Europe in the early Middle Ages.

36 GOD OF MANY NAMES

as "they are now" (*Il.* 12.381–83, 445–49). In the *Odyssey* this golden age based on the violent, agonistic play of a warrior group is largely replaced by another golden age, the Phaeacian model, which Odysseus brings to Ithaca at the end of the epic and which is based on the relatively quiet competition of a wealthy, urbane aristocracy "secure in power." Hesiod shares these quieter values in the *Theogony* and the *Works and Days*, presenting them from the viewpoint of the well-to-do Boeotian farmer.[60] From this perspective, the median notion of work seems to be emphasized over the aristocratic notion of (violent) play, and Hesiod's poetry, no less than Homer's, seems to point to an opposition between play and work that in modern times becomes central to Western culture as a whole.

Before examining Hesiod's poems, it would be helpful to recall briefly the historical record of Hellenic median values. In the archaic *oikos* as described by Homer median values seem to have been required mostly of the *basileus'* dependents, including old men, women, and children (hence

60. The traditional view of Hesiod as a poor peasant (see, for example, Werner Jaeger, *Paideia: The Ideals of Greek Culture*, 3 vols., trans. G. Highet [Oxford, 1939–45], 1:55–73) has recently been challenged. See, among others, C. G. Starr, *The Origin of the Greek Civilization* (New York, 1961); Marcel Detienne, *Crise agraire et attitude réligieuse chez Hésiode* (Brussels, 1963); and Pietro Pucci, *Hesiod and the Language of Poetry* (Baltimore, 1977). In addition to these studies, my discussion is partly based on Francis M. Cornford, *Principium Sapientiae* (Cambridge, 1952); Frisch, "Hesiod," in *Might and Right in Antiquity*, 81–99; Friedrich Solmsen, *Hesiod and Aeschylus* (Ithaca, N.Y., 1949), pt. 1: "Hesiod"; Eric A. Havelock, "The Justice of Hesiod," in *The Greek Concept of Justice from Its Shadow in Homer to Its Substance in Plato* (Cambridge, Mass., 1978), 193–217, and "Hesiod and Poetry," in *Preface to Plato*, 97–114; J. P. Vernant, "Hesiod's Myth of the Races: An Essay in Structural Analysis," in *Myth and Thought among the Greeks* (London, 1983), 3–33, and "Hesiod's Myth of the Races: A Reassessment," in the same book, 33–72; G. P. Edwards, *The Language of Hesiod in Its Traditional Context* (Oxford, 1971); Heinz Neitzel, *Homer-Rezeption bei Hesiod* (Bonn, 1975); Kurt von Fritz, G. S. Kirk et al., *Hésiode et son influence*, Fondation Hardt, vol. 7 (Geneva, 1960); Detienne, *Les maîtres de vérité*, chaps. 2 and 4; Annie Bonnafé, *Eros et Eris: Marriage divins et mythe de succession chez Hésiode* (Lyon, 1985); as well as M. L. West's Prolegomena and Commentary to the *Theogony* (Oxford, 1966) and to *Works and Days* (Oxford, 1978). The controversy over whether Homer composed before Hesiod or Hesiod before Homer remains, I believe, inconclusive and, in view of my general thesis, of secondary importance: no less than Homer, Hesiod (should he indeed prove to be a historical rather than a legendary figure) is an authorial convention for a body of oral poetry that, before and after being written down, must have undergone constant changes well into the classical period, if not throughout Antiquity (none of the extant Greek manuscripts is earlier than the eleventh century A.D., and the majority of them date from the fifteenth and the sixteenth centuries). As in the case of Homer, median values are superimposed on their archaic counterparts, lending the Hesiodic texts a divided, double perspective.

the precarious situation of Odysseus' household during his absence, in the *Odyssey*); they were also invoked by shaman-priests in dealing with the warriors (see, for instance, the beginning of the *Iliad*) and by some of the traditional sages, as well as by certain commoners, including rich farmers, poets, tradesmen, craftsmen, and so forth. In Hesiod, such terms as *metrios* (moderate), *mesos* (in the middle), and *kairos* (due measure) primarily describe the life proper to a farmer (for example, in *Works and Days*, 40, 306–7, and 694; see my discussion later in this section).

In the early sixth century B.C., sayings such as "Know thyself" (*Gnothi sauton*), "Nothing in excess" (*Mēden agan*), "Measure (*metron*) is best," "Understand due measure (*kairos*)," "Honor moderation (*sōphrosunē*)," and "Flee from sensuous pleasure (*hedonē*)" are attributed to some of the Seven Sages, such as Cleobulus, Chilon, Pittacus, and Solon. During the same century, "Know thyself" and "Nothing in excess" are inscribed over the entrance to the Alcmaeonid temple of Apollo and Apollo's shaman-priests at Delphi preach due measure and restraint.[61]

With the growth of the *polis*, these injunctions become more and more common, for example in the poetry of Theognis, Alcman, Pindar, Phocylides, Bacchylides, and others, as well as in fifth-century Greek tragedy. Although their origins are aristocratic and as such are used by statesmen like Pittacus of Mytilene and Solon to support *eunomia*, these proverbs seem gradually to acquire a democratic flavor, being placed in the service of *isonomia*.[62] From the very beginning, however, median gnomic wisdom seems designed to temper excessive agonistic values rather than do away with them altogether, and therefore, in the city-states no less than in the Homeric and Hesiodic worlds, cooperation remains at all times subordinated to competition.

As we have seen from this brief overview, Hesiod is one of the first thinkers that promote median values in the Hellenic world. In the *Theogony*, traditionally seen as his earlier opus, Hesiod employs epic language and, implicitly, heroic values, but only in order to question them, attempting, however ineffectively, to replace them with median values. Through this attempt, Hesiod makes explicit what in the *Iliad* and

61. For a full discussion of the proverbs that deal with the Mean, see, among others, H. J. Mette, *Mēden agan* (Munich, 1933), and H. W. Parke and D. E. W. Wormell, *The Delphic Oracle* (Oxford, 1956).
62. For the link of the Delphic wisdom to middle-class ideology, see Thomson, *Aeschylus and Athens*, 283 and 350. But the doctrine of the golden mean obviously transcends any single social class, as is evidenced in the philosophy, the arts, and the crafts of the classical period.

the *Odyssey* largely remains implicit: the divided, contradictory nature of all values belonging to a mentality of power. The *Theogony* can be seen as consisting of two (interrelated) sections: the first examines the nature of epic poetry and the cultural role of the poet, whereas the second examines the nature of divine and human power in the archaic community.

In the Proem (*Theog.* 1–115), Hesiod supplements the traditional epic invocation of, and hymn to, the Muses with an account of his encounter, on Mount Helicon, with the Muses themselves: "These are the Muses who once taught Hesiod beautiful song/ as he was pasturing his flock in the foothills of holy Mount Helikon./ This is the speech with which I was first addressed by these goddesses,/ the Muses who sing on Olympos, the daughters of Zeus of the Aigis:/ 'Shepherds who dwell in the fields, base creatures, disgraces, mere bellies,/ we know how to tell numerous lies which seem to be truthful,/ but whenever we wish we know how to utter the full truth' " (*Theog.* 22–28).

By dramatizing his encounter with the Muses, Hesiod separates himself from them, having them speak to him, rather than through him. He thus allows the Muses to reflect upon the nature of their art. In turn, he becomes their representative, rather than a mere vehicle of their song, and as such he implicitly enters in competition with other poets (Homer or the Homeridae?) for the privilege of being their authorized spokesman. And this authority is no longer based merely on divine inspiration, but also on knowledge and truth. Like all the other gods, the Muses can both lie and tell the truth, and thereby they can favor some poets over others; in turn, the poet has to show discrimination, or a critical ability to separate the truth from the lie, and therefore he assumes an enormous cultural responsibility in contrast to his predecessor, the singer of tales, who probably was the mere unconscious voice of the Muses.

By separating himself from the Muses, therefore, Hesiod in effect distances himself from the epic tradition and is able to view it critically. At the same time, however, the Muses do breathe a divine voice into his mouth and order him to sing (*Theog.* 33–34), and so Hesiod finds himself in a paradoxical situation: he, a baseborn shepherd (a disgrace, a mere belly), is chosen by the highborn Muses as a vehicle for their song about almighty Zeus and the Olympian gods, a divine and heroic world that must surely be alien to him. This paradoxical situation actually reflects the paradox of any archaic rhapsode who turns into a poet, and can also apply to Homer: although the poet harks back to a heroic age, he is no longer part of that age, thus changing into a nightingale who sings (and at the same time reflects upon) a hawk's song.

This paradox becomes particularly manifest in Hesiod's (unsuccessful) attempt to separate the poet (*aoidos*) from the lord (*basileus*), or to separate poetic speech from political speech. In a heroic community the poetic and the political functions remain largely indistinguishable, and this original unity between lord and poet is reflected in Hesiod's statement that Calliope is the "most important of the [Muses], for she grants her ready attendance to honorable kings [*basileis*, lords]," breathing into them the gift of poetic speech: "Every Zeus-graced lord they look on with favor at birth,/ receives from them on his tongue a sweet pouring of heavenly dew,/ and from his mouth flow honeyed words. Then the people/ all look in honor to him interpreting the customs [*themistes*]/ with straight verdicts; and he by his smooth and unerring speech/ swiftly brings even to great disagreements a skillful solution./ Lords are considered wise because whenever their people/ need some redress they in assembly see that they gain it/ easily, using their skill in the art of mollifying persuasion" (*Theog.* 81–90).

This passage has frequently been compared to the one in the *Odyssey*, where Odysseus, in response to the challenge of one of his Phaeacian hosts (deriding the stranger's ungainly appearance), describes a gifted lord as one who elicits obedience in the assembly not through his looks but through the power of his mellifluous speech (*Od.* 8.158–74); Hesiod's description, no less than that of Odysseus, seems to point to the original interchangeability of poetry and (political) rhetoric as immediate forms of power.

In Homer, as in Hesiod, the archaic voice has a major performative role, for it is less what the speaker says than how he says it that impresses an archaic audience. Both in the *Iliad* and in the *Odyssey* one gets a glimpse of the function of the voice as power when the gods manifest themselves to the heroes, telling them what to do. In turn, the gods and the heroes differ from ordinary men not only by their special, vision-blurring, radiance but also by the overwhelming strength and, therefore, authority of their voices. Achilles' war cry suffices to keep the Trojan army away from his ships, Apollo and Ares sow panic in the ranks of the armies through their thunderlike voices, and Stentor remains to this day proverbial for his battle cry. In historical or recorded times, when the gods seem reluctant to show themselves to men (except during periods of stress, such as during the Persian wars), their authoritative voices live on in the oracles, as "belly-voices," and in the hypnotic chants of the rhapsodes, as "muses" (who can also be viewed as a form of ventriloquism in the sense that they take over or *possess* the singer of tales, speaking through him rather than to him).

Yet the voice can not only frighten but also coax into obedience, as in the *Odyssey*, where the Sirens lure Odysseus by their rhythmic, hypnotic chanting, and where Odysseus himself, no less than the gifted lord he refers to in book 8, sways his audience by the peculiar quality of his voice and speech, so much so that this audience forgets his ungainly physical appearance.[63] And it is this mellifluous, incantatory quality of lordly speech that Hesiod also refers to in the Proem of his *Theogony*.

In the very next lines, however, Hesiod attempts to separate the lord from the poet, attributing to each a different genealogy: "For by the power of the Muses and far-shooting Apollo/ men who sing and play on the lyre [*aoidoi*, minstrels] are brought to earth;/ lords are from Zeus" (*Theog.* 94–96). The function of the lord (in the assembly, *not* in war) is to give straight verdicts, in keeping with customary law. This function he

63. Socrates preserves this archaic trait in Plato's dialogues, where his unattractive physique is compensated by his seductive rhetoric (e.g., in the *Phaedrus*, the *Symposium*, and the *Republic*). For a median mentality, therefore, speech and voice remain an important source of authority, in the form of persuasion, and *peithō* becomes a goddess. (For a detailed discussion of the *peithō* semantic group the reader can consult, among others, A. Oguse, "A propos de la syntaxe de *peithō* et de *pisteuo*," *Revue des études grecques* 78 [1965]: 513–41; and George M. Pepe, "Studies in Peitho," [Ph.D. diss., Princeton University, 1966]; most semantic studies of the *peithō* group point out its dynamic, performative nature, generally conveying the idea of "prevailing or being prevailed upon," usually not by physical force, but by offering rewards, gratification, or favors. Significantly, Peitho as a goddess appears for the first time in Hesiod, in *Theog.* 349 and *Works and Days* [hereafter *WD*] 73.)

In classical times and even later, the *technē* of rhetoric itself remains closely bound to poetry and to oral, mnemonic practices. In fact, rhetoric deliberately traces its history back to and justifies its authority upon orality, as for instance in Isocrates, who praises the power of speech as being able to make people cry or to move stones—hackneyed metaphors that once may have been inescapably literal. Even Plato, who attempts to undermine the archaic (rhythmic, incantatory) power of rhetoric by infusing it with logo-rational self-knowledge and justice (for instance, in the *Protagoras* and the *Sophist*), still considers speech to be superior to writing: for him writing is only a pale, unreliable and inauthentic duplication of speech (for instance, in the *Phaedrus*). On the other hand, when Plato praises rhetoric, he does so precisely because it prevails upon men through logo-rational means rather than through physical violence. Thus "the art of persuasion (*peithein*) is superior to all arts: for she overwhelms all things not through physical force (*dia bias*) but with their consent (*di' hekonton*)" (*Phil.* 58a). Note, however, that the art of rhetoric remains power oriented even as it decries physical violence.

performs not by physical compulsion, but by the persuasive power of poetic speech. Although the lord descends directly from Zeus (in contrast to the poet, who descends from him only indirectly through Apollo and the Muses, Zeus' children), he often adopts the honeyed speech of the minstrel to settle disputes and to rule over his community in times of peace. The function of the minstrel, on the other hand, is to make the community forget its troubles, to soothe people's grief, to "divert their minds": "Sweet is the voice that flows from [the singer's] mouth./ So if someone is stricken with grief of a recent bereavement/ and is torturing his heart with mourning, then if some singer/ serving the Muses sings of past glory and heroes of old and/ tells of the blessed immortals who have their homes on Olympos,/ swiftly the grief-stricken one is forgetful and remembers/ none of his sorrow; quickly the gifts of the Muses divert him" (*Theog.* 97–103).

Hesiod here emphasizes the cathartic function of poetry as mimesis-play that is also apparent in the *Iliad* and the *Odyssey*. Although there are no singing contests at the funeral games for Patroclus, such contests were often part of these games, and for obvious reasons: the mourners could relieve their grief through *methexis*, a mimetic process of identification with the singer, often leading to catharsis. (Hesiod himself may have composed the *Theogony* for the funeral games of Amphidamas at Chalcis, where apparently he won the first prize in the singing contest).[64]

Despite his genealogical and functional distinctions, however, Hesiod has a hard time separating poetry from immediate power. Both lord and poet employ traditional, poetic speech (used also by the shaman-priests in oracles) because of its powerful effect on the listener. In the case of the *basileus*, it has the power to quell inflamed tempers and smooth out differences; in the case of the poet, it can alleviate pain and restore good spirits. More importantly, in both cases poetic speech has the power to "divert" or "bend."[65] As one can see particularly in *Works and Days*,

64. Compare Hesiod, *WD*, 654–59. For a discussion of this point, see West, Prolegomena to the *Theogony*, chap. 3, "The Date and Occasion of the *Theogony*," 40–48.

65. Pucci, for example, notes: "the word for 'persuading,' *paraiphamenoi*, means literally 'to speak to deflect,' 'to deviate someone.' The idea of persuasion in Homeric Greek is often expressed by words connoting an act of deflection, bending the mind or will of others. In *Iliad* 2.14 this notion is expressed by a verb that literally means 'to bend.' . . . The implication of the idea of persuasion, therefore, is 'to move the others from the path of their minds,' and it focuses on the power of bending and deflecting rather than on an overriding concern for truth" (*Hesiod and the Language of Poetry*, 17–18). Earlier scholars have also pointed out certain similarities between the speech of the lord and that of the poet in Hesiod; see, for example, Hermann Fränkel, *Dichtung und Philosophie des frühen*

persuasion has little to do with justice in a modern sense; rather it is the ability to bend the hearer's mind, to bring him around to the speaker's point of view. (Of course, this is also true of modern jury trials, where both the defense and the prosecution attempt to sway the juror's minds, by putting various, often conflicting, interpretations on the factual evidence.) The ability to bend or "make crooked" can be valued either positively or negatively, depending on which side of the dispute one chooses, and is not yet related to impartial, eternal truth in the Platonic, logo-rational sense (although we shall see that Hesiod awkwardly attempts to relate it to the justice of Zeus). Poetic speech, the vehicle of the lord's "straight verdicts," in effect turns out to be a potent drug (*pharmakon*), which can be used by both lord and poet to sway the minds of the hearers at will, to either the hearers' or their own advantage.[66] Both lord and poet are performers in the full sense of the word. Through mimesis as play, they control and manipulate the emotions of their audience, goading it into or diverting it from violent emotion. And what better example of a poet's attempt at controlling his audience than Hesiod's own *suasio*, in *Works and Days*, addressed to his brother Perses, whom he tries to discourage from proceeding with the legal action the latter presumably brings against him?[67]

Hesiod does, however, separate the performative power of poetic speech from physical violence, which he condemns in the crooked, shameful deeds and the bad eris, characteristic of both the pre-Olympian gods in the second section of the *Theogony* and the "arrogant" lords of *Works and Days*. Long before Plato, Hesiod seems to be aware of the potential violence embedded in mimesis-play and he attempts to purge it

---

Griechentums, 2d ed. (Munich, 1962; hereafter cited as Fränkel, *DPFG*), who remarks that Hesiod employs parallel words for "das Tun des Königs und des Sängers" (quoted by Pucci, 39); and Friedrich Solmsen, "The 'Gift' of Speech in Homer and Hesiod," *TAPA* 85 (1954): 11–12.

66. Here Pucci again is illuminating: "Strange *logos*, then, that of the good basileus! It stands firm and straight, but it constitutes a deflecting speech" (Pucci, *Hesiod and the Language of Poetry*, 18). Pucci, however, does not connect poetic speech with archaic, immediate power, preferring instead to deconstruct Hesiod's concept of *logos* in a Derridian fashion. He thus places Hesiod squarely in a rationalist, onto-theological tradition, which is something of an anachronism. The difference between the modern "logocentrist" and the Hellenic logo-rational thinker is that the latter attempts to moderate archaic agonistic values rather than assert the primacy of Reason at all costs. In other words, the Hellenic logo-rational thinker is not so much "rational" as "reasonable."

67. For a cogent discussion of the relation between *eris* (strife, dispute), justice, and the power of archaic poetry as "praise" and "blame," see Nagy, *BTA*, esp. 219–42.

of this violence by clothing the agonistic nature of aristocratic values in a relatively quiet garb. Indeed, the *Theogony*, no less than the *Odyssey*, can be read as a mythical narrative of the shift in emphasis from archaic to median values in Hellenic thought.

In the Hymn to the Muses of the first section, Hesiod presents Zeus securely in charge of Olympus, being as serene in power as King Alcinous. The Muses, and therefore poetry-music-dance, are directly related to Olympian power, being Zeus' daughters (whom he begets by Mnemosune, memory), and fulfill the normal functions of a singer of tales in a heroic community. They praise Zeus, the supreme authority, "telling how he excels all the other gods, how great in strength [he is]" (*Theog.* 49), and they glorify "the special empowerments [*nomoi*, ordinances] and manners of all the immortals" (*Theog.* 66). Like all minstrels, the Muses are "powers that make evils forgotten and bring rest from sorrows" (*Theog.* 55). After Zeus seizes the divine throne from his father Cronus, the Muses go to Olympus to become part of the new order and sing its praises: "From under their feet a lovely sound rose/ as they went to their father, to him who lords over heaven,/ for he controls the thunder and smoldering bolt of the lightening./ and he had defeated Kronos his father by force [*kratos*] and fairly allotted/ to the immortals equally and granted them provinces [*timai*, spheres of influence]" (*Theog.* 70–74).

The new order, glorified by the Muses, is an idealized picture of Olympian rule which stands in sharp contrast to the succession myth that is at the center of the second part of the *Theogony*. In this myth, the "honey-sweet-voiced" Muses help Hesiod tell the gruesome story of the violent contest for supremacy among the Hellenic gods. Uranus "abuses" his power until his genitals are reaped with a sickle by his son Cronus, with the full cooperation of Gaia, Uranus' wife and Cronus' mother. In turn, Cronus attempts to stay in power by eliminating the competition of his children. He swallows all of them as soon as they are born, but is in turn tricked by Rhea and Zeus, his youngest son, who defeats him "by craft and violence" (*technēsi biēphi te*, *Theog.* 496). Hesiod thereby reveals the violent foundations of Zeus' orderly, serene rule, at the same time that he attempts to justify these foundations by the abuses of the previous ruler, who "first thought of shameful acts" (*Theog.* 172; 166).[68] This

68. Nietzsche, among others, points out the double character of Hellenic culture, invoking the horrifying spectacle of the Hesiodic world of myth in support of his thesis that behind the slightest cultural advancement lies a murder or an iniquitous act: "Let us imagine the suffocating atmosphere of Hesiod's poem, still thickened and darkened and without all the mitigations and purifications, which poured over Hellas from Delphi and

double strategy of any succession myth—of presenting the old, defeated dispensation in an unfavorable light while justifying and legitimizing the new, victorious one—is typical of any mentality of power, and has been repeated ad nauseam by ancient and modern political regimes alike.[69]

In the *Theogony* Hesiod attempts to deal with the ambiguous question of the relationship of the poet and his art to power, a question that would probably not have occurred to the singer of tales, who was part and parcel of the archaic, mythopoeic world and, as such, its unreflective instrument. In *Works and Days*, Hesiod tackles the no less ambiguous question of the relation of power to justice.

The issue of justice arises in a concrete manner as Hesiod is possibly faced with legal action initiated by his brother Perses over their paternal inheritance. Perses has apparently squandered his share, presumably by neglecting his farm and associating with idle and crooked *basileis* in the agora, and now he seeks a redistribution of the family estate. To this end, he has presumably enlisted the help of his dissolute aristocratic friends, who can bend justice in his favor, for a price.[70]

the numerous seats of the gods! If we mix this thickened Boeotian air with the grim voluptuousness of the Etruscans, then such a reality would extort from us a world of myths within which Uranos, Kronos, and Zeus and the struggles of the Titans would appear as a relief. Combat in this brooding atmosphere is salvation and safety; the cruelty of victory is the summit of life's glories. . . . Behind that bloody age stretches a wave-furrow deep into Hellenic history ("Homer's Contest," 55). But it is Homer and Hesiod themselves who begin the process of "mitigating" and "purifying" (that is, covering up) this horrifying world of myth by idealizing and glorifying it in epic poetry. For a detailed examination of the succession myth of the *Theogony*, see Bonnafe, *Eros et Eris*, although the author does some covering up of her own by seeing the Olympian rule as a delicate balance between Strife and Eros, or as an earlier version of Empedocles' contest between Neikos and Philotes (see below, chapter 2).

69. The reverse movement is equally common: after the new dispensation has proven as unacceptable as its predecessor, the latter becomes idealized and nostalgia for the good, old times sets in. Consider, for example, Hesiod's myth of the ages in *Works and Days*, or Socrates' ideal Republic.

70. Another possible scenario is that after Perses squanders his share (which in Hesiod's opinion he had obtained by questionable means in the first place), he comes to his brother for help, alternating begging with threats of another legal hearing. Hesiod is reluctant to help him, urging him instead to leave the bad company of his aristocratic friends and apply himself to work. For the various modern theories regarding the legal context (historical or fictional) of *Works and Days*, see West, Prolegomena to *WD*, esp. 33–40. There is also Adkins' intriguing theory (in *Moral Values and Political Behavior*, 22–35) that Hesiod represents the values of an *agathos* in decline, who is forced to work because of the changed circumstances of his environment. Although my reading is, in many respects, sympathetic to that of Adkins, it presupposes a diametrically opposite view-

The real or imagined threat of a legal hearing offers Hesiod an excellent opportunity to reflect upon justice in general, upon the nature of divine and human order, and upon the status and interaction of various social groups in his community. The poet runs into serious problems from the start, however, partly because he lives in a society controlled by aristocratic values, according to which might still largely makes right, and partly because he does not yet have an adequate abstract vocabulary to reflect with. The result is a contradictory mixture of archaic and median thought which, again, seems to indicate the transitional nature of Hesiod's poetry.

The poet's invocation to the Pierian Muses concerns their father Zeus, who is said to uphold justice through his superior might. Here Hesiod opposes the religious notion of divine retribution to the heroic notion of justice as the arbitrary will of the powerful. Yet when he attempts later to explain the origins of human injustice, he inevitably traces it back to Zeus and the myth of Pandora (*WD* 59–105).[71]

---

point: far from being an *agathos*, Hesiod shares all the median values of a well-to-do farmer. He looks up to the *agathos*, just as Perses does, but unlike Perses, he does not believe in "upward mobility" and attempts literally to make a virtue out of a necessity (work). In this sense, it is people like Perses, rather than people like Hesiod, who will eventually demand to have more say in the affairs of their community. Adkins, however, seems justified in his implicit assumption that a change in prevailing values can occur only when the *agathoi* themselves acknowledge its inevitability. In terms of my reading, they are now willing to rub shoulders in the agora with aspiring young commoners like Perses.

71. A brief semantic history of the word *dikē* is relevant here. In Homer and to a certain extent in Hesiod, to administer justice or to "speak a verdict" (*dikazein*) among equals largely means to point or direct to the outcome of a past dispute or dilemma as a model of conduct for the current one; the verdict thus has an advisory rather than a judicial function and can rarely be enforced. Because of this Homeric use, some etymologists have related *dikē* to speech (orality), regarding it as the ancestor of the Latin *dicere*. Other scholars, such as Johan Huizinga, relate *dikē* (from *dikein*, to throw, cast) to a game of dice, in an effort to account for the seemingly aleatory character of justice in archaic Greece. In any case, the Homeric aristocratic world often behaves as if might and right were indistinguishable, and it is only in classical times that the two notions appear gradually to diverge. For example, such moralists as Socrates, Plato, and Aristotle seek to develop a concept of justice somewhat similar to our own, in which might should protect right, moral responsibility toward the community should overrule individual claims against it, and reciprocity should prevail over retribution. But even this median concept of justice is based on competitive values, which in the classical *polis* seem to resemble Hesiod's good *eris* (strife, contest). One competes with one's peers in being just (*dikaios*) and philosophers such as Socrates and Plato attempt to relate the old agonistic concept of *aretē* (excellence) to *dikaiosunē* (justice). Despite these attempts, even in classical Greece

Similarly, when Hesiod tells the fable of the hawk and the nightingale, he apparently attempts to protest against the ethics of the hawk, identifying with the victim, who speaks with a "minstrel's voice" (*WD* 203–12). He associates the hawk with arrogance (*hubris*) and warns Perses against the dangers of the predator's argument, immediately after he recounts the fable: "But you Perses, hearken to Right [*Dike*] and don't honor arrogance [*hubris*]/ Arrogance is a bad thing for the common man, for not even the nobleman/ easily bears it but staggers under its burdensome weight and/ meets with calamity. Better it is to take/ the other road to Right. Right in the end wins the contest over arrogance./ The fool by suffering learns this" (*WD* 213–18).

This passage shows, however, that Hesiod conceives of Dike in competitive terms, as being engaged in a race with Hubris. Likewise, a little later, Horkos the oath-god runs faster than a crooked verdict because, even when Dike seems to be disqualified and dragged out of the race by "gift-eating men who interpret the customs with bent decisions," she will return to haunt the city where the crooked verdicts have been spoken (*WD* 219–21). Hesiod thus sets the tone for an agonistic view of justice that will persist throughout the archaic and the classical periods. Note also that Hesiod says "gift-eating men" (*andres dōrophagoi*) and not "gift-eating *basileis* or *agathoi*." He cannot use the latter terms in a derogatory

the goddess Dike seems to remain an ambiguous figure, with her blindfolded eyes and unevenly tipped scales. And as late as the fifth and fourth centuries B.C., the Athenian law courts appear very different in practice from the ideal ones advocated by Socrates and others (for example, it was not unusual for the defense to demand acquittal on the strength of a defendant's prominent family, his wealth, or his usefulness to the state). For the various meanings of the word *dikē* in the archaic period, out of which I have mentioned only those strictly relevant to this discussion, see, among others, Michael Gagarin, "*Dike* in Archaic Greek Thought," *CP* 69 (1974): 186–97; and Garner, *Law and Society in Classical Athens*, esp. 4–10. For the concept of justice in ancient Greece in general, the reader can consult G. Glotz, *La solidarité de la famille dans le droit criminel en Grèce* (Paris, 1904); Louis Gernet, *Recherches sur le développement de la pensée juridique et morale en Grèce* (Paris, 1917); Frisch, *Might and Right in Antiquity*; Dodds, *The Greeks and the Irrational*; Adkins, *MR*; Havelock, *The Greek Concept of Justice*. For a view that challenges somewhat the accepted one, see Lloyd-Jones, *The Justice of Zeus*. For the relationship of justice to religious taboo, blood-revenge, and scapegoat ritual in archaic Greece see, among others, V. Gebhard, *Die Pharmakoi in Ionien und die Sybakchoi in Athen*, Ph.D. diss., Munich, 1926; Dodds, *The Greeks and the Irrational*; Mary Douglas, *Purity and Danger: An Analysis of Concepts of Pollution and Taboo* (London, 1966); Girard, *La violence et le sacré*; Burkert, *Homo Necans*, and *Structure and History in Greek Mythology and Ritual* (Berkeley, 1979); and Robert Parker, *Miasma: Pollution and Purification in Early Greek Religion* (Oxford, 1983).

context because in his culture the powerful are also the virtuous.[72] He can therefore express his disapproval of a *basileus'* verdict only in an oblique fashion. This obliqueness also comes through in the way in which Hesiod uses the fable of the hawk and the nightingale. Although he seems at first to address the "lords who understand," he abruptly switches to Perses, for whose benefit the story is actually told. All Hesiod ends up saying is that hawks will be hawks, but because Perses himself is not a hawk, he should stop imitating one and behave instead according to his station.[73]

In support of his cause, Hesiod can shift the argument to the religious level, but even there he dwells mainly on the divine punishments that result from breaking an oath or swearing falsely (compare *Il.* 23.586–95, where Antilochus refrains from perjuring himself before Menelaus, thereby abiding by the divine rules that govern human oaths). First, Hesiod says that the crooked verdicts of the *basileis* will be punished by Zeus in the form of some calamity befalling the whole community, an accepted religious belief that is equally shared by Homer. Then, he extols the civic benefits of Dike almost in the same terms that Homer describes the just lord's miraculous effects on his kingdom in *Od.* 19.75–79, at the same time that he has Zeus mark out for great punishments those "whose care is violence and evil deeds (*erga*)" (*WD* 238–39). Finally, Hesiod states the matter in the most general religious terms available to him, again attempting to persuade Perses, rather than the lords:

Perses I beg you carefully to ponder these things in your heart and

72. Nietzsche makes this point well when he remarks that contrary to common belief the concept of moral goodness does not originate with "those to whom the good has been done." On the contrary, it is the "good" themselves, "that is to say the noble, mighty, highly placed, and high-minded who decreed themselves and their actions to be good, i.e., belonging to the highest rank, in contradistinction to all that was base, low-minded, and plebeian" (Nietzsche, *Genealogy of Morals: An Attack*, trans. F. Golffing [New York, 1956], 160). For a recent debate around *dikē* and justice in *WD*, see among others Michael Gagarin, "*Dikē* in *Works and Days*," *CP* 68 (1973): 81–94; David B. Claus, "Defining Moral Terms in *Works and Days*," *TAPA* 107 (1977): 73–84; and M. W. Dickie, "*Dikē* as a Moral Term in Homer and Hesiod," *CP* 73 (1978): 91–101.
73. Compare West, Commentary to *WD*, 209, as well as my concluding remarks to this section. Given Hesiod's traditional views, I find it difficult to see him as a voice of social protest (see Sarah. C. Humphreys, *Family, Women, and Death: Comparative Studies* [London, 1982]). In all likelihood, Hesiod represents the viewpoint of the wealthy farmer rather than that of the poor one, and as such he probably advocates *eunomia*, that is, vertical rather than horizontal cooperative values.

hearken to Dike and think not of insolent might.
For this law is alloted to men by Zeus, son of Kronos:
fish and beasts of the wild and birds that fly in the air
eat one another, since Dike has no dwelling among them;
but to men he gives Dike, which is the greatest of blessings.
If one is willing to speak what he sees to be righteous,
what he knows is the right thing,
far-seeing Zeus grants him a blessed life.
But if he witnesses falsely and willfully perjures himself,
being a liar, a harmer of Dike, incurably blind,
he is leaving his family a gloomier future existence.
He who swears truly creates for his family future prosperity.
(WD 274–85)

Hesiod nowhere mentions that the justice Zeus provides for men (which differs from the one he provides for animals) is binding for gods as well. As in Homer, moreover, this justice must be observed because of fear of divine retribution and not because of an inner sense of fair play, or because a legal mechanism of crime and punishment similar to ours is operative in Hesiod's archaic community. In this regard, Hesiod follows traditional religious thinking which, far from dispensing with the principle of might makes right, simply moves it from the human to the divine plane.[74]

That Hesiod never really renounces the agonistic mentality which he decries in Perses is evident from his parenthetic observation, or "paradox-wish," just before his seemingly quiet conclusion: "Now neither would I myself be just in my dealings with men nor/ hope that my son be, since it will be a bad thing to be just,/ if the deviser of greater injustice will have greater justice./ But I hope Zeus of the Counsels will not yet bring this to pass" (WD 270–73). Again, it is not some inner moral drive,

74. The religious notion of a supreme, unassailable, divine power that can override all individual power claims and, therefore, can effectively arrest the formation of orders of rank based on individual contest is partly the reason for the success of monotheistic religions in modern, predominantly median societies; it is also an important weapon in the hands of nonaristocratic social groups. Although Hesiod's Zeus is not yet as "just" as the Christian god, he differs considerably from the Zeus of the epic tradition and even from that of the *Theogony*, probably because in *Works and Days* he appears mainly in his role of protector of suppliants and punisher of perjurers, that is, in relation to humans and not to other gods. An excellent description of the workings of a Christian religious power mechanism employed as a weapon against an aristocratic, agonistic mentality can be found, for example, in Alessandro Manzoni's novel *I promessi sposi*.

but Zeus that guarantees justice. Consider also the irony of Hesiod's position vis-à-vis his brother, with whom he engages in a (bad) competitive relationship or in what René Girard calls, in a different context, "conflictive mimesis."[75] Throughout his poem, Hesiod attempts (unsuccessfully) to turn bad emulation into good emulation, setting himself up as a model for Perses (in place of the crooked noblemen, whom the latter has been imitating in the agora) at the same time that he himself has a hard time escaping the mimetic double-bind. His *suasio* is a clear case of the mixed signals that any model conveys to his emulator: "imitate me, don't imitate me" (in this regard, Perses must surely be a younger brother). This *suasio* makes it equally obvious that the ambiguity of Hesiod's view of justice derives from his ambiguous view of agon itself.

Immediately following his invocation to the Pierian Muses, Hesiod takes up the question of *eris* (strife, competition, contest). Because it is unthinkable in his, as well as in any other power-oriented, world to advocate a complete renunciation of competition, Hesiod no less than Homer makes a distinction between a bad *eris*, associated with violent, predominantly aristocratic agon, and a good *eris*, associated with the peaceful contest among members of various trades and crafts, including poets (note that at *Theog.* 226, Eris is all negative, being one of the great evils pestering both the divine and the human worlds). Bad Eris "stirs up the evil of war and/ conflict of battle, and no mortal loves her, but under compulsion,/ as the immortals decree, we honor the burdensome Eris" (*WD* 14–16). This is a far cry from the love of battle (*charmē*) experienced by the Homeric warrior, and Hesiod plainly shares not the aristocrat's but the commoner's view of war. On the other hand, good Eris, who is "the older daughter of black Night," proves beneficial to humans: "She sets a man to his work in spite of the fact that he's shiftless,/ for it makes him eager to work whenever he sees/ another prospering, one who is hastening to plow and/ build an excellent homestead. Neighbor is envious of neighbor/ hastening to wealth, and this is the Eris that benefits mortals./ Potter fiercely challenges potter, carpenter carpenter,/ beggar enviously strives with beggar, singer with singer" (*WD* 19–26).

In this passage, Hesiod contrasts the heroic values of a warrior group (such as that of the *Iliad*) with the quieter values of the commoners, by relating *eris* to work, rather than to play as agon. The *basileis* are excluded from the province of the good *eris*, being relegated, by implication, to the

75. See, for example, René Girard, *Des choses cachées depuis la fondation du monde* (Paris, 1978), and *"To Double Business Bound"* (Baltimore, 1978).

province of the bad one. Yet the good Eris is said to be the older daughter of black Night and, if we return for a moment to the *Theogony*, we realize that in effect she is indistinguishable from the bad one, at least in terms of its origins: "Baneful Night also bore Nemesis, an avenging plague for/ mortal men; and then Deceit and Sexual Love and/ baneful Old Age and Eris, a hard-hearted demon./ And the stygian Eris produced burdensome Labor/ and the curse of Forgetfulness, Hunger, and tearful Pains,/ Conflicts of Battle and Fights and Murders and Killings of Men, Disorderly Government and her accomplice, the power of Ruin,/ and the oath-god Horkos, who is the greatest plague for/ every man who wilfully swears a false oath" (*Theog.* 223–32).

This second passage emphasizes the close relationship between bad *eris* and work, as one is said to engender the other. Work (*ponos*) is seen as an evil rather than a blessing, and a comparison of the two passages reveals the conceptual difficulties that Hesiod encounters in separating the two kinds of *eris*. His value system cannot separate between *ponos* and evil any more than it can separate between *agathos* (noble) and good. Although Hesiod wishes to emphasize work over aristocratic play, he can conceive of the former only in terms of contest (good *eris*), since *agon* is the main generator of cultural values in his world. In other words, under the pressure of the dominant, aristocratic ethical code, Hesiod must conceive of work itself as a specific form of (competitive) play.[76] In essence, then, Hesiod's ambiguous attitude toward work is similar to that of Homer, and is shared by all Greek thinkers from Heraclitus to Plato to Aristotle. Nevertheless, there are certain differences between Hesiod's and Homer's treatment of work, stemming from Hesiod's position as a spokesman for the Boeotian well-to-do farmer.

In the Homeric epic, aristocratic play as freedom is implicitly opposed to work (*Il.* 15.362). In *Works and Days*, on the other hand, Hesiod presents this opposition explicitly, for example, in his description of the golden race of mortals: "And they lived like gods without any care in their

76. Ironically, this is also the position of certain theorists of play in the contemporary behaviorist sciences. Under the pressures of a postindustrial society where the work ethic becomes slowly eroded and play is again favored as a generator of cultural values, these theorists argue that work is really only a form of play. See, for example, Michael J. Ellis, *Why People Play* (Englewood Cliffs, N. J., 1973) and Joseph Levy, *Play Behavior* (New York, 1978). Modern play theorists have thus come full circle to the aristocratic notions of play that Hesiod wishes to replace, at least in part, with a Hellenic quasi-equivalent of the Protestant work ethic. But even in classical capitalism "competition" plays a major role in creating cultural values; in turn, socialism appears as a movement from below to curb this competition.

hearts,/ free and apart from labor and misery. Nor was the terror of/ old age upon them, but always with youthful hands and feet they/ took their delight in festive pleasures apart from all evil;/ and they died as if going to sleep. Every good thing was/ theirs to enjoy: the grain-giving earth produced her fruits/ spontaneously, abundantly, freely; and they in complete satisfaction/ lived off their fields without any cares in blessed abundance" (*WD* 112–19).

This ideal model, which is appropriate for the commoners rather than for the aristocracy, is a community of fruit-gatherers, based on nonviolent play (festive pleasures), from which work, associated with pain, illness and misery is completely excluded (compare *Theog.* 215–16). This playful golden age is, moreover, contrasted to the iron age, where "men never cease from labor and woe" (*WD* 176–77). In its last stages, the iron age turns into a nightmare of violence and civic disorder, where father will quarrel with son, guest will quarrel with host, one man will destroy another man's city, might will be right, and Envy will attend upon men, "causing commotion, rejoicing in evil, with face full of hate" (*WD* 180–96). The nonviolent play of the golden age turns into both hard labor and the violent play or bad eris of the iron age.

Hesiod also adds a race of heroes to the traditional myth of four races. This heroic race is "much juster and better" than the previous, bronze one (*WD* 158), although it is equally plagued by "the evil of war and terrible battle" (*WD* 161). Hesiod seems to make a concession to the epic tradition, which must have commanded considerable cultural authority in his age. He is close enough to the Homeric world to attempt to distance himself from it, and yet far enough to look at it nostalgically and presumably prefer it to his own age of iron: "Would that I now were no longer alive in the fifth age of men, but had died earlier or had been born at a later time" (*WD* 174–75).[77]

In Hesiod's treatment of the myth of the ages one can also find the beginnings of an "as if" approach to knowledge, which is closely linked to the notion of nonviolent, median play as an ideal way of life. For example,

77. Again, the distance implied here is both temporal and social. As we have seen, in Homer we can encounter the same kind of nostalgic idealization of the heroic age, especially in the *Odyssey*, and the Homeric poet is possibly as far removed both temporarily and socially from the Homeric world as Hesiod is. For detailed discussions of Hesiod's myth of the races see, among others, A. Mirgeler, *Hesiod: Die Lehre von den fünf Weltaltern* (Düsseldorf, 1958); B. Gatz, *Weltalter, goldene Zeit und sinnerwandte Vorstellungen, Spudasmata* 16 (1967); Arthur W. H. Adkins, *From the Many to the One: A Study of Personality and Views of Human Nature in the Context of Ancient Greek Society, Values, and Beliefs* (Ithaca, N. Y., 1970), 50–52; and E. R. Dodds, *The Ancient Concept of Progress* (Oxford, 1973), chap. 1.

in *WD* 112–19 quoted above, Hesiod presents the golden race in terms of its likeness to the divine world. Men live *like* gods, free from work, pain, and old age; they die *as if* they fell asleep, and so forth. Hesiod contrasts an ideal state of affairs to a historical one, seeing the iron age as a fall from the golden one, which functions as its logical opposite. Prefiguring Plato, Hesiod attempts to separate play ("festive pleasures") from violent agon (bad *eris*) and link it, within an ideal setting, to less violent, median values.

As a rule, Hellenic ideal societies (as opposed to modern utopias) exclude work from their positive set of values, thereby revealing their nostalgic, aristocratic origins. Yet whereas for the Homeric, heroic mentality work has mostly negative connotations, being associated either with punishment and disgrace or with the lower classes and the slaves, for Hesiod it is almost a virtue, proper to these lower classes. For example, in his exhortation to work addressed to Perses, he says: "Men by the doing of work [*ergon*] are rich in flocks and successful,/ and if you work you will be much dearer to the immortals and to mortal men, for they very much hate the shiftless./ Working is not a reproach [*oneidos*], but not working is a reproach./ If you will work, the nonworker soon will be envious of you,/ seeing you prosper; fame and honor attend upon wealth./ But whatever your god-given lot it is better to work,/ better to turn your ruin-prone mind from others' possessions" (*WD* 308–15). Later on, the poet assures his brother that the way to riches does not lie in crookedness and bribes, but only in piling "work on work and still more work" (*WD* 382). Nor does it lie in begging, to which Perses is now reduced because of his improvidence. The poet will no longer help him, because he wants to teach him a lesson: "Work, foolish Perses, work at the works which the gods have given to men as their portion,/ so that you with your children and wife in distress may never/ seek to subsist off the kindness of neighbors and find them unhelpful" (*WD* 397–400).

In these passages, Hesiod seems to contrast a life of idleness and excess, usually associated with the *aristoi*, to the productive and moderate life of a well-to-do farmer. Nevertheless, one should again tread lightly here.[78]

---

78. For a slightly different view, see G. Nussbaum, who says in relation to the passage I have just quoted: "To Hesiod as to Homer physical work is not degrading. But it is interesting to find [Hesiod] say so explicitly, as though he felt that some might think it was" ("Labour and Status in the *Works and Days*," *CQ* 10 [1960]: 217). But this is precisely the point: Hesiod has to defend his attitude toward work in the poem because the *basileis* (and Homer) do regard physical work as a disgrace, especially if it is imposed on them by others. This does not mean, however, that they do not, in turn, impose it on their inferiors, or that these inferiors cannot make the best of a bad *moira*. But, then, Nussbaum does qualify his statement: "It would be quite wrong, however, to imagine

Hesiod hardly ever implies that working should be the *aretē* of the *basileus*; he simply says that Perses is not a *basileus* and therefore cannot behave like one without going beyond his portion and incurring *hubris*. The portion of the farmer is to work; hence, although working may be shameful for the *basileus*, it is not so for the farmer, being his only means of acquiring honor and fame. In sum, since fame and honor are dependent upon wealth, and since the only way of accumulating wealth for a farmer is through work (rather than, say, through war booty and prizes), it is better for Perses— *not* for the *basileis*—to work rather than not to work. Note, however, that even here Hesiod emphasizes competition, since the nonworking (common) man will soon envy the working one for his prosperity and, thereby, also for his honor and fame. Thus Hesiod shrewdly appeals to the dominant agonistic mentality of his culture in order to goad Perses into working.

Despite his arguing for the necessity of work, Hesiod's attitude toward this activity remains ambiguous, precisely because he lives in a society permeated by aristocratic values (work is pointedly absent from his golden age). Furthermore, the notion of work in Hellenic culture differs considerably from ours, and here we can speak only of family resemblances. Just as in the case of "play," there is no word in ancient Greek that fully describes what we understand by "work." The words that denote specific kinds of work have mostly negative connotations: *ponos* and *ergon* involve as a rule painful effort and can best be translated as "toil" or "labor." Finally, even though the Greek notion of *ergon* can include production and therefore can perhaps also be translated, in certain contexts, as "creative work" (as Solmsen translates it), it rarely produces and measures cultural values as it does, for example, in classical capitalism.[79]

---

that work is positively honorable to Hesiod" (217). Regarding the notion of work in Homer and Hesiod, see also A. Aymard, "L'idée de travail dans la Grèce archaique," *Journal de psychologie* 41 (1948): 29–45; as well as Finley, *World of Odysseus*, chap. 3, "Wealth and Labor."

79. Even during the classical period and later, as evidenced, for instance, in Aristotle's discussion of *scholē* (leisure, play), *diagōgē* (diversion), *paidia* (play), and *ascholia* (occupation, work), it is play rather than work that produces most Hellenic values (see chapter 5). Work coupled with a Protestant ethic becomes a main source of Western cultural values only with the rise of the industrial societies in Western Europe and the United States. In contemporary postindustrial cultures, on the other hand, play tends again to replace work as primary generator of value. Many contemporary entrepreneurs see themselves as *playing* the market and money becomes again a stake in a power game against both other entrepreneurs and the stock exchange, which functions as the secular, commercial version of a celestial casino.

There is one sense, however, in which Hesiod's notion seems to come close to ours, and that is in relation to tilling the land (*ergon* originally also meant "field"). Agriculture has always had religious associations, involving seasonal cycles and fertility rites, and has preserved its relatively high cultural status to the present day in such sentimental notions as the return to the land and its pristine values, pastoralism, and the like.[80] Outside this religious context, however, Hesiod sees work in terms of good *eris*, that is, in terms of play as (nonviolent) agon. In this respect, Hesiod favors work over play less than he favors good play over bad, an ethical polarization that will reach its full conceptual development in Plato and Aristotle.

Hesiod's concern in *Works and Days* with the "justice of Zeus" has often led scholars (both ancient and modern) to emphasize Hesiod's deep piety in contrast to Homer's allegedly more lighthearted attitude toward religion. Such emphasis, however, seems unjustified. Leaving aside the question of whether we can know anything at all about the relative piety of the two poets, surely one does not appear more "pious" than the other. Hesiod has to emphasize the justice of Zeus more than Homer does because he belongs to a social group which must almost entirely depend on this justice to defend its claims successfully. Hesiod needs piety in order to persuade his brother Perses that his portion as a farmer, even though not as good as an aristocrat's, can still be an enviable one. In fact, given the agonistic context of the poem (a real or imagined legal hearing), piety can easily be viewed as a rhetorical means of persuasion or dissuasion: we never hear Perses' side of the story and therefore we cannot impartially judge the merits of the poet's case. It is not inconceivable that the poet may be reluctant to help his impoverished brother (well-to-do farmers are proverbially tightfisted), justifying this reluctance by delivering a pious sermon before sending him away empty-handed.

Like Homer, Hesiod never seems to question the order of rank in his community, but simply demands that each station behave according to its assigned place in the Great Chain of Being. It is quite possible, therefore,

80. For a detailed treatment of the religious implications of work in ancient Greece, see Vernant, "Work and Nature in Ancient Greece," in *Myth and Thought*, 248–70, and "Some Psychological Aspects of Work in Ancient Greece," in the same book, 271–78. A similar connection between work and religion is preserved in modern times, in the so-called Protestant work ethic. This work ethic is as ambiguous as that of Hesiod, maintaining its negative-positive features through its close link to the Hellenic (and Christian) notions of suffering and sacrifice (see, for example, such influential modern thinkers as Kant, Hegel, and Marx). The best known study of this problem is Max Weber's *Protestant Ethic and the Spirit of Capitalism* (New York, 1958).

that Hesiod no less than Homer and Solon champions aristocratic *eunomia* rather than democratic *isonomia*. As with women and children, the farmer is allotted quieter values than those of the *basileus* and a poem dealing with a farmer's world will naturally emphasize a farmer's values. The fact that a farmer gets to voice his opinions in a poetic work at all can of course be an indication that his social group has gained a certain cultural prestige, but is no indication of the extent of this gain within the archaic community as a whole. As I have already suggested, we can speak of a real shift in cultural emphasis only when the *aristoi* themselves are forced to adopt a median behavior, not only in relation to each other but also in relation to other social groups.

Nevertheless, by emphasizing work, nonviolent agon, and the separation of might from right in human affairs (a separation that is, however, guaranteed by divine authority and not by a communal legal system), Hesiod contributes to the rise of a median mentality in Hellenic thought. But far from renouncing power, this mentality will simply enable the hawk to assume the (dis)guise of the nightingale.

2 ▪ Agōnes Logōn: *Power and Play* in Presocratic Thought ▪

▪ The contest between archaic and median values present in Homer and Hesiod is carried on in the work of the cosmologists, doctors, and sophists who lived in various *poleis* during the sixth and the fifth centuries B.C. and who are generally labeled "Presocratics." It is certainly tempting to argue that this label still bespeaks the predominantly archaic nature of their thought, in contrast to that of later, predominantly logo-rational Socratics, such as Plato and Aristotle. But Presocratic thought exhibits many logo-rational features as well, and the Presocratic thinkers are too heterogeneous to fit any single label.[1]

Presocratic thought reaches us only indirectly and distortedly, in the form of quotations and paraphrases inserted in the work of later thinkers, such as Plato, Aristotle, Theophrastus, Diogenes Laertius, and Simplicius. Hence, we can reconstitute this thought with even less certainty than it is usually the case when dealing with remote historical periods. Nevertheless, what has come down to us indicates that the Presocratic notions of power and play become increasingly impersonal and abstract, at the same time that their concrete, archaic forms are not yet completely obscured.

On the one hand, the Presocratics extend human agonistic values to the physical world, which is at first conceived of as "full of gods" (by Thales) and then as a play of natural forces (*dunameis*)—the latter notion undergoes a logo-rational transformation when Aristotle calls the natural forces "elements" and "principles." Western science comes into exis-

---

1. Insofar as the term "Presocratic" implicitly (and often unfavorably) contrasts Socrates and his predecessors, it also contains a biased, rationalist value judgment, stemming mainly from a Platonic and an Aristotelian version of the history of Hellenic thought. For further references to this bias, which is carried over into modern histories of Greek philosophy, see below, throughout this chapter.

tence, and the notion of the physical world as an interplay of various forces remains current in modern physics as well. The Presocratics inherit it from Homeric, mythopoeic thought, but gradually separate it from its concrete religious context of divine personifications, and turn it into a somewhat more impersonal, scientific truth. This scientific tendency can be discerned particularly in the thought of such *phusikoi* as Anaximander, Anaximenes, and Heraclitus as well as in Xenophanes and the Hippocratic Corpus.[2]

On the other hand, the Presocratic notion of power as agonistic play gradually loses its immediacy or its connection with the physical world, approaching the status of an abstract, transcendental principle. This idealizing tendency seems to be present in such thinkers as Pythagoras and the Pythagoreans, Parmenides, Zeno, Melissus, and Anaxagoras. This chapter will first examine the metamorphoses of power as play (and play as power) in Presocratic thought, in relation to such conceptual *topoi* as strife and love, equality and justice, and chance and necessity; it will then consider the *agōnes logōn* (verbal contests) among the Presocratic thinkers themselves, who devise ingenious theories, subtle arguments, and shrewd rhetorical stratagems, indeed a whole eristic, perhaps not so much because of their love of wisdom (*philosophia*) as because of their love of getting the better of their intellectual opponents. In this regard they behave like Homeric heroes, even though their battles are waged with winged words rather than with deadly weapons.

■ *Strife and Love, Equality and Justice*

One of the key concepts in understanding Presocratic thought is "strife" (*eris*, *agōn*, *polemos*, *neikos*), which recurs with great frequency in both the Ionian and the Italian schools. The Presocratic notions of strife are undoubtedly the philosophical versions of their Homeric and Hesiodic counterparts and bear a strong family resemblance to them. Whereas in the epic tradition these notions are often expressed in a personified, anthropomorphic guise, being assigned a divine origin, as in Homer's Ares or Hesiod's Eris, in Presocratic thought they tend gradually to lose this

2. Here, however, the stress is on the word "tendency," because the Presocratics listed do not yet make a distinction between "matter" and "spirit," and generally conceive of the world order as a live organism. It is for this reason that the so-called New Physics of the twentieth century turns to them for support in refuting the rationalist Cartesian dichotomy between subject and object, and in positing a holistic view of the universe, or a unity between the observer and the observed.

guise and become impersonal, being extended to the physical elements (*stoicheia*), to use a later, Aristotelian term. Not unlike Homeric *aristoi* and Hesiodic commoners, however, these physical elements or material substances compete among themselves for supremacy, and it is their agon that accounts for physical changes both in the human body and in the world order at large.

Anaximander is the first known *phusikos* who seems to have explained change in terms of warring forces: "Destruction too happens by necessity [*kata to chreōn*, in due order] for they [the warring forces] pay penalty to each other for their injustice according to the assessment of Time."[3] Although the word "strife" does not appear as such in this longest extant fragment of Anaximander, what does appear is "*didonai . . . dikēn kai tisin*" ("to pay penalty and retribution"), a phrase that implies strife or conflict, perhaps of a legal nature. Later reactions to Anaximander's thought, such as that of Heraclitus (as I discuss below) seem also to indicate that the

3. Anaximander, B 1. The Presocratic texts cited here are from H. Diels and W. Kranz, *Die Fragmente der Vorsokratiker*, 3 vols., 6th ed. (Berlin, 1952) as well as from Kathleen Freeman, *Ancilla to the Pre-Socratic Philosophers: A Complete Translation of the Fragments in Diels* (Oxford, 1956). Unless otherwise specified, the English translations of the fragments quoted are from Kirk and Raven, *Presocratic Philosophers*, although I have collated them with Diels and Kranz's German and Freeman's English translations, and have occasionally modified them according to my own sense of the Greek original. The numeration of the fragments, unless otherwise indicated, is that of Diels-Kranz (hereafter cited as *DK*). I have made use of their classification: "A-fragments" contain later biographical and cultural narratives; "B-fragments" contain relatively certain *ipsissima verba*.

For general introductions to the Presocratics, in addition to the works already mentioned one can consult Theodor Gomperz, *Greek Thinkers: A History of Ancient Philosophy*, vol. 1, trans. L. Magnus (London, 1901); John Burnet, *Early Greek Philosophy*, 4th ed. (London, 1930); Karl Reinhardt, *Parmenides und die Geschichte der griechischen Philosophie* (Bonn, 1914), hereafter cited as Reinhardt, *PGGP*; Eduard Zeller, *Die Philosophie der Griechen in ihrer geschichtlichen Entwicklung*, pts. 1 and 2, *Vorsokratische Philosophie*, 7th ed. (Hildesheim, 1963); Olof Gigon, *Der Ursprung der griechischen Philosophie* (Basel, 1945); Fränkel, *DPFG*; Charles H. Kahn, *Anaximander and the Origins of Greek Cosmology* (New York, 1960), hereafter cited as Kahn, *AOGC*; William K. C. Guthrie, *A History of Greek Philosophy*, vol. 1, *The Earlier Presocratics and the Pythagoreans* (Cambridge, 1962), vol. 2, *The Presocratic Tradition from Parmenides to Democritus* (Cambridge, 1965), and vol. 3, *The Fifth-Century Enlightenment* (Cambridge, 1969), hereafter cited as *HGP 1*, *2*, and *3*; Adkins, *From the Many to the One*; A. P. D. Mourelatos, ed., *The Pre-Socratics: A Collection of Critical Essays* (New York, 1974), hereafter cited as Mourelatos, *The Pre-Socratics*; R. E. Allen and D. J. Furley, eds., *Studies in Presocratic Philosophy*, 2 vols. (London, 1975), hereafter cited as Allen and Furley, *Studies*; Raymond A. Prier, *Archaic Logic: Symbol and Structure in Heraclitus, Parmenides, and Empedocles* (The Hague and Paris, 1976); and Jonathan Barnes, *The Presocratic Philosophers*, rev. ed. (London, 1982), hereafter cited as Barnes, *TPP*.

Milesian probably imagined the world order to be an outcome of the interplay of warring physical substances. G. S. Kirk, for example, comments:

> The constant interchange between opposed substances is explained by Anaximander in a legalistic metaphor derived from human society: the prevalence of one substance at the expense of its contrary is "injustice," and a reaction takes place through the infliction of punishment by the restoration of equality—of more than equality, since the wrongdoer is deprived of part of his original substance, too. This is given to the victim in addition to what was his own, and in turn leads (it might be inferred) to *koros*, surfeit, on the part of the former victim, who now commits injustice on the former aggressor. Thus both the continuity and the stability of natural change were motivated by Anaximander, by means of this anthropomorphic metaphor.[4]

Kirk's surmise about the agonistic nature of Anaximander's cosmic mechanism of stability and change seems plausible enough, although his characterization of Anaximander's language as "metaphorical" may be anachronistic. Whereas this language also belongs to the juridical and the political sphere, it would perhaps be more accurate to call it "metonymic," rather than "metaphorical": Anaximander unconsciously extends a political and juridical notion from the human to the divine and physical spheres, as is often the practice of an archaic, mythopoeic mode of thought (which makes no distinction, as we do, between these spheres).[5]

As Kirk implies, the traditional physical substances are earth, water, air, and fire, but of primary interest to us are the so-called opposites (*ta enantia*), that is, the forces (*dunameis*) through which these physical substances act upon one another. The four primary forces are the hot, the

---

4. See Kirk and Raven, *Presocratic Philosophers*, 119.
5. Of course, in a certain sense all language can be seen as metaphorical or analogical, but this is not the sense that Kirk and others have in mind here. It is probably Aristotle and the Peripatetics that impute metaphoricity to Anaximander and other early *phusikoi* (whom, significantly, Aristotle calls *phusiologoi*), in the same way that they impute other abstract formulations to them, as Kirk himself cautions us. But some Presocratic thinkers, such as Xenophanes and Protagoras, do become aware of the metaphoric character of logo-rational language in general. For a full examination of the Aristotelian ideological distortions of Presocratic thought, often adopted uncritically by later commentators, see Harold Cherniss, *Aristotle's Criticism of Presocratic Philosophy* (1935; rptd. New York, 1976); and Michael C. Stokes, *One and Many in Presocratic Philosophy* (Cambridge, Mass., 1971), esp. chap. 1, "Aristotle and the Analysis of Unity and Plurality."

cold, the wet, and the dry, and most scholars (including Kirk) agree that in Anaximander and other *phusikoi* these forces should be conceived of not as abstract attributes, but as substantive things: it is only later in Plato and Aristotle that warmth, dryness, and the like become "qualities" (*poioteis*), which are clearly distinguished from substances, and that as a result the *dunameis* become abstract.[6]

Charles Kahn points out, moreover, that the scientific term *ta enantia* can be traced back directly to the language of the epic, where it describes "hostile warriors facing each other in battle." The opposites are really "opponents" or enemies and "their confrontation is a battle." This notion appears again and again not only in the Presocratic fragments (particularly in the Hippocratic Corpus), but also in the tragic poets, as well as in Plato and Aristotle. Indeed, "there is practically no limit to the number of texts which could be cited in illustration of this view of nature as a dynamic interplay between conflicting powers."[7]

In Anaximander, then, it is probably the strife of the substantive opposites (hot, cold, wet, dry) rather than that of the "elements" that leads to the formation "of existing things" (*tōn ontōn*), when these opposites "pay penalty and retribution to each other," that is, when they rule in turn, according to the principle of *isomoiria* (equal shares, balance of forces).

Despite numerous modern hypotheses, however, Anaximander's fragment remains silent about the relationship between the warring opposites and *to apeiron* (the boundless, the unlimited, the indefinite), and therefore it is impossible to assess the overall importance of the idea of strife in

6. Thus Cornford: " 'The hot' was not warmth, considered as an adjectival property of some substance which is warm. It is a substantive thing, and 'the cold,' its contrary, is another thing. Hence it was possible to think of the hot and the cold as two opposed things which might be fused together in an indistinct condition, like a mixture of wine and water." (*Principium Sapientiae*, 162). Compare Guthrie, *HGP I*, 78–80; and Kahn, *AOGC*, chap. 2, "Elements and Opposites: The Members of the World." For an early study of the Hellenic notion of physical forces, see J. Souilhé, *Etude sur le terme dunamis* (Paris, 1919).

7. Kahn, *AOGC*, 130–32. Kahn, however, believes that the scientific term originates in a metaphor, whereas for me it is, rather, a metonymy or a *pars pro toto*, pointing to the Hellenic mentality of power as a whole. The distinction is not as trivial as it may seem, because most modern scholars never pause to consider its implications. For example, Guthrie says: "The conflict of the opposites is an undeniable fact of nature" (*HGP I*, 79). Yet all we can reasonably say is that the conflict of opposites is an undeniable fact of Hellenic (and our own) culture. In other words we should be wary of reading our own cultural biases into "nature," not least because nature seems to respond to us in any way we choose to approach it.

Anaximander's cosmology. In the Heraclitean fragments, on the other hand, strife (*eris*) and war (*polemos*) seem to constitute the very foundation of the Heraclitean world order.

We have seen in chapter 1 how Heraclitus echoes Homer when he says that "it is necessary to know that war is common [or shared] and right [*dikē*] is strife, and that all things happen by strife and necessity" (B 80). This Homeric paraphrase is somewhat ironic in view of the fact that Heraclitus himself is reported by Aristotle to have rebuked Homer for saying: "Would that strife might be destroyed from among gods and men" (*Il.* 18.107). For without strife, Aristotle continues, "there would be no musical scales [*harmonia*], nor living creatures without female and male which are opposites" (*Eudemian Ethics* 1235a25). But despite Heraclitus' repeated attacks on Homer (or perhaps on the rationalizing tendencies in reading Homer that had already become fairly common in his time),[8] the Ephesian seems to have stayed closer than any other Presocratic thinker to a Homeric, archaic mentality.[9] For example, Heraclitus shares the heroic ideal of *aien aristeuein*, when he says: "One man is to me ten thousand, if he be best" (B 49), or when he thunders against his fellow Ephesians who banished Hermodorus, "the best man among them, saying, 'Let no one of us excel, or if he does, be it elsewhere and among others'" (B 121). Heraclitus sums up the agonistic nature of Homeric

8. For instance, William B. Stanford notes that allegory was used as early as the sixth century B.C., citing the example of Theagenes of Rhegium. See Stanford, *The Ulysses Theme: A Study in the Adaptability of a Traditional Hero* (Oxford, 1954), 125–26.

9. The present view of Heraclitus as an archaic, proto-logo-rational thinker seems to find some support (admittedly inconclusive) in the doxographical reports about his aristocratic background—he seems to have belonged to the royal clan at Ephesus, which gave him certain rights, such as choice seats at the games. He also appears to have been haughty towards his fellow citizens and to have harbored contempt for humanity in general. These reports should, however, be understood as later, logo-rational interpretations of his scorn for the lower classes, which comes through in some of the extant fragments. For example, Heraclitus says: "What sense or mind have they? They put their trust in popular bards and take the mob for their teacher, unaware that most men are bad, and the good are few" (B 70; compare also B 1, B 17, B 19, B 29, and B 34). "Most men are bad, and the good are few" seems moreover to be a quotation from Bias of Priene, one of the Seven Wise Men and seems to be directed against the equalitarian claims of the lower classes rather than against all mankind. As Guthrie points out in relation to B 43 ("Insolence must be quelled more promptly than a conflagration"), Heraclitus' concept of hubris "must have been much the same as that of Theognis, namely a failure by the lower orders to keep their proper station" (*HGP 1*, 409–10). For further discussion of Heraclitus' aristocratic background see, in addition to Guthrie, G. S. Kirk, *Heraclitus: The Cosmic Fragments* (Cambridge, 1954), 3–5, and Kirk and Raven, *Presocratic Philosophers*, 182–84.

values when he observes: "War is the father and the king of all, and some he shows as gods, others as men; some he makes slaves, others free" (B 53). No less than Homer, Heraclitus seems to conceive of war as a circle of conflicting elements, bringing all contestants up and then down, and producing the kind of negative justice or retribution that Homer's Hector ascribes to Ares, and to which Anaximander seems to have referred as well.

Because B 80 and B 53 seem to link the notion of strife to that of justice, they can also be discussed in terms of *isonomia* and *isomoiria*. These fragments seem to indicate that in some *poleis* the concept of *isonomia* (equality before the law, balance of forces) and its relative, *isomoiria* (equal political shares, balance of forces) might have developed as temporary, expedient solutions of curbing the unpredictable, disruptive effects of political contest. When the warring parties prove to be of equal strength, they seek to reach a mutually advantageous agreement, ruling by rotation.[10]

10. Historically, the notions of justice and equality are inextricably linked to the notion of contest. The modern scholars who examine the concept of *isonomia* have a tendency to see it in evolutionary, rationalist terms as a sign of a desirable, "progressive" development of Hellenic society from aristocratic or autocratic to democratic forms of government. For example, contrasting the democratic *isonomia* to the aristocratic, Solonian *eunomia*, Gregory Vlastos notes: "[*Isonomia*] was not an aristocratic idea, for though the nobles at times made common cause with the people against the tyrant, their goal was not an advance to the equality of *Isonomia* but a retreat to traditional inequalities sanctioned by *Eunomia*. . . . When in due course [*Isonomia*] was displaced as a proper name by the more prosaic and more precise *Demokratia*, [it] still remained the favorite slogan of democracy, for it alone expressed its greatest achievement, its pursuit of the goal of political equality to the farthest limits envisaged by the Greek mind, and this not in defiance, but in support, of the rule of law" ("*Isonomia*," *AJP* 74 [1953], 366). Here the emphasis should not be on "advance," "greatest achievement," and the "people" (the last word being too vague to possess anything more than an emotional value), but on "slogan," that is, on the propagandistic intent of *isonomia*. Although we may naturally favor democratic forms of government, surely these forms are equally power-oriented. Watchwords like the "will of the people," and "liberty, equality, fraternity," often acquire the same propagandistic value in the modern world that *isonomia* had in the ancient. The Romans, for example, were perfectly aware of the power-oriented nature of *isonomia* when they translated it as *aequilibritas*, equilibrium or balance (of forces)—see Ostwald, *Nomos*, 96 n.1. Ostwald himself, however, shares Vlastos' democratic bias (see esp. *Nomos*, pt. 3, chap. 2, "The Originality of Cleisthenes"). Vlastos comes closer to my view when he points out that to the Hellenic mind "justice was an affair between equals and . . . its settlement involved an equation of compensation to injury" ("Equality and Justice in Early Greek Cosmologies," in Allen and Furley, *Studies*, 1:83). On the other hand, in a debate with Kurt von Fritz, Vlastos draws a distinction between the balance of power among classes and governing bodies and the idea of equality among individual

It is perhaps in this sense that "right is strife." As Heraclitus seems to
imply in his rebuttal of Anaximander (if he indeed refers to the latter in B
80), warring forces create "justice" rather than "injustice" in at least two
senses. In one sense (also implicit in Anaximander), they create a sort of
negative justice (compare *Il.* 18.309), whereby the killer may in turn get
killed. In another sense, however, the warring forces do not have to pay
penalty to each other, and it is in this sense that Heraclitus may differ
from Anaximander (at least in Kirk's account of Anaximander's cosmic
mechanism). As soon as one contestant gets the upper hand, the others
hasten to match or, rather, outmatch him. Hence when the balance of
forces is upset, a reshuffling takes place until a new balance is established.
This compensatory, rather than retributive, concept of justice offers a
more elegant explanation than that of Anaximander (in Kirk's version)
not only of stability and change—or order and disorder—in the physical
world, but also of the isonomic mechanism in the fifth-century *polis* (as we
have seen, Anaximander seems to rely on legalistic terms in his account of
cosmic stability and change, in which case his mechanism would not be
strictly self-regulatory, but would need some sort of outside, impartial
arbiter such as the Homeric "god of war").

Heraclitus' self-regulating mechanism of justice by strife can also be
seen as eventually generating the Hellenic (and Western) concept of
reason in general. The word *metron*, measure, which occurs twice in the
Heraclitean fragments (B 30 and B 94) may convey the idea of regulated
competition, being closely related to the Homeric notion of *moira*, not as
fate, but as share or portion in a power game.[11] What the Hellenic

citizens, saying that only the latter "would be characteristic of democracy in its mature
form" ("Equality and Justice," 85 n.140). Although Vlastos' distinction is historically
correct, it should be remembered that the idea of equality among the individual citizens
originates in the aristocratic, agonistic notion of justice among equals. In this respect, the
slightly different shades of meaning inherent in *isomoiria* and *isonomia* are instructive:
whereas *isomoiria* or equality of shares perhaps still preserves the idea of competition,
isonomia seems somewhat to obscure this idea, since it appears to imply that all citizens
are entitled by law to equal political shares. In modern America, those who speak of
"equal opportunity before the law," rather than "equality before the law," return to the
older, agonistic meaning of the Greek terms, which contemporary socialist ideologies
tend to obscure. Finally, the notions of *isonomia* and *isomoiria* tend to erase the distinction
between vertical and horizontal cooperative values (although vertical, one-way cooperation is still required of noncitizens and slaves). This convergence of cooperative values
occurs in modern democracies as well.
11. As Kahn points out in *The Art and Thought of Heraclitus* (Cambridge, 1979), 149, the
words *metron* in the sense of "measure, proportion," and *logos*, which can also mean,
among many other things, "measure, proportion," are at times interchangeable in

thinkers understood by "reason" (*logos*), then, is equally the *metron* (later, the Latin *ratio*, which gave our "reason") which attempts to preserve a given balance of forces by always keeping the middle course through a distribution of equal shares among the contestants, and thus avoiding surfeit (*koros*), which inevitably leads to imbalance. Consequently, to go *huper moron*, "beyond one's share or appointed fate," means to overstep the mark and thereby disturb the balance of power, in short to go beyond reason.

It is by no means clear, however, that for Heraclitus "measure" is anything more than a temporary state in an ever-changing power game: strife incessantly sets up world orders, which it then destroys and replaces with new ones, and in this sense *metron* or "reason" is subordinated to the restless play of warring forces.[12] Like Homer, Heraclitus describes the

---

Heraclitus; later on, especially in Plato and Aristotle, and then in the early Christian fathers, *logos* seems largely to replace *metron* in denoting the faculty of reason and becomes the code word for a predominantly rational mentality. The close semantic kinship of *metron* and *logos*, therefore, justifies my use of the term "logo-rational" to characterize postarchaic Hellenic thought. For me, then, "logo-rational" denotes not so much the primacy of Reason in a rationalist Cartesian sense, as the median, tempered quality of Hellenic philosophical thought (compare chaps. 4 and 5). On the other hand, Heraclitus' way of thinking can best be characterized as proto-logo-rational, because it is much closer to an archaic than to a median mentality. For a list of the various meanings of *logos* during the archaic and the classical periods, see Guthrie, *HGP 1*, 419–24. For *metron* see also Raymond A. Prier, "Some Thoughts on the Archaic Use of Metron," *CW* 70 (1976): 161–69.

12. It is this point that rationalist commentators on Heraclitus do not sufficiently take into consideration. These commentators focus, as a rule, on Heraclitus' ontology, on his notions of Flux and the Unity of Opposites, without pausing to examine the power-oriented nature of this ontology. Jonathan Barnes, for example, defends an extreme rationalist position when he declares: "And yet both these theories [Flux and Unity] seem idiotic in themselves, and rest upon idiotic arguments; they are not worth a moment's attention from a rational man" (*TPP*, 76). And later on: "It will not do to suggest that 'we need not expect Heraclitus' thought to be by our standards completely logical and self-consistent' [Guthrie, *HGP 1*, 461], and to intimate that by Heraclitean logic the Unity thesis is consistent. The standards of logic are not 'our' standards: they are the eternal standards of truth; and any statement which fails by those standards fails to be true whether its utterer spoke in knowledge or in ignorance of the standard he flouted" (*TPP*, 79). Here Barnes takes the same position that certain Christian theologians do in the Middle Ages, when they condemn all non-Christians to the eternal flames of hell. Of course, the key term in these passages is "rational man," as Barnes, but not as a reasonable rationalist like Guthrie, understands the term. To the Barnesian rational man, Heraclitus' thought must necessarily appear as a pitiful groping in the dark for the saving light of Reason. Other less dogmatic scholars, such as Kahn, regard Heraclitus as an early representative of the rationalizing tendency in Hellenic scientific thought that

arbitrary, spontaneous and unpredictable character of strife in terms of a
child's play: "Lifetime (*aiōn*) is a child at play, moving pieces in a game.
The kingship belongs to the child" (B 52). Perhaps it would not be too
farfetched to interpret *aiōn* in this particular context as cosmic (physical)
force because, according to some scholars, *aiōn* may have originally meant
something like "vital force." It is, perhaps, only later that Plato redefines
aiōn to mean "the immutable eternity of the Forms," thus further
obscuring the fact that his idealist philosophy is rooted in a mentality of
power.[13] In any case, Heraclitus associates *basileie*, kingship, with the
innocence of a child at play, an association which we have already
encountered in Homer (*Il.* 15.361–66)—if *aiōn* were here interpreted as
cosmic force then the fragment would become perfectly understandable,
seeing that *basileie* and *aiōn* would be homologous terms, echoing and
reinforcing each other. In B 52, then, Heraclitus seems to operate with an
archaic, Homeric notion of play as agon, which in other contexts he calls
polemos and *eris*, and which he turns into a fundamental cosmic principle.[14]

stresses cosmic unity and order over flux and disorder. But it is far from clear whether
Heraclitus is a "progressive" thinker (like, say, Xenophanes), departing from Homeric
values, or a "conservative" one, returning to them. Although I favor the second position,
I believe the general thesis of this chapter remains valid in either case: like other
Presocratic thinkers, Heraclitus stands poised between an archaic or a proto-logo-
rational mode of thought and a logo-rational one, at the same time that he never reflects
upon the mentality of power underlying both of them, as Euripides, for example, does
later on.

13. See Kahn, *AOGC*, 188–89. For a possible etymological sense of *aiōn* as "vitality, vital
force," see Emile Benveniste, "Expression indo-européenne de l'éternité," *Bulletin de la
Société de Linguistique* 38 (1937): 103. One can therefore also link the Western notions of
time and duration to the notion of power, and the image of Cronus devouring his
children in order to secure his continuous and undisputed dominion is a highly
appropriate one.

14. For a different interpretation of this fragment, see Kahn, *Heraclitus*, 227–29. Kahn
starts from the thesis that Heraclitus combines the ideal of self-assertion present in
Homeric epic, and the morality of self-restraint present in the sayings of the Seven Sages,
Greek tragedy, and classical Hellenic ethics, a combination that Heraclitus then rein-
terprets through the natural philosophy of the Milesians. Although Kahn's view parallels
to a certain extent mine, there are important differences. Kahn, not unlike Adkins and
his followers, chooses not to trace the development of the Hellenic mentality from an
ideal of self-assertion to a median morality in terms of power or, more specifically, in
terms of a shift in cultural emphasis from immediate to mediated forms of power, and
thus tends to idealize the nature of Hellenic logo-rationality. Kahn argues, moreover,
that the traditional Sages "did not see—and could not see before the birth of natural
philosophy— . . . that the pattern of human life and the pattern of cosmic order is one
and the same" (*Heraclitus*, 22). This argument seems implicitly to deny the holistic

Whereas the Ionian school generally sees strife as generating both stability and change, and places it at the very foundation of Becoming, the Pythagoreans and some of the Eleatics seem to reject it as a grounding principle. Instead, the latter thinkers introduce the philosophical, logo-rational notion of Being, denying the ultimate reality of change, motion, and chaos, and affirming eternal stability, harmony, and order. At the same time some of them, especially the Pythagoreans but, apparently, also Parmenides, attempt to replace strife by love as a fundamental cosmic principle. This love, however, is conceived, on the model of Hesiod's Eros or Philotes, as unifying force and thereby remains closely bound to a mentality of power. More often than not, the Pythagoreans and the Eleatics seem to have ended up positing a thoroughly agonistic world, divided between Love and Strife, Being and Becoming, between the eternal realm of immutable forms and the ever-changing realm of deceiving appearances.[15]

Even though the Italian school often downplays the cosmological role

---

character of Homeric mentality in general. To me it makes more sense to say that Heraclitus goes against the relatively impersonal character of the Milesian cosmos, returning to the older, anthropomorphic view, which implies the unity of the human, divine, and natural spheres.

As far as Kahn's specific discussion of B 52 goes, he stresses the presumed regularity and predictability of the Heraclitean world order: "The fundamental thought [of this fragment] is not the childlike and random movements of the game (as some interpreters have supposed) but the fact that these moves follow a definite rule" (Heraclitus, 227). In the best logo-rational tradition, then, Kahn emphasizes games over play, and thus favors the view of the Heraclitean cosmos as an orderly, rule-governed manifestation of the divine Logos. Again, the question here is not whether the Heraclitean world order can appear as regular and harmonious, but whether this order remains always the same or identical with itself, being continuous and indestructible as, say, in Parmenides. My answer to this question is obviously in the negative.

15. For eros in Parmenides, which seems to be, as in the case of the Platonic concept, of Pythagorean provenance, see, for example, Karl Deichgräber, "Parmenides' Auffahrt zur Göttin des Rechts: Untersuchungen zum Prooimion seines Lehrgedichts," Akademie der Wissenschaften und der Literatur: Abhandlungen der Geistes- und Sozialwissenschaftlichen Klasse, Jahrgang 1958, no. 11 (Wiesbaden, 1959): 629–724. In my study eros remains necessarily confined to the use to which it is put by a mentality of power. Yet there are crucial, underground aspects of the Hellenic notion that can be seen as pointing to something other than this mentality. A study of these aspects (which cannot be undertaken here) would undoubtedly uncover values completely "alien" from the ones upon which my present investigation has focused. For the amphibolous nature of eros in the Hellenic world, see especially Anne Carson, Eros, the Bittersweet (Princeton, N.J., 1986), and Jean-Pierre Vernant, L'individu, la mort, l'amour: Soi-même et l'autre en Grèce ancienne (Paris, 1989), particularly chaps. 8, 9, and 10.

of strife, agonistic values remain its constant feature, especially in relation to the Ionian school. In fact, the philosophical monism of the Eleatics may partially have developed as a strategem of blocking the pluralistic theories of their Milesian rivals, and Parmenides' doctrine of Being reveals a number of agonistic elements that deserve closer examination.

Parmenides presents his logical view of Being in his poem traditionally titled *Peri phuseōs*, "On Nature." This poem, of which only fragments have come down to us, apparently consisted of three parts: the Proem, which describes a youth's journey in a horse-drawn chariot to the abode (?) of an unknown goddess; part 1, "Truth" (*Alētheia*), in which the goddess initiates the youth into the nature of Being; and part 2, "Opinion" (*Doxa*), in which the goddess teaches him about the nature of Becoming.

In part 1, by formulating the central question of his philosophical inquiry in terms of logical exclusion, "either [it] is (*esti*) or [it] is not (*ouk esti*)," Parmenides has his guide, the unknown Goddess, reject the possibility that "[it] is not." In turn, what-is (*eon*) is indivisible, immovable and continuous, precluding change, discontinuity and becoming:

> But, motionless within the limits of mighty bonds, [what is] is without beginning or end, since coming into being and perishing have been cast out by true belief. Abiding the same in the same place it rests by itself, and so abides firm where it is; for strong Necessity holds it firm within the bonds of the limit that keeps it back on every side, because it is not right that what is should be unlimited . . . for there is not, nor shall be, anything else besides what is, since Fate [*Moira*] fettered it to be entire and immovable. Wherefore all these are mere names which mortals laid down believing them to be true—coming into being and perishing, being and not being, change of place and variation of bright color. (B 8.26–41)

In this passage, which is crucial for the subsequent history of Western philosophy, (absolute) power and "what is" are interchangeable. Parmenides rejects the notions of void, transitoriness, and motion in favor of plenitude, continuity, and immobility. Being fills up the cosmos, banishing nonbeing. Order and Justice exclude chaos, chance, and the unlimited, which are identified, as in the Pythagorean Table of Opposites (Aristotle, *Metaphysics*, A5 986a23–27), with evil, disorder and injustice. Justice itself is significantly described in the mythopoeic terms that are as a rule reserved for Necessity and Fate: "it looseth not its fetters . . . but holdeth it fast." Indeed, Dikē, Anankē, and Moira are used interchangeably (note here the departure from Homer and the family resemblance to Hesiod), because "strong Necessity [*Anankē*] keeps Being firm within the bonds of the limit . . . because it is not right [*themis*, customary right] that what is should be unlimited."[16]

But even in the case of Parmenides one cannot be absolutely certain of his firm monistic commitment, because the second part of his poem is concerned with the "way of opinion," that is, with the contradictory world of Becoming, process, and change, which has just been refuted in the first part. Why this concern with the world of nonbeing, once its logical impossibility has been proven beyond the shadow of a doubt? Scholars have offered various answers to this question, but the fact remains that Parmenides could not, any more than his successor Plato could, lay the world of becoming to rest (so to speak), once and for all. He thus seems to remain divided between the two worlds, even as he seems to subordinate one to the other.[17]

Note also that in Parmenides Being is presented much like an unassailable, circular stronghold, "bounded on every side, like the bulk of a well-rounded sphere, from the center equally balanced in all direction" (B 8.11–13). Despite his tendency toward abstract thinking, Parmenides still formulates his notion of Being in concrete, agonistic terms. Consequently, he does not yet entirely obscure the immediate relationship between Being and power, and it is only in Plato and the Neoplatonists that power seems largely to emancipate itself from corporeality, becoming a full-fledged transcendental principle.[18]

16. For further discussion of Parmenides' notion of chance, necessity, fate, and justice in relation to other Presocratic philosophers, see the following section.

17. What seems to have influenced subsequent thinkers most is Parmenides' doctrine of Being, but this is no decisive argument regarding the nature of his own beliefs. For the most recent ontological interpretations of Parmenides' poem, which, however, mostly overlook the inseparable link between Being, Becoming, and power, see, among others, Leonardo Tarán, *Parmenides: A Text with Translation, Commentary, and Critical Essays* (Princeton, N.J., 1965); David Furley, "Parmenides of Elea," in *The Encyclopedia of Philosophy* (New York, 1967); Alexander P. D. Mourelatos, *The Route of Parmenides: A Study of Word, Image, and Argument in the Fragments* (New Haven, 1970); Prier's chapter on Parmenides in *Archaic Logic*; David Gallop, *Parmenides of Elea, Fragments: A Text and Translation with an Introduction* (Toronto, 1984); and Scott Austin, *Parmenides: Being, Bounds, and Logic* (New Haven, 1986). For an interesting view of Parmenides as the originator of both the doctrine of Being and the dichotomy of *nomos* and *phusis* in relation to the world of Becoming, see Reinhardt, *PGGP*, 5–64.

18. Compare Kirk and Raven: "Had [Parmenides] been asked whether his Being was solid (or 'body') his answer would have been a hesitant negative" (*Presocratic Philosophers*, 270). Other scholars deny that for Parmenides the dichotomy of corporeal and incorporeal, or matter and mind would have been an issue at all (see, for instance, Tarán,

The concrete, immediate nature of Parmenidean Being-power is particularly apparent in what is usually called the "Allegory of Truth" in the Proem, which despite its presumed allegorical intent seems to come much closer to the archaic poetry of Homer and Hesiod than to the intellectual, allegorizing language of the Neoplatonists—Parmenides, like Hesiod, still composes in epic hexameters. In fact, his encounter with the unknown goddess (Aletheia?) in the Proem recalls Hesiod's encounter with the Muses on Mount Helikon. The differences between the two encounters, however, are as important as their similarities. Hesiod still has relatively easy access to his Muses, who can tell both truth and lies. By contrast, Parmenides undertakes a long and laborious (perhaps even magic) journey, gaining access to his goddess by penetrating a formidable portal.[19] In addition to being almost impossible to reach, Parmenides'

Parmenides, 194–95). For Parmenides' notion of circularity and boundedness, see Austin, *Parmenides*, chap. 6, and Lynne Ballew, *Straight and Circular: A Study of Imagery in Greek Philosophy* (Assen, 1979), chap. 3. For truth as a military metaphor in Parmenides, see G. Jameson, " 'Well-Rounded Truth' and Circular Thought in Parmenides," *Phronesis* 3 (1958): 15–30. Mourelatos objects to Jameson's thesis that "truth can face any attack [because of its circular shape] fully confident of victory," arguing that in Parmenides "falsehood and ignorance are never pictured as rivals, competitors, or enemies of truth." Far from conspiring against truth, "mortals are only pitiable in their 'wandering' and 'helplessness' " (*Route of Parmenides*, 149 n.38). One can reply that although Parmenides may present truth as being above all competition (a shrewd rhetorical move), he still takes great care in fortifying it against any potential enemies. It is therefore conceivable that Parmenides does not guard truth from but *through* falsehood or the way of seeming: he defends truth by exclusion, by showing that everything else is falsehood. In this respect, falsehood is an ally rather than a competitor of truth (La Rochefoucauld makes this point in a different way when he says that a lie is the greatest compliment one can pay to truth).

19. The youth's journey in the Proem has been associated with that of a shaman, whose spirit travels out of his body in order to communicate with the world of demons. See Cornford, *Principium Sapientiae*, 118; Guthrie, *HGP 2*, 11; and Walter Burkert, *Weisheit und Wissenschaft: Studien zu Pythagoras, Philolaos und Platon* (Nuremberg, 1962), 263. A refutation of this shamanistic connection in Parmenides can be found in Tarán, 28–29. For Parmenides, Hesiod, and the epic tradition, see E. A. Havelock, "Parmenides and Odysseus," *HSCP* 63 (1958): 133–43; E. F. Dolin, Jr., "Parmenides and Hesiod," *HSCP* 66 (1962): 93–98; Hans Schwabl, "Hesiod und Parmenides: Zur Formung des parmenideischen Prooimions," *Rheinisches Museum für Philologie* 106 (1963): 134–42; Jaap Mansfeld, *Die Offenbarung des Parmenides und die menschliche Welt* (Assen, 1964) and "Parmenides Fr. B2, I," *Rheinisches Museum für Philologie* 109 (1966): 95–96; as well as B. A. van Groningen, *La composition littéraire archaïque grecque* (Amsterdam, 1958), and more recently, Robert Böhme, *Die Verkannte Muse: Dichtersprache und geistige Tradition des Parmenides* (Berne, 1986).

goddess, unlike Hesiod's Muses, would never tell a lie, an indication that for Parmenides and his contemporaries truth has become elusive and is no longer easily accessible. Indeed, barring a few initiates, truth has become impenetrable and impregnable. In Parmenides, then, one can dimly see emerging a logo-rational philosophical hermeneutics or the science of truth (versus the nescience of falsehood), whose initially crude, agonistic character will later be chiseled and refined in the Academy and the Lyceum.[20]

Other Eleatics continue Parmenides' attempt to replace the arbitrary play of physical forces or Becoming with an orderly and harmonious Being. For example, despite a certain tendency of reconciliation with the Milesian notion of change, Anaxagoras basically follows Parmenides when he posits Mind (nous) as a first cosmic principle and describes it in terms of power that are almost identical to those in which Parmenides describes Being: "All things have a portion of everything, but Mind is infinite and self-ruled, and is mixed with nothing but is alone by itself. . . . For it is the finest of all things and the purest, it has all knowledge about everything and the greatest power; and mind controls all things, both the greater and the smaller, that have life" (Anaxagoras, B 12.1–12). Here, nous cannot yet be regarded, any more than Parmenidean Being can, as a totally incorporeal entity; nevertheless, for Anaxagoras, mind and sheer physical

20. Here, the close link between agon, interpretation, and truth in a mentality of power becomes evident. In Hellenic thought, the notions of truth and falsehood probably come into existence as hermeneutical instruments of establishing and preserving authority by an increasingly influential logo-rational mentality. The Greek word alētheia, which originally seems to have meant "unforgetfulness" and later on, "unhiddenness" or "unveiledness," points to the hermeneutical (and hermetical) nature of truth in classical Hellenic thought: truth becomes something hidden or veiled that has to be revealed. As we can see in Parmenides, alētheia turns into an agonistic notion both because thinkers need to gain access to it or force it open and because, once they take possession of it, they need to defend it constantly. For a logo-rational mentality, truth assumes a performative function both in the sense of stabilizing and legitimizing a certain verbal construct or state of affairs and in the sense of triggering a mechanism of belief based on persuasion (the logo-rational, mediated equivalent of the direct power of speech present in an archaic community). Truth thereby replaces or, rather, supplements the traditional automatic mechanism of command and compliance based on an immediate display of physical force. On the other hand, falsehood or lie seems to assume a negative performative value: it becomes a mechanism of suppression and exclusion by which a verbal construct or state of affairs appears illegitimate, unethical, or destabilizing. For a different notion of philosophical truth and interpretation, see Martin Heidegger, especially "Logos" and "Alētheia," in Vorträge und Aüfsatze (Pfullingen, 1954), vol. 3.

matter do not appear as equal terms, one being given priority over the other.[21]

Through their incipient idealist monism, then, the Eleatics seek to arrest strife and raise Being above all competition. But another Italian, Empedocles, goes back to the *dunameis* (which he now calls *rizōmata*, roots) as cosmological fundamentals, restoring strife to its central place in Hellenic thought. He subordinates the four roots to two contrary forces, *Neikos* (Strife) and *Philotēs* (Love). In turn, Strife and Love generate a never-ending cosmic cycle, whereby the One becomes Many and the Many become One. In this respect, his poem *Peri phuseōs* recounts a "double tale" and can, at least to a certain extent, be described as dualistic:

> A twofold tale I shall tell: at one time it grew to be one only from many, and at another again it divided to be many from one. There is a double birth of what is mortal, and a double passing away; for the uniting of all things brings one generation into being and destroys it, and the other is reared and scattered as they are again being divided. And these things never cease their continual exchange of position, at one time all coming together into one through love, at another again being borne away from each other by strife's repulsion.[22]

21. On the other hand, if we stress Anaxagoras' Ionian connection and posit change as the fundamental idea of his cosmology, then Anaxagoras becomes a Heraclitean or a proto-logo-rational thinker. This is Nietzsche's route in *Philosophy in the Tragic Age of the Greeks*, where he sees Anaxagoras' *nous* as a precursor of his own Will to Power. Nietzsche interprets *nous* as a random, playful cosmic force: "*Nous* has no duty and hence no purpose or goal which it would be forced to pursue. Having once started with its motion, and thus having set itself a goal, it would be . . . a game [*Spiel*, also play]" (112). According to Nietzsche, it is precisely because Anaxagoras believes that *nous* has "free, arbitrary choice" that he resorts, like Heraclitus, to the idea of play: "Absolute free will can only be imagined as purposeless, roughly like a child's game or an artist's creative play impulse" (116). Here Nietzsche probably reads his own archaic notion of play into Anaxagoras' thought, as we have no conclusive proof that the latter saw the cosmos, as Heraclitus did, in ludic terms. Nevertheless, Nietzsche seems fully justified in seeing *nous* as free of teleological implications, because teleology appears as a later, Platonic and Aristotelian development.
22. Empedocles, DK 17.1–8, in M. R. Wright, *Empedocles: The Extant Fragments* (New Haven, 1981), 166. Subsequent translations refer to this edition. In addition to the general studies on the Presocratics already mentioned, one can consult, specifically on Empedocles, Wright's introduction, and D. O'Brien, *Empedocles' Cosmic Cycle* (Cambridge, 1969).

If we accept M. R. Wright's recent interpretation, Strife and Love are powers with expanding and contracting spheres of influence, inextricably bound to the roots, in the sense that "they are manifest in the pattern of balance and movement of the roots, and [that] they are contained within the same limits as them." Strife "takes up less and less place as its power subsides, in that less and less of the root masses are held apart." At the same time, Love "takes up more and more place insofar as more and more parts of roots are brought together and mingle further."[23] It seems clear, then, that irrespective of how many cycles Empedocles' contrary principles may generate (two, three, or four), his cosmological view remains consistently agonistic throughout these cycles. Love itself "rules" or "reigns," being conceived of as a unifying force, which ceaselessly disputes its dominion with Strife, seen as a dividing force. In this respect Philotes is little more than Hesiod's good Eris. Ultimately, Empedocles seems to return to Ionian pluralistic cosmology, but without renouncing the Parmenidean doctrine of Being, which he now applies equally to Strife and Love.

Empedocles' theory of the roots is taken over by the medical writers, who posit a certain number of *dunameis* (which in later medical literature will be called "humors") as making up the human body. According to these writers, the health of the human body depends, just as that of the body politic, on the equilibrium between forces or on *isomoiria*, and physical changes or diseases are the result of an imbalance between these forces. For example, the author of *The Sacred Disease* explains epileptic seizures as a war between the heat (of the blood) and the cold (of the phlegm): The symptoms occur "when cold phlegm streams into the blood, which is warm; for it chills the blood and stops its flow. And if the stream is great and thick, death takes place immediately; for it overpowers the blood by its coldness and solidifies it. But if the stream of the phlegm is less considerable, it overpowers the blood temporarily and cuts off respiration; then as it is gradually dispersed into the veins and mingled with a great deal of warm blood, if it is itself overpowered in this way, the veins receive air and consciousness is restored." In turn, the function of the physician is "to stand up to the morbid power as to an enemy and to treat it by opposite influences."[24]

23. Wright, *Empedocles*, 34.
24. W. H. S. Jones, ed., *The Medical Writings of Anonymous Londinensis* (Cambridge, 1947), 160–62.

Alcmaeon of Croton, another medical theorist who is influenced by Milesian cosmology, believes that an "equal distribution" (*isonomia*) of conflicting forces indicates a state of health in the body, whereas the "monarchy" (*monarchia*) of any single force produces illness.[25] The fundamental principles of ancient Hippocratic medicine, therefore, are as power-oriented as those of the magicians or the "medicine men" whose cultural authority it largely replaces, and have been uncommonly persistent throughout the history of Western medicine.

In conclusion, the notion of strife seems to have played an important role in the development of both the pluralistic and the monistic cosmological models of the Presocratics. Indeed, one can establish a direct correlation between these models and the archaic notion of power, which gradually moves from immediate or concrete forms to mediated or abstract ones. On a political level, this movement, which is by no means irreversible, corresponds to a no less reversible movement from strictly hierarchical to democratic systems of government. The concrete, physical monism of such Milesians as Thales and Anaximenes (who place a material principle [*archē*] at the foundation of the universe) seems to parallel the hierachical structure of the archaic *oikos*, where the father (*pater*) is also the lord and master of the household—both progenitor and source of all authority.[26] In turn, this *archē* can become a physical element or a *primus inter pares*, vying for supremacy with other elements, according to the isonomic principle of government by rotation, possibly in Anaximander and Heraclitus, and certainly in Empedocles and the Hippocratic Corpus. Finally, Parmenides and the Eleatics again attempt to raise the *archē* above all contest, by moving it to an unreachable, unassailable

25. For further discussion of the Hippocratic corpus in terms of *neikos*, *dunameis*, and *isomoiria* see, among others, Jones, *Medical Writings* and *Works of the Hippocratic Corpus*, 4 vols. (Loeb Classical Library, Cambridge, Mass., 1923–31), as well as *Philosophy and Medicine in Ancient Greece* (Baltimore, 1946); K. Deichgräber, *Hippokrates über Enstehung und Aufbau des menschlichen Körpers* (Leipzig, 1935); Vlastos, "*Isonomia*," 363–64; Kahn, *AOGC*, 126–28 and passim; and G. E. R. Lloyd, *Magic, Reason, and Experience* (Cambridge, 1979), 247–56. The most extensive collection of Hippocratic texts is in Hippocrates, *Opera Omnia*, 10 vols., ed. E. Littré (Amsterdam, 1961–62).

26. Although what Aristotle calls *archē*, material principle (*Metaphysics* A3 983b6), seems to be an anachronistic imputation to Thales and others of an abstract, logo-rational category, what is significant here is the Presocratic genealogical view (present already in Homer and Hesiod) according to which one thing "comes-to-be" from and is consequently controlled or governed by another. The notion of primogeniture consistently recurs throughout Milesian cosmological thinking, even though each individual thinker may postulate an *archē* different from that of his predecessor (Thales—water, Anaximenes—air, and so forth).

position. Plato completes this task and the concept of power as transcendental Being is ready for use in postclassical, Hellenistic monarchies. Avatars of Greek monistic and pluralistic modes of thought have persistently recurred throughout the history of the Western world, often (but not necessarily) in relation to their counterparts, the various forms of absolute monarchy and dictatorship on the one hand, and their rivals, the democratic forms of government, on the other.

■ *Necessity and Chance*

In chapter 1, I have suggested that the Homeric mentality does not draw a firm line between necessity and chance, and that the Homeric world order appears as a play of chance-necessity or a game of chutes and ladders. From the standpoint of ordinary mortals, world events may often seem predetermined by divine forces or, rather, contingent upon their arbitrary will, whereas from the standpoint of the gods (and of some heroes), these events may often seem fortuitous, because of the ongoing power contest between divine forces—for instance, between the Olympians and the older gods—which determines their (temporary) shares or *timai*. The archaic notions of necessity and chance seem thus inextricably linked to the notion of archaic agon and do not yet acquire the abstract and static nature of their late, classical counterparts. In Presocratic thought, these notions still seem much closer to their Homeric than to their classical versions, despite a certain rationalizing tendency, as evident in their case as it is in that of other archaic notions (*aretē*, *agōn*, *eris*, *kosmos*, *moira*, *psuchē*, *nous*, and so forth). However, the terms expressly denoting "necessity" and "chance," *anankē* (or *heimarmenē*) and *tuchē*, occur only infrequently in the Presocratic fragments; moreover, some of these occurrences are perhaps later additions or interpretations, and therefore may obscure their original meaning.[27] Here, then, in addition to a restrictive

27. In regard to the archaic concepts of necessity and chance, the English translations of the Presocratic fragments have been particularly misleading. To give one example, the archaic phrase *to chreōn*, occurring in Anaximander's longest extant fragment and in several Heraclitean fragments, is often translated as "by necessity." As Hermann Fränkel points out, however, "Wollte man *chreōn* hier [in Anaximander] mit 'Notwendigkeit' wiedergeben, so hatte man der Sache und der Sprache Gewalt angetan. Wir sind ja nicht im Bereich einer sinnfrei zwingenden Mechanik (*anankē*), und die Wörter des Stammes *chre-* bezeichnen ein 'Sollen' und 'Schuldigsein,' ein 'Gebrauchen' und 'Brauchbar sein.' Durch den Zusatz *kata to chreōn* wird also diese Regel des Geschehens nicht als finstere Macht auf den Thron des Despoten erhoben, sondern als berechtigt und einsichtigt legitimiert. 'Wie es in der Ordnung ist' meinen die Wörte" (*Wege und Formen frühgriechis-*

semantic analysis of *ananke* and *tuche*, one should attempt broader conceptual inferences that go beyond a purely positivistic idea of what constitutes textual evidence.

The semantic history of *ananke* shows the usual development of the
word from concrete to abstract meanings. As already mentioned, this
word seems originally to have conveyed the idea of binding. Heinz
Schreckenberg, for example, lists a considerable number of Homeric
phrases in which *ananke* means "fetters," "yoke," or "bonds."[28] He also
points out the affinity between *moira* and *ananke* throughout archaic and
later literature.[29] This affinity becomes particularly close when the two
words acquire a more abstract meaning in religious thought, where both
Ananke and Moira personify divine powers that hold the cosmos together
in inescapable bonds. It is probably at this point that *tuche*, which
originally also seems to have conveyed the idea of binding, begins slowly
to be separated from *ananke*, personifying Fortune.[30] Although the original affinity between Ananke and Tuche will remain recognizable precisely
because of their mutual bond to Moira, they will eventually become
specialized, as it were. In later literature, personified Ananke primarily
conveys the idea of inescapable fate or doom, whereas Tuche primarily
conveys the idea of the arbitrary dispensation of *moirai* or lots.[31]

Outside a religious context, *ananke* and *tuche* can also be used interchangeably in everyday language, especially once the Greek thinkers set
up an opposition (during the fifth century B.C.) between *nomos* and *phusis*,
culture and nature, or between *techne* and *phusis*, art and nature.[32] In this

---

chen Denkens, 188). In English, Anaximander's phrase can be rendered as "in due order"
or even "in due course." As to the interpretation of archaic *ananke* and *tuche*, the
doxographers seem to have been as perplexed as modern scholars are. While *ananke*
occurs in several fragments, *tuche* appears mostly in Democritus, and there only in an
ethical context, denoting "fortune." In other cases, the word *tuche* is supplied by the
doxographers themselves, and therefore it is probably used in a logo-rational, philosophical sense (as that which is unpredictable and arbitrary in its effects).

28. Schreckenberg, *Ananke*, 17–18.
29. Ibid., 79–82.
30. Compare Onians, *OET*, 450 and passim.
31. For example, in Democritus: "those who rejoice at the misfortune of their neighbors
do not realize that what fortune (*tuche*) sends is common to all" (B 293). Compare also B
197, B 210, and B 269. For a discussion of the negative connotations of *tuche* for a logo-
rational mentality, see Paul Joos, *Tuche, Phusis, Techne: Studien zur Thematik frühgriechischer
Lebensbetrachtung* (Winterthur, 1955), especially the chapters on Democritus (77–94;
with specific reference to *tuche*, 90–91), and Isocrates (94–108; with specific reference
to *tuche*, 98–99).
32. The Greek terms *phusis* and *nomos* (conveying, when employed antithetically, the idea

context, both *anankē* and *tuchē* can denote the blind and purposeless interplay of natural forces, as opposed to planned, goal-oriented cultural activities, and therefore are closely associated with the notion of *phusis*. Here *tuchē* is often used interchangeably with *automaton*, conveying the idea of spontaneous coming into being, without the agency of a cosmic intelligence.[33]

of "nature" versus "custom" or "convention") are originally unrelated but, like *anankē* and *tuchē*, they become increasingly abstract and then begin to be used as an antithetical pair in fifth-century political and moral thought, especially after the cosmologists and the doctors correlate them in their scientic treatises. From the beginning of the fifth century, *nomos* seems to develop along two lines: on the one hand it can designate the "unwritten law" (*agraphos nomos*) that is divinely ordained and beyond dispute, and on the other hand it can denote "custom," varying from community to community, or from nation to nation. In the latter sense, *nomos* is associated with *doxa* (common opinion) rather than with *alētheia* (truth, reality). The relativization of *nomos* under the pressure of the cosmologists, doctors, and ethnologists of the latter half of the fifth century ultimately leads to the Sophistic antithesis of *nomos* and *phusis*, in which *nomos* loses its implication of universal validity and comes to denote mere convention or common opinion.

   Phusis, on the other hand, originally conveys the idea of "birth," "growing," "becoming," or "that which arises spontaneously," and as such it is relegated by the Eleatics to the realm of appearance and nonbeing. The Ionian *phusikoi*, however, value it very highly as the "true essence or inner nature of a thing." This true essence or inner nature should be understood as dynamic, rather than static, involving becoming and appearance, and it is here that one should look for the origin of the *phusis* part of the Sophistic antithesis. In the latter part of the fifth and the beginning of the fourth century, under the pressure of the Eleatics, *phusis* also comes to denote either "nature" in the sense of a static inner being, or "Nature" in the sense of a personified, exterior power or order of things.

   The Sophists finally bring the *nomos-phusis* antithesis into the ethical and political doctrines of the Greek *polis*, where it becomes a commonplace throughout the classical period. The semantic development of the two terms can be related to the widening gap, in philosophical and scientific thought, between the physical or the "natural" world and the moral one or, in psychological terms, between the body and the soul. This gap can in turn be connected to the slow but steady gains of a logo-rational mode of thought. For detailed treatments of the *phusis-nomos* dichotomy, the reader can consult Felix Heinimann, *Nomos und Physis: Herkunft und Bedeutung einer Antithese im griechischen Denken des 5. Jahrhunderts* (Basel, 1945; rptd. Darmstadt, 1965); M. Pohlenz, "Nomos," *Philologus* 97 (1948): 135–42, and "Nomos und Phusis," *Hermes* 81 (1953): 418–38; Ostwald, *Nomos*, *passim*; Guthrie, *HGP* 3, chap. 4, "The 'Nomos'-'Physis' Antithesis in Morals and Politics"; and G. B. Kerferd, *The Sophistic Movement* (Cambridge, 1981), esp. chap. 10, "The Nomos-Physis Controversy."
33. Compare my discussion of the atomists, in this section. For a history of the conceptual development of *technē* in relation to *phusis, nomos, sophia*, and so forth, see Jörg Kube, *Techne und Arete: Sophistisches und Platonisches Tugendwissen* (Berlin, 1968). For the development of the opposition between *technē* and *anankē*, see Kube, *Techne und Arete*,

Given the primary and the secondary meanings of *ananke* and *tuche* listed above, it is not difficult to see how they can convey both complementary and opposite ideas. But what is crucial for our argument is that, irrespective of their later, more abstract semantic development, both necessity and chance are direct products of a mentality of power and can initially be understood only in terms of the archaic notion of contest.

It has also been noted that the philosophical meanings of *ananke* and *tuche* differ considerably from ours. For example, Guthrie points out that "the Greeks saw things so differently that to them the expression 'necessary chance' was perfectly natural." He adds that Aristotle was "not cheating when he at the same time spoke of the earlier natural philosophers as disallowing a teleological view of nature by attributing everything to *necessity* . . . and criticized this position by an argument designed to show that natural events are not at the mercy of *chance*, but exhibit a certain constancy and regularity."[34] From a modern rationalist's standpoint, this Aristotelian argument appears as a "horrible muddle" (Barnes' phrase), which no amount of rationalist exegesis could effectively disentangle. On the other hand, by distinguishing between an archaic and a logo-rational notion of necessity and chance, things may fall into place. In this respect, in the passage from *Physics* to which Guthrie refers above, Aristotle seems to struggle with the archaic meaning of the two words, which he is in the process of redefining in logo-rational terms.[35]

The Homeric notions of necessity and chance are inextricably linked to that of contest, and this also seems to be the case for Heraclitus (and possibly for Anaximander), who bases his entire cosmology on the idea of agon. Although *ananke* and *tuche* as such do not appear in the extant

33–35. For *techne* and *tuche*, see Joos, *Tuche, Phusis, Techne,* passim. Joos, however, generally underestimates the place of *tuche* in Hellenic thought; he presents only a partial, logo-rational account of the Greek thinkers' attempt to offset the arbitrariness of *tuche* through *techne*, and his treatment of chance remains superficial, for example in his remarks on Thucydides. In this, he is probably misled by Plato and Aristotle who had, however, good reasons to downplay the notion of archaic chance in their philosophies (see below, chapters 4 and 5). *Tuche* experiences a resurgence in the Hellenistic period, when it becomes the object of a cult as Fortune (the equivalent of the Latin Fortuna). 34. Guthrie, *HGP 2,* 415. Guthrie also lists some of the places where the phrase *anankaia tuche* occurs, mostly in Greek tragedy. An interesting occurrence is in Plato, *Laws* 889c: *kata tuchen ex anankes* (in accordance with chance from necessity). This passage as well as the whole question of necessity and chance in the Presocratics is discussed also by Barnes, *TPP,* 418–20. But both Guthrie and Barnes seem to me to rely too much on the modern scientific concepts of necessity and chance, especially as they appear in contemporary physics (for a discussion of these concepts see Spariosu, *Dionysus Reborn,* pt. 2, sec. 2). 35. For an examination of this passage in the *Physics,* see chapter 5.

Heraclitean fragments, one can discuss them, by implication, in B 53 and B 80, where conflict is seen as engendering all things, and in B 52, where *aiōn* is called a child at play.[36] If conflict is the "father and king of all," it also creates necessity and chance as two complementary ways of viewing the outcome of the contest among physical forces, and one can provisionally distinguish between them in terms of temporal sequence. In this light, chance appears as the first moment of a power game, during which the new configuration of forces is established. All things come to pass (*gignomena*) in accordance to conflict: rather than being predetermined, they are subject to the ups and downs of contest. In a dice game, this moment corresponds to the casting of the dice (assuming that Heraclitus' child-king of B 52 plays backgammon). In this sense, as Nietzsche points out, "chance itself is only the clash of creative impulses," or the clash of active forces.[37] In turn, necessity appears as the second moment of the power game, an *après coup*, during which the new configuration of forces settles in and takes its course, until the next clash. In a dice game, such as that presumably played by the *aiōn* in B 52, necessity corresponds to the moving of the pieces to a new position, after the fall of the dice. Chance, therefore, is the more dynamic, whereas necessity is the more static element of the contest of physical forces and its outcome.[38]

We can readily see wherein lies the difference between an archaic and a

36. The word "necessity" does, however, occur in B 137, "utterly decreed by Fate [*heimarmena*, necessity, destiny]" (Aetius, *Opinions* I, 27, I). In turn, Aetius may depend on Theophrastus' *Doctrines of Natural Philosophers*, frag. 1, containing the phrase *kata tina heirmarmenen anankēn*. But Diels lists this fragment among the doubtful ones, as being of Stoic derivation. For a full discussion see, among others, Kirk, *Cosmic Fragments*, 303–5. Kirk basically agrees with Diels that we have no evidence that Heraclitus spoke of cosmic *anankē* and adds that if the fragment were genuine, then it should be seen as evidence of Heraclitus' concept of *metra*: "It is perfectly possible for Heraclitus to have said 'all things are absolutely (or inevitably) apportioned,' meaning nothing more than that there were *metra* of all natural events, which could not be transgressed" (304). For me, however, Heraclitean *metra* are not absolutely but only temporarily apportioned, according to the vagaries of contest. On the other hand, their provisional character does not necessarily exclude their inevitability.

37. See Nietzsche, *The Will to Power*, sec. 673, 355.

38. The distinction between "dynamic" and "static" that I employ here is, of course, also of logo-rational provenance. Note the semantic development of the Greek word *stasis*, which can mean both "conflict, intestine strife" (e.g., in the Hippocratic corpus) and "balance, stability" or stasis in the modern sense (although the old sense is preserved in the modern medical term *metastasis*). Hence even static concepts of the universe can be traced back to dynamic ones, because "stasis" indicates stability as balance of forces, rather than as absolute lack of movement or conflict. But logo-rational philosophers like Parmenides, Plato, and their followers essentialize or eternalize the temporary, provi-

logo-rational idea of the interplay of necessity and chance. A proto-logo-rational mode of thought, such as that of Heraclitus, will as a rule emphasize the first moment, or the clash itself, subordinating necessity to chance; a logo-rational mode of thought, on the other hand, will as a rule emphasize the second moment, subordinating chance to necessity. Consequently, whereas for an archaic mentality chance events become necessity only after they occur, for a logo-rational mentality these events are always predetermined, although their determining agency (such as a god) or their causal chain may remain obscure.[39]

If we must rely mostly on educated guesses as to Heraclitus' notion of chance-necessity, in Parmenides we seem to be on somewhat firmer ground, because the notion of *ananke* is central to his poem *Peri phuseōs* and exhibits a marked rationalizing tendency. As Mourelatos, following Schreckenberg, points out, the Eleatic attempts to formulate his "concept of logical-metaphysical necessity . . . on the model of the [traditional] theme of Fate-Constraint."[40] We have seen that, like Hesiod, Parmenides relates Ananke and Moira to Dike, describing all of them in terms of bonds, shackles, and fetters, and thereby points to the agonistic origins of logo-rational thought in general.[41] At the same time, Parmenides confers

sional character of any balance of forces (which also means that they eternalize or essentialize "necessity") and thus obscure the agonistic origins of their static worldview.

39. It is precisely this logo-rational meaning that Guthrie (also followed by Barnes, *TPP*, 425–26) attributes to the atomistic concept of necessity and chance: "We conclude that Democritus' theory of causality comprised the following three points: (1) Every event is determined. There is no such thing as chance if the term is used in an absolute or objective sense. (2) The notion of chance may be retained and used in a qualified sense to mean a cause which is, and must remain obscure to us. (3) The incomprehensibility of such a cause lies in the fact that it is always, so far as we are concerned, one of an indefinitely large number of possibilities" (*HGP 2*, 419). But here Guthrie sounds too much like Planck and other modern physicists to whom he refers in the conclusion to his chapter on the fifth-century atomists (*HGP 2*, 498–500).

40. Mourelatos, *Route of Parmenides*, 46.

41. In his interpretation, Mourelatos often downplays the agonistic nature of Parmenidean thought and emphasizes its "congeniality," by opposing the traditional theme of Ananke to the relatively new theme of Peitho, or Persuasion. For Mourelatos, "the use of language of fidelity and persusasion in Parmenides has the same rationale as the use of the language of love as a metaphor of knowledge and understanding in Plato" (*Route of Parmenides*, 162). He acknowledges that the Parmenidean relationship of trust or faith (*pistis*) between reality-truth and mortals is unequal, because the real "does the active *peithein* [persuading], and we do the obliging *peithesthai* [compliance]." But he goes on to say that "the moral compulsion which is the ruling principle in the prephilosophic worldview is progressively civilized in Greek thought into congeniality and rational persuasion," and that "the conception of the world as a congenial—if more powerful

upon Necessity an absolute ontological status, eliminating chance from what-is and banishing it to the realm of nonbeing, that is, to the realm of Becoming and appearance. Thereby, Parmenides paves the way for the logo-rational, idealist philosophy of Plato, where Ananke becomes more abstract and remote, but also more "inevitable," being associated with the irresistibly seductive power of the Logos, which conquers and subdues by logical necessity rather than by brute force.

Parmenides' concept of Ananke as unavoidable Necessity also goes hand in hand with the Eleatic concept of the One, further developed by Plato and the Stoics. We have seen that Parmenides attempts to raise Being as One above all competition, which also means above all *chance*. The outcome of contest is always unpredictable and uncertain, and the victor constantly runs the danger of being in turn defeated. Just as any successful political configuration of forces attempts to perpetuate itself indefinitely by eliminating the very process that has brought it into being, so does the Parmenidean One attempt to eliminate or subordinate the Many and present itself as immovable Necessity, no longer open to change, that is, to chance. *Moira* as portion to be won in a contest turns into Moira or Fate, which is no longer subject to but, rather, arrests competition. If all portions are predetermined, or allotted in advance by a supreme power, then there is no reason to compete but passively accept one's "fate," and this is precisely the rationale, say, behind Stoic fatalism.[42] Thus the mythopoeic notion of Ananke as predetermined, inexorable, and inescapable Fate becomes the most appropriate philosophical agent of the logo-rational One, which literally takes no chances in its attempt to anchor itself in eternity.

Since Empedocles seeks to reconcile the Ionian Many with the Eleatic One, bringing together Strife and Love in a dualistic system, one can expect that his notion of necessity and chance will be a dualistic one. Indeed, a quick look at the pertinent Empedoclean fragments confirms this expectation. For example, Empedocles borrows Parmenides' image of Ananke as holding what-is together by strong bonds, and applies it to the relationship between Strife and Love: "There is an oracle of Necessity, ancient decree of the gods, eternal and sealed with broad oaths" (B 115.1–2). What the oracle of Ananke decrees is that Strife and Love rule in turn, an idea which recurs in B 30, where "great Strife" becomes a

---

and superior—partner is central in Greek philosophy" (162). Here Mourelatos seems uncritically to adopt the modern rationalists' version of the history of rationality as a history of human progress and ever higher civilization.

42. Compare Adkins, *From the Many to the One*, 230–32.

ruler again, in accordance with the time "which is fixed for them [Love and Strife], in alternation, by a broad oath."[43] Moreover, Charis (Grace or Love) "hates unbearable necessity" (B 116), when it is time for her to give way to Strife.

On the other hand, the mixing of the four roots, which produces all existing physical things, occurs by chance rather than by necessity, that is, it follows the vagaries of the agon between Love and Strife: "But as one divinity [daimon] grappled closer and closer [in combat] with the other (viz. Love and Strife), these things fell together as each chanced, and many additional things were incessantly produced" (B 59).[44] Likewise, the various parts of animals and plants are fitted together by chance, rather than by design. B 57, for example, describes the first generation of beings: "Here sprang many faces without necks, arms wandered without shoulders, unattached, and eyes strayed alone, in need of foreheads." And, again, in B 61, where perhaps the second generation of beings is described: "Many creatures were born with faces and breasts on both sides, man-faced ox-progeny, while others again sprang forth as ox-headed offspring of man, creatures compounded partly of male, partly of the nature of female, and fitted with shadowy [or sterile, according to Diels] parts."

Apart from offering an explanation of mythological creatures and of monsters and deformities, these Empedoclean fragments also stress the role of chance in the struggle for survival (an idea that some modern commentators have seen as foreshadowing Darwin's theory of evolution by natural selection). As Aristotle notes, according to Empedocles only

43. For a discussion of the relationship between these two fragments in terms of Ananke, see Schreckenberg, *Ananke*, 111–12.

44. Compare Empedocles, B 53, where air (one of the roots) is not always separated off—from the vortex—upwards, "but often in other ways." Aristotle, who refers to this passage in *Physics* 196a19–24, goes on to say that Empedocles also believes that the parts of various animals come into existence mostly by chance (see below). Simplicius, in *Physics* 331, lists several other Empedoclean fragments where chance seems to play a role: B 75, B 85, B 98, B 103, and B 104. All these fragments have in some way to do with the mixing of the roots during the combat between Love and Strife. B 103, "Thus all (creatures) have intelligence by the Will of Fortune [*Tuchē*]," shows that *phronēsis* itself is the chance product of the mingling of the roots rather than an all-encompassing, quasi-transcendental, cosmic principle (like Anaxagoras' *nous*). On the other hand, the four roots themselves, as well as Strife and Love, are held together by the inseparable bonds of *Anankē*, which can also appoint the times when they begin to mix or to separate (see Schreckenberg, *Ananke*, 112 and passim). What is subject to chance, therefore, is the various ways in which the four roots mingle and separate.

those creatures survived that were fortuitously equipped to do so: "Wherever, then, everything turned out as it would have if it were happening for a purpose, there the creatures survived, being accidentally compounded in a suitable way; but where this did not happen, the creatures perished and are perishing still" (*Physics* B7 198b29).

This Aristotelian account is particularly interesting for us because it draws a logo-rational distinction between necessity and chance which is certainly not Empedoclean, but which implicitly favors necessity over chance: according to Aristotle, the creatures survived only in those cases in which "everything turned out as it would have if it were happening for a purpose," that is, only in those cases in which chance coincided with necessity.

These examples show that although Empedocles is not concerned with the philosophical question of necessity versus chance (as it is posed by Aristotle and his pupils), he seems in effect to be divided between the archaic and the logo-rational sense of these notions. When he follows the Ionian *phusikoi*, he subordinates necessity to chance, and therefore operates with the Homeric notion of chance-necessity. When he follows Parmenides, he attempts, like the latter, to employ the mythopoeic notion of Ananke in a logical-metaphysical way.[45]

The atomists also seem to move back and forth between the archaic notions of chance and necessity and their logo-rational counterparts, and it is from this standpoint that we can best clarify the apparently confusing account of these atomistic concepts given by the doxographers. For example, Leucippus and Democritus are reported to have believed that "everything happens by necessity," an interpretation that seems to be supported by the only extant atomistic fragment (from Leucippus) that mentions *anankē*: "Nothing occurs at random (*chrēma matēn*), but everything for a reason (*ek logou*) and by necessity (*hup' anankēs*)" (Leucippus, B 2). Likewise, Diogenes Laertius, among others, says that for Democritus "all things happen according to necessity (*kat' anankēn*; for the cause of the

45. Although his argument has a completely different thrust, Schreckenberg nevertheless makes a somewhat related point when he concludes: "Jedenfalls ist der strenge ontologische Standpunkt des Parmenides zugünsten einer mehr pluralistischen Deutung aufgegeben: vier Elemente (Feuer, Wasser, Luft, Erde), zwei Kräfte (Philia, Neikos) und eine alles steuernde Gewalt (Ananke) machen die Gesamtheit des Seins aus" (*Ananke*, 113). But the "four Elements" are also forces and, therefore, what Empedocles apparently wishes to accomplish is an isonomic model that is ultimately deferred to a supreme authority; in other words, he apparently seeks to keep competition going and at the same time to regulate it.

coming-into-being of all things is the vortex (*dinēs*, whirl), and this he calls necessity."[46]

On the other hand, Leucippus and Democritus are reported to have ascribed the coming-into-being and the destruction of the physical world(s) to chance. Aristotle seems to refer to the atomists (among others) when he says that "There are some who make chance the cause both of these heavens and of all the worlds; for from chance arises the whirl and the movement which, by separation, has brought the universe into its present order" (*Physics* B4 196a24). Simplicius takes over Aristotle's remark and mentions Democritus by name: "When Democritus says that 'a whirl was separated off from the whole, of all sorts of shapes' (and he does not say how or through what cause), he seems to generate it by accident or chance."[47]

These statements are only seemingly contradictory once it is realized that, at least in their cosmology, the atomists probably treat chance and necessity as complementary rather than as opposite notions (although, like Empedocles and unlike the Aristotelians, they do not seem to be primarily concerned with them as philosophical concepts). Since Leucippus and Democritus believe that the physical world is the result of the motion of atoms that collide and combine in the void, one should not impute to them any notion of cosmic necessity in the logo-rational, Aristotelian sense (present, for example, in the teleological concept of the natural world as the necessary design of a divine intelligence). They do not need to explain the original cause and nature of the motion of the atoms, as Aristotle and Simplicius demand of them, because they simply do not think in terms of Aristotelian necessity, bound up with cause and effect. In fact, as Simplicius' text seems to imply, the atomists conceive of the motion of the atoms as a sort of strife that is ceaselessly carried on among them from the outset.[48] Like all strife, therefore, this motion

46. Diogenes Laertius, *Lives of Eminent Philosophers* 9.45, trans. R. D. Hicks (Loeb Classical Library, London, 1925), modified.

47. Simplicius, *Physics* 327.24, cited by Kirk and Raven, *Presocratic Philosophers*, 420.

48. See Simplicius, quoting Aristotle's book *On Democritus*, in *Physics*, DK A 37. In this passage, Simplicius uses *stasiazein* to describe the motion of the atoms, a word that suggests *stasis*, intestine strife. If Simplicius interprets the atomists correctly, they see the natural world, like the Milesians, Heraclitus, and Empedocles, as a product of the *agon* of physical forces. In this sense, "motion" and "collision" would be an Aristotelian interpretation of atomistic Strife. Several extant Democritean fragments suggest that the atomists indeed saw the collision and the congregation of various atoms in agonistic terms. If we were to apply an Anaximandrean metonymy to the atomists, then we could say that, in political terms, the "collisions" are clashes between opponents while

would be subjected to chance-necessity, in the Homeric and the Heraclitean sense.

But even if one does not accept the equivalence between motion and strife in atomistic cosmology, the world of atoms remains governed by the blind, spontaneous play of physical forces coming into being and perishing at random. In this sense, Diogenes' argument that everything happens by necessity because the "whirl" is a cause of all that comes into being and because Democritus calls it "necessity" is the kind of logo-rational tautology that Aristotle and Simplicius avoid: the latter two correctly interpret the whirl as the product of chance (in their own, logo-rational sense of the word).

On the other hand, in their ethics, the atomists stress the goal-oriented nature of both human culture and (human or divine) consciousness, that is, they stress the concept of necessity in its Aristotelian, teleological sense. It is from this cultural perspective that one ought to interpret Leucippus' *logos* and *anankē*. If in the physical world blind and purposeless necessity-chance rules supreme, in the cultural world everything can be traced back to an intelligent purpose and in this respect man "makes himself," or determines his own fate.[49] Democritus says: "Men have

---

"congregations" are (temporary) alliances. In turn these alliances, in which like seeks out like (see Democritus, B 164), would be based on the archaic concept of *philia*, understood not as love in the modern sense but as friendship based on mutual interest. (For archaic *philia* in relation to guest-friendship, *philotēs*, and *xeniē*, see Adkins, *From the Many to the One*, 16–19) If Democritean "ethics" corresponds (in a limited sense) to his "physics," then one can mention, in support of strife as the creator of both separation and congregation, B 249, B 250, B 252, B 258, and B 267.

The relation between Democritean ethics and physics has been discussed by Vlastos in "Ethics and Physics in Democritus," Allen and Furley, *Studies*, 2:381–98. One can note here Vlastos' insight that in the atomists nature is "de-humanized, de-moralized as never before in the Greek imagination" (397). On the other hand, I remain sceptical of Vlastos' logo-rational attempt to reconcile Democritean physics with the "law of measure," the knowledge of which presumably "empowers the soul to build upon nature goodness and justice which would otherwise not be found in nature at all" (398). It seems to me that Vlastos' argument largely depends on the polysemy of words like *phusis*, *anankē*, and *tuchē*, and I believe that one should distinguish between the meanings of these words in Democritus' ethics and in his physics. Democritus already seems to operate with a dichotomy between *phusis* and *nomos*, nature and culture, found also in modern science, for example in contemporary evolutionary theory (see Spariosu, *Dionysus Reborn*, pt. 2, sec. 1).

49. Vlastos, "Ethics and Physics," 390–92. It is therefore unnecessary to dismiss the Leucippus fragment as a mistaken attribution by later doxographers (as Freeman does in *Pre-Socratic Philosophers*, 289). Consider that this fragment is supposed to belong to *On Mind* rather than to *World-Order* (Leucippus' cosmological treatise, of which *On Mind*, if it

wrought an image of chance [*tuchē*] as an excuse for their own stupidity. For chance rarely conflicts with intelligence [*phronēsis*], and most things in life can be set in order by an intelligent sharpsightedness."[50] Or again: "Fools are shaped by the gifts of chance, but those who understand these things by the gifts of wisdom" (B 197).

But physical necessity (*anankē*) finds a place in Democritus' ethics as well, and is mainly connected with the body rather than the soul, acting as a limit or a boundary to what an individual can do (that is, to his power). As such, it is up to the soul to negotiate this limit through the careful guidance of the body (B 159). It is in this connection that the "law of the measure" (Vlastos' phrase) applies in human life. Nothing in excess, everything in moderation, and measure is best are maxims that Democritus shares both with the old sages and with the fifth-century tragedians. Although he retains "pleasure" (which, as we have seen, is immediately connected with the feeling of power in the Homeric world) as the guiding principle of his ethics, he redefines it in median terms: pleasure is not to be sought in "mortal things" (B 189), including desire for excessive wealth and power, which breeds envy, jealousy, and spite (B 191); rather, it is to be found in moderation (B 211). Cheerfulnesss (*euthumiē*), the chief characteristic of the healthy soul (and body), is attained "through moderation of enjoyment and harmoniousness of life," whereas things that "are in excess or lacking are apt to change and cause great disturbance in the soul" and, therefore, also in the body (B 191).[51]

It appears, then, that the atomistic notions of chance and necessity assume a double (archaic and logo-rational) aspect precisely because Leucippus and Democritus already operate with the logo-rational dichotomies of body and soul, nature and culture, art and nature, and so

---

was not a separate book, may have been a chapter) and therefore does not deal with the world of atoms, but with the world of intelligent beings (human and divine). I part ways with Vlastos, however, when the latter argues (against Cyril Bailey) that atomistic chance "is not only consistent with physics . . . [but] it can only be correctly explained through physics," and goes on to say that "the misunderstanding of the relative reality of chance means an absolute reduction in our natural power" (391–92). This line of argument favors a logo-rational over an archaic notion of necessity and chance that seems alien to atomistic thought. For general studies of the atomists, see Cyril Bailey, *The Greek Atomists and Epicurus* (Oxford, 1928); V. Alfieri, *Atomos Idea* (Florence, 1953); and D. J. Furley, *Two Studies in the Greek Atomists* (Princeton, N.J., 1967).

50. Democritus, B 119. All translations of Democritus' ethical fragments are, with slight alterations, from Freeman, *Ancilla*.

51. In this respect, Democritean ethics is almost identical with its Platonic and Aristotelian counterparts. See below, chapters 4 and 5.

forth. It should be stressed, however, that the atomists, whose allegiances seem to be evenly divided between the Milesians and the Eleatics, generally accord an equal status to the terms of their dichotomies (in this sense, the soul still preserves something of its archaic, corporeal nature in the atomists) and it is only subsequent thinkers that begin to favor one term over the other.

■ The Play of the Presocratics

The world view of the Presocratics is an obvious extension of their lives, of their public and private activities, which are through and through competitive. It is common knowledge that the archaic and classical city-states were constantly at war both within and outside their walls, in their assembly debates, law courts, agorae, theaters, symposia, and palaestrae, as well as on the battlefield and at the Panhellenic games. War as contest shaped the mentality of their citizens, their way of thought and behavior, their philosophy of life.[52] It seems hardly unreasonable, therefore, to assume (as I do in this chapter) that the play of the Presocratics is primarily agonistic and that the notion of play as contest determines all the other Presocratic notions of play.

The Presocratics were the first, to our knowledge, to have developed critical thinking, which is essentially an agonistic activity, relying on distinctions, oppositions, appropriations, and exclusions. As forms of critical thought, philosophy and science thrive on competition among various thinkers, on warring theories contending for authority, which in this case assumes the guise of objective, scientific truth.[53] The competi-

52. "Pour les Grecs de l'époque classique, la guerre est naturelle," writes Jean-Pierre Vernant in Mythe et société en Grèce ancienne (Paris, 1974), 31. In the wake of Nietzsche, Burckhardt, and others, Vernant draws a graphic picture of the competitive nature of Hellenic society in general.

53. Assessing what he calls the "weaknesses" and the "strengths" of Hellenic science in modern, rationalist terms, G. E. R. Lloyd remarks with a caution and restraint that lend all the more rhetorical weight to his conclusions: "The way in which evidence and 'experiment' were often used to support, rather than to test, theories, a certain over-confidence and dogmatism, above all a certain failure in self-criticism, may all be thought to reflect the predominant tendency to view scientific debate as a contest, like a political or a legal agōn. Aristotle noted in De Caelo (294 b 7ff) that 'we are all in the habit of relating an inquiry not to the subject-matter, but to our opponent in argument.' This remains true, no doubt, today, but the observation appears especially relevant to early Greek science. The sterility of much ancient scientific work is, we said, often a result of the inquiry being conducted as a dispute with each contender single-mindedly advocat-ing his own point of view. This is easy to say with hindsight: but an examination of the

tive nature of philosophical and scientific thought comes through, for example, in its frequent attacks against Homer and Hesiod as promoters of an archaic mentality. Even before Socrates and Plato, Xenophanes criticizes the poets, from a logo-rational standpoint, because they "have attributed to the gods everything that is a shame and reproach among men, stealing and committing adultery and deceiving each other" (B 11). Likewise, Heraclitus caustically remarks that "Homer deserves to be expelled from the competition and beaten with a staff—and Archilocus, too" (B 42, trans. Kahn).

Heraclitus, moreover, attacks not only the poets but also the philosophers, including Xenophanes: "Much learning does not teach understanding. For it would have taught Hesiod and Pythagoras and also Xenophanes and Hecateus" (B 40, trans. Kahn). Pythagoras in particular seems to be the helpless butt of Heraclitus' polemical wit, being styled a "prince of impostors" (B 81), whose reputed "much learning" is in fact "artful knavery" (in Greek this is a play on words: *polumathein, kakotechnien*; B 129, trans. Kahn). This polemical display is undoubtedly part of the contest for cultural authority that is carried on among various thinkers and is, ironically, in full accord with the traditional, archaic values supported by Homer and Hesiod. We have seen, for example, that Heraclitus upholds the very same values when he defends the Homeric notion of *aretē* (B 49, B 104, and B 121). That Homer is attacked by one of his own cultural heirs can also be regarded as an ironical example of negative or retributive justice: he who lives by the sword, dies by it, too.

Heraclitus' polemical stance is shared by all the other *phusikoi* (as Aristotle complains in *De caelo*), which perhaps explains why each of them chooses a different *archē* (Thales—water, Anaximenes—air, and so on), to which he then subordinates all the others. But the group that became most (in)famous for their polemical spirit are the fifth- and fourth-century Sophists and rhetoricians, who openly indulged in this kind of verbal contest. They stage interminable debates over such beloved topics as *nomos* versus *phusis, technē* versus *phusis*, and so forth, and these debates can best be seen in terms of the larger contest between archaic and median values in Hellenic culture.

The advocates of *phusis* against *nomos*, for example, often seem to argue from an archaic position, and they include Protagoras, with his relativist

---

Greek evidence suggests that this very paradigm of the competitive debate may have provided the essential framework for the growth of natural science" (*Magic, Reason, and Experience*, 266–67). Here Lloyd applies to Greek scientific thought the insight that Nietzsche and others have applied to all Hellenic (and Western) thought.

doctrine of man as the "measure of all things"; Thrasymachus and Callicles, with their revival of the aristocratic notion of the right of the stronger; Antiphon, with his theory of *phusis* as "enlightened self-interest"; and finally Gorgias, with his playful theses on nonbeing and with his contention that the word is "a mighty despot" and that the art of persuasion "far surpasses all the others and is far and away the best, for it makes all things its slaves by willing submission, not by violence" (Plato, *Philebus* 58a–b). Lysias and Thucydides seem often to join this group as well, with their situational ethics and their notion of political expediency or profit (*to sumpheron*).[54] On the other hand, the advocates of *nomos* against *phusis* appear to defend a median position. They interpret *nomos* positively, not as arbitrary convention, but as universal, logo-rational law which triumphs over a savage and uncouth *phusis*, nature.

The idea of progress also seems to arise in the context of the *nomos-phusis* debate. This idea is another intellectual offshoot of the contest between archaic and median values in the fifth century and replaces the archaic notion of cultural regression present, for instance, in the Homeric and Hesiodic myths of the ages of mankind. The so-called fifth-century "enlightenment"—a modern rationalist label that describes only one strand of thought in an extremely diverse and complex age—presents archaic times not as a golden age (as Homer and Hesiod generally do) but as an age of savagery that is superseded by a cultivated age, in both an agricultural and an intellectual sense. Prometheus becomes the central symbol of the enlightened spirit, teaching humanity how to elevate itself from a natural, savage state to the civilized *polis*. One of the first thinkers to advocate the logo-rational idea of progress is Xenophanes, who, moreover, relates it to the logo-rational notion of human perfectibility through scientific investigation: "Yet the gods have not revealed all things to men from the beginning; but seeking men find better in time" (B 18). His criticism of the Homeric view of the gods as violent and amoral should thus be understood in the same progressive spirit.

Xenophanes is echoed by some of the older Sophists, such as Protagoras, who is believed to have written a tract called "The Original State of Man," in which he rejects the savagery and the ignorance of the natural state and praises reason, law, and order as the best foundations for a social contract. These ideas become commonplace by the end of the fifth century: for example, Critias (d. 403 B.C.) places them in the mouth of Sysiphus, the title character of his play: "There was a time when the life of

54. Some of these Sophists can also situate themselves on the opposite, logo-rational side of the issue. See my discussion below, in this section.

men was disorderly and beastlike, the slave of brute force, when the good had no reward and the bad no punishment. Then, as I believe, man laid down laws to chastise, that justice might be ruler and make insolence its slave, and whoever sinned was punished" (B 25.1–8).

In this speech *nomos* prevails over *phusis*, as it does, later, in the speeches of such rhetoricians as Lysias, Isocrates, and Demosthenes. For instance, in a funeral oration for the Athenians who died in the Corinthian War, (pseudo?) Lysias praises the "early" citizens of Athens for their way of handling public affairs, "by law honoring the good and punishing the wicked, for they thought it the action of beasts to prevail over one another by violence." Lysias then goes on to say that men in general should "make law the touchstone of what is right and reasoned speech the means of persuasion, subjecting themselves in action to these powers, with law for their king and reason their teacher."[55]

The arguments of both Critias and Lysias show that the median values themselves have now become projected into the past nostalgically, as an ethical golden age. But at the very moment that the two orators decry violence in human affairs, they condone it under the auspices of the "law," which has a retributive and repressive function. Their logo-rational language remains agonistic: laws "chastise," justice is a "ruler" who "make[s] insolence its slave," men "subject themselves [to] the powers" of law and reasoned speech, and so forth.

Yet it is precisely the "beastly" and "savage" condition, deplored by the orators, that such Sophists as Thrasymachus and Callicles praise under the form of *phusis* as the justice of the stronger, and it is by no means clear what the prevailing view of the ruling class was in the fifth-century *polis*. Judging, for instance, from parts of Thucydides' account of the Peloponnesian War, it is quite possible that many rulers paid lipservice to logo-rational ideas and democratic sentiments, at the same time that they ruled according to the archaic principle of might makes right—in this sense, lipservice to democracy would have been part of the *mētis* of a ruler, a shrewd way of wielding political power.

Neither is it possible to determine with certainty what the Sophists' true political beliefs were, because they often composed speeches, for practical purposes, defending opposite viewpoints. Protagoras, Gorgias, and Lysias, for example, were notorious for their delight in arguing on both sides of an issue, and the Sophist treatise known as the *Dissoi logoi* (*Double Speeches*) ought to be regarded less as a proof of cognitive and

55. Quoted in Guthrie, *HGP 3*, 74–75.

ethical relativism than as a playful, agonistic exercise. What the Sophists taught their pupils was how to function in a political, ethical, and intellectual climate in which contest, violent and nonviolent, determined all other values.[56]

Another example of rhetorical playfulness, one which is not explicitly agonistic but which nevertheless remains linked to contest, can be found in a form of epideictic oratory called *paignion*, "playful" or "sportive speech." The best known *paignion* or rhetorical display is Gorgias' *Encomium on Helen*, widely imitated by subsequent rhetoricians (notably by Isocrates, although in a less playful spirit). In this sportive speech, Gorgias undertakes the difficult task of defending Helen's conduct before and during the Trojan War. After a brilliant tour de force, the Sophist concludes: "By this discourse I have freed a woman from evil reputation; I have kept my promise which I made in the beginning; I have essayed to dispose of the injustice of defamation and the folly of allegation; I have prayed to compose a lucubration for Helen's adulation and my own delectation."[57]

In this passage, Gorgias' playful spirit comes close to what, in the wake of Kant and Schiller, becomes a permanent component of modern definitions of play: its "disinterestedness" or "for-its-own-sake-ness." Gorgias and other Sophists may occasionally have composed speeches for their

56. For the so-called Sophistic relativism, see, for example, Kerferd, *Sophistic Movement*, esp. chap. 9. But Kerferd largely misses the playful dimension of the Sophistic movement, being too intent on demonstrating its philosophical seriousness or respectability. The relativist and nihilistic implications of some of the Sophistic speeches are undeniable, but these rhetorical pieces should not be taken out of their agonistic context. The rise of rhetoric itself has been connected with the increasingly litigious character of life in the democratic *polis*, where even the rank-and-file Greek citizen was well-advised to learn how to defend himself, or how to defeat his opponent in court. The Sophists therefore taught their pupils how to argue on both sides of a question not in order to arrive at the "truth" but to get the better of their opponents. It was only later, in Plato, that these rhetorical exercises were divorced from their concrete agonistic context and condemned as cognitive and ethical relativism. Plato seeks to redefine Sophistic rhetoric in terms of his own median goals. In this respect, despite Kerferd's frequent questioning of the Platonic evaluations of the Sophists, he occasionally shares a Platonic logo-rational bias in his defense of the Sophistic movement. The standard works on Greek rhetoric are R. C. Jebb, *The Attic Orators from Antiphon to Isaeos*, 2 vols. (London, 1876); Friedrich Blass, *Die attische Beredsamkeit*, 3 vols. (Leipzig, 1887–98); and more recently, George Kennedy, *The Art of Persuasion in Greece* (Princeton, N.J., 1963). For the agonistic nature of the Hellenic system of justice and law courts, see Garner, *Law and Society in Classical Athens*, esp. 58–94.

57. Quoted in G. Norlin, ed. and trans., *Isocrates*, 3 vols. (Cambridge, 1961), 1:56.

own "delectation" or for the sheer fun of it, rather than for any immediate utilitarian purpose (although they did eventually use these speeches as rhetorical exercises for their pupils). A modern aestheticist critic would say that the Sophists sometimes practised "oratory for oratory's sake."[58] This notion of play as pleasurable activity in and for itself, beyond immediate utility, is undoubtedly present in the fifth and fourth centuries, when such words as *paidia* (play, leisure, pastime, dancing), *paignia* (play, sport, game), *paigma* (play, game), *paignion* (plaything, toy, rhetorical display) also begin to be set in opposition to words like *spoudē* (difficulty, seriousness) and end up carrying less ethical prestige than the latter.

An ethical polarization also occurs within the play concept itself, and just as one finds good and bad *eris* in Hesiod, one can find good and bad play in Protagoras, Gorgias, Aristophanes, Isocrates, Xenophon, Plato, and Aristotle.[59] When such logo-rational philosophers as the Pythagoreans and, in their wake, the Platonists begin to favor *theoria* (contemplation) over agon, the play concept increasingly takes on cooperative, nonviolent features and ultimately becomes separated altogether from immediate power and violence.[60]

An early example of the link between play and (the pleasure of) contemplation can be discerned in Plato's predecessor, Pythagoras, who is reported by Diogenes Laertius to have likened life to a festival or the games—a play metaphor reminiscent of the Renaissance and Baroque *theatrum mundi*: "He [Pythagoras] compared life to the Great Games (*panēgurei*), where some went to compete for the prize and others with wares to sell, but the best as spectators; for similarly, in life some grow up with slavish natures, hunting for fame and gain, but the philosophers for

58. Again, however, we should not lose sight of the agonistic context of these playful speeches: the Sophists composed many of them as displays of rhetorical virtuosity at symposia, festivals, and other public competitions. Like *aristeia*, therefore, the *paignion* is a manifestation of the pride of power not only for its own sake but also for the purposes of establishing (in this case, intellectual) hierarchies.
59. For a partial examination of the evidence for these polarizations, see, for example, Joachim Dalfen, *Polis und Poiesis: Die Auseinandersetzung mit der Dichtung bei Platon und seinen Zeitgenossen* (Munich, 1974). Dalfen, however, does not concentrate on play, but on poetry and *mimēsis*, which he only incidentally considers ludic forms. For further discussion of the polarizations undergone by the play concept in the classical period, see chapters 3, 4, and 5.
60. This is not to say, of course, that even as Plato's dialogues advocate cooperation and median values, they are not themselves, at least in part, agonistic or eristic forms of play.

truth."[61] Note, however, how Diogenes Laertius mixes archaic and median values in the antithesis between the slavish man and the philosopher, the implication of which is that the process of arriving at truth is as noncontemplative and agonistic as that of arriving at fame or gain.[62] It is clear, then, that the philosophical notion of play as developed by some of the Sophists, Pythagoras, Socrates, Plato, Aristotle, and others can best be understood in terms of the contest between archaic and median values in Hellenic thought.

The ethical polarization of good and bad play goes hand in hand with the logo-rational opposition between play and seriousness, reality and illusion, and truth and fiction. That the Sophists were already familiar with these oppositions seems obvious from Gorgias' famous *paignion* about the nature of tragedy: "By its myths and emotions, tragedy creates a deception in which the deceiver is more honest [just] than the non-deceiver, and the deceived is wiser than the non-deceived" (B 23). Although Gorgias plays on the logo-rational dichotomy between illusion and reality (compare also B 26, where he plays on the logo-rational distinction between being and seeming, or essence and appearance), he nevertheless implies that both his play and the play of tragedy are ethically serious (insofar as they reveal truth, be it only in an oblique, paradoxical fashion). In his playful way, Gorgias attempts to defend tragedy against accusations of falsehood, deception, and irresponsible play; in the course of his defense he also dissolves the opposition between play and seriousness.[63]

The question of the relationship between play and median morality or

61. Diogenes Laertius, *Lives of Eminent Philosophers* 8.8, trans. Hicks, modified.
62. Most Hellenic, logo-rational as well as modern, rational concepts of play will have a hard time steering clear of their archaic competitors, which, when pushed out the front door, sneak in through the back. See the chapters on Plato and Aristotle below, as well as my discussion of Kant and Schiller in Spariosu, *Dionysus Reborn*, pt. 1, sec. 1.
63. In this respect, Gorgias is the ancient precursor of Schiller, who in *Aesthetic Education* also attempts to exonerate play and literature of charges of deception, irresponsibility, and levity brought against them by neoclassical rationalist philosophy. Unlike Schiller, however, Gorgias does not seem to embrace a rationalist creed. Consider, for example, B 12, wherein Gorgias says: "One must destroy one's adversaries' seriousness with laughter, and their laughter with seriousness." Because Gorgias teaches eristics (the art of winning an argument) one cannot be sure what his own view of tragedy was. It seems clear, nevertheless, that he provided what was demanded of him, that is, strong arguments for defending the art of tragedy against its detractors. For a somewhat different view of Gorgias and the concept of fictionality in Hellenic thought, see Charles P. Segal, "Gorgias and the Psychology of the Logos," *HSCP* 66 (1962): 99–155.

seriousness is also raised by the symposium, a widespread form of Hellenic play (equally practised by the Presocratics), which receives ample literary treatment throughout Antiquity and which exhibits both archaic and median features. Having its roots in archaic ritual, the symposium combines orgiastic wine drinking and sex, that is, Dionysian revelry, with quieter forms of play, such as artistic performance (singing, poetry reciting, mime, dancing, acrobatic acts, and the like), society games, and philosophical debate.[64] Socrates, for example, was fully aware of the potential role of this central Hellenic institution in disseminating median values, but also of its considerable dangers. By the fourth century B.C., the opposition between play and seriousness shifts to the center of both Plato's and Xenophon's literary treatments of the symposium. For example, Xenophon begins his Symposium with this very issue: "In my opinion, it is not only the serious [spoudēs] actions of gentlemen [kalōn kagathōn andrōn] that merit commemoration, but also their games [paidiai]."[65] Here he appears, at first sight, to polemicize with Plato, who seems deliberately to downplay the archaic elements (the often excessive wine drinking and occasionally vulgar tomfoolery) of the traditional banquet, infusing it with median values, notably through a philosophical debate on love (which is pointedly directed against sympotic sexual practices) and the sober, exemplary behavior of Socrates during the proceedings.[66] Unlike Plato, Xenophon seems to imply that sympotic play is a worthwhile activity in its less philosophical aspects as well, and he is far from idealizing his master, Socrates. He does not refrain from presenting Socrates as cracking bad jokes (about his own ungainly physical appearance), trading sexual innuendoes with his younger male companions, and generally playing the fool. But even Xenophon visibly

64. For historical and literary background on the symposium, which has substantially contributed to the rise of Hellenic lyric poetry, the reader can consult, among many others, Peter von der Mühll, "Das griechische Symposium" (1926), reprinted in Mühll, Ausgewählte kleine Schriften (Basel, 1976), 483–505; J. Martin, Symposion: Geschichte einer literarischer Form (Paderborn, 1931); H. Jeanmaire, Couroi et courètes (Paris, 1936), 85–97; and more recently, F. Dupont, Le plaisir et la loi (Paris, 1977); K. J. Dover, Greek Homosexuality (London, 1978); and Massimo Vetta, ed., Poesia e simposio nella Grecia antica (Rome and Bari, 1983).

65. Xenophon, Symposium 1, Greek edition by F. Ollier (Paris, 1972), my translation. Further citations refer to this edition.

66. On the other hand, if Xenophon's Symposium is dated earlier than that of Plato (a less plausible, but not indefensible, hypothesis), then Plato can conversely be seen as seeking to revise his peer's presentation of the banquet as a traditional mixed bag of low and high entertainment. For Plato's attempt, in the Laws, to infuse this central Hellenic institution with median values, see the last section of chapter 4.

disapproves of sympotic Dionysian excesses and has Socrates moderate the drinking of his companions as well as debate the merits of spiritual love versus physical. More importantly, Xenophon's symposium ends with nothing more unseemly than a sexual pantomime (the nuptial rites of Dionysus and Ariadne—the resplendent ephebe Autolycos, in whose honor Callias holds the banquet, is by now safely out of harm's way, chaperoned by his father), after which the aroused participants leave either to rejoin their wives or to cool off by means of a night walk. Even in Xenophon, then, moderation and sobriety prevail over shameless, self-indulgent Dionysian play.

Although the historical symposium probably never became the kind of logo-rational play that both Plato and Xenophon would have wished it to be,[67] philosophy devised other median forms of playfulness, for instance, in what I have called an *as if* approach to knowledge. In all likelihood, this approach was developed, at least in part, as a logo-rational response to a certain cognitive nihilism and axiological relativism that allowed the kind of playful inversions encountered in Gorgias' paradoxes. It starts from the premise that whereas man cannot attain absolute truth or knowledge, he can at least act *as if* truth or knowledge were accessible. Xenophanes is the first thinker known to us to employ this epistemological approach, in connection with his critique of Homeric values. After he criticizes the violence and amorality of the Homeric gods (B 11), he dismisses the Homeric view of religion as a projectional fallacy (or what, in modern times, Kant calls *symbolischer Anthropomorphismus*). Noting that mortals "consider that the gods are born, and that they have clothes and speech and bodies like our own" (B 14), and that, moreover, the "Ethiopians say that their gods are snub-nosed and black, the Thracians that theirs have blue eyes and red hair" (B 16), Xenophanes extends his argument, by analogy, to the animal world: "But if cattle and horses or lions had hands, or were able to draw with their hands and do the works that men can do, horses would draw the forms of the gods like horses, and cattle like cattle, and they would make their bodies such as they each had themselves" (B 15).

From the fact that men imagine the gods to be like themselves, Xenophanes apparently infers that all knowledge is relative, that man can never know (absolute) truth and, hence, that he can hardly know any-

---

67. See, for example, Plutarch's *Sumposiaka* (probably written around the second decade of the second century A.D.), in which Plutarch equally disapproves of (stubbornly persistent) Dionysian orgiastic practices. In turn, he favors moderate drinking and high entertainment, including sober philosophical conversations.

thing about the gods either: "No man knows, or ever will know, the truth about the gods and about everything I speak of: for even if one chanced to say the complete truth, yet oneself knows it not; but seeming is wrought over all things [or fancy is wrought in the case of all men]" (B 34). This inference, however, does not prevent Xenophanes from retaining the symbolical projection in epistemology, under the refined form of the good analogy (corresponding to Kant's good symbolical anthropomorphism): "Let these things be stated as conjectural only, resembling truth [or reality]" (B 35, my translation). On this *as if* basis, Xenophanes declares divinity to be not many, but one, "greatest among gods and men, in no way similar to mortals either in body or in thought." He thus introduces what Hans Vaihinger calls a "useful philosophical fiction" in epistemology, a fiction that Vaihinger, following Plato, regards as a form of intellectual play.[68]

In Xenophanes, then, we can, perhaps for the first time in the history of philosophy, discern a form of play that is entirely rational: the play of analogical thought, through which what by now has become inaccessible truth is rendered at least partly accessible, in an *as if* or imaginary mode of being. Plato will also employ this analogical artifice in order to transform the archaic notion of mimesis-play into the logo-rational concept of mimesis-imitation or simulation. In modern philosophy, Xenophanes' epistemological approach based on an *as if* ludic notion becomes not only a major cognitive instrument from Kant to Vaihinger, but also an expedient answer to the vexed question of truth in the theoretical and practical sciences.

But even Xenophanes' *as if* form of play remains tied to agon, both because of its polemical context and because of its close kinship with the Sophistic strategy of arguing from probability or from appearance. The classical example of this type of argument is provided by Plato (*Phaedrus* 273b) and then taken over by Aristotle: "If a weak man is accused of assault, his defense will be that it is not probable that he would attack a stronger man. But if he is likely to be guilty, if he is himself the stronger, he may argue that the crime is still not probable for the very reason that it was bound to appear so" (*Rhetoric* 1402a). Another well-known example, highlighting not only the playful nature of the argument from probability but also its immediate link to agon, is the anecdote about the (alleged)

68. Vaihinger, *Die Philosophie des Als Ob* (Leipzig, 1920), passim. Vaihinger employs *Spielbegriffe* as an alternative term for "fictions." For Plato's playful *as if* approach, see chapter 4. For a full discussion of the modern *as if* cognitive method, including Vaihinger's, see Spariosu, *Dionysus Reborn*, passim.

fathers of rhetoric, Corax and his pupil Tisias, both of Sicily. Dragged into court by Corax because he refused to pay for his rhetoric lessons, Tisias pleaded that if he won the case he did not have to pay by virtue of the court's decision, but if he lost, payment would be unfair since Corax's teaching would have proven worthless. Corax's plea, of course, reversed the argument. The court, in turn, threw the case out with an equally playful pun: "A bad egg from a bad crow" (*korax*).[69]

The essentially agonistic nature of the Presocratic mode of thought and behavior is finally underscored by the fact that the Sophists took part in the Hellenic games, competing for prizes in organized contests, just as the athletes, the dramatic poets, and the singers of tales did.[70] Moreover, the Sophists themselves often sang the praises of contest, regarding it as the main generator of values in their culture. As Guthrie points out,

> For Protagoras any discussion is a "verbal battle," in which one must be victor and the other vanquished (*Prot.* 335a), in contrast to Socrates' expressed ideal of the "common search," one helping the other that both may come nearer to the truth. The contest, said Gorgias, needs both boldness and wit, for the argument, like the herald at Olympia, summons whoever will come, but crowns only those who can succeed. Thucydides is contrasting himself with the Sophists when he says that his own work is not intended as a "competition-piece for a single occasion" but a possession for all time. As often, Euripides makes his characters speak in true contemporary sophistic style when Creon's herald sings the praises of monarchy as opposed to democracy and Theseus replies (*Suppl.*, 427 f.): "Since you yourself have started this competition, listen to me; for it is you who have proposed a battle of words."[71]

One might add that Socrates' expressed ideal of a common search for

69. See Kennedy, *The Art of Persuasion*, 34.
70. For instance, Kerferd remarks in relation to the Sophistic public display lecture (*epideixis*): "Hippias gave such performances regularly at the Panhellenic games at Olympia in the sacred precinct where he offered to speak on any one of a prepared list of subjects, and to answer any questions . . . and it appears that this may have been a regular feature there. . . . Gorgias offered to speak on any subject whatsoever in the theatre at Athens . . . and he spoke also at Olympia and at the Pythian games at Delphi. . . . On occasion both Hippias and Gorgias adopted the purple robes of the rhapsode, as though to emphasize their continuation of the functions of poets in earlier days" (*Sophistic Movement*, 28–29). These and other examples also underscore the spectacular, playful character of the Sophistic *technē* over its strictly utilitarian purpose.
71. Guthrie, *HGP 3*, 43.

truth remains, at best, only an ideal: Socrates is equally competitive, so much so that his appeal for help can be seen as just another tactical move, particularly effective in disarming his opponent and eventually winning him over to his own position (compare my discussion of the *Republic* in chapter 4). In turn, when Thucydides contrasts himself to the Sophists, claiming that his work, unlike theirs, will endure, he implicitly challenges them or engages them in a contest for everlasting fame—a Presocratic, intellectual version of heroic *timē*.[72]

Theseus' "battle of words" is also a dramatic device (*stuchomachia, stuchomuthia*) and, as such, it is a playful, self-conscious reference to the playwright's own dramatic skill. This dramatic device is favored not only by Euripides but also by Sophocles and Aristophanes, remaining part of the technical dramatic repertory well into the Renaissance and the Baroque. In turn, *agōn* becomes a technical term in tragedy, just as it does in rhetoric (for instance, in Corax). Indeed, one can say that Greek tragedy itself comes of age only when Aeschylus introduces a second actor, the antagonist, to face the protagonist, thus enhancing the action's dramatic, that is, agonistic character.

Philosophers such as Socrates, Plato, and Aristotle, historians such as Thucydides, rhetoricians such as Corax and Tisias, and dramatic poets such as Aeschylus, Sophocles, Euripides, and Aristophanes are thus no less competitive than the cosmologists, doctors, scientists, and Sophists that we have considered in this chapter, and it has by now become obvious that Hellenic thought continues to preserve its mentality of power in the classical period as well. The rise of median values affects the ways in which power is perceived and presented, but does not change its agonistic nature. The same holds true for play, insofar as a median mentality foregrounds certain cooperative and nonviolent ludic forms but, eventually, places them in the service of agon, just as an archaic mentality does. Nevertheless, the Presocratic median values, which perhaps find their clearest expression in the democratic ideal, indicate a gradual shift from the naked and shameless play of power within the archaic world to the increasingly self-conscious and veiled (but still transparent) power play of the warring factions within the classical *polis*.

72. The Greek historians are thus as competitive as other Presocratics, and historiography, through its struggle with myth, greatly contributes to the development of critical thinking. For Thucydides, see *Historiae*, 2 vols., ed. H. S. Jones (Oxford, 1900–1901).

3 ■ Masks of Dionysus: The Bacchae
and The Frogs ■

■ During the fifth century B.C., the increasingly complex structure of the *polis* brings about a metamorphosis of power, which appears more and more decentered, dispersed, and mediated. On the political level, this metamorphosis corresponds, in some *poleis*, to a replacement of monarchies and tyrannies by oligarchies and democracies; on the intellectual level, the metamorphosis parallels a shift from concrete to abstract modes of thought. Power tends less to present itself in the *basileus* than to represent itself in the agora, especially through the democratic ideal of *isonomia*. In turn, the archaic and the median values remain engaged in a heated competition, and poetry, whose cultural authority goes largely undisputed in the archaic age, becomes one of the main battlegrounds, first in literate epic, and then in Greek drama, which flourished mainly in Attica and was contemporary to much Presocratic thought.[1]

1. It should be stressed that the agon between archaic and median values is not carried on mainly along disciplinary lines, with philosophy and science as the main promoters of median values and with poetry as the chief promoter of archaic values. We have seen, for example, that the Presocratic thinkers are still quite divided between archaic and logo-rational modes of thought or, indeed, between a poetic and a philosophical language. We have also seen that median values permeate epic poetry and they are certainly present in drama, the very existence of which is based on the conflict between an archaic and a median mentality. On the other hand, even though the agon between archaic and median values is carried on within the domain of poetry itself, the latter is perceived by philosophers like Plato and Aristotle as the chief repository and, therefore, promoter of archaic values. It is only after philosophy and science become the dominant forms of discourse in Western thought that the agon between the two mentalities will be carried on along disciplinary lines as well, precisely because philosophy and science define themselves in opposition to poetry (for example, in Plato).

Yet the Greek theater can both be a reflection of and reflect upon the agonistic process that produces it. It can stage a far-reaching intellectual debate, exploring the nature of the Hellenic mentality as a whole and thus opening (in an imaginary space) the possibility of cultural alternatives. In drama, the double nature of power, which determines the double nature of Hellenic values in general, is aptly embodied in its patron, Dionysus. As Nietzsche points out in *The Birth of Tragedy*, "in his existence as a dismembered god, Dionysus shows the double nature of a cruel savage daemon and a mild gentle ruler."[2] In turn, Dionysus himself can become a dramatic figure, for instance in Euripides' *Bacchae* and Aristophanes' *Frogs*. By placing the patron of drama at the center of their action, these two plays comment, self-reflectively, on the nature not only of the Greek theater but also of the Greek mentality as a whole. It cannot be pure coincidence that they appear at the very end of the development of Greek

2. Nietzsche, *Birth of Tragedy*, 66. For the double nature of Dionysian experience, see also Erwin Rohde, *Psyche* (1894; trans. W. B. Hills, New York, 1966); Jane Harrison, *Prolegomena to the Study of Greek Religion* (Cambridge, 1903) and *Themis* (Cambridge, 1912); Martin Nilsson, *Studia de Dionysiis atticis* (Lund, 1900) and *The Dionysiac Mysteries of the Hellenistic and Roman Age* (Lund, 1957); Walter F. Otto, *Dionysos, Mythos und Cultus* (Frankfurt, 1931; trans. R. B. Palmer, *Dionysus: Myth and Cult* [Bloomington, Ind., 1965]); H. Jeanmaire, *Dionysos: Histoire du culte de Bacchus* (Paris, 1951); Dodds, *The Greeks and the Irrational*; and K. Kerenyi, *Dionysos: Archetypal Image of Indestructible Life* (Princeton, N.J., 1976). A useful review of the various cultural anthropological and religious interpretations of the figure of Dionysus is offered by Park McGinty in *Interpretation and Dionysos: Method in the Study of a God* (The Hague and New York, 1978). For the double nature of Dionysus in Euripides see, among many others, Albin Lesky, *Die Tragische Dichtung der Hellenen* (Göttingen, 1972), 449–50; R. P. Winnington-Ingram, *Euripides and Dionysus* (Cambridge, 1948), 31–39; A. J. Festugière, "Euripide dans les 'Bacchantes'" *Eranos* 55 (1957): 127–44; Robert Dyer, "Image and Symbol: The Link between the Two Worlds of the 'Bacchae,'" *Journal of Australasian Universities Language and Literature Association* 21 (1964): 15–26; Girard, *La violence et le sacré*, passim; J.-P. Guépin, *The Tragic Paradox: Myth and Ritual in Greek Tragedy* (Amsterdam, 1968); Marcel Detienne, *Dionysos mis à mort* (Paris, 1977), esp. chap. 4, and *Dionysos à ciel ouvert* (trans. A. Goldhammer, *Dionysus at Large* [Cambridge, Mass., 1989]); Albert Henrichs, "Greek and Roman Glimpses of Dionysos," in C. Houser, ed., *Dionysos and his Circle* (Cambridge, Mass., 1979), 1–11; Charles Segal, *Dionysian Poetics and Euripides' Bacchae* (Princeton, 1982), 19–20 and passim; Helen P. Foley, *Ritual Irony: Poetry and Sacrifice in Euripides* (Ithaca, N.Y., 1985), esp. chap. 5, "The *Bacchae*"; and, most recently, Arthur Evans, *The God of Ecstasy* (New York, 1988), esp. chap. 1. The ensuing discussion of the *Bacchae* is particularly indebted to those of Winnington-Ingram, Dodds, Kirk, Girard, Segal, Foley, and Evans (although its underlying premise is rather different from theirs) and is a substantially revised and expanded version of my paper, "The Concept of Play in Greek Tragedy: Euripides' *Bacchae*" (1983), published in E. Fischer-Lichte, ed., *Das Drama und seine Inszenierung* (Tübingen, 1985), 94–105.

drama. As Charles Segal, for example, observes, "the latter part of the fifth century saw the increasing importance of conceptual thought, logical definition, prose. In Athens the prolonged attrition of the Peloponnesian War took its toll. The last two great tragedians died within a year of one another. The exuberant playfulness of Old Comedy also came to an end about the same time with Aristophanes' *Frogs*, roughly contemporary with the *Bacchae*. Indeed the *Bacchae*, Sophocles' *Oedipus at Colonus*, and the *Frogs*, all among the last works of their genre and all written about the same time, have the same retrospective cast, the same sense of the passing of an era."[3]

Not long thereafter, both tragedy and comedy turn into highly stylized and conventional genres, gradually losing their central cultural position in the Hellenic community and becoming largely entertainment in the modern sense. Drama itself is partly responsible for this cultural development. The *Bacchae*, for example, discloses the purely nontranscendental source of the tragic mechanism and thereby renders it largely inoperative; *The Frogs* tends, perhaps, to defend the cultural authority of drama, but in the process it raises disquieting questions about the latter's nature and goals. That the authority of poetry is beginning to be challenged is already obvious in Gorgias' defense of tragedy. In *The Frogs*, Aeschylus and Euripides deploy their own defense, and roughly along the same lines that Gorgias does. Their attempt must, however, remain a failure as Aristophanes himself probably realized. By the end of the fourth century B.C. and in the wake of Socrates and Plato, poetry is largely subordinated to

3. Segal, *Dionysian Poetics and Euripides' Bacchae* (hereafter *DP*), 268–69. For general background on Greek drama the reader can consult, among many others, F. R. Adrados, *Festival, Comedy, and Tragedy: The Greek Origins of Theatre* (Leiden, 1975); A. W. Pickard-Cambridge, *The Dramatic Festivals of Athens*, 2d. ed., rev. by J. Gould and D. M. Lewis (Oxford, 1968; originally published in 1953) and *The Theatre of Dionysus in Athens* (Oxford, 1946); Francis Cornford, *The Origin of Attic Comedy* (Cambridge, 1914); Victor Ehrenberg, *The People of Aristophanes: A Sociology of the Old Attic Comedy* (Oxford, 1943; rptd. London, 1974); Gerald F. Else, *The Origin and Early Form of Greek Tragedy* (Cambridge, Mass., 1965); Simon Goldhill, *Reading Greek Tragedy* (Cambridge, 1986); H. D. F. Kitto, *Greek Tragedy* (London, 1939); Bernard Knox, *The Heroic Temper: Studies in Sophoclean Tragedy* (Berkeley, 1964) and *Word and Action* (Baltimore, 1979); Lesky, *Die Tragische Dichtung*; Max Pohlenz, *Die griechische Tragödie*, 2d. ed. (Göttingen, 1954); Thomas G. Rosenmeyer, *The Art of Aeschylus* (Berkeley, 1982); Oliver Taplin, *Greek Tragedy in Action* (Berkeley, 1978); Thomson, *Aeschylus and Athens*; Brian Vickers, *Toward Greek Tragedy* (London, 1973); T. F. Gould and C. J. Herington, eds., *Greek Tragedy* (Cambridge, 1977); Cecil J. Herington, *Poetry into Drama: Early Tragedy and the Greek Poetic Tradition* (Berkeley, 1985) and *Aeschylus* (New Haven, 1986); and J. J. Winkler and F. Zeitlin, eds., *Nothing to Do with Dionysos?: Athenian Drama in Its Social Context* (Princeton, N.J., 1989).

logo-rational discourse, a subordination that becomes complete with Aristotle's philosophical treatment of tragedy in the *Poetics*. And philosophy silences the unsettling questions raised by poetic drama through the same scapegoat mechanism that allegedly brought the theater into existence. Hence the cultural alternatives suggested by Greek drama at the end of its development remain only virtual possibilities embedded in the Hellenic imagination.

■ *Dionysus' Tragic Mask*

It is often argued that the *Bacchae* marks Euripides' return not only to the traditional tragic forms and language but also to the traditional values of the archaic world, which he himself, no less than Aeschylus and Sophocles, presumably questions in other plays. Aged, disillusioned, and in exile, Euripides experiences a spiritual conversion, repudiating the ambiguous wisdom of the fifth-century Age of Logos and returning to the old religion of fear, wrath, and violent vengence.[4] This may partially be the case, but I believe that Euripides' "return" is also a revelation, and therefore can hardly be intended as a reaffirmation of archaic values. Rather, Euripides places himself in a no man's land from which he can view the archaic and median values of his contemporaries with equal detachment.

The dramatic action of the *Bacchae* can be considered from a double perspective: human and divine. Both these perspectives, however, are part of the same mentality of power, the difference between man and god residing in their degree of power. As in Homer, from a human perspective power appears laborious, painful, elusive, and potentially (self-)destructive, whereas from a divine perspective it appears both as ecstatic experience and as free and effortless play. In turn, these two perspectives create two generic frameworks. The human perspective creates a tragic framework within which power presents itself in the guise of cultural order, in constant danger of collapsing but, in principle, always restorable. The divine perspective, on the other hand, creates a comic framework within which power appears as exuberant, impersonal violence, arbitrarily building and erasing all cultural differences. The two frameworks

---

4. This is the so-called palinode theory of the nineteenth-century scholars (see E. R. Dodds' introduction to the Greek text edition of the *Bacchae* [2d ed., Oxford, 1960], xl–xli). Gilbert Murray's *Euripides and His Age* (London, 1913) is an early twentieth-century version of this theory, greatly refined and modified. For arguments against it, see Winnington-Ingram, *Euripides and Dionysus*, 149–71.

overlap in the bacchantes, who provide both the title of the play and its chorus—a common convention in Greek drama. What is, however, less conventional and, perhaps, even a deliberate play on conventions is the fact that the maenads themselves are in turn divided into two groups, embodying the double nature of power. The first group or the chorus is made up of the Asian women, who have accompanied Dionysus to Thebes and who mostly appear, at least at first sight, in their peaceful guise.[5] The second group is made up of the Theban women, who are infused with violent Dionysian frenzy and of whom the chorus seems to disapprove.

The play presents human power in its three main sociopolitical guises: administrative-military (Pentheus), patriarchal (Cadmus), and religious (Teiresias). The social order threatened in the play has been founded on violence, and Euripides suggests this fact in several ways. The royal house of Thebes follows the usual road from war to political (self-) legitimation. Pentheus' grandfather, Cadmus, has founded Thebes by killing a dragon and sowing its teeth and, finally, by defeating the army that sprang out of those teeth and forming shrewd political alliances with the survivors (the five *Spartoi*). Pentheus himself is the result of this alliance, being the son of Cadmus' daughter Agave and Echion, one of the Sown Men—the name of the latter is, appropriately enough, the male equivalent of Echidna, the serpentine monster. Euripides does not fail to draw out the ironic implications of this violent founding of Thebes when, toward the end of the play, he has the Messenger who announces Pentheus' death refer to Cadmus as the "old man from Sidon who sowed in the earth/ the earthborn crop of the serpent, the snake."[6] The implied moral of the *Bacchae* seems to be that he who sows violence will reap destruction: Cadmus is no less "responsible" for the fall of his house than the other members of his family, including Dionysus, are.[7]

5. The exceptions, however, are highly significant and will be examined in some detail later in this chapter.

6. Euripides, *Bacchae*, trans. G. S. Kirk (Englewood Cliffs, N.J., 1970), lines 1025–26. Unless otherwise specified, further references are to this translation, which I have occasionally modified to convey my own interpretation of a particular Greek passage. I have used, in parallel, the Greek text edited, with an indispensable commentary, by E. R. Dodds (2d ed., Oxford, 1960). I cite from Euripides, *Fabulae*, 3 vols., ed. G. Murray (Oxford, 1900–1901).

7. I would therefore hesitate to describe Cadmus as a "true civilizer," as a "farmer, a 'sower,' not a killer," and his "foundation of the city [as] a deed not of war but of agriculture, which for the Greeks is the privileged model for the settled, stable quality of civilized life" (Segal, *Dionysian Poetics*, 138). In the founding of Thebes, as in that of many an ancient and modern city, war seems to precede agriculture. In this sense, Cadmus' crop is indeed of a "fantastic and unpromising sort" (ibid).

Because violence is at the origin of the Theban social order, the restoration and maintainance of this order will also require violence, and the three Theban leaders, Pentheus, Cadmus, and Teiresias, quarrel solely over the kind of violent remedy they propose to employ. In dealing with a potentially explosive situation, Pentheus advocates direct military force—he has already given orders for the arrest and imprisonment of the Theban bacchantes and of the stranger who instigates them. In his eyes, this stranger is a usurper who, taking advantage of the king's absence from the city, attempts to undermine his authority and possibly unseat him. Pentheus remains unconvinced by the rumor that the troublemaker is the legitimate messenger of a new god, who, moreover, is a relative and therefore a potential contender for power; instead, Pentheus chooses to believe the other rumor about his aunt Semele, who, according to family gossip, got pregnant out of wedlock and imputed the child to Zeus—a highly plausible story from a logo-rational standpoint, one might add. Pentheus favors this second rumor not only because it sounds more plausible, but also because it best suits his own political interests, or at least so he thinks.[8]

Teiresias and Cadmus, on the other hand, suggest that in this instance power needs to be exercised with caution and the religious safety valve needs to be left wide open. In one respect, the choice is between governing either according to new scientific and logo-rational methods or according to traditional, religious, "irrational" ways. Pentheus partly represents the newfangled, Sophist-trained leader who openly proclaims—or, rather, secretly believes?—that "force alone prevails with men" (Bacchae 310), and relies on his authority with the army to restore law and order in Thebes. He reads the civil outbreak in Thebes in political rather than in religious terms, and it is for this reason that he cannot, later, deal with this outbreak in an effective manner. By contrast, Teiresias reads the events correctly and proposes to rely on the old, proven ways of the religious mimetic mechanism as a cathartic remedy against gener-

8. Here I can partially see the point of those critics who view Pentheus somewhat sympathetically and attempt to justify his actions. See, for instance, E. M. Balaiklock, The Male Characters of Euripides (Wellington, New Zealand, 1952) and Bernard Seidensticker, "Pentheus," Poetica 5 (1972): 35–63. For the opposite view, see especially Kirk, who throughout his commentary on the play seems, ironically, to join forces with Dionysus and the Asian bacchantes in scapegoating Pentheus. The point (in principle acknowledged by Kirk) is that Pentheus and Dionysus are antagonistic doubles and therefore are equally violent. If this point is granted, then Euripides certainly cannot take the side of Dionysus (as Kirk and others do) against Pentheus or vice versa.

alized violence (and Cadmus backs him, not without adding his own pragmatic reasons).

Teiresias attempts to persuade the hotheaded king that, under the circumstances, the Theban leaders would do well not to discount the possibility that they are indeed dealing with a god, and join the crowd of revelers: "But be persuaded by my advise, Pentheus:/ Do not be over-confident that "force [*to kratos*] alone prevails with men";/ nor if you hold an opinion [*doxa*], but your judgment is awry,/ take that opinion for good sense. Receive the god into this land/ and pour offerings, and be a bacchant, and garland your head./ . . . Therefore I and Cadmus, whom you make fun of,/ shall crown ourselves with ivy and shall dance—/ a grey-haired couple, but all the same dance we must" (*Bacchae* 309–23, trans. modified). In his speech, Teiresias clearly strikes at the precepts of modern government advocated by certain Sophists, drawing a traditional distinction between learning and wisdom and generally taking the traditional position appropriate for a religious leader.[9] Although he does not

9. Interestingly enough, however, even Teiresias is visibly affected by a logo-rational mode of thought. For example, he offers a rational explanation for the birth of Dionysus out of Zeus' thigh (*Bacchae* 286–97), probably because he is aware of his interlocutor's Sophistic persuasion and hopes to prevail upon him by employing logo-rational arguments as well. I would not, however, go as far as labeling him a Sophist, which seems to be the prevailing view (see Winnington-Ingram, Dodds, Kirk, Segal, and, most recently, Evans). For a full list of the proponents of this view, see Segal (*Dionysian Poetics*, 294 n.27), who in turn expands it in his interpretation of Teiresias' speech (292–305). Despite Teiresias' employment of "rationalizing sophistry" (Segal's phrase), he seems to criticize what he perceives as a might-makes-right mode of behavior on the part of Pentheus, to which he opposes the wisdom of the Seven Sages and the Delphic oracle ("know thy limits," "measure is best," and the like). This religious wisdom has certain logo-rational features and probably stands in the background of the development of a later secular, median mentality; it must not, however, be confused with the latter, as the case of the Asian maenads shows. In order to avoid confusion of the various ideological positions taken by Pentheus, Teiresias, and Cadmus, one should further keep in mind that the Sophists are not a homogeneous camp and can roughly be divided into two groups: the ones who, like Callicles and Thrasymachus, seem to have advocated the primacy of *phusis* over *nomos* and, therefore, may have favored archaic values, and the ones who, like Protagoras, seem to have insisted on *nomos* over *phusis* and thus may have favored median values. Finally, Pentheus, Teiresias, and Cadmus are public leaders and not philosophers, and consequently, their political practice and beliefs may differ considerably from their rhetoric. In this regard, they can argue in a logo-rational manner for or against a certain course of action and then completely reverse both their arguments and their actions according to momentary expediencies. In one sense, it is precisely these ever-shifting gaps between power and (logo-rational) discourse that Euripides dramatizes in the *Bacchae* as well as in other plays. The well-known words of

say so directly, he implies that it would be unwise to go against the crowd (by refusing to dance) because one would then run the risk of being singled out as a scapegoat.

What Teiresias only implies is openly affirmed by Cadmus, who stresses the wisdom of joining the crowd and attempting to direct its violence from within, for one's own political ends: "My son, Teiresias exhorted you well;/ dwell with us, not outside the accustomed ways [tōn nomōn]./ . . . Even if this is no god, as you assert,/ let him be called one by you—tell a lie in a good cause,/ that he is Semele's child, so that it may seem [dokei] that she bore a god/ and we gain honor for our family" (Bacchae 330–36). Cadmus' speech is appropriate for a fifth-century pragmatic leader, who may have his doubts about the old Homeric gods, but is nevertheless aware of the political usefulness of religion, holding traditional mētis in high esteem. Like Teiresias, then, Cadmus should be only partially identified with the new logo-rational way of thinking.

Pentheus' reply to his grandfather, on the other hand, is typical of a self-assured rational young leader who has been taught to believe that "man is the measure of all things" and therefore can achieve perfect control over himself and others. (His position, however, in no way precludes the might-makes-right mentality imputed to him by Teiresias: "man is the measure of all things" is hardly incompatible with "power is the measure of all things.") Pentheus promptly gives orders to correct what he judges to be a clear case of civil unrest:

> Keep your hands off me—go and perform your bacchic rites
> and don't wipe off your foolishness on me!
> Teiresias here, the instructor of your folly,
> I shall punish [dikēn meteimi]. Go, someone, with all speed,
> and when you come to his throne where he takes omens,
> prise it with levers and turn it upside down;
> mix everything in utter confusion,
> and fling his sacred fillets to the winds and storms:
> by doing this I shall affect him most!

Phaedra in Hippolytus, "we understand what is right and proper [ta chrēst], and know it, but do not work it out in acts" (380–81) are not so much a critique of Socratic rationalism as a profound insight into the divided nature of any mentality of power. My view of Teiresias and Cadmus as traditional leaders is partly shared by Hans Diller, "Die Backen und ihre Stellung im Spätwerk des Euripides," Akademie Mainz 5 (1955): 453–71, translated as "Euripides' Final Phase: The Bacchae," in E. Segal, ed., Oxford Readings in Greek Tragedy (Oxford, 1983), 357–89. Diller also offers a helpful review of the traditional critical approaches to the play.

The rest of you go through the city and track down
the effeminate stranger, who is introducing a new disease
for our women and dishonoring their beds.
And if you catch him, lead him here
in chains to get his deserts by stoning
and so die, after seeing a bitter end to bacchanals in Thebes.
(*Bacchae* 343–57)

Far from showing "a kind of spitefulness, a total lack of magnaminity"
(as Kirk states) in his manner of dealing with Teiresias, Pentheus acts, it
can be argued, in perfect accordance with his position as a secular leader.
He sees the prophet as an old but shrewd quack who attempts to gain
political advantage from the introduction of a new deity in Thebes, and
therefore he seeks to hit the priest where it hurts him most, by destroying
his professional paraphernalia and, consequently, his authority.

Ironically, Pentheus also takes the old man's lesson to heart and seeks
to turn the stranger into a political scapegoat by pointing to him as the
main culprit for the unrest in Thebes. Of course, the stranger will
ultimately turn the tables on him, substituting himself for Pentheus as a
religious scapegoat. The king will appear as a lion to his mother, Agave, and
the other bacchantes and will therefore become identified with Dionysus,
the god of violence. In the form of Pentheus-lion, the women will tear
apart the symbol of violence (the scapegoat) and thereby will restore
peace and order in the city. This ritual is the homeopathic remedy of
healing the wound by the spear that inflicted it, a remedy also favored, as
we have seen, by Teiresias and Cadmus; it cures random violence by
organized violence, through tearing apart and eating the sacrificial victim
(*sparagmos* and *omophagia*).[10] As Cadmus and Teiresias point out, and as
Dionysus sets out to demonstrate at the expense of the Theban maenads,
one must become mad before one can become sane.[11]

10. For a full discussion of this point see, among others, Dodds, *The Greeks and the Irrational*, app. 1, "Maenadism," 270–82; Burkert, *Homo necans*, passim; Girard, *La violence et le sacré*, passim; and Detienne, *Dionysos*, passim.

11. For a discussion of women, maenadism and madness, see especially Evans, *God of Ecstasy*, 11–13. Although I am sympathetic to parts of Evans' argument, especially when he examines the nature of power in its patriarchal manifestations, I am not sure I can share his feminist position nor his view of Euripides as a mediator between emotion and intellect. Evans' central thesis is that in the *Bacchae* Euripides appeals "to the traditional Greek ideal of *sōphrosynē*, intelligent balance or moderation in leading one's life. But in contrast to the rising intellectualism of his time, Euripides sees as an essential part of that balance the validation of deep-seated emotional needs. By so validating emotion, Euripides presents a striking alternative to the later teachings of Plato and his school,

It is also in terms of the scapegoat ritual that one can best understand the ambivalent role of the Asian bacchantes throughout the play. Critics have often noticed the shift in the chorus' behavior as the action progresses. At the beginning of the play, the Barbarian maenads seem, ironically, to decry violence, stressing the gentle, beneficial side of the Dionysian cult. No less ironically, they are also the carriers (together with Teiresias) of the traditional Delphic wisdom of moderation and knowing one's limits. As Pentheus gradually reveals himself powerless in dealing with his infinitely superior adversary, the Asian bacchantes become increasingly aggressive, finally hurling insults at him and demanding his victimization. After the sacrifice takes place, they exult in their victory and sardonically taunt Agave and the Theban bacchantes. They remain thereby completely unaware of their own vulnerability in the face of divine violence (unlike, say, Odysseus in Sophocles' *Ajax*). In this regard, they behave like many common citizens who are timid and self-effacing in everyday life but may, on occasion, become deadly, for instance when gathered together in large, anonymous crowds or when given the certainty of acting in the name of a higher authority.[12]

---

who interpreted moderation as requiring the sublimation of passion. A moderation based on emotional denial, Euripides argues, is an invitation to madness" (11). By stating the problem of the *Bacchae* in contemporary psychoanalytic terms, Evans does not seem to take into account sufficiently the cultural conditioning of emotion, the origins of which can be traced back to a mentality of power that is equally shared by men and women. Furthermore, Plato seems fully aware of the dangers of repressing violent emotion, for example that of the guardians of the Socratic ideal republic, and has Socrates turn this emotion outside the city, on foreigners and the enemies of the state. Valuable investigations on sex, desire, and education are currently being conducted by John Winkler, Froma Zeitlin, and David Halperin. See, for example, J. J. Winkler, F. Zeitlin and D. M. Halperin, *Before Sexuality: The Construction of Erotic Experience in the Ancient Greek World* (Princeton, N.J., forthcoming); and John J. Winkler, *The Constraints of Desire: The Anthropology of Sex and Gender in Ancient Greece* (New York: Routledge, forthcoming).

12. For a review of the critical positions on the choral odes and the role of the Asian maenads in the play, as well as for a full analysis of the choral odes themselves, see especially Marilyn Arthur, "The Choral Odes of the *Bacchae* of Euripides," *YCS* 22 (1972): 145–79. Although I find much of her discussion illuminating, I am not sure I agree with Arthur's larger cultural historical assessment of Euripides' objectives in employing the Bacchic choral odes the way he does. Arthur seems to argue that through the ambiguous attitude of the chorus Euripides shows (not unlike Thucydides) the adverse effects of the return of a revenge mentality in ancient Greece as a result of the Peloponnesian War. It is true that archaic values, including the ideology of revenge, resurface during periods of sociocultural stress, but this does not necessarily mean that Euripides himself advocates a return to median, democratic normalcy. Arthur seems to miss the essential otherness

In view of the fact that the other Theban leaders, as well as the Asian bacchantes, equally advocate violence (be it only in a religious form), Pentheus appears "unjust," "unrighteous," and "mad" in their eyes not because he employs violence, but because he attempts to do so against somebody or something that proves to be more powerful than himself. In Theban society, as in the Homeric world, what matters is not intentions but results. Pentheus loses his contest with Dionysus, and therefore he becomes *kakos*, bringing *aiskron* (shame, misery) on his house. His threats against the stranger prove empty and ridiculous only because he cannot carry them out. His hubris is perhaps less some kind of ethical flaw (as Kirk and others seem to imply) than a matter of miscalculation in his game of power.

Human tragedy in the *Bacchae*, then, reminds us of its counterpart in the *Iliad*: it is the outcome of an agonistic game of wagering against infinite power, which takes either the form of the gods or, ultimately, the form of chance (*tuchē*). Hubris is the limit or the end of the game, where chance reveals itself as necessity (*anankē*). In this respect, one can apply the Heraclitean model of the dice game, or Adkins' metaphor of chutes and ladders, not only to the epic hero but also to his tragic counterpart. The casting of the dice is the act of wagering, while the outcome of the throw reveals the next move, up and down, but always binding in its necessity. By choosing not to believe in the story of Dionysus' divinity—in this sense, Pentheus cannot but remain blind to the repeated warnings that he receives from all quarters about the latter's divine manifestations—the Theban king wagers against Dionysus, loses the game, the stakes of which also involve enforcing a certain version of reality, and thus comes to grief, fulfilling the vocation of his name.[13]

On the other hand, a philosophy of moderation, such as is espoused by Teiresias and the Asian bacchantes, is largely an attempt to minimalize the effect of chance, to avoid reaching the limit, or to delay the outcome of the game by hedging one's bets (compare the Presocratic notion of *metron* discussed in the previous chapter). This philosophy is also naturally hostile to tragic truth—even as it constitutes one of its conditions of

---

of the play's standpoint, concluding that "nevertheless the chorus remains dedicated throughout the play to the principles of justice, wisdom, order and piety" (170)—an obviously modern, rationalist interpretation.

13. As critics have often pointed out, Euripides sustains the game-contest metaphor throughout the play. Winnington-Ingram, for example, suggests that Euripides employs the language of the Olympic games in describing the power contest between Dionysus and Pentheus (*Euripides and Dionysus*, 27 and 128). See also Segal, *Dionisian Poetics*, 266–71.

possibility—because it obscures the fact that, irrespective of the strategy of the players, sooner or later the human game invariably ends in defeat or death; in this respect, it recoils from affirming the full truth of tragedy.[14]

In the *Bacchae* Euripides shows us not only the other side of Greek tragedy—human action from the standpoint of the gods or of the dice, as it were—but also its profoundly ambivalent nature. He fully underscores this ambivalence by bringing the patron of tragedy himself into (the) play. From the outset, Dionysus presents himself, and is presented by the Asian maenads, as both gentle and violent. He appears in the guise of a young, effeminate, soft-spoken stranger, an ideal victim for Pentheus' vengefulness. He makes no secret, however, of his violent intentions: he wants to prove his godhead by cruel action against his mother's family, who fail to recognize him as a god. In this sense, Teiresias' traditional, anthropomorphic view of Dionysus—and of divinity in general—ultimately proves to be correct. As the prophet points out in his *suasio* addressed to Pentheus, "You see how you are pleased, when the multitude/ throngs the gate-towers, and the city magnifies the name of Pentheus;/ so Dionysus, too, in my opinion delights in being honored" (*Bacchae* 319–21). Dionysus is certainly no more competitive, vengeful, and violent than most *aristoi*; it is simply that he can inflict more damage than ordinary mortals because of his superhuman powers. Finally, like Thebes, Dionysus has violent, ambiguous origins: half-god and half-human, he is born out of Zeus' lightning bolt, which also kills his mother, Semele.[15]

14. Nietzsche, on the other hand, realizes the necessity, from the standpoint of an archaic mentality, of joyfully embracing the ghastly truth of tragedy; see, for example, his "Versuch zur Selbstkritik," published in the second edition of the *Birth of Tragedy*. It is this realization that distinguishes his affirmative pessimism from the negative pessimism of Schopenhauer, as well as his view of tragedy from that of Aristotle. For the role of truth in tragedy see also Timothy J. Reiss, *Tragedy and Truth* (New Haven, 1980). In the wake of Foucault, Reiss points out the transitional nature of tragedy, which appears at moments that are "marked by a kind of 'hole' in the passage from one dominant discourse to another" (284). Arising at points of crisis in the life of a community, tragedy creates a shift from one mode of discourse about social order to another. It produces "rationality by showing what can be termed the irrational within that rationality," and thus it both hides and discloses "what is unspoken in the law that is the order of discourse." Reiss' view seems to corroborate my view of tragedy as the product of a shift in cultural emphasis from archaic (what Reiss calls "irrational") to median values.

15. In his stychomythia with Cadmus at the end of the play, Dionysus again makes it very clear that he has been motivated by revenge, because he has been "slighted" as a god, not being accorded proper *timē* in Thebes. When at *Bacchae* 1348 Cadmus objects that "Gods should not resemble men in their anger" (an obviously logo-rational concept of divinity—compare Xenophanes), Dionysus simply brushes him aside with another

Dionysus engages his cousin Pentheus in an unequal contest, playing with him a cat-and-mouse game in which the latter does not have the slightest chance of winning (even though he does not know it). Dionysus is a successful Pentheus who can make his power-claims good, and he eliminates his rival without any qualms, just as Pentheus would have eliminated him. In this light, his meekness (like that of his votaries) seems only a deceptive mask. Dionysus transfers his gentle role, together with his effeminate appearance, to Pentheus, who quickly turns from hunter into quarry, from victimizer into victim.

After punishing Pentheus and his family, Dionysus does not resume his meek aspect but, on the contrary, takes steps to restore the old violent order. He decrees that the house of Cadmus, which he has almost destroyed, will rule again, but not before the old king goes into exile. This exile, however, seems to have little of its usual healing, reconciliatory effect on the community (as, say, in Sophocles' Theban cycle) or, if it has any, this effect seems to be short-lived. Ironically, Cadmus will return to Thebes in the form of the dragon that he had killed, in other words, in one of the animal guises of Dionysus himself. He will institute a new dispensation that is in no way different from the previous one. The ending of the play (despite some textual gaps and corruptions) seems to suggest that the cycle of violence will plague the city ad infinitum, while Cadmus himself will find peace only in an ideal setting, the Isles of the Blessed.

Dionysus reveals himself not only as a violent godhead but also as a playwright, director, and leading actor or protagonist in Pentheus' tragedy: only from the god's point of view—as well as from that of the chorus—the play is a comedy since it ends in his apotheosis. Like a dramatist (and a Sophist), he deals in appearances or "phantoms" and he himself assumes various identities, never revealing his true nature (*phusis*). To Pentheus he appears as a young stranger, a skillful and cool Sophist, a bull; to the maenads he appears as a handsome seducer, a chorus leader (*chorodidaskalos*), and then as a lion and a serpent. When Pentheus sees double, he sees the god in both his animal and his human guise; later on,

---

traditional religious argument: "Long ago Zeus my father approved these things" (*Bacchae* 1349). This passage seems again to show that in the *Bacchae* Euripides returns to an archaic, anthropomorphic view of the gods, but the question remains why he does so. Part of the answer, I believe, lies in the fact that Euripides constantly reminds his spectator that divinity, or at least its representation, is a *human* invention, and as such it will take any form that humans choose to give it, be it benign or violent, rational or irrational. If this is so, then humans must stop blaming the gods for their own representations or, more importantly, for their own mode of behavior.

Dionysus will take the form of Pentheus himself, while Pentheus will assume his cousin's identity (as already mentioned, he appears to Agave and to the Theban bacchantes in the form of a lion).

Dionysus also plays with lightning and sets fire to the royal palace but, apparently, without burning it down.[16] He thereby proves to be an illusionist, a juggler or a thaumaturgos, a player of shadows, a trickster, a puppeteer. He tells the chorus the story of his escape from Pentheus' prison with obvious relish, gloating over the fact that he made a fool of the king: "This was just the ignominy I did him, that he thought he was binding me/ but neither touched nor laid hands on me, but fed on empty hopes./ He found a bull by the stalls where he took me and locked me up,/ and round his knees and hooves he cast his knots,/ panting out his rage, dripping sweat from his body,/ setting his teeth to his lips. But I close by/ was peacefully sitting and watching" (Bacchae 616–22).

In the last two lines of his speech (Bacchae 640–41), just as Teiresias has done before, Dionysus appears to regard Pentheus as a (manqué) disciple of the Sophists, mockingly citing against him one of their famous precepts that the young king has so obviously failed to follow: he has lost his composure. Dionysus, on the other hand, will "take [Pentheus] lightly, even if he comes breathing arrogance;/ for it is the quality of a wise man [pros sophou . . . andros] to exercise restrained good temper" (Bacchae 640–41). And immediately afterwards, he coolly instructs Pentheus: "Hold it, and put a quiet brake to your rage" (Bacchae 647). In these lines, therefore,

16. This fact has led some critics, notably Gilbert Norwood in The Riddle of the Bacchae (Manchester, 1908), to see the entire course of events in the second part of the play as the product of mass hallucination. Even though Norwood later partially recanted his views (in Essays in Euripidean Drama [Berkeley and Los Angeles, 1954]), I believe that in a certain sense he was not entirely off the mark the first time. Under the psychedelic influence of Dionysus and his potent pharmaka, everyday reality becomes like a dream, and the worst (logo-rational) nightmares turn into everyday reality. In our terms, the archaic mentality that is pushed into the background by its median counterpart erupts with renewed force onto the historical stage, bringing with it a radical change in the perception of reality, which, indeed, it restructures altogether. One should, therefore, not overemphasize the interplay of reality and illusion (or fiction) in the Bacchae, as recent criticism tends to do. Euripides seems to strip his audience of all illusion in the face of Dionysiac reality (naked, unashamed power), without recuperating any part of this illusion through the rational order of the work of art itself (see Dodds, Winnington-Ingram, Foley, and Segal). Instead, the playwright seems to reveal the very process by which we ceaselessly create and destroy various realities. In this sense, illusion is simply a discarded reality, and reality is an illusion currently in force or, as the etymology of the word "illusion" indicates, in play. Finally, it is the play of power, Euripides seems to suggest, that indifferently creates reality and illusion.

Dionysus also presents himself as a true Sophist, who never loses his temper, and is always in control of himself and others. Pentheus himself remarks this during his first stychomythia with his rival: "How brazen is the bacchic fellow, and not untrained in argument [*kouk agumnastos logōn*]!" (491). The stranger gets the better of the king not only in their physical contest, but also in their *agōnes logōn*.

But does Dionysus properly speaking have any one true *phusis*? In the prologue, Euripides has the god repeat several times that he has assumed human form, but we are not really told what his divine form is (the allusion to his being born "bull-horned," can only be another metaphor, in the original sense of transference: it refers to one of the god's animal forms and it is in this form that, later on, a "hallucinating" Pentheus will see him). When Pentheus presses the stranger, asking: "Since you claim that you saw the god plainly, what was his nature?" (*Bacchae* 477), the latter evades the answer: "Whatever he wished to have; not what I arranged" (*Bacchae* 478). Dionysus' power is a display of (re)semblances, an illusionist's act and he invariably assumes the gentle or violent nature of the other (the Asian bacchantes, Pentheus, Agave, and the Theban maenads). He truly shows himself as a "god of many names," as the limitless, as the ever-changing, as an eternal play of simulacra. He is the god of Becoming par excellence. To him truth and appearance are interchangeable because he manufactures them both. In this sense, for Dionysus knowledge is not power, as it is for some of the Sophists or for rational thinking in general; rather, power is knowledge as he plays with human toys for whom he poses as fate.

Dionysus' play, then, is an archaic game of power, very similar to that of Apollo in *Iliad* 15.361–66, or to that of the hawk in Hesiod's fable. On the other hand, the ecstatic singing and dancing of the Asian maenads reveal the psychological and phenomenological aspects of this game of power, aspects that belong to what I have called mimesis-play. The maenads themselves repeatedly refer to their bacchic activities as "playing" (*paizein*). For example, they conclude the epode of the parode by chanting: "O onward bacchants,/ onward bacchants!/ Ornamented with gold of Tmolus' river/ to the deep beat of drums/ sing and dance to Dionysus/ exalting the god to whom you cry '*euoi*'/ amid Phrygian cries and incantations/ when the holy melodious flute/ sounds out its holy playings [*hiera paigmata*], accompanying/ you on your way to the mountain, the mountain. Joyfully/ then, as a foal with its grazing mother,/ the bacchant leaps around with nimble feet" (*Bacchae* 152–69, trans. modified).

This passage abounds in play imagery, associating the swift, exuberant movement of the Dionysian votary with the nimble, joyful leaps of a foal frisking at its mother's side. The same play imagery reappears in the first strophe of the third stasimon, where the ecstatic bacchic dancer compares herself to a "fawn playing [*empaizousa*] in the green pleasures of a meadow" (*Bacchae* 866–67). Thus mimesis as play—and we recall that in this context *mimēsis* does not refer to imitating or representing, but to expressing or bringing something forth—is associated with the sheer joy of leaping (which is also one of Plato's definitions of play), or an exuberant manifestation of physical energy—the body rejoicing in its own strength. Under the Dionysian spell, even venerable men like Teiresias and Cadmus turn light of foot, casting off the grave dignity of old age and breaking into a youthful, bacchic dance.

This expense of energy for its own sake appears harmless enough as long as it remains "disinterested" or "undirected." But in the *Bacchae* the joyful manifestation of an enhanced feeling of power is only a prelude or foreplay to a more sinister kind of game, since it is harnessed to the scapegoat ritual. The Theban maenads are no less playful when they hunt down Pentheus (hunting is a form of violent play that is as a rule tolerated by a median mentality as long as it remains directed toward animals rather than toward human beings), or even when they tear him apart: "One was carrying a forearm,/ another a foot with the boot still on; his ribs/ were being laid bare by the tearing; and each of the women, with hands/ all bloody, was playing ball with Pentheus' flesh [*diesphairize*, made it her handball; compare Nausicaa harmlessly playing ball with her companions on the shores of Scheria in *Odyssey* 6.115–16]" (*Bacchae* 1133–36, trans. modified). Euripides, therefore, constantly and relentlessly reminds us of the violent origins of play in an archaic mentality, at the same time that he breaks down all the (logo-rational) dichotomies between playfulness and seriousness, morality and entertainment, fiction and reality, and so forth.[17]

17. Compare Segal, who justly remarks in connection to Huizinga's definition of play in *Homo ludens*: "As metatheater, the *Bacchae* calls into question that process of 'hedging off' a sacred space for play separate from reality. It allows the one to break through into the other. In contrast between the parode and the later ode it also shows the other side of the firm belief that 'the action actualizes and effects a definite beatification, brings about an order of things higher than that in which [the participants] customarily live' [Huizinga, 14], for that conviction of being in a heightened state, a higher order or beatification, can equally characterize homicidal psychosis" (*Dionysian Poetics*, 270). Segal seems, however, to draw back from the full consequences of his insight. For example, he quotes Roland Barthes on "the pleasure of the text" to support his argument that Dionysiac play (which can be extended to art) undermines warlike values: "Le plaisir du

If the nature of Dionysus is pure, unmediated power which manifests itself as violent, arbitrary play, then one may wonder about the function that Euripides assigns to his mask. We know that throughout the play (*his* play), Dionysus wears a smiling mask and this mask, as well as his illusion making, have been discussed at length by critics. Dodds, for example, observes that there is "a psychological miracle at the center of the action," implying that theatrical or psychological illusion is the only means by which Dionysus can be understood.[18]

Helen Foley seems to endorse Dodds when she argues that "by suggesting throughout the action of the play that we have access to the god by theatrical means—through mask, costume, voice and music, or through illusion, symbol and transformation—Euripides seems to make a strong claim for art's ability to represent a reality inaccessible to ordinary human sight." According to Foley, through the smiling mask, Euripides creates a double perspective, one for the characters, to whom the mask signifies benignity, and one for the audience, to whom the mask signifies destruction (given Dionysus' stated intention in the prologue). "Dionysus' divinity in the *Bacchae*," Foley concludes, "can be understood through this power to control representation. Euripides makes his 'anomalous' (untragic) mask become the central mocking image of what we as men can understand of a force that cannot be fully captured by human vision."[19]

In turn, Charles Segal extensively develops Dodds' and Winnington-Ingram's theses (independently of Foley), concluding that the tragedy itself functions as a mask, a self-conscious fiction that points to an inexpressible truth: "The tragedy includes all the points of view on Dionysus and all of the ways in which men try to grasp the god: rationalization, gesture, ritual, music, dance. . . . In reflecting its own

---

texte (la jouissance du texte) est au contraire comme un effacement brusque de la valeur guerrière" (in *Dionysian Poetics*, 267). But any act of undermining seems to belong equally to an agonistic mentality, constituting a *valeur guerrière*. We have seen that pleasure itself is inextricably bound with power, indeed, often *is* an enhanced feeling of power, and much art is certainly not free of this feeling.

18. See the introduction to Dodds' edition of the *Bacchae*, xxvii.

19. See Helen P. Foley, "The Masque of Dionysus," TAPA 110 (1980): 132–33. One can also consult Foley's more recent work on the *Bacchae*, in *Ritual Irony*, 205–58. Here Foley seems equally to support Dodds' and Winnington-Ingram's (as well as Kirk's) general thesis that the *Bacchae* is "an eclectic demonstration of Dionysiac religion that ultimately takes no firm moral position, but emphasizes the overpowering reality and amorality of the divinity and the forces that the god represents in human existence" (*Ritual Irony*, 205 n.1). For Euripides as self-conscious artist, see also Winnington-Ingram, "Euripides: *Poietes Sophos*," *Arethusa* 2 (1969): 129–42.

status as a fiction that speaks truth, a mask that conceals the surface to reveal hidden depths, it spans the two poles of the Dionysiac spell or 'drug,' the destructive and the beneficient, the delusive madness and the cleansing intensity. It includes all points of view, but in its dialectical structure, prevents any single one from emerging as unambiguously correct and definitive."[20] Segal comes as close as possible to seeing that in the *Bacchae* (and elsewhere), Euripides offers an extensive description of the power-oriented mentality of his world. Yet Segal seems reluctant to name power as the primary concern of the play and, more often than not, he appears to use the word "power" in a "natural," unproblematic way.

As long as power remains hidden through its very transparency, it never loses its transcendental status and is still able, through Dionysus' mask, ceaselessly to reproduce the signification that it destroys. The play, and the work of art in general, appears in turn as a balanced repository of conflicting cultural values, a paradoxical nexus of tensions, an inscrutable oracle that remains for ever in suspense. The assumption behind this view seems to be that although Euripides is fully aware of his culture's mentality of power, he cannot but endorse it, or even embrace it joyfully, in the absence of any clearly (or vaguely) formulated alternatives. But Euripides speaks from exile, from no man's land—the very decision to leave Athens (if indeed he went into physical exile) points to Euripides' unhappy consciousness in relation to his world—and therefore he may have the necessary distance to view his culture with detachment.[21]

From this detached, atopian standpoint, I would like to suggest that the mask of Dionysus in the *Bacchae* is far from remaining an ambivalent, paradoxical symbol; on the contrary, it symbolizes nothing, it conceals no "depths" behind it. The mask itself is not a sign, it does not signify, although it arbitrarily creates and destroys all systems of signification. At the end of Greek tragedy, power reaches, as the true god of many names, its ultimate guise as play of simulacra, as an impersonal interplay of necessity and chance. Fiction and reality, nature and culture, Being and Becoming again collapse together in the ecstatic, violent play of Dionysus. Through the god's mask, Euripides points to the nature of the tragic mode

20. Segal, *Dionysian Poetics*, 307.
21. The question can be raised as to what alternatives Euripides (as well as I) might have in mind. The answer is that there are no ready-made alternatives since power-oriented worlds are all *we* know. In this respect Euripides, or anyone else, can offer no specific alternatives but, rather, can only affirm the possibility of other worlds by gradually moving away from his own. Once we begin to entertain rather than exclude this possibility, new worlds and new values will slowly begin to emerge as we muddle along.

itself, in which power reveals itself most when it obscures itself most.[22] Thereby, he also points to this mode as a direct cultural product of the mechanism of power, which divides itself against itself in order to recreate itself perpetually.

It is perhaps in this sense that Euripides brings tragedy to an end. The latter is possible only when the right hand, as it were, does not know what the left hand is doing, when power splits itself into a concrete and a transcendental world, and then pitches one against the other. Once the common source of these two worlds is revealed, neither agon nor agony, neither conflict nor pity are possible. In simple (perhaps even simple-minded) ethical terms, when men can no longer blame the gods for their own actions, they alone must face these actions in all their consequences, and it is at this point that tragedy starts melting into nothingness.

■ *Dionysus' Comic Mask*

If in the *Bacchae* Euripides seems to reflect, through the figure of Dionysus, on his world's mentality of power, revealing the tragic mechanism itself as a product of this mentality and thereby turning away from tragedy altogether, in *The Frogs* Aristophanes can be seen, initially, as attempting to restore the tragic mechanism and revive tragedy. But because his attempt is carried out indirectly, through comic means, it becomes highly ambiguous, revealing the amphibolous, reversible nature of both tragedy and comedy.

Like Euripides, Aristophanes brings the figure of Dionysus as well as the Dionysian cult(s) into his play in order to comment on the state of tragedy and, indirectly, comedy at the end of the fifth century B.C.[23]

22. It is crucial to remember, as Foley points out, that Dionysus "was worshipped in Greek cult as a mask (among many examples the *kalpis* signed by Hypsis, ca. 510 B.C. . . . is particularly appropriate for the *Bacchae*, in that it portrays the worship of the mask of Dionysus in both its benign and bestial incarnation). The final scenes of the *Bacchae* help to clarify precisely why the god was worshipped as a mask" ("Masque of Dionysus," 133 n.43). I would add that Euripides also reveals the essential emptiness of this mask and, implicitly, worship. The mask of Dionysus has also been seen as a symbol of "mimetic desire" that creates and destroys all signification (see Girard, *La violence et le sacré*, passim). But "mimetic desire" is only one kind of agonistic manifestation of power. See Spariosu, *Dionysus Reborn*, pt. 1, sec. 1.2.

23. It is not inconceivable that Aristophanes was familiar with Euripides' *Bacchae* because the play may have been performed in Athens soon after Euripides' death in late 407 or early 406 B.C., and we know almost for certain that *The Frogs* was first performed in the winter of 405 B.C. As Carlo Pascal, Cornford, Van Leeuwen and others have pointed out, there are several linguistic parallels between *The Frogs* and the *Bacchae*, even though these

Because both Sophocles and Euripides have recently died, thereby allegedly leaving the tragic profession in a sorry state, the comic poet has
Dionysus conceive a craving (*pothos*) for Euripides and undertake a trip to
Hades in order to bring him back to Athens. Once in Hades, however,
Dionysus changes his mind, ostensibly as a result of a poetic contest
between Euripides and Aeschylus—for which he acts both as umpire and
as judge—and decides to revive Aeschylus instead, as the better poet of
the two (it is precisely the idea of what constitutes a "better poet" that
will presently concern us).

As has often been pointed out, *The Frogs* is divided into two main
sections that seem to be only loosely connected. The first section deals
with Dionysus' and his slave Xanthias' journey to Hades, which includes a
visit to Hercules' house, as well as several adventures during the crossing
and upon arrival. The second section deals with the poetic contest itself,
being separated from the first section by a famous parabasis, in which the
chorus exhorts the poet's fellow Athenians to adopt certain urgent
political measures designed to save the city from complete debacle, and
which reportedly was so popular with its Athenian audience and jury that
they caused the play to be performed a second time.[24]

---

parallels may be due, as Segal observes, to a conventional way of writing hymns to
Dionysus; see Charles Segal, "The Character and Cults of Dionysus and the Unity of the
Frogs," *HSCP* 65 (1961): 207–42, 241–42 n.96, and passim. But even if *The Frogs* was
performed before the *Bacchae* and therefore could not have been a direct response to it,
Aristophanes was thoroughly familiar with Euripides' other tragedies and fully understood their potentially destabilizing effect on the tragic tradition. The fact that both the
Bacchae and *The Frogs* center on Dionysus as the patron of drama also justifies my
choosing this Aristophanian comedy to illustrate the theme of play and power. This
theme could equally well have been illustrated by *The Clouds*, which reveals the close link
between sophistry, law and contest, or by *The Birds*, which parodies the Hellenic
mentality of power in general.

24. The present discussion is particularly indebted to the following studies on
Aristophanes and *The Frogs*: Ludwig Rademacher, introduction to and commentary on
the Greek text of *The Frogs* (German ed., Vienna, 1954); W. B. Stanford, introduction to
and commentary on his edition of the Greek text (2d ed., London, 1963); Cornford, *The
Origin of Attic Comedy*; C. W. Dearden, *The Stage of Aristophanes* (London, 1976); Kenneth J.
Dover, *Aristophanic Comedy* (London, 1972); Ehrenberg, *The People of Aristophanes*; Eduard
Fraenkel, *Beobachtungen zu Aristophanes* (Rome, 1962); Thomas Gelzer, *Der epirrhematische
Agon bei Aristophanes*, *Zetemata* 23 (Munich, 1960); Rosemary Harriott, *Aristophanes: Poet
and Dramatist* (Baltimore, 1986); Jeffrey Henderson, "The *Lekythos* and *Frogs* 1200–1248,"
HSCP 70 (1972): 133–44, which is a refutation of Cedric Whitman's "*Lekythion apolesen*,"
HSCP 73 (1969): 109–12; Hans Herter, *Vom Dionysischen Tanz zum komischen Spiel* (Iser-
lohn, 1947); J. T. Hooker, "The Composition of the *Frogs*," *Hermes* 108 (1980): 169–82;
Douglas MacDowell, "Aristophanes, *Frogs* 1407–67," *CQ* 9 (1959): 261–68, and "The

To the modern, Aristotelian critic this somewhat loose structure poses problems of unity, particularly of plot and character. The journey to Hades is episodic and seemingly has little connection with the contest, of which Dionysus (as well as the spectator) learns only subsequently, upon his arrival in the kingdom of the shades. The figure of the god himself appears as a heterogenous composite of contradictory mythic, ritualistic, and popular representations and has posed difficult interpretive puzzles: one has somehow to account for the fact that the ridiculous braggart, the bibulous, lecherous bon vivant of the first section is called upon to arbitrate and judge, in the second section, in such serious matters as the tragic contest between the greatest poets of Hellas and the best political course for the embattled Athenian polis. One seems therefore confronted with the choice of either allegorizing the play (looking for thematic and symbolical unity beyond the narrative or plot level) or discarding the question of unity altogether, on the not implausible grounds that it is an Aristotelian logo-rational concept that probably did not concern either Aristophanes or the jury that awarded him the first prize. Nevertheless, there is a third interpretive choice, which I propose to follow here and which neither depends on an Aristotelian notion of unity nor allegorizes the play. Outside an allegorical or metaphorical interpretation, *The Frogs* can lend itself to a metonymic and holistic reading, if one assumes that for Aristophanes, just as for Euripides, Dionysus does not represent or symbolize anything, but *constitutes* everything at the same time and in the same movement: he is both coward and hero, quack and magician, man and god, comedy and tragedy, play and seriousness, gentleness and violence, in other words, he is literally a god of many names (and masks). As in the case of the *Bacchae*, then, the action of *The Frogs* can be seen from a series of double perspectives that are nevertheless facets of the same Janus-like figure: comic and tragic, peaceful and violent, human and divine, worldly and otherworldly, and so forth.

The double-faceted nature of Dionysus is made obvious from the

Frogs' Chorus," *CR* (1972): 3–5; Gilbert Murray, *Aristophanes: A Study* (New York, 1964); Kenneth J. Reckford, *Aristophanes' Old-and-New Comedy* (Chapel Hill, N.C., 1987); Segal, "The Character and Cults of Dionysus and the Unity of the *Frogs*"; Lois Spatz, *Aristophanes* (Boston, 1978); Cedric H. Whitman, *Aristophanes and the Comic Hero* (Cambridge, Mass., 1964); Garry Wills, "Why Are the Frogs in the *Frogs*," *Hermes* 97 (1969): 306–17, and "Aeschylus' Victory in the *Frogs*," *AJP* 90 (1969): 48–57; and Leonard Woodbury, "Aristophanes' *Frogs* and Athenian Literacy: *Ran.* 52–53, 1114," *TAPA* 106 (1976): 349–57. I should also mention the valuable contributions included in H.-J. Newiger, ed., *Aristophanes und die alte Komoedie* (Darmstadt, 1975), and David J. Littlefield, ed., *Twentieth Century Interpretations of the Frogs* (Englewood Cliffs, N.J., 1968).

outset, when the god appears on stage, complete with yellow *krokos* (habitually worn by his votaries in religious precessions) and cothurni, incongruously matched with a Herculean lion skin and club. This apparel has naturally been seen as a grotesque, comic disguise and is commonly interpreted as an indication that Aristophanes either undercuts or, on the contrary, reinforces the heroic values embodied by Hercules, as well as by tragedy in general. These symmetrically opposed interpretations are further supported by the fact that Dionysus turns out to be a complete coward, a *miles gloriosus* who shies away from any violent confrontation. For example, when faced with Hercules' angry creditors in Hades, Dionysus exchanges costumes with Xanthias, wishing to cull all the benefits but face none of the perils of a heroic life. The bacchic god could thus become identified with the Athenian democracy, which, Aristophanes seems to suggest, would like to reap all the benefits of power without paying its customary high price.

Neither of these readings, however, can by itself satisfactorily account for Dionysus' apparent change of heart and character at the end of the play, when he shows his true colors and gives the first prize to Aeschylus. But far from having to decide between these two interpretations, one can see them as complementary, just as the mild, effeminate features of Dionysus' comic persona complement its tragic, terrifying counterparts (compare the *Bacchae*, in which Dionysus also appears at first as a gentle, effeminate stranger and then transfers his role to Pentheus). In this sense, Dionysus' costume at the beginning of the play is both human and divine, grotesque and heroic, comic and tragic, that is, both mimetic affectation and an indication of his real nature (endless Becoming or play of simulacra).

Like the *Bacchae*, *The Frogs* presents Dionysus both in his human and in his divine guise, and from this perspective there seems to be no development of his character in the course of the play, no search for identity, as critics have argued.[25] Rather, throughout the play, Dionysus incessantly dons and doffs his masks, assuming and discarding a variety of roles. In the first section, Dionysus is mostly presented in his human (dis)guise, and it is in this disguise that he appears as an effeminate coward, as an

25. See Charles Segal and, in his wake, Whitman and Reckford. But to say that in *The Frogs* Dionysus is in search of his identity, which he finally finds in the latter part of the play, is a little bit like saying that, in the *Bacchae*, Dionysus finds his true identity after he transfers his gentle, effeminate persona to Pentheus. The point is that the god has no one true identity, although he himself creates and destroys all identities, as Aristophanes seems to be aware.

intellectual esthete who is "quite crazy" about Euripides and his tragic turns of phrase, as a rotund sybarite addicted to wine, women, and song. From the very first lines of the play, Aristophanes leaves no doubt as to which Dionysian mask he intends to employ here. Complaining about his slave (just as Xanthias complains about his master), Dionysus addresses the audience in an effort to gain their sympathy: "Now isn't this a sassy slave [*ubris*]? I've spoiled him./ Here am I, Dionysus, son of Grapejuice,/ wearing out my own feet, and I let him ride/ so that he won't get tired carrying the bundles."[26]

The "son of Grapejuice" (*huios Stamniou*, son of [Wine] Jar) is a mundane representation of the bacchic god that is always played up in comedy and played down in tragedy—in the *Bacchae*, for instance, Pentheus' charges of drunkenness and sexual promiscuity are repeatedly belied by the firsthand reports of the Theban bacchantes' behavior in the wilderness. It is this earthy and rowdy Dionysus that wears a preposterous Herculean disguise, gets involved in petty squabbles with his slave, and generally plays the fool both in the world above and in the world below. Hercules himself draws attention to Dionysus' human disguise when he mockingly suggests possible shortcuts for the journey to the underworld (hanging oneself, taking hemlock, hurling oneself down from a tower, and the like), shortcuts that are obviously more appropriate for men than for immortal gods (*Frogs* 120–35).

It is also in his earthly, human guise that the Bacchic god spurns his votaries on two occasions during his journey to Hades: when the chorus of frogs engages him in a croaking (singing) contest and when he is approached by the second chorus of the Eleusinian Mystae or initiates. Critics have offered elaborate explanations for Dionysus' failure to acknowledge his worshipers. It is, I believe, commonly accepted, for example, that his failure to recognize them is in effect a failure to recognize himself (on this psychological reading, he becomes a modern hero in search of a stable identity; yet my point here, as in my discussion of the *Bacchae*, is that Dionysus is a multiplicity of masks that hide nothing behind them; he is pure difference creating and destroying identity, rather than the other way around).

26. Aristophanes, *Frogs* 21–24, trans. R. Lattimore (Ann Arbor, Mich., 1962). Further English citations refer to this translation, which I have often revised substantially in order to convey my own sense of the Greek passage in question. In addition to that of Rademacher and Stanford, I have also consulted Victor Coulon's Greek edition of *The Frogs*, in *Aristophane*, vol. 4 (Paris, 1928). I cite from Aristophanes, *Comoediae*, 2 vols., eds. F. W. Hall and W. M. Geldart (Oxford, 1900–1901).

But perhaps the god is simply playing, and as such he delights in his disguises, he enjoys pretending to be a mortal, involved in mortals' serious and not so serious affairs—much as in the sundry "prince and pauper" tales in Western literature royal personages enjoy sampling, under a temporary, safe disguise, the lives of their less fortunate subjects.[27]

In the case of the frogs, it is conceivable that Dionysus delights in teasing them by trying to overpower them through loud farting and croaking, purely for the sake of the contest (the frogs themselves are no less eager to compete, boasting their art as much as Dionysus does). In the second case, the god avoids his worshipers so that he can safely and leisurely enjoy their choral performance from his hiding place (compare Zeus in the *Iliad*, where he seldom takes part in human or divine contests, preferring to watch them from Olympus; there is also a parallel, here, with Pentheus' eagerness to watch in secret the Theban bacchantes at play in the woods, *Bacchae* 810–16). In fact, the two choruses appear, not unlike the Euripidean maenads, as two faces of the same coin. The frogs are a comic extension of the wild and violent nature of the bacchic cult (note, in this respect, that the outcome of the contest between the frogs and Dionysus remains inconclusive: the god seems to prevail over them only because he arrives on the other side of the Styx, leaving their natural habitat, the marshes, behind). The chorus of initiates, on the other hand, embodies his relatively gentle, lighthearted side.

The choral performances, no less than their counterparts in the *Bacchae*, abound in play imagery, and one should not forget that the inscription at Eleusis describing the nature of the god read: *Dionusos parapaizon*, "Dionysus, the play-loving." In this regard, Aristophanes' use of the Eleusinian mysteries is certainly not parodic; rather it underscores

27. This delight in being the Other is also acknowledged by the so-called rituals of reversal where, for example, during carnivals, the oppressors temporarily become the oppressed and vice versa. Anthropologists often assume that these ceremonies are organized mostly for the enjoyment and benefit of the oppressed in order to release social tensions. But it may also be that within clearly defined limits or within the relatively safe space of a cultural game, the masters equally enjoy switching roles with their servants. Apart from the obvious parodic functions that disguise and role-playing have in *The Frogs*, Dionysus' trading roles with Xanthias can also be regarded in terms of such a ritual of reversal. For anthropological and literary interpretations of this kind of ritual see, for example, Victor Turner, *The Ritual Process: Structure and Anti-Structure* (Ithaca, N.Y., 1969); V. Turner, ed., *Celebration: Studies in Festivity and Ritual* (Washington, D.C., 1982); Hedwig Kenner, *Das Phaenomen der verkehrten Welt in der griechischen-roemischen Antike* (Bonn, 1970); B. A. Babcock, ed., *The Reversible World* (Ithaca, N.Y., 1978); and Jean Claude Carrière, *Le carnaval et la politique* (Paris, 1979).

the ludic, festive character not only of the Dionysian cult, but also of its poetic product, Old Comedy.[28] But this ludic or festive character has also become problematic, since the chorus of Mystae needs to defend its playfulness, pointing to the logo-rational opposition of play and seriousness—an opposition that later Plato will thoroughly exploit, turning it against both the Sophists and the poets. For example, in their invocation to Demeter, the initiates chant: "Demeter, ruler of holy orgies [*hagnōn orgiōn anassa*],/ stand by me, save your chorus./ Grant me to play on and do my dances/ in safety throughout the day/ To say many things in fun and many in earnest [*polla men geloia . . . polla de spoudaia*]; and/ after playing [*paisanta*] and joking worthily of your festival/ grant me the victor's garland" (*Frogs* 384–95, trans. modified).

In other words, under the pressure of competition, the chorus (which self-consciously addresses not only Demeter but also the judges in Aristophanes' dramatic contest) feels the need to be serious in addition to being playful, thus foreshadowing the double nature of the agon between Aeschylus and Euripides in the second part of the play. It can nevertheless be argued that in Aristophanes the playful spirit prevails, as can be seen in the third song of the Mystae, where the chorus addresses Iacchus/Dionysus (as well as Aristophanes' spectators-judges) in an entirely flippant way: "It was you who, for laughs and economy,/ ripped up this shirt and little sandal/ it was you who showed me how/to play and dance with impunity" (*Frogs* 405–9). Then, casting a glance aside, the chorus draws attention to a pink nipple peeping out of a young girl's tattered clothes— a zestful play companion (*Frogs* 410–15). Xanthias and Dionysus, who make playful, irreverent remarks throughout the choral performance, are equally appreciative of the girl's charms, expressing a fiery desire to join in the play (*Frogs* 416–18).

Because Dionysus is a god in human disguise he is not only a *miles gloriosus* or an *alazōn* (as critics have often seen him) but also an *eirōn*—he delights in pretending to be less than he is. For a while, he even enjoys swapping attires with his slave in Hades and one can imagine him doing so less in order to escape beatings than to deflect them onto his partner.

28. For the view of *The Frogs* as satire of the Eleusinian mysteries, see Etienne Lapalus, "Le Dionysus et l'Heracles des *Grenouilles*," *Revue des Etudes Grecques* 47 (1934): 1–20. As critics have rightly pointed out, Aristophanes could not have caricatured the mysteries since they were an extremely well-kept secret, and even if he had, there would be no way for the modern critic to know it, because the secret of Eleusis disappeared with its last hierophants. For a reasonable approach to the question of the Eleusinian mysteries, see George E. Mylonas, *Eleusis and the Eleusinian Mysteries* (Princeton, N.J., 1961).

Xanthias is fully aware of Dionysus' game of *mētis* and answers him in kind
by urging Aeacus to flog the disguised god (*Frogs* 615–25). He continues
the game even after Dionysus thinks it has gone far enough and changes
the rules by claiming divine inviolability (*Frogs* 628–32). The shrewd slave
assures Aeacus that a god would feel no physical pain from being whipped
(a tongue-in-cheek contention—consider the pain inflicted by Diomedes
on Aphrodite, or Poseidon and Apollo's travails at Troy, in the *Iliad*—here
Aristophanes probably plays on the changing religious beliefs of his
contemporaries, who tend to imagine gods as less anthropomorphic and
more abstract than they appear to an archaic, Homeric mentality). Then,
unexpectedly, Xanthias accepts the god's challenge to an agon of endurance (*Frogs* 637–39). Despite his low tolerance to pain, Dionysus will
not pass up the contest and heroically endures Aeacus' flogging. As
Xanthias proves no less competitive, the infernal overseer is finally forced
to defer the matter to his divine superiors, thereby putting an end to
Dionysus' human game (*Frogs* 668–71).

In the second part of the play, we find Dionysus presiding over the
contest between the two tragic poets, and the farce seems suddenly to
take a serious turn. As noted before, this alleged suddenness has caused
considerable critical uneasiness, but does it have to? If Dionysus as patron
of comedy and tragedy is all at once human and divine, cowardly and
heroic, playful and serious, farcical and sublime, then his switching of
roles is natural, creating a paradox only at the human level, or rather, at
the critical level: his presence within a dramatic piece will always erase
the distinctions between comedy and tragedy, or play and seriousness,
revealing them as purely arbitrary, and rendering all criticism, that is, all
decision, irrelevant. In the *Bacchae*, Euripides achieves precisely this paradoxical effect, playing on the double nature of the god through his smiling
mask. Aristophanes achieves the same effect by opposite means, because
he brings Dionysus into a comedy and then has him judge the relative
merits of two modes of writing tragedy. Thereby, like Euripides, he seems
(intentionally or unintentionally) to point to the artificial, man-made
nature of tragedy in general, a revelation that has not only rhetorical but
also profoundly ethical implications: tragic situations, no less than tragic
composition, are entirely of human making, and humans must not blame
the gods but only themselves for any tragic dilemmas in which they might
get themselves involved.[29]

29. Note that Aristophanes' Dionysus does *not* propose to help Athens in her hour of
need through either direct advice or direct action, but only indirectly, by bringing back

And just how serious is Dionysus in the second part of the play? No more and no less so, it seems, than he was in the first part. One should not lose sight of Dionysus' amphibolous nature either when he plays the fool in his human guise or when he plays the divine judge. Indeed, in this latter role he has no good reason to turn particularly serious, since he is dealing only with humans, not with his divine peers. He obviously delights in his dual role of umpire and judge, egging on the contestants and indis-criminately making inane and judicious, naive and sarcastic, dull and witty asides. Although the contestants will ultimately have to abide by his decision, they do not treat him with the reverence due to a god or, for that matter, to a human judge. Both of them are haughty and condescend-ing, constantly questioning his good judgement. For example, when Dionysus praises Aeschylus' studied long silences on stage, Euripides calls him a dupe, and the god takes the insult in good part (*Frogs* 917–18). Likewise, when Dionysus teasingly threatens Aeschylus with a good thrashing for having portrayed the Thebans as being greater warriors than the Athenians, the old poet remains undaunted and alludes to the god's cowardliness, urging him to acquire something of the true grit of his own warlike characters (*Frogs* 1023–36).

In view of these and other examples, it is hard to see how Dionysus has developed in the course of the play to the point where he allegedly acquires the dignified seriousness of a divine judge. On the other hand, his decision of proclaiming Aeschylus a victor does appear rather sudden and arbitrary, since he himself acknowledges he cannot make up his mind. His words to Pluto, who presses him into a decision, reflect his ambivalence: "They are friends [*andres philoi*; also allies] and I cannot decide [*ou krinō*] between them./ For I do not wish to quarrel with either of them: one I regard as clever [*sophos*; but also wise), the other as pleasing" (*Frogs* 1411–13). Although some translators apparently cannot bear the ambivalence, ascribing the cleverness to Euripides and the pleasing quality to Aeschy-lus, a good case can be made for the opposite interpretation.[30] Dionysus makes no secret of his love for Euripides and his distaste for Aeschylus, whom he finds clever, but rather pompous and heavy-handed. Obviously, then, one must distinguish between Aristophanes' and his characters'

---

one of her illustrious poets and giving him his vote of confidence. Besides, the most crucial political advice to the city is given by the chorus in the parabasis, rather than by the god or the poets themselves.

30. Dudley Fitts, for example, translates: "Euripides is *so* sophisticated/ and Aeschylus so rewarding"; see Aristophanes, *Four Comedies*, trans. D. Fitts (New York, 1957), 146.

view of Aeschylus.[31] Judging from his fairly balanced presentation of the two opponents, Aristophanes seems to imply that, from the standpoint of a purely artistic contest, the two contestants run neck in neck, with comparable handicaps.

If we turn, for a moment, to the contest itself, we again see that we have no good reason to believe that this contest, any more than its judge, tends to "lean toward seriousness."[32] On the contrary, it is, if anything, broad farce and can hardly be taken as a genuine battle of wits between two of the most respected minds of the fifth century. Aristophanes is primarily interested in making his audience laugh and therefore mostly reduces the contestants to hilarious caricatures.[33] Their literary joust is all the more amusing because it is announced by the chorus as an *agōn sophias* (*Frogs* 884), in the heroic tradition of the contest between Homer and Hesiod, but then is treated as a mock combat. The chorus itself sets the mock heroic tone in its prologue to the battle, which is a delightful parody of the high-flown, Aeschylean tragic style: "Fearful shall be the spleen now of Thundermutter withinside/ when the riptooth-sharpening he sees of his multiloquacious/ antagonist to encounter him. Then shall ensue dread eyewhirl of fury./ Horse-encrested phrases shall shock in helmtossing combat,/ chariots collide in whelm of wreckage and splinter-flown action,/ warrior beating off brain-crafted warrior's/ cavalried speeches" (*Frogs* 814–21).

One can plainly see, however, that even as it is parodying Aeschylus, the chorus takes his side and will continue to do so throughout the contest, thus heavily loading the dice in his favor. Some critics have been

31. All the more so because the chorus situates itself at the opposite side from Dionysus, visibly favoring Aeschylus over Euripides. Of course, the question remains why Aristophanes creates all these conflicting views, and even more importantly, why he has Dionysus lean toward Euripides and yet award the first prize to Aeschylus. For possible answers, see the end of this section.

32. Reckford, *Aristophanes' Old-and-New Comedy*, 424.

33. In stressing the comedy and playfulness of Aristophanes' theatrical piece, I do not mean to overlook its seriousness. I am simply saying that, in discussing *The Frogs*, it is impossible to separate play from seriousness and seriousness from play, be it in the first or in the second part of the comedy. Although he is aware of the opposition between play and seriousness, Aristophanes himself seems to ignore this opposition deliber-ately—he simply does not operate with logo-rational, moral categories. I have chosen to overemphasize his playfulness because others have overemphasized his seriousness, and it seems to me that this is one instance in which the stronger critical case should be made weaker, in order to restore the balance. The underlying assumption of my argument, however, remains the same. Like Dionysus' mask, *The Frogs* presents two inseparable faces: a playful and a serious one.

fooled by the chorus' *parti pris* into believing that Aristophanes himself
roots for Aeschylus by giving him a more dignified attitude than Euripides' during the contest. But surely the older poet occasionally maintains a dignified silence only for heightened dramatic effect, in obvious
imitation of the behavior of his own characters. Despite Dionysus'
somewhat patronizing view of Aeschylus, Aristophanes shows him to be
not only pompous and abstruse but also wily and versatile (as Euripides
does not fail to point out—set a tragic pro to catch another): like
Antilochus in the chariot race of *Iliad* 23, Aeschylus will employ any kind
of ruse to win. No less than Euripides, who is supposedly the more crafty
of the two, being trained by the Sophists, Aeschylus constantly hits under
the belt, going for the easy shots (and laughs). For example, he scores an
effective, if underhanded, opening punch when he implies that he is
handicapped in competing in the underworld because, although he is
dead, his poetry is still alive, whereas Euripides' poetry has died with him
and, therefore, can be easily marshalled in support of its maker (yet later
we find Aeschylus reciting gustily from his own plays, which, despite his
previous claim, have apparently made their way to Hades after all; *Frogs*
1126).

Aeschylus also shows considerable political acumen when, asked at the
beginning of the contest to say a prayer, he addresses Demeter, the patron
goddess, together with Persephone and Dionysus, of Eleusis—now one
can understand why the chorus, made up of Eleusinian Mystae, naturally
favors him over Euripides, who invokes such abstract, scientific divinities
as Aether and Comprehension (*Xunēsis*). Aeschylus displays the same *mētis*
when he tags his *lekuthion* or little bottle of oil onto the tail of Euripides'
lines or when he delivers bombastic verses fraught with ponderous
references to death, corpses, battle chariots, and the like, in order to tip
the rhetorical weight in his favor (a feat of dubious distinction, one might
add). During the final stretch of the contest, he even attempts to trick
Dionysus into bringing him back to Athens *before* having supplied the
advice required of him to save the city and win the competition (*Frogs*
1454–62). Finally, after the decision goes his way, Aeschylus attempts to
keep his throne in the underworld as well, by entrusting it to Sophocles
(Sophocles, it is suggested, is too gentle-hearted to compete in the first
place and therefore is likely to surrender the throne without a fight,
should the older poet return).

The agon between Euripides and Aeschylus is certainly not a contest of
sophia in our sense of "wisdom," but in the archaic sense of "shrewdness"
or savoir faire (in the technical sense as well), and what is praised is the

ability to win, by fair or foul means alike. In this regard, their battle of wits is not much different from a wrestling match, as the chorus plainly states in its pep talk to the contestants: "Up from your places! Into the ring again!/ Wit must wrestle wit once more in fall upon fall./ Fight him, wrestle him, throw the book at him,/ talk at him, sit on him, skin him alive,/ old tricks, new tricks, give him the works./ This is the great debate for championship. Hazard it all" (Frogs 1103–8).[34]

All the same, words neither kill nor inflict visible wounds, and therefore Dionysus is confronted with a tough decision, as he confesses to Pluto. By the end of the contest, despite his sarcastic asides, the god of drama still shows a great deal of sympathy for Euripides, to whom he feels much closer in spirit and whose lines he knows by heart. One may wonder, then, why he nevertheless awards the first prize to Aeschylus, and the explanation most commonly given by critics is that his decision is motivated by ethical rather than aesthetical considerations. But it is possible that his verdict is motivated by neither, and that one has to look for an answer in the archaic values that the god seems to embrace.[35]

It is noteworthy that Dionysus never explains his choice of victor directly but only through lines borrowed, again, from Euripides. For example, Dionysus replies with a verse from Hippolytus (612) to Euripides' accusation that he has broken his vow by choosing Aeschylus: "My tongue swore, not my heart" (Frogs 1471). When Euripides keeps reviling him, wondering how Dionysus has the gall to look him straight in the face after committing such a shameful act, the god counters with: "What's shameful?—unless it seems so to the audience?" (Frogs 1475). This question is a modified version of a line from Aeolus (now lost), which reads: "What's shameful unless it seems so to those who do it?" and I shall later explore the possible meanings of this modification. In his sarcastic answers, therefore, Dionysus taunts Euripides with the kind of Realpolitik

34. Although Lattimore's translation is somewhat free here, it certainly preserves the wrestling imagery of the original and accurately renders the kind of competitive spirit that animates the two contestants. Even though both the chorus and Dionysus urge them, in other places, to behave like "gentlemen," this is clearly no gentlemanly fight, at any rate no more so than the ones between Homeric heroes.
35. G. M. A. Grube, for example, is fully aware of this problem when he says that Dionysus' decision is "explicitly subjective, it is based neither on poetic merit nor on moral-didactic grounds"; see The Greek and Roman Critics (Toronto, 1965), chap. 2. Grube, however, does not seem to offer an explanation for this decision, simply remarking that "Aristophanes could hardly have made it clearer that both are great poets, and that no choice is possible on aesthetic or artistic grounds." Grube's observation should nevertheless be dealt with.

that the lines the god quotes from his tragedies seem to advocate. He reminds Euripides that a god can change his mind and words at will since no mortal has the power to bind him to them, that is, Dionysus reminds him of the might-makes-right principle.

The god's change of mind is primarily motivated by self-interest (and as such it can hardly indicate his moral development in the course of the play). As Dionysus informs the two contestants a little earlier, he has descended to Hades in order to find a poet that would, through his advice, save Athens so that the city can continue holding *his* festivals (*Frogs* 1419). This seems to contradict Dionysus' original explanation for his trip, which he undertakes out of boredom: Euripides has died, nobody writes good plays any more, hence the god wishes to bring the poet back so that the latter can entertain him (in this respect, the word *pothos*, craving, which Dionysus uses to express his need for Euripides is entirely appropriate—just as Hercules craves for good soup, the god of drama craves for good drama). But that explanation was given to Hercules and a god is not bound to account for his actions to mortals in the same way that he will account for them to his peers (compare his dialogue with Pluto, to whom he admits that he does not know whom to choose). As it turns out, however, the two explanations are not entirely incompatible, because Dionysus is interested in keeping his festivals going in order to keep himself entertained and decides that Aeschylus is the suitable man for the job. The god may save Athens in the process, but this is not his primary goal. Again play and seriousness are indistinguishable: what to the god appears as a matter of play and entertainment can appear to humans as a matter of grave consequence (compare the Dionysus of the *Bacchae*, who stages a comedy that turns into a tragedy for the humans with whom he plays).

Before Dionysus comes to Hades he has no idea that he will be appointed a judge and asked to choose in a poetic contest; the circumstances have now changed and, being the pragmatist that he is, the god will not be held to his word any more than an imperial power would. Aristophanes seems to suggest that in real life, and specifically in artistic contests—pointedly, his play is also engaged in such a contest—self-interest often prevails over other considerations (such as "disinterested," aesthetic ones) and Dionysus ends up choosing the contestant who in his opinion will best serve his festival. Contrary to what some critics think and what Dionysus' additional quotation from Euripides seems to suggest ("I shall choose him, whom my soul desires," *Frogs* 1468), the god's decision comes from the mind, and not from the heart—the kind of reasoned, pragmatic decision that would presumably be more to the liking of the Sophists, Socrates, and Euripides himself than to that of Aeschylus and his "old-fashioned" admirers.

If the better poet is the one who serves Dionysus' festival best, then political considerations seem to prevail over aesthetic ones in awarding the first prize. On the other hand, the political advice given by the two poets fails to act as a determining factor in the choice of the winner, and in this sense Aristophanes seems to suggest that the poet's primary function (outside the parabasis, which is, in turn, outside the play proper) is not necessarily a political one. In fact, the advice given by the two poets is politically worthless, as critics have often remarked.

Each poet, moreover, gives the kind of advice that appears to be more appropriate for the fictional character of the other. For example, apropos of Alcibiades, Euripides (elsewhere scoffed at by Dionysus as not being a friend of democracy and, in other plays, accused of being a demagogue)[36] gives the kind of advice that one would perhaps have expected from Aeschylus: "I hate the citizen who, by nature well endowed,/ is slow to help his city, swift to do her harm,/ to himself useful, useless to the community" (Frogs 1427–29). Aeschylus, in turn, seems to give the kind of advice that would be more in keeping with Euripides (at least as often presented by Aristophanes, a friend of those Sophists who presumably advocated a might-makes-right morality): "We should not rear a lion's cub within the state./ But if we rear one, we must do as it desires" (Frogs 1431–32).[37] As to the next piece of advice, Euripides seems to voice Aristophanes' own opinion and, therefore, it would presumably have been more properly placed in Aeschylus' mouth: "If we mistrust those citizens

36. Frogs 952–52, and Rademacher's commentary, Ranae, 280–81, as well as Stanford's, The Frogs, 156. Admittedly, Dionysus' remark has also been seen as being addressed to Aeschylus (for example, Lattimore, The Frogs, 61). In fact, modern scholars have been at great pains emending the Greek text in such a way that it would render the two poets' characters more consistent with a logo-rational, Aristotelian notion of unity. My assumption, on the other hand, is that the text may be naturally ambivalent and that the two poets' positions are presented as largely interchangeable because, under the pressure of the contest, they are both hypocritical or demagogical. Note also Dionysus' role as a deflator of the high claims of either poet in support of his art.

37. Or Frogs 1431b: "Lions are lords. We should not have them here at all." Of course, Aeschylus' words can also be interpreted as advising against the return of Alcibiades (compare Coulon, The Frogs, 152 n.4), in which case line 1432 would run: "For if we rear one, we must do as it desires." Even this interpretation, however, would not invalidate my main point, because both poets would give the same advice and, therefore, Dionysus could not choose the winner on this basis.

whom now we trust,/ and use those citizens whom we do not use now, we might be saved" (*Frogs* 1446–48). This piece of advice seems to correspond to that offered by the chorus in the parabasis, through its metaphor of the old and the new coins (*Frogs* 717–37). On the other hand, Aeschylus' advice to Athens is that of Pericles (as presented by Thucydides in his history of the Peloponnesian War) and is hardly suited for 405 B.C., a historical moment that seems to call for prudent entrenchment rather than aggressive expansion.

In view of these apparent illogicalities, the fictional identities of the two poets seem considerably garbled—a disturbing state of affairs for those critics who have seen in *The Frogs* Aristophanes' quest for political and dramatic unity. It may be that the text here is corrupt beyond repair, but it may also be that it deliberately plays on a certain ambivalence (or, indeed, equivalence) as far as the two contestants are concerned.[38] As in the case of Dionysus and Xanthias, Aristophanes perhaps has the two poets switch roles in order to show them as interchangeable. Note, again, that Dionysus mercilessly teases both of them, constantly undermining the validity of their statements and treating them as equally biased. It is also possible that both poets are presented as skillful demagogues, being as opportunistic as Dionysus himself. In order to win the contest, they will say whatever they assume the judge (and the audience) wants to hear, thus ending up with reversed cues. Finally, one should not discount Aristophanes' own opportunism: a comic poet will say and do just about anything that would make his audience laugh. Hence it is not impossible that in constructing the personae of the tragic poets, Aristophanes was led primarily by contextual rather than by overall artistic considerations. Be it

38. For a discussion of the textual and interpretive difficulties with this entire passage, see Wills, "Aeschylus' Victory in the *Frogs*." I remain, however, unconvinced by Wills' argument that Aeschylus does not offer any specific political advice in this passage and that what he has to offer instead is "himself," that is, his own kind of lofty and heroic tragic poetry as opposed to the "Palamedes-type invention[s]" offered by Euripides (Wills, "Aeschylus' Victory in the *Frogs*," 57). Wills seems to opt for the traditional view, according to which Aristophanes gives the palm to the conservative Aeschylus over the liberal Euripides, seeking the salvation of Athens in the revival of its heroic past. Although this interpretation is not implausible, it needs to be refined considerably without excising (as Wills proposes to do) those parts of the text that do not fit our interpretive models. In fact, Wills' (well-reasoned) proposal of rejecting *Frogs* 1442–50 and 1463–65 can serve as a modern example of how logo-rational concepts slowly made their way into and eliminated archaic notions from archaic and early classical texts. In the name of unity and logic, Wills eliminates or tries to "improve" what seems intolerable to a logo-rational mentality (contradictions, nonsequiturs, and so forth).

as it may, most critics seem at least to agree that the contestants' political opinions, regardless of how they are assigned between the two of them, are by themselves insufficient in establishing a clear winner, and that to provide specific solutions to specific political problems does not seem to be the main function of the poet in Aristophanes' eyes (or, for that matter, in ours).

But if tragic (and comic) poetry does not seem to have primarily a political function for Aristophanes, does it then have a more general, educational function? At first sight, this certainly appears to be the case. In reply to Aeschylus' question as to what the poet's duty is and why he is respected by his community, Euripides says: "For his dexterity and his exhortations [*dexiotētos kai nouthesias*], for making men better in the poleis" (*Frogs* 1009–10, trans. modified). Aeschylus later utters the famous lines according to which "the little boys have their teachers to instruct them,/ but young men have poets [as their instructors],/ and we must say only high-minded things [*chrēsta legein*, later repeated by Euripides as *chrēsta didaskein*, teach high-minded things]" (*Frogs* 1054–57, trans. modified). Both poets, therefore, agree that their mission is to educate the public, and they accuse each other only of not properly carrying out this mission. Finally, after a victor is chosen, both Pluto and the chorus offer their blessings and then urge him to go and instruct the "foolish majority."[39]

39. The didactic notion of poetry was mainly developed by the Sophists and does not seem to have much to do with the historical Aeschylus himself. In fact the first time we hear about it in any detail is precisely in *The Frogs*. Again, we see that the comic poet is indeed "aristophaneuripidizing," bringing into play a notion that is developed by his own contemporaries. This does not mean, however, that either Euripides or Aristophanes himself necessarily shares the Sophistic view of the educational role of poetry. For a brief outline of the history of the Hellenic notion of teaching (*didaskein*) in relation to wisdom (*sophia*) up to the Sophists and *The Frogs*, see, for instance, Leonard Woodbury, "The Judgment of Dionysus," 244–49. Woodbury also offers a balanced view of the question of orality and literacy in the play. One can add, however, that insofar as Aristophanes presents Aeschylus mostly as a symbol of the heroic age and oral mentality (because of his poetic language, which seems to have become almost unintelligible for a late fifth-century audience) and Euripides as a symbol of the literate mentality and Sophistic rationalism, the comic poet again simplifies history in favor of schematic contrast: the two tragic poets exhibit both oral and literate elements in their work. On the other hand, Aristophanes at times presents both poets as Sophists (for example, in their exchange about the educational role of poetry). But the historical Euripides was no less than Aristophanes put off by excessive sophistry and, therefore, the comic poet's presentation of him as a Sophist is purely self-serving. Finally, I am not so sure that Aristophanes should be unqualifiedly identified with Dionysus when the latter chooses Aeschylus over Euripides (see Woodbury, "The Judgment of Dionysus," 252).

Yet Dionysus repeatedly points out that if instruction is indeed the function of poetry, then both Aeschylus and Euripides have failed miserably in changing the ways of their fellow citizens. For example, when Aeschylus argues that "from the earliest times/ incitement to virtue and useful knowledge have come from the makers of rhymes/ . . . Homer, divinely inspired,/ is a source of indoctrination to virtue. Why else is he justly admired/ than for teaching how heroes armed them for battle?" (*Frogs* 1030–35), Dionysus remarks sarcastically: "He didn't teach Pantakles though./ He can't get it right. . . . He was called to parade, don't you know,/ and he put on his helmet and tried to tie on the plume when the helm was on top of his head" (*Frogs* 1036–38). Aeschylus defends himself in the next lines, giving the counter example of Lamachos (who is bitterly satirized in the *Acharnians*, but becomes a hero after his death in the expedition against Syracuse) and arguing that "the man in the street simply has to catch something from all my heroics and braveries" (*Frogs* 1039–41). But he has already admitted that his fellow Athenians could have learned much more from him in this and other respects than they actually did (*Frogs* 1025). Euripides, on the other hand, has taught the Athenians only bad things, such as endless chatter, which makes them desert the palaestra for the agora, endless questioning and criticism, which leads them to insubordination or even impiety toward the gods, and so forth. Of course, from Euripides' point of view (and, no doubt, from the point of view of at least some of the spectators), endless chatter is a sign of a healthy democratic spirit, and the critical faculty is an indispensable instrument of a mature, self-governing community. But as the whole debate of who-taught-what-to-the-Athenians-and-with-what-results seems to imply, there is a great gap between what poetry might claim to teach and what is actually learned. Not unlike Euripides, Aristophanes seems to suggest that, poetry or no poetry, we all seem to know "what's right" but do not necessarily act upon that knowledge.

The debate on the educational nature of poetry in *The Frogs*, therefore, should not be taken out of its immediate context (the agon between the two poets) and presented as Aristophanes' own views; one should further take into consideration the fact that the poetic contest appears to remain as inconclusive in this round as in all the others. That poetry is not deemed altogether effective in setting things straight in the *polis* is again underscored at the end of the play when Pluto sends Aeschylus to instruct the Athenians, but furnishes him with such unpoetic instruments of persuasion as a handful of halters: "Here is a rope to give Kleophon/ here's one for the revenuers/ . . . they are waited for here, today,/ and if they delay/ I, in person, will go brand them, sting them,/ sling them each in a thong/ and bring them/ here to Hades', where they belong" (*Frogs* 1504–14).

Since in *The Frogs* dramatic poetry seems to play neither a major political nor a major educational role, does it perhaps have the communal function that the scapegoat ritual used to perform in a not too distant past? Again, one can make an excellent case for this conjecture without having to look for evidence any farther than Hades' instigation to violence in the preceding quotation. Sacrificial ritual and drama have such close affinities that many scholars consider the one to be the origin of the other. In *The Frogs*, Aristophanes seems to stage the kind of scapegoat ritual that is also discernable in much tragedy, including the *Bacchae*. If the play appears to achieve some form of communal unity, as critics have recently argued, this unity is undoubtedly due to the sacrificial victim (who in this case seems to be Euripides and his tragic poetry), and as such it remains tenuous and short-lived.[40]

The dramatic situation in the second part of the comedy contains several sacrificial elements. According to Aeacus, Euripides is an arrogant impostor who, with the help of the rabble, has unseated Aeschylus from his legitimate throne. As we have seen, the chorus (but not Dionysus) indirectly reinforces this view of Euripides by cheering for Aeschylus during the competition. The contest in itself is a legitimate means of establishing one's claims to power, and we remember that the whole tragic action of the *Bacchae* also revolves around a contest. But in both works this contest is played with loaded dice: just as in the *Bacchae* the dice are loaded against Pentheus, in *The Frogs* they are loaded against Euripides. Once the god declares Aeschylus a winner, he is crowned and celebrated the way a great hero would be, and the festivities include a feast at Pluto's, from which Euripides is excluded. In fact, Euripides the loser is all but expelled from the poetic community: he is not even given second place, a point emphasized when Sophocles is entrusted with Aeschylus' throne in the latter's absence. Depending on his sympathies,

---

40. Because much comic action reverses or parodies tragic action, its sacrificial features are often (but not always) attenuated and consequently do not as a rule have the same emotional impact that they do in tragedy. Comedy often employs the double mechanism of the scapegoat ritual (the unification of the community through the exclusion of the victim) without dwelling on the violent sacrificial deed itself. It is therefore sufficient to dethrone and isolate Euripides (rather than, say, stone him to death) in order to achieve a comic scapegoating effect. The point is, however, that Aristophanes seems to lay bare this comic device deliberately.

then, the spectator can regard Aeschylus' victory and Euripides' defeat as either a "tragic" or a comic ending (here the similarity with the *Bacchae* is again striking).

The question, of course, is to decide how Aristophanes himself views this ending, and the interpretation of *The Frogs* as a symbolic enactment of a scapegoat ritual has no trouble in deciding: Aristophanes hates Euripides (as much as he hates Socrates), turning the competition between the two tragic poets into an indictment of the younger one. And the comic poet does it all in the name of higher principles, such as rescuing Athens from political and military defeat.[41] Even though these are compelling arguments, the question of Aristophanes' sympathies proves to be much more difficult than it might at first sight appear, not least because we are, again, dealing with the slippery world of comic play. But let us further examine the evidence for the presence of a sacrificial mechanism in *The Frogs*, before we decide what to make of this mechanism.

We have seen that Dionysus, as opposed to the chorus, does not really side with either of the contestants (even though he seems much fonder of Euripides than of the older poet) and then decides in favor of Aeschylus at the last minute, in a rather arbitrary, self-serving manner. One also has

41. This is, in a somewhat oversimplified form, the influential thesis of Bruno Snell in "Aristophanes and Aesthetic Criticism," in *The Discovery of the Mind*. Although Snell's discussion abounds in valuable cultural historical insights, I do not agree with his judgment that Aristophanes is a precursor of Plato insofar as he "measure[s] tragedy by the standard of morality," nor that the comic poet hates Euripides. In this respect, Gilbert Murray seems better to convey Aristophanes' feelings toward his contemporary, which are, at worst, ambiguous: "It is mere blundering to say that Aristophanes thinks Euripides a bad poet and Aeschylus a good, or that he hates the one and loves the other. He sees that both are great poets; he admires both, loves both, but at the end of the count, old Aeschylus, with the glow of Marathon still upon him, Aeschylus, who had triumphed with Miltiades and Aristides the Just, remains on his throne, shaken a little but not displaced. . . . Yet, naturally enough, the verses that ran continually in his head, and seemed to weave about him a spell from which he had neither the power nor the desire to escape, were of his great contemporary" (*Aristophanes*, 134).

Actually, it is not very clear how much Aristophanes loves Aeschylus, but it seems fairly obvious that he is obsessed by Euripides. It is not impossible that Aristophanes has toward Euripides the ambiguous feelings that one has toward a model-rival: someone to emulate and, at the same, distance oneself from (was not tragedy the high and comedy the low genre and did not most poets aspire to write the former even when their talent possibly directed them to the latter?). With Euripides' death, however, Aristophanes is deprived of his model, and he may well experience the emptiness and boredom that he ascribes to Dionysus; consequently, he sets out to revive his old rival, even if in the end he ruefully decides to kill him again, with the help of Aeschylus. The meaning of this ritual killing, however, is by no means clear.

difficulties, from a strictly political point of view, in telling the two poets apart and one would invariably have to suggest some kind of emendation of an allegedly corrupt text to get around these difficulties. Both points seem to argue in favor of a sacrificial mechanism operating in the play, given the arbitrary nature of this mechanism. These points, however, are far from conclusive because, in the first case, Dionysus' show of impartiality during the contest is not inappropriate for his position as a judge and, in the second case, it is generally agreed, after all, that the text shows marks of corruption (even though there is no general agreement as to what the original version sounded like). Nevertheless, there are other troubling aspects in the presentation of the two poets that can speak more conclusively in favor of reading *The Frogs* as a comic staging of a sacrificial ritual.

For example, it is a common assumption that the historical Euripides was only moderately successful in dramatic contests, being rather unpopular with Athenian audiences (this relatively poor reception of his drama may have played a role in Euripides' decision to go into self-exile in Macedonia); Aeschylus was, on the contrary, consistently successful, being the only tragic poet whose plays were allowed to compete, after his death, alongside with those of the living poets. In *The Frogs*, however, what is generally construed as the real-life situation seems reversed: Euripides is the successful one, and even though Aeacus contends that the poet is popular only with a few infernal thiefs and thugs, the latter seem to carry enough influence to cause Aeschylus to surender his throne to his younger opponent.

As has often been noticed, moreover, Aristophanes makes it clear that Euripides rather than Aeschylus has educated the taste of the audience addressed in the play, to such an extent that this audience is trusted to follow and enjoy a relatively sophisticated and often highly technical poetic debate. Aeschylus himself seems comfortable with the new thought (even though he is accused of obscurity by the new standards) and raises logorational objections to certain Euripidean passages. For example, he counters blow for blow Euripides' charges of logical inconsistencies in his prologues by pointing out similar inconsistencies in his opponent's work. But even though there is little difference between them in regard to the nature of their arguments or the manner in which these arguments are conducted, Aeschylus is chosen over Euripides, and thus we seem to have another bit of evidence for the sacrificial nature of the comic denouement in *The Frogs*.

As it has perhaps become clear from the preceding two paragraphs, our problem of determining Aristophanes' own position in the contest is part of the larger problem of determining what sort of audience he was addressing and what his own attitude toward this audience was, a problem that scholarship still has to solve; in turn, this uncertainty raises another, related question: does Aristophanes' hypothetical audience coincide with his real one? More specifically, does he, in the famous choral passage in *Frogs* 1113–19, mock his audience or does he actually attempt to hold its attention by flattery? Or, perhaps, does he do both? I am not sure that these questions can ever be answered satisfactorily.

Nevertheless, Aristophanes' fictitious reversal of what is commonly construed as the historical reception of the two poets can support a sacrificial reading of the play. If Aristophanes generally panders to his audience (even though he may attack it viciously at times), as comic poets often do, then he distorts historical fact in order to facilitate the comic scapegoating of Euripides: the majority of his audience must have believed that Aeschylus was actually the better poet and must have derived great satisfaction from his being restored to his throne by the god of drama himself (otherwise, the play would have lost its comic effect). In turn, this would mean that Aristophanes is indeed the conservative thinker that most scholars have portrayed him to be. This traditional Aristophanes believes, like Teiresias and Cadmus in the *Bacchae*, that in dangerous times the community should achieve unity and make a common front against the enemy, and then chooses the most obvious way of achieving this unity: blaming the new mode of thought (represented in this play by Euripides) for all the troubles of the *polis* and advocating a return to the archaic values, allegedly promoted by Aeschylus' plays.

But we are still confronted with the problem of Aristophanes' audience and the fact that he is working (or should I say playing?) in the comic mode, where fair is foul and foul is fair. Another interpretive possibility thus suggests itself, which does not go against the theory of dramatic scapegoating, and yet it turns it upside down. What if Aristophanes, not unlike Euripides in the *Bacchae*, is only *staging* a scapegoat ritual, doing it in a way that will reveal its arbitrary and violent nature and, therefore, render it ineffective?

Perhaps Aristophanes reluctantly points out how drama can indeed achieve communal unity by at least partially reverting to archaic practices, at the same time that he himself no longer firmly embraces either the new or the old values, because he has come to understand only too well the nature of both. Hence he would also exhibit an ambiguous attitude toward his audience (turning its demands against itself): when you had Euripides, you learned nothing from him, so I give you back that old windbag, Aeschylus; and if you demand scapegoats, I can easily give you scapegoats as well.

This mocking, ambiguous attitude can be read in Aristophanes' modification of a Euripidean line mentioned earlier. Instead of the Euripidean original "What's shameful unless it seems so to those who do it?" Dionysus' second barb against its author reads: "What's shameful, unless it seems so to the audience?" Could it be that the god simply gives the audience what it has wanted all along? (Compare the Dionysus of the *Bacchae*, who always assumes the form of the Other.) And could it be, the god implies, that what this audience wants *is* shameful? Through a dexterous twist worthy of the Sophists and Euripides, Dionysus seems to throw the ball into the audience's court and challenges the latter to find a reason for his decision.

Along similar lines, one can reconsider the god's parting shot to Euripides. When the tragic poet appeals to his mercy, begging to be rescued from the kingdom of the shades, the god equivocates: "Who knows if life be death indeed or death be life, or breathing [air] be [eating] dinner [a word play on *pnein* and *deipnein*]" (*Frogs* 1477–78). Although mocking the kind of Sophistic paradox often found in Euripides' plays, Dionysus' barb nevertheless contains a deeper irony, at the level of the audience, questioning a whole mode of thought and behavior. In the end, is there any difference between winning and losing, between being dead and alive, between the world above and the underworld? Is Aeschylus, or any other of the old sages, going to make a difference this time around, or will he continue preaching in the wind? And, most disturbingly, is he preaching the right thing? If not, is there any point in returning to Athens in order to defend a mode of life that would eventually bring one full circle back to Hades?

In a certain sense, Dionysus offers Euripides the possibility of living *hors concours*, and his exclusion from the play's agonistic society finds its atopian parallel in Cadmus' Isles of the Blessed or in Euripides' own exile at the court of the Macedonian king. At any rate, the indirect, equivocal manner in which the above questions are raised seems to cast doubt, if not on the agonistic notion of difference itself, at least on the way in which ethical differences are being established. In fact the god himself points to this doubt when he stands poised between the two contestants without being able to choose, and finally doing so only at the request of a higher authority, his uncle Pluto. And could the imposssibility, or indeed, the irrelevance of choice (this kind of choice, anyway) have been Aristophanes' own predicament as well? Knowing fully well that tragic poetry works the emotions rather than the intellect (in this sense, one might add, old Attic drama is definitely mimesis-play rather than mimesis-imitation, despite Aristotle's theses in the *Poetics*), Aristophanes advocates its return to emotion, as a manifestation of the will to power, by giving a Pyrrhic victory to Aeschylus. At the same time, however, he wonders, like Plato's Socrates, if under the circumstances tragic poetry is worth salvaging after all.

Finally, however, regardless of Aristophanes' intention (which we shall probably never know since it has left no trace in the historical record and is effectively covered up, in the comedy itself, under layers of playful equivocation), we need not decide between the various interpretations of *The Frogs*, any more than we need decide between the various interpretations of the *Bacchae*, because all these interpretations can equally be seen as metonymic effects of the two-sidedness of the Dionysian mask. This mask continuously effaces the boundaries between tragedy and comedy, and its reversible, double nature ceaselessly avoids, even as it haunts, the high grounds of ethical decision. Independently of Aristophanes' or Euripides' beliefs, their plays pose questions across the centuries, revealing their full ambivalence particularly during times of axiological crisis such as our own. In this respect, both *The Frogs* and the *Bacchae* seem to be the amphibolous products of a juncture in Hellenic thought when a different kind of choice presents itself, of either completely renouncing power as a founding principle of all that is or transforming it again into an inaccessible, transcendental truth. Greek philosophy appears to have chosen the second path, through Plato, Aristotle, and their logo-rational successors.

4 ■ Plato and the Birth of Philosophy from the Spirit of Poetry ■

■ Plato challenges poetry, especially Homer, Hesiod, and the tragic poets, presumably because he sees in it a still undefeated stronghold of the archaic values; these values are also present in myth and ritual, which he equally challenges.[1] Indeed, at the beginning of the fourth century B.C., the poets in general and the Homeric corpus in particular seem still to hold a tight grip on Hellenic culture. During the fifth century, the Sophists help to strengthen this grip both by using examples from Homer and other poets in their teachings and, at least some of them, by openly supporting the archaic values embedded in Greek epic and drama. Through the teachings of some of the Sophists, "the Homeric values have returned; or rather, since the basic framework of Homeric values has persisted unchanged, these values have been stripped of their accretions: the long-lived accretion of divine retribution, the recent one of quiet moral *aretē*. This being so, the values of the *Iliad* remain naked and unashamed."[2]

In retrospect, one of Plato's objectives seems to have been again to

1. Here I generally use the term *poetry* interchangeably with the Greek term *mousikē*. In Plato *mousikē* often still denotes, in addition to "music" (in the modern sense), the archaic mythopoeic unity of poetry reciting, music making, and dancing, as well as ritualistic and dramatic performance. Myth and ritual are thus inextricably linked to it. In the English translations of Plato's works, on the other hand, *mousikē* is mostly rendered by "music." Needless to say, both "poetry" and "music" convey only partially the meaning of *mousikē*, and the problem is compounded by the fact that in Plato's time archaic cultural unity was already breaking down and various disciplines were coming into being, claiming exclusively for themselves what in the past had been common territory. The reader is urged to keep these problems in mind throughout this chapter and the next, in order to avoid confusion.
2. Adkins, *MR*, 238.

cover up the heroic values embedded in Homer under the shamefaced garb of logo-rationality. His attack on poetry necessarily goes hand in hand with his attack on some of the Sophists (as well as on archaic myth and ritual) because he regards all of them as ideological allies, as promoters of an archaic, violent rather than a median, persuasive way of ruling.[3] One of his tasks, then, is to undermine the educational claim of poetry, or its authority as knowledge and truth, and to replace it with a logo-rational kind of authoritative discourse that he calls "philosophy." The concepts of imitation and play (which Plato partially borrows from the Sophists and the poets) will prove to be important instruments in carrying out this task.

But drama is Plato's first love: although he allegedly gives it up in order to follow Socrates, does he not remain, like so many of us, marked by this first love? For the most part, his thought assumes the shape of dramatic dialogue, thus maintaining the ambivalent and self-questioning nature of Euripidean and Aristophanic dramatic poetry. In this sense, it can be argued that, in the wake of the dramatic poets, Plato *stages* a series of trials against poetry and in favor of logo-rational philosophy, with all the ambiguous, double effects that one can expect from such self-conscious staging. I shall attempt to trace Plato's ambivalent wrestling with poetry in the *Republic*, with an excursus on the *Phaedrus* and brief references to other dialogues as well. Finally, I shall discuss Plato's theory of play in the *Republic* and the *Laws*, showing the inseparable link between this theory and his views on poetry, which he equally regards as a ludic form.

■ *Politeia: Philosophy's Agon with Poetry*

In the *Republic*, Socrates turns most poetry away from his ideal state, and the little of it that he lets in he places under house arrest, under the

---

3. Plato's perception of poetry and of the Sophists is naturally as biased as Aristophanes' presentation of Euripides, Socrates, and the Sophists in his comedies. In order to create an effective scapegoat, one must not only play up the hated features of the prospective victim, but also play down or simply omit its less hateful ones. We have seen, for example, that dramatic poetry itself is a stage for the contest between archaic and median values. Moreover, some of the Sophists (for example, Protagoras) can also be seen as "enlightened" promoters of logo-rational concepts. These fine nuances necessarily get lost in the heat of the *agōnes logōn*, in the contest for cultural authority in which all Hellenic thinkers, including Socrates and Plato, were deeply involved. More often than not, these thinkers differed less radically from their opponents than they were prepared to admit and, not infrequently, they would quietly absorb each other's insights at the same time that they would profess irreconcilable antagonism. Of course, this

strict surveillance of logo-rational, educational ideals. The Socratic arguments through which poetry is subordinated to metaphysical truth because it is *mimēsis* (understood as a play of appearances far removed from the eternal, changeless Forms) are well known. What is less often discussed is the agonistic nature of these arguments, which, although conducted from the standpoint of universal goodness and justice, serve the interests of a philosophical (largely aristocratic) elite in charge of defining what is good and just.

Let us briefly recall some of the main issues in this dialogue.[4] Socrates

---

remains equally true of modern intellectual debates. For a brief account of the background of Plato's feud with the poets, see Dalfen, *Polis und Poiesis*, esp. chap. 1, "Hintergrund und Rahmen der platonischen Dichterkritik."

4. An overwhelming number of Platonic studies are relevant to my discussion, and here I can mention only a few. In addition to Adkins' *Merit and Responsibility* and *From the Many to the One* as well as Dalfen's *Polis und Poiesis*, the following stand out: U. von Wilamowitz-Moellendorff, *Platon: Sein Leben und seine Werke*, 2 vols. (Berlin, 1920); E. E. Sikes, *The Greek View of Poetry* (New York, 1931); Paul Shorey, *What Plato Said* (Chicago, 1933); J. W. H. Atkins, *Literary Criticism in Antiquity*, 2 vols. (London, 1934); G. M. A. Grube, *Plato's Thought* (London, 1935); Wilhelm Nestle, *Vom Mythos zum Logos: Die Selbstenfaltung des griechischen Denkens vom Homer bis auf die Sophistik und Socrates* (Stuttgart, 1942); Richard McKeon, "The Concept of Imitation in Antiquity," in R. S. Crane, ed., *Critics and Criticism* (Chicago, 1952); Richard Robinson, *Plato's Earlier Dialectic* (Oxford, 1953); Rupert C. Lodge, *Plato's Theory of Art* (London, 1953); Paul Friedländer, *Platon*, 2 vols. (Berlin, 1954); Elfriede Huber-Abrahamowicz, *Das Problem der Kunst bei Platon* (Winterthur, 1954); John Gould, *The Development of Plato's Ethics* (London, 1955); Dodds, *The Greeks and the Irrational*; W. K. Wimsatt and C. Brooks, *Literary Criticism: A Short History* (London, 1957); Hermann Koller, *Die Mimesis in der Antike: Nachahmung, Darstellung, Ausdruck* (Berne, 1954); Jaeger, *Paideia*, vol. 2; Havelock, *Preface to Plato*; W. J. Verdenius, "L'Ion de Platon," *Mnemosyne* 3 (1963): 241–58 and *Mimesis: Plato's Doctrine of Artistic Imitation and Its Meaning to Us* (Leiden, 1949); Gerald Else, " 'Imitation' in the Fifth Century," *CP* 53 (1958): 73–90; W. D. Ross, *Plato's Theory of Ideas* (Oxford, 1966); Gilbert Ryle, *Plato's Progress* (London, 1966); Göran Sörbom, *Mimesis and Art: Studies in the Origin and Early Development of an Aesthetic Vocabulary* (Uppsala, 1966); A. E. Taylor, *Plato: The Man and his Work* (London, 1969); Guthrie, *History of Greek Philosophy*, vol. 3; Rosemary Harrison, *Poetry and Criticism before Plato* (London, 1969); G. Vlastos, ed., *Plato II* (Garden City, N.Y., 1971); Whitney J. Oates, *Plato's View of Art* (New York, 1972); Victor G. Menza, "Poetry and the 'Techne' Theory: An Analysis of the *Ion* and the *Republic*, Books III and X," Ph.D. diss. Johns Hopkins University, 1972; Nicholas P. White, *Plato on Knowledge and Reality* (Indianapolis, 1976); Alan F. Blum, *Socrates, the Original and Its Images* (London, 1978); Jean-François Mattéi, *L'étranger et le simulacre: Essai sur la fondation de l'ontologie platonicienne* (Paris, 1983); Stanley Rosen, *Plato's Sophist: The Drama of Original and Image* (New Haven, 1983); Kenneth M. Sayre, *Plato's Late Ontology: A Riddle Resolved* (Princeton, 1983); and Morimichi Kato, *Techne und Philosophie bei Platon* (Frankfurt and New York, 1986). Particularly relevant to my discussion of the *Republic* are Jakob Barion, *Macht und Recht: Eine Platon-Studie* (Krefeld, 1947); N. R. Murphy, *The Interpretation of Plato's Republic*

is challenged by the Sophist Thrasymachus and by his own pupils Glaucon and Adimantus to prove that because right is independent of might, committing injustice leads to misery and behaving justly leads to happiness; more specifically, Socrates is required to firmly relate *aretē*, *agathos*, and *aristos* (the highest terms of praise in the Hellenic system of values) to *dikaiosunē* and *sōphrosunē*, justice and wisdom-moderation. Although Socrates manages if not to persuade, at least to confuse and silence Thrasymachus, he certainly does not fool Glaucon and Adimantus, who are quick to point out that he has in fact tricked the Sophist into conceding defeat (in the verbal contest to which the latter has challenged Socrates) by employing a sophism himself. Socrates has been arguing by opinion (*doxa*) rather than nature (*phusis*), and Adimantus asks him to prove not only that it is more profitable for a man to be just than unjust in the eyes of his fellow-citizens, but also that justice or injustice is inherently good or bad.[5]

Yet for the better part of the dialogue Socrates does precisely what Adimantus asks him not to do. The latter has asked him to define justice in the context of the individual. Socrates circumvents the question by proposing to look at the individual in relation to other individuals, that is, as a social component.[6] For this purpose he constructs a fictional model

(Oxford, 1951); T. L. Thorson, ed., *Plato: Totalitarian or Democrat?* (Englewood Cliffs, N.J., 1963); Karl R. Popper, *The Open Society and Its Enemies*, vol. 1, *The Spell of Plato* (London, 1966); Eric Voeglin, *Plato* (Baton Rouge, 1966); R. C. Croos and A. D. Woozley, *Plato's Republic* (London, 1966); Richard L. Nettleship, *Lectures on the Republic of Plato* (New York, 1968); James Adam's indispensable commentary to his Greek edition of the *Republic*, 2 vols. (London, 1969); Iris Murdoch, *The Fire and the Sun: Why Plato Banished the Artists* (Oxford, 1977); Mary Margaret Mackenzie, *Plato on Punishment* (Berkeley and Los Angeles, 1981); F. J. Pelletier and J. King-Farlow, eds., *New Essays on Plato* (Guelph, Ontario, 1983), esp. Richard B. Parry, "The Craft of Justice," 19–38, and Elizabeth Belfiore, "Plato's Greatest Accusation against Poetry," 39–62; Julius A. Elias, *Plato's Defence of Poetry* (Albany, N.Y., 1984); and Stanley Rosen, *The Quarrel between Philosophy and Poetry: Studies in Ancient Thought* (New York/London, 1988).

5. See Plato, *Republic* 2.367a–c, trans. P. Shorey, in E. Hamilton and H. Cairns, eds., *The Collected Dialogues of Plato* (Princeton, N.J., 1961). I have used in parallel two Greek editions: Adam, *Republic*, and E. Chambry, *Republique*, in Platon, *Oeuvres complètes* (Paris, 1949), vols. 6, 7. Further references are to Shorey's translation, which I have occasionally modified to convey my own sense of a certain passage. Greek citations are from Platon, *Opera*, 5 vols., ed. J. Burnet (Oxford, 1900–1907).

6. For example, in book 7, Socrates says: "The law is not concerned with the special happiness of any class in the state, but is trying to produce this condition in the city as a whole, harmonizing and adapting the citizens to one another by persuasion and compulsion, and requiring them to impart to one another any benefit which they are severally able to bestow upon the community, and . . . it itself creates such men in the

or paradigm, his ideal republic, which then allows him to define justice (not unlike Solon's *eunomia*) as keeping one's assigned place in the social hierarchy. The Socratic ideal republic is ideal, as Adkins observes, only from the point of view of the rulers: "Socrates never admits that he is evaluating sophrosyne and dikaiosyne as aretai from the point of view of the ruling class and so can conveniently assume that he has proved that sophrosyne is the arete of the third class, from the point of view of that class. . . . The trick is exactly similar in the case of dikaiosyne. . . . Sophrosyne is the acknowledgement of the rulers that they should rule, of the defenders that they should defend, and of the rest that they should acquiesce."[7]

As Adimantus shrewdly remarks, moreover, Socrates comes full circle to Thrasymachus' position (that justice is the other man's good or the advantage of the stronger), but quietly and without the Sophist's cynicism. In fact, Thrasymachus' loud advocation of such archaic principles makes it impossible for the rulers effectively to rule in a democracy, and their open affirmation is entirely counterproductive. On the other hand, Socrates' quiet concealment of these principles under the transcendental values of universal good, love, nonviolence, and justice is the ultimate Sophistic political (if not philosophical) move: from Pericles to the modern technocrats, rulers have always found it more convenient to rule in the name of an abstract idea (God, the People, Communism, Freedom, Equality, Justice, and the like) rather than in their own name, as surrogates or representatives rather than as unmediated presences.

With his overman's morality, Thrasymachus rudely strips off the mask of power as representation, which goes hand in hand with the new disguise of the hawk as nightingale.[8] One recalls that Socrates puts on this

---

state, not that it may allow each to take what course pleases him, but with a view to using them for the binding together of the commonwealth" (*Rep.* 7.519e1–520a4). Socrates omits to say, however, that in practice laws are usually made by the ruling class and, consequently, tend to serve its interests. (Of course, this fact also contradicts Thrasymachus' and other Sophists' assertion that laws are instruments of the weak against the strong). Note also the combination of persuasion and compulsion, or rationality and violence, through which Socratic law operates.

7. *Adkins, MR*, 288. Unlike Adkins, however, I believe that Plato's and Socrates' viewpoints ought not to be seen as identical.

8. Even though Thrasymachus enjoys winning a verbal contest as much as Socrates does, it is by no means clear that the doctrine of might makes right is his own belief. For instance, when Socrates asks him whether he is only "mocking" them or telling them his "real opinions about the truth," Thrasymachus replies: "What difference does it make to you . . . whether I believe it or not? Why don't you test the argument?" (*Rep.* 1.349a4–10).

mask, for example, in the *Protagoras*, where he argues against another Sophist, Callicles, that it is better to suffer than to inflict injustice, a totally un-Hellenic attitude, which is nevertheless a useful ideological instrument in maintaining social order. Socrates repeats this argument in the *Republic* as well, for instance when he proves that the shepherds guard the sheep for the latter's benefit, or that in ruling the ruler does not consider his own advantage but that of the one whom he rules (*Rep.* 1.342e). It is almost as if Socrates mimicked the Sophists' own strategy and delighted in making the weaker argument stronger. By presenting both arguments, however, Plato seems to make it possible, at least theoretically, to conceive of a third alternative. The question then would no longer be whether it is "better" to suffer or to inflict injustice, "better" to be a victim or an aggressor, but whether one should not turn away from this dialectic altogether. For this purpose, however, one would have to turn away from the Hellenic mentality of power as a whole, a path that neither Socrates nor, perhaps, Plato himself seems prepared to take.[9]

Far from giving up power, Socrates retains it as an operating principle in his ideal republic at the same time that he deflects its more unsavory, violent aspects outside the confines of this republic (thereby coming back

9. The *Republic* seems to pose more questions than it solves, perhaps because Plato himself does not know the answers to these questions and is honest enough to admit so, by implication. For example, Thrasymachus' accusation that Socrates employs a "petti-fogging" manner of arguing is not entirely unjustified and can again be ascribed to a prevailing agonistic mentality toward which Plato has ambiguous feelings. In this regard, the dialogue between Socrates and Thrasymachus in *Republic* 1.341a–b is highly revealing:

> So then, Thrasymachus, said I [Socrates], my manner of argument seems to you pettifogging?
> It does, he said.
> You think, do you, that it was with malice afterthought and trying to get the better of you unfairly that I asked that question?
> I don't think it, I know it, he said, and you won't make anything by it, for you won't get the better of me by stealth and, failing stealth, you are not of the force to beat me in debate.
> Bless your soul, said I, I wouldn't even attempt such a thing.
> (*Rep.* 1.341a5–b3)

Socrates, however, not only attempts but actually manages to get the better of Thrasymachus by his wily manner of questioning, as Adimantus points out afterwards (6.487b–c). This and other examples show that it would be unwise to identify Plato's views completely with those of his character Socrates. Could it be that Plato, like Adimantus, is another bright Socratic pupil, who, despite his love of his master, is not that easily fooled by him?

full circle to Cephalus' definition of justice as that which benefits friends and harms enemies, *Rep.* 1.334d). This becomes evident in Socrates' notion of the guardian of the state who is supposed to be trained, in the manner of watchdogs, to be friendly and gentle toward his fellow citizens and vicious toward foreigners and outsiders:

> [Socrates:] It may be observed in other animals, but especially in that which we likened to the guardian. You surely have observed in well-bred hounds that their natural [*phusei*] disposition is to be most gentle to their familiars and those whom they recognize, but the contrary to those whom they do not know.
> [Adimantus:] I am aware of that.
> The thing is possible, then, said I [Socrates] and it is not an unnatural requirement that we are looking for in our guardian (*Rep.* 2.375d–e).

The question of poetry arises in the *Republic* precisely with regard to the education of the guardian-watchdog. In the *Ion*, Socrates attacks poetry because of its mimetic nature, in the double sense of ecstatic performance and simulation of other *technai*.[10] He brings up this issue in the *Republic* as well, but now he begins his attack, in books 2 and 3, primarily by emphasizing poetry's (lack of) educational value, indeed its potentially negative, pernicious influence on the very young.

As Aristotle does in the *Poetics*, Socrates discusses poetry first in terms of *dianoia*, its content, and then in terms of its manner and means of presentation (imitation and rhythm). Poetry will first of all affect the guardians through the tales (*logoi*, *muthoi*) they are taught in their infancy, even before they are taught gymnastics, and these tales come mainly from Homeric and Hesiodic epic.[11] Consequently, in order to educate the guardians properly, one must begin by censoring the story-makers, and induce mothers and nurses to tell only those stories that are on the accepted list and "so shape their souls by these stories far rather than their bodies by their hands" (*Rep.* 2.377b11–c4).

10. I discuss these issues at some length in "Plato's *Ion*: Mimesis, Poetry, and Power," in R. Bogue, ed., *Mimesis in Contemporary Theory*, vol. 2, *Mimesis, Semiosis, and Power* (Philadelphia and Amsterdam, 1990), 13–26.
11. For an examination of the various meanings of *muthos* and *logos* in Plato, see Robert Zaslavsky, *Platonic Myth and Platonic Writing* (Washington, D.C., 1981). Zaslavsky concludes that the "assumed separation out of the meanings of *logos* and *muthos* into respectively true account and false account may not be as clearcut as it seems" (220). This conclusion seems to corroborate my thesis that Plato does not distinguish between philosophy and poetry primarily on epistemological criteria. See below, in this section.

When Adimantus wants to know what kind of stories must be censored as false, Socrates mentions the "lies" that Homer, Hesiod, and others tell about the gods; these poets should be particularly censored if they do not lie prettily or beneficially (*kalos pseudētai*, *Rep.* 2.377d9). The ugly or harmful lies turn out to be connected with the violent, unjust, and agonistic nature of the gods in traditional epic. For example, according to Socrates, Hesiod tells improper lies when he recounts what Uranus did to Cronus, or how Cronus in turn took his revenge, to say nothing of the doings and sufferings of Cronus himself at the hands of Zeus. But even if these stories were true, they should not be told to thoughtless young persons. On the contrary, "the best way would be to bury them in silence, and if there were some necessity of relating them, only a very small audience should be admitted under pledge of secrecy" (*Rep.* 2.378a3–5).

When asked about the kind of religious tales that one *should* teach young warriors, Socrates playfully objects that he and Adimantus are "founders of a state and are not required to compose fables" (*Rep.* 2.378e7–379a4). Nevertheless, when pressed further, Socrates presents a nonanthropomorphic picture of the gods that is identical to that of Xenophanes and Parmenides, reflecting logo-rational, philosophical values and rejecting the archaic notion of divinity as an agonistic, violent, and arbitrary play of power (*Rep.* 2.379–81). In sum, children must not be taught that the gods are indifferent perpetrators of good and evil but, rather, that they are the cause of only what is good (*Rep.* 2.380c6–9).

Socrates is, then, fully aware that he, no less than the poets, "composes fables" (his ideal republic itself is little more than a pretty fable, as he himself indirectly suggests).[12] He censors poets not because they tell lies, but because they tell ugly or harmful ones rather than pretty or beneficial. For Socrates philosophy, in contradistinction to (some) poetry, is the discourse that promotes pretty lies for the sake of the community. At the beginning of book 1, he points out to Cephalus that certain lies are "just," and here he repeats and elaborates on this argument. He draws a distinction between a "deception in words" and a "deception in the soul" (*Rep.* 2.382a1–d3). Under certain circumstances, the deception in words is necessary in the case of humans (although not in that of the gods); for

12. For example, in *Rep.* 5.472 Socrates says: "A pattern, then, said I [Socrates], was what we wanted when we were inquiring into the nature of ideal justice and asking what would be the character of the perfectly just man, supposing him to exist. . . . We wished to fix our eyes upon them as types and models. . . . Our purpose was not to demonstrate the possibility of the realization of these ideals" (*Rep.* 5. 472c4–d2). Also compare *Rep.* 3.414b1–415c7 and 7.511b3–c2, which I examine below.

example, it is serviceable in defeating an enemy or in averting an evil done by a friend who has lost his senses, in which case the lie is useful (*pseudos chrēsimon*) and becomes a "medicine" (*Rep.* 2.382c6–10). Since it is a medicine or a drug (*pharmakon*), it is also a poison, and therefore it has to be strictly controlled or regulated. This is precisely the function of the rulers:

> The rulers then of the city may, if anybody, fitly lie on account of enemies or citizens for the benefit of the state; no others [including the guardians] may have anything to do with it. But for a layman to lie to rulers of that kind we shall affirm to be as great a sin, nay a greater, than it is for a patient not to tell his physician or an athlete his trainer the truth about his bodily condition, or for a man to deceive the pilot about the ship and the sailors as to the real condition of himself or a fellow sailor, or how they fare (*Rep.* 3.389b7–c6).

It is because Socrates is fully aware of the dangers of lying, be it only in the interest of the good, that he will later require that rulers be appointed only from among philosophers, who will then become philosophers-kings. And it is also because of this awareness that he requires that poetry be placed under the strict surveillance of a philosophy-queen. Thereby Socrates provides "good" (logo-rational) reasons not only for expelling poetry from his ideal state, but also for replacing it with philosophy as the guiding, authoritative discourse of this state.

Socrates' distinction between a pretty or good (*kalos*) lie and an ugly or bad (*kakos*) one is based on Xenophanes' *as if* approach to knowledge and truth, and is in turn a beautiful fiction or a form of aesthetic play. For example, speaking of the permissible, pretty lie, Socrates observes: "Owing to our ignorance of the truth about antiquity, we liken the false to the true as far as we may and so make it edifying" (*Rep.* 2.382d1–3). Because humans cannot know and, therefore, cannot speak the truth, they can do the next best thing: they can attribute this ability to the gods and then attempt to act *as if* it were given to human beings as well. Even though, as Socrates says, "there is no lying poet in God" (*Rep.* 2.382d9), our representations of divinity are, apparently, products of a poetic lie. For him, there are good fictions, which are of value in helping rulers govern the community, and bad fictions, which are useless or even counterproductive in carrying out the (good) rulers' goals of creating a harmonious and orderly state. In turn, what Socrates calls good fictions are the median values that are generally supported by philosophy, and what he calls bad fictions are the archaic values that are mostly promoted, in his view, by poetry.[13]

Poetry, in its uncensored form, can negatively affect the soul of the future guardians not only through its content or tales (*logoi, mythoi*), but also through its diction (*lexis*) or its manner of presentation, and here again, Socrates argues, one must carefully sift the good from the bad. It is at this point that Socrates introduces the notion of *mimēsis*, which, to begin with, he seems to use as a technical, poetic term. He draws a distinction between narrative and dramatic form, between *diēgēsis* and *mimēsis*, arguing that in the first case the poet speaks in his own name and that in the second case he "hides" behind his characters, assuming their voice. According to Socrates, *mimēsis*, in this sense, is "likening oneself to another in speech [*lexin*] or bodily bearing" (*Rep.* 3.393c1–3). Here, therefore, Socrates partially retains the archaic meaning of *mimēsis* as "miming" or "impersonation," albeit in the modified, logo-rational form of "dissimulation" (thus stripped of its magical powers, because the poet no longer assumes the god's voice or speaks through it). It is also this modified form that allows Socrates to condemn it as a protean activity devoid of any definite *technē* at the same time that it irresponsibly dabbles in all *technai* (compare the *Ion*, in which Socrates condemns poetic activity in general on the same grounds, but without mentioning the term *mimēsis*).

Mimesis is far from being all bad, however, and Socrates leaves the avenue open for the philosophical, logo-rational interpretation of the term, later in the dialogue, as good mimesis of the eternal Forms. When he states that "we must reach a decision whether we are to suffer our poets to narrate as imitators or in part as imitators and in part not," Adimantus hazards a guess that what his mentor actually means is deciding whether one should suffer tragedy and comedy to remain in the ideal state, but Socrates replies evasively: "Perhaps . . . and perhaps even more than that. For I certainly do not know yet myself, but whithersoever the wind, as it were, of the argument blows, there lies our course" (*Rep.*

13. The political dangers of this philosophical position have been repeatedly pointed out. See, for example, Popper, *The Open Society and Its Enemies.* Popper, however, presents Plato from a modern point of view and therefore misreads the Platonic historical moment, which marks the (temporary) victory of median over archaic values. On the other hand, Popper does to Plato exactly what Socrates does to Homer: in order to keep power-oriented values going (in Popper's case, a certain brand of critical rationalism), one must isolate and sacrifice at least some of these values. For the debate around Popper's book see especially R. Bambrough, ed., *Plato, Popper, and Politics: Some Contributions to a Modern Controversy* (New York, 1967).

3.394d7–9). So when Socrates goes on to ask whether "we wish our guardians to be good mimics or not," the answer is both yes and no: yes, if they mimic good and honorable persons and actions; no, if they mimic bad and shameful ones. This ambiguity comes from the fact that mimicry does not have a nature (*phusis*) of its own but, like Dionysus, it takes on all shapes and forms. It will thus allow Socrates not only to condemn dramatic poetry as bad mimesis, connected with appearance and simulacrum, but also to commend philosophy as a good mimesis of the ideal Forms, directly related to Xenophanes' *as if* approach to knowledge: one must pretend or simulate access to that which remains inaccessible (transcendental Being).

From the imitation, moreover, the imitator may "imbibe the reality": "Or have you not observed that imitations, if continued from youth far into life, settle down into habits and second nature in the body, the speech and the thought?" (*Rep.* 3.395d1–3). The young warriors ought not to mimic those of an inferior status, such as women and slaves, nor bad and cowardly men, nor madmen (*Rep.* 3.395d5–396a6). But here Socrates leaves one more way open to the imitator, because the imitation can be done either "seriously" (*spoudē*) or "playfully" (*paidias charin*, *Rep.* 3.396d3–e2). He therefore opposes play to seriousness and he does not seem, at least at first sight, to ascribe greater value to one over the other explicitly, as he will do in book 10. On principle, Socrates ought to discourage all mimicry of bad character and action, whether performed in earnest or in jest, because of the contagious nature of mimicry as such. Apparently, however, he approves of playful mimicry of this kind and thus opens a way for much poetry to sneak back into his republic, because it is only in jest that some poetry mimics bad or reprehensible action and character (this is the argument that has been employed, ever since Plato, by the apologists of comedy: *ridendo castigat mores*).

Socrates must nevertheless be aware of the fact (even though he omits mentioning it) that comic or satirical mimicry is by its very nature too slippery to aid his educational goals effectively; for if it can be directed against objectionable actions, it may equally well be directed against good actions and characters, casting them in a flippant, questionable light (consider Socrates' own unflattering portrait in Aristophanes' comedies). Hence, in book 3 no less than in book 10, Socrates *must* subordinate play to seriousness after all and he does not fail to do so, for example when he stipulates that the poetry allowed in his *Politeia* should consist mostly of diegesis, with very little mimesis mixed therein. He admits that the evenly "mixed type" is the most pleasing, but he recommends its avoidance on the ground that it is also the most exposed to the dangers of mimicry, which he again condemns for its protean nature, devoid of *technē*:

> If a man, then, it seems, who was capable by his cunning of assuming every kind of shape and imitating all things [*mimeisthai panta chrē-mata*] should arrive in our city, bringing with himself the poems which he wished to exhibit, we should fall down and worship him as a holy and wondrous and delightful creature . . . [yet] we should send him away to another city . . . [and] we ourselves, for our souls' good, should continue to employ the more austere and less delightful poet and taleteller, who would imitate the diction of the good man and would tell his tale in the patterns which we prescribed in the beginning, when we set out to educate our soldiers. (*Rep.* 3.398a1–b3)

In this quotation, then, the "delightful" kind of poetry, that is, poetry as mimesis-play (in the sense of both an enhancement of the feeling of power and impersonation or mimicry), is condemned as a luxury that has no place in a healthy, simple city. The many-rused poets, skilled in all sorts of delightful impersonations, should be covered with laurels but taken beyond the precincts of this city, and the education of the citizens should be turned over to the more austere and less playful poets, who would employ simple and straightforward mimesis of good character and action.

Socrates again takes up the idea of playful (mimetic as opposed to diegetic) poetry as a dispensable luxury when he discusses the kinds of rhythms (*ruthmoi*) to be allowed in his ideal state. He starts from the logo-rational premise that "rhythm and harmony follow the words and not the words these" (*Rep.* 3.400d1–4), a premise that is hardly shared by the archaic singers of tales (if we are to believe Milman Parry's theory of formulaic oral poetry). This premise equally allows Socrates to postulate that "seemliness and unseemliness are attendant upon the good rhythm and bad" (*Rep.* 3.400d11–e3), and he predictably defines the good rhythm as the one that best suggests brave and temperate character and action (*Rep.* 3.399a5–c4). In turn, the best presentation of the latter is achieved through the simple or monotonous rhythm rather than the mixed or varied one, just as in the case of the *logoi* diegesis is preferable to mimesis because of its simplicity. Correspondingly, the simple musical instruments are preferable to the many-stringed or polyharmonic ones. In this manner, Socrates rightly says, "we have all unawares purged our city which a little while ago we said was luxurious" (*Rep.* 3.399e5–6).

Socrates thereby harks back to book 2, where he favors the simpler city over the more complex one because excessive wealth, no less than its inevitable counterpart, excessive poverty, contributes to the ruin of the just city. This is the old, Delphic wisdom of "everything in moderation," and it seems quite natural for the son of a stonemason to promote median values and condemn aristocratic excess. Socrates' educational program is obviously aimed at inculcating median values into the Athenian aristocracy (values that are, one might add, profoundly incompatible with it). Like many an ancient and modern conservative, Socrates does not want to do away with the aristocracy, but simply make it a little more like the middle class, so that it will become more accessible to the latter.[14] If the basic principle of founding a state is "our needs," (*ep' allou chreiai*, literally "for the service of the other," *Rep.* 2.369c1–4; an obviously median notion), then poetry is, like all aristocratic play, a luxury. This luxury is characteristic of a "fevered state," and one must severely curtail or completely dispense with it, if one wishes to build a just or "healthy" state.[15]

In book 10, Socrates returns to poetry and poets (after occasional critical references to them in other books) in order to give them the coup de grace. In the preceding books he prepares the way for the philosopher-king as a new type of political and spiritual leader who bases his authority on knowledge and truth, arrived at through dialectic rather than through eristic. For Socrates, dialectic is the philosopher's master *technē*, with the aid of which median morality and civic virtue (*aretē*) in the sense of moderation (*sōphrosunē*) can be taught. Through dialectic, the philosopher discerns the various parts of the soul and their order of rank, which parallels the proper social hierarchy in a healthy, well-organized polity. It

14. Note that Socrates divides his ideal society into three classes and opens the ruling class to the other two: membership to the former does not depend on birth but on merit or virtue (*aretē*), which is, however, redefined in the median terms of *sōphrosunē*. In other words, Socrates' aristocracy becomes a meritocracy.

15. Throughout the dialogue Socrates employs an analogy between the physical body and the body politic that is strongly reminiscent of Presocratic medicine. In addition, he attempts to develop a medical science of the soul, on which, according to him, the welfare of the two bodies equally depends. The philosopher-king is also a physician, whose doctrine of being and immortality of the soul replaces that of *phusis* as ceaseless physical Becoming, which is held by his Presocratic counterpart; whereas the Presocratic doctor sees *isonomia* (in the sense of a continuous adjustment of the balance among agonistic forces) as a condition of physical health, the Socratic doctor sees *harmonia* (in the sense of a hierarchical ordering of the physical parts of the soul under its immaterial, logo-rational part) as a healthy condition of both body and soul.

is also dialectic that allows its practitioner to overcome Becoming by fixing his eyes on Being, to sift reality or truth from the play of semblances or appearance. Because, for Socrates, the mimetic poet deals in appearances par excellence and therefore cannot have any claim to real knowledge, he must naturally be replaced by the philosopher-king as a moral and political leader in the ideal republic.

At the beginning of book 10, Socrates observes to Glaucon that their examination of the various parts of the soul and the conditions under which a particular soul attains inner concord or harmony has again revealed the wisdom of their previous decision of banishing the mimetic poets from the model state (Rep. 10.595a). Because this statement sounds rather cryptic, having the appearance of a paradox (Glaucon asks Socrates what he means by it), Socrates undertakes to explain it in a roundabout way. He begins by relating mimesis to his newly developed theory of Forms. Whereas in book 3, he sees mimesis mainly as "impersonation" or "mimicry," applying it to poets as counterfeiters of character, here he sees it, at least in the first part of his demonstration, mainly as "copying" or "duplicating," applying it to painters as counterfeiters of real objects. He attempts to define mimesis in relation to production and craftsmanship, that is, in relation to technē. Employing the well-known example of the couch as artifact, Socrates distinguishes between two kinds of legitimate maker (poiētēs, dēmiourgos) of this artifact: god and the carpenter. The painter, on the other hand, is not a creator or producer but, rather, a mimētēs, an imitator or, more properly, a duplicator or counterfeiter of the couch:

> [Socrates]: Shall we also say that the painter is the creator and maker [dēmiourgon kai poiētēn] of that sort of thing?
> [Glaucon]: By no means.
> [Socrates]: What will you say he is in relation to the couch?
> This, said he [Glaucon] seems to me the most reasonable designation of him, that he is the imitator [mimētēs, duplicator] of the thing which those others produce.
> Very good, said I [Socrates]. The producer of the product removed from nature [apo tēs phuseōs] by three degrees you call the imitator?
> [Glaucon]: By all means.
> (Rep. 10.597d11–e5)

Socrates then immediately substitutes, through a paralogism, the dramatic poet for the painter in his demonstration: "This, then, will apply to the maker of tragedies also, if he is an imitator and is by nature third in rank after the king and truth [*apo basileōs kai tēs alētheias*], as are all other imitators" (*Rep.* 10.597e6–8).[16]

Critics have pointed out that Socrates' comparison between the painter and the poet is inadequate even by his own standards: the dramatic poet presumably "imitates" persons, whereas the painter "imitates" objects, one impersonates voice, the other conjures up visual resemblances. Although this criticism is certainly justified, one must keep in mind that Socrates can apply his definition of mimesis to both, because he preserves the archaic meaning of *mimeisthai* at the same time that he interprets this meaning negatively: both the poet and the painter mime or conjure up persons or objects with the intention to deceive. They carry out their deception by laying hold of "only a small part of the object [or person], that part which is a phantom [i.e., appearance]" (*Rep.* 10.598b1–2). In this respect, the painter (and, by extension, the dramatic poet) duplicates or simulates the work of the craftsman, rather than that of the divine demiurge, "appearance as it appears," rather than "reality as it is" (*Rep.* 10.598b).

The painter no less than the poet can also duplicate, or present the semblance of, persons. He can, for example, paint a craftsman at work, without really understanding anything of the nature of his craft. Again, the skill of his art consists in an uncanny ability to deceive, to present only the semblance of reality: "For example, a painter, we say, will paint us a cobbler, a carpenter, and other craftsmen, though he himself has no expertness in any of these arts, but nevertheless if he were a good painter,

16. Here I should like to depart from the traditional translation of *mimēsis* as "imitation," proposing "simulation" instead. "Simulation" has the advantage of both preserving, to some extent, the archaic meaning of *mimēsis* (that is, bringing something forth through miming, assuming the shape of a person or object in order to master it or deceive others) and conveying the new, logo-rational meaning (that is, replicating or duplicating something). "Simulation," then, partly covers both mimesis-play and mimesis-imitation, although it does lose the connection between mimesis-play and the ecstatic enhancement of the feeling of power—a loss that is deliberately brought about by Socrates himself. "Simulation" also conveys the ethical polarization present in Socratic mimesis: dissimulation when used in relation to poetry, and an *as if* mode of behavior and/or cognition when used in relation to philosophy (the latter sense is preserved to this day in such terms as "computer simulation," in game theory and elsewhere). The translation of *mimēsis* by "simulation" also eliminates the apparent contradiction between Socrates' use of the term in book 3, where he understands by it mostly impersonation, or miming of character, and his use of it in book 10, where he associates it with the duplication of an "object," giving it a visual or pictorial sense. But whether the translation of *mimēsis* as "simulation" is accepted or not, it must at all times be remembered that the Greek term retains its archaic, dynamic, or performative aspect in Plato as well.

by exhibiting at a distance his picture of a carpenter he would deceive children and foolish men, and make them believe it to be a real carpenter" (Rep. 10.598b8–c4).

In this passage, Socrates picks up the *technē* argument that he uses against poetry in book 3 of the *Republic*, as well as in the *Ion*, now directing it against both painters and poets. These artists are confidence men who make believe that they know everything, when in reality they know nothing. But they can fool only children and simpletons, who cannot "distinguish knowledge, ignorance, and imitation [*mimēsis*, simulation]" (Rep. 10.598d4–5). At this juncture, Socrates tacitly reintroduces the figure of the philosopher in the background of his discussion, as the implicit ideal of a wise man, in contrast to the spurious pretender to knowledge that is the poet. It is in the name of the philosopher that Socrates takes up again his critique of tragedy and "its leader Homer." He proposes to (re)examine the assertions of "some people" (presumably the Sophists and other apologists of poetry) that the poets "know all the arts and all things human pertaining to virtue and vice, and all things divine" (Rep. 10.598d6–e2). This is precisely the domain of expertise claimed by Socrates for his newly created discipline, philosophy, and its establishment presupposes, in a first phase, the elimination of similar claims (real or imagined) on the part of a rival field, such as poetry.

Socrates first argues that because the poet can only produce appearance rather than reality, there is no good reason to honor him at all. For if a man "were able to produce both the exemplar and the semblance," would he "be eager to abandon himself to the fashioning of phantoms and set this in the forefront of his life as the best thing he had? . . . If [the poet] had genuine knowledge of the things he imitates [*mimeitai*, simulates] he would far rather devote himself to real things than to the imitation [simulation] of them, and would endeavor to leave after him many noble deeds and works as memorials of himself, and would be more eager to be the theme of praise than the praiser" (Rep. 10.599a6–b7). Here Socrates employs the archaic notion of *timē*, which he combines with the logo-rational notion of the useful, *ophelia*, as Glaucon himself indicates (Rep. 10.599b8). As in Hesiod's *Theogony*, the function of the poet is to praise the *basileus*, and therefore he should not be honored simply because he enhances the honor (*timē*) of those he sings about. Now one can also better understand Socrates' rather cryptic statement in *Rep.* 10.597e6–8 that poetry comes third in rank not only after the truth but also after the *basileus*: when Socrates says that poetry only simulates reality or Being, what he in effect says is that it only simulates, and therefore is only a pale shadow of, power.

That Plato equates Being or reality with power is clear not only from the fact that in the *Republic* Socrates defines *technē* as *dunamis* (*Rep.* 1.346a1–3), as what somebody can do, but also, for instance, from the Stranger's definition of reality in the *Sophist*. *To on* (a thing that is), which is usually translated as "being" or "the real" (according to Cornford), is explicitly defined by the Stranger as power: "I suggest that anything has real being [*to kai hopoianoun*] that is so constituted as to possess any sort of power either to affect anything else or to be affected, in however small a degree, by the most insignificant agent, though it be only once. I am proposing as a mark to distinguish real things [*ta onta*] that they are nothing but power."[17] The Stranger, moreover, defines production as "any power that can bring into existence what did not exist before" (*Soph.* 265b9–10). In turn, he traces this productive or engendering power back to divinity as the supreme demiourgos (*Soph.* 265c1–5), thus reinforcing Socrates' definition of *technē* in the *Republic*. Consequently, Socrates' argument in the *Republic* that the poets simulate real persons and objects rather than create them (which parallels the similar argument offered by the Stranger in regard to the sophist in the *Sophist*), has less an ontological than a political import, separating mimetic poetry from power and authority in the state.[18]

The *technē* argument that follows has a similar political import and serves to separate the poets from such men of power as Lycurgus, Charondas, and Solon, who, unlike Homer (or Ion), do not simulate, but actually possess the art of government (*Rep.* 10.599b9–e4). Homer is found lacking even when compared to men "wise in practical affairs," and according to Socrates, no "ingenious inventions for the arts and business of life" are reported of Homer as they are, say, of Thales and Anacharsis (*Rep.* 10. 600a1–7). As to Homer's ability to create a following because of

17. Plato, *The Sophist*, 247d6–e3, trans. F. M. Cornford, in Hamilton and Cairns, *The Collected Dialogues of Plato*. The poets have throughout the ages attempted to challenge Socrates' argument that they lack effective power, for example in the well-known topos of *exegi monumentum* in the Latin poets and in the Renaissance sonnet or, later on, in Shelley's defiant statement that the poets, not the philosophers, are the true, if unacknowledged, legislators of mankind.

18. In this light, to say that "the quarrel between the poet and the philosopher is the deep end of the quarrel between the poet and the moralist" (Wimsatt and Brooks, *Literary Criticism*, 10) is to blur the issue. What is primarily at stake in this agon is not morality but something that in fact determines the nature of it: authority or power.

his educational virtues, he again falls short not only of Pythagoras but also of such Sophists as Protagoras and Prodicus (*Rep.* 10.600a10–e3).

Next Socrates attempts to explain why some of his contemporaries (including himself) can nevertheless fall under the spell of the poets, and he concludes, as he does in the *Ion*, that their power resides in their words (rather than in their deeds), indeed not in the meaning of these words, but in the way they arrange them, according to rhythm, meter, and harmony. So "mighty is the spell that these adornments naturally exercise," that they make one forget that they simply serve to cover up a lack of essence, just as the bloom of youth serves to conceal the lack of genuine beauty in certain adolescent faces. Socrates draws a logo-rational distinction between verbal form and content, associating form with appearance and content with reality and thereby again demonstrating that poetry is nothing but a pleasurable play of appearances, devoid of any true knowledge (*Rep.* 10.601a–c). Stripped of its "adornments," poetry is also stripped of its power—one recalls that Socrates does not allow Ion to recite Homer, in other words he does not allow the rhapsode to cast his mimetic spell or exert his power over him. In this light, Socrates' little rhetorical exercise of retelling "without meter, for I am not a poet" the beginning of the *Iliad* (*Rep.* 3.393e11–394b1) is far from gratuitous: by transforming poetry into prose, Socrates attempts to show not only how one can easily dispense with an excessive and therefore dangerous luxury, but also how one can dispel its quasi-magical power.

But why does Socrates insist on the dangerous nature of mimetic poetry as a play of appearances? And why does he go to such lengths in proving that the mimetic poets lack any power-knowledge and therefore have no place in a tightly organized community? After all he may discard epic and tragic poetry, in the manner that he has discarded it in the *Ion*, as a form of harmless play, not to be taken seriously, and indeed, this is what his argumentative strategy appears to be throughout book 10. For example, in *Rep.* 602b, it turns out that the poets mime or simulate persons and objects not so much in order to deceive (although they can lead fools and children astray) as to delight their audiences; in other words, they are motivated by play. In the mimetic poet's case, moreover, play cannot have anything to do with knowledge. Because the poet as *mimētēs* takes orders from neither the user nor the maker of artifacts, he "knows nothing worth mentioning of the things he imitates," remaining ignorant of the goodness and badness of his images. The poet presents "the thing that appears beautiful [*kalos*, also good] to the ignorant multitude," only to please them, not to instruct them. Consequently, his mimesis is a "form of play, not to be taken seriously, and . . . those who attempt tragic poetry, whether in iambics or heroic verse, are all altogether imitators [simulators]" (*Rep.* 10.602b1–10).[19] Glaucon himself understands the ironic, somewhat condescending spirit of the Socratic critique of poets and poetry, and he cracks a joke of his own at the expense of Homer's only known disciple and, perhaps, kinsman, Creophylus, punning on the latter's name ("friend [or member of the tribe] of the flesh," *Rep.* 10.600b6–c1).

Glaucon's pun is quite revealing, however, because Socrates does take mimetic art seriously and attacks the archaic poets precisely because they are "friends of the flesh," appealing to the senses, rather than to the intellect. Glaucon's pun suggests a possible answer to the questions raised in the previous paragraph, and it is highly significant that after Socrates dismisses poetry as mimetic play, as a sort of "witchcraft and jugglery" (*Rep.* 10.602c10–d4), he comes back to it once more, this time examining it in terms of the division of the soul that he has established in book 9 and elsewhere. His conclusion is, not unexpectedly, that poetry appeals to the "inferior," rather than to the "nobly serious" part of the soul (*Rep.* 10.603b9–c2). This inferior part is the one that is connected to the slippery world of the senses, being prone to excessive emotion and thus becoming involved in division and strife (*en tais praxesi stasiazei te kai machetai*; *Rep.* 10.603c10–d8). Defining mimetic poetry as a simulation of compulsory or voluntary human action that results in either grief or joy (compare Aristotle's definition of drama in the *Poetics*), Socrates argues that it encourages, for example in the face of calamity, intemperate feelings, rather than the solace of reason. The theater appeals to the "irrational and idle part [*alogiston . . . kai argon*] of us" (*Rep.* 10.604d9–10), hindering the soul from properly playing the game of life: "to deliberate . . . about what has happened to us, and, as it were in the fall of the dice, to determine the movements of our affairs with reference to the numbers that turn up, in the way that reason [*ho logos*] indicates it would be best" (*Rep.* 10.604c5–7).[20] As in the *Ion*, Socrates accuses poetry of jeopardizing reason-moderation

19. This passage clearly establishes the link between poetry and play at the same time that it severs the link between poetry as play and power in Western thought. For further discussion of this point, see the last section of this chapter.
20. This passage could be seen as a protoformulation of what contemporary mathematicians call "game theory," which can be described as a rational attempt to deal with the interplay of necessity and chance in human affairs, being generally directed toward attenuating the effects of chance in these affairs. For a detailed examination of this theory, see Spariosu, *Dionysus Reborn*, pt. 2, secs. 1 and 2.

by pandering to the pleasures of the senses, which is equivalent to pandering to the taste of the ignorant multitude. Rather than "stumbling like children . . . and wasting the time in wailing," as the theater encourages the soul of both the community and the individual to do, the nobler, logo-rational part of this soul must take over and master its lower counterpart, "banish[ing] threnody by therapy" (*Rep.* 10.604c7–d2).

Socrates seems, then, to indict mimetic poetry because it promotes archaic thought (which he calls the "irrational," *alogiston*). He feels justified in not admitting the mimetic poet in a "well-ordered state, because he stimulates and fosters this [irrational] element in the soul, and by strengthening it tends to destroy the rational part." Just as a thought-less community puts bad or tyrannical men in power with ruinous consequences for all, so the mimetic poet "sets up in each individual soul a vicious constitution by fashioning phantoms far removed from reality, and by currying favor with the senseless element that cannot distinguish the greater from the less, but calls the same thing now one, now the other" (*Rep.* 10.605a8–c3).[21] The effect of mimetic poetry is all the more insidious because it allows the spectator to enjoy vicariously, through mimetic identification or participation (*methexis*), the spectacle of some-body else's excessive feelings without fear of incurring shame himself, that is, with neither external nor inner restraint.[22] Finally, mimetic poetry insidiously plays on the feelings of pleasure and pain, that is, on the feeling of power. It abets and nourishes "the emotions of sex and anger, and all the appetites and pains and pleasures of the soul . . . when what we ought to do is to dry them up, and it establishes them as our rulers when they ought to be ruled, to the end that we may be better and happier men instead of worse and more miserable" (*Rep.* 10.606d1–7). And therewith Socrates seemingly completes his critique of poetry as mimesis-play directly linked with archaic, immediate power.

But even after he dismisses mimetic poetry from his ideal polity, Socrates continues to justify himself, confessing that, for his part, he is

21. For Socrates the definition of the tyrannical man (including the political tyrant) is very similar to that of a singer of tales. In book 9, for example, Socrates says: "Then a man becomes tyrannical in the full sense of the word . . . when either by nature or by habits or by both he has become even as the drunken, the erotic, the maniacal" (*Rep.* 9.573c7–9); in other words, when he has become intoxicated by power. The singer of tales may in this respect be doubly guilty, because he transmits this drunkenness to others.

22. Here one can discern the origins of Freud's theory of art as play in the "Creative Writer and Day-Dreaming." For an examination of this theory, see Spariosu, *Dionysus Reborn*, pt. 2, sec. 1.2.

well aware of her spell and that he has always loved her. Yet "reason constrained" him to expel her because "there is from old a quarrel [*diaphora*, dispute] between philosophy and poetry" (*Rep.* 10.607b5–6). This "quarrel," it appears, is really a contest (*agōn*), being in turn part of a greater competition: "Yes, for great is the struggle [*agōn*, competition], I [Socrates] said, dear Glaucon, a far greater contest than we think it, that determines whether a man prove good or bad, so that not the lure of honor or wealth or any office, no, nor of poetry either, should incite us to be careless of righteousness and all excellence" (*Rep.* 608b3–8).

Socrates reminds his audience that he has never given up his contest with Thrasymachus, and that the contest between philosophy and poetry is inextricably linked to this original agon between the philosopher and the Sophist. But Socrates' claim that there is an ancient quarrel between philosophy and poetry is hard to document before his time. What is much easier to document, however, is philosophy's quarrel with poetry, its repeated attacks on the archaic poets, of which Socrates' is the latest and the most extensive. Then why would Socrates appeal to the ancestry of this dispute?

One answer can be found in Socrates' general strategy of substitution in the *Republic*. He conceals the fact that he substitutes philosophy for poetry as the authoritative discourse in the state by implying that both of them are ancient *logoi*, having always played the neatly distinguishable roles that he assigns them in his argument.[23] Socrates seeks to install philosophy as cultural authority not only in terms of its claims to knowledge and truth, but also in terms of primogeniture. He transforms his logical principle of origin and derivation (according to which poetry, insofar as it is a bad mimesis of Being, is subordinated to philosophy, the true science of Being) into a historical principle as well. Socrates has used the same strategy in book 8 in regard to his ideal state, which undergoes a similar process of historicization: this ideal state suddenly turns out to be a traditional form of rule, an "aristocracy or the government of the best" (*Rep.* 8.544e7–8), superior to all the other traditional forms (timocracy, oligarchy, democracy, and tyranny). Employing the mythical analogy of the four ages of mankind (golden, silver, brass, and iron), Socrates presents his constitutional forms as deriving from each other, in regressive

23. We have seen that "philosophy" in its Socratic sense of the science of Being comes into existence only with certain Presocratics (Pythagoras, Xenophanes, Parmenides) and therefore cannot claim the ancestry of Homeric or Hesiodic poetry. Moreover, despite Socrates' arguments to the contrary, poetry itself, including epic and tragedy, substantially contributes to the development of median values in ancient Greece.

order, not only logically but also historically. In this sense, it can be argued that he uses the fictional construct of his ideal polity to purge the aristocratic constitution of the poet-king and replace him with the philosopher-king, thereby disguising the violent origins of this constitution. After he effects this purification (*katharsis*), Socrates reintroduces his model into history as the original, unadulterated form of constitution from which all the other forms have derived or, rather, regressed.[24]

Socrates' alleged love of Homer and the tragic poets also points to a scapegoat-like mechanism of substitution. After he confesses his love for poetry, Socrates goes on to argue that this love is harmful and therefore needs to be suppressed: one must refrain from "slipping back into the childish loves of the multitude, for we have come to see that we must not take such poetry seriously as a serious thing that lays hold on truth [and Being], but that he who lends an ear to it must be on his guard fearing for the polity in himself [*tēs en autōi politeias*]" (*Rep.* 10.608a). At the same time, however, one's love of poetry can find a proper substitute in philosophy and the words *philosophia* and *philosophos* themselves point to this substitution, in which the aggressor assumes, as it were, the identity of his victim. In the late sixth century B.C., *sophos* and *sophia* describe the attributes of the singer of tales, meaning something like "skill of speech" and "skill of mind." It follows that *philosophia* is properly "love of poetic wisdom," while a *philosophos* is properly a "lover of poets," and indeed Socrates professes to be such a lover. But he transfers the skill of speech and the skill of mind from the poet to the philosopher and turns poetic *technē* into an abstract or scientific one.[25] Socrates' double move of usurping and then scapegoating poetry leads not only to the birth of literature (as a bad simulation of Being and, as such, the false discourse of appearance or Becoming), but also to the birth of philosophy (as the legitimate discourse of Being).

Finally, through the poets Socrates challenges not only the Sophists but also the *phusikoi*, who equally subscribe to a philosophy of Becoming rather than one of Being. For example, at the end of book 5 and the beginning of book 6, Socrates draws a distinction between *philosophous* and *philodoxous* (*Rep.* 480a11–12), with the first fruitfully pursuing the science of Being and the second vainly pursuing the nescience of Becoming; a

24. Hence, in a certain sense, the *Politeia* is literally philosophy's *Odyssey*, if the latter is seen as Odysseus' final substitution of the world of the nightingale for the world of the hawk. See the concluding remarks to my discussion of the *Republic* in the last section of this chapter.

25. Compare Havelock, *Preface to Plato*, chap. 15, "The Supreme Music Is Philosophy."

little later, Socrates notes that "we must accept as agreed this trait of the philosophical nature, that it is ever enamored of the kind of knowledge which reveals to them something of that essence which is eternal, and is not wondering between the two poles of generation and decay" (*Rep.* 6.485a10–b3). It is also the philosopher rather than the doxophile who should be placed at the helm of the ideal polity, and Socrates asks Glaucon a question the answer of which we know by now in advance: "Since the philosophers are those who are capable of apprehending that which is eternal and unchanging, while those who are incapable of this, but lose themselves and wonder amid the multiplicities of multifarious things, are not philosophers, which of the two kinds ought to be leaders in a state?" (*Rep.* 6.484b2–7).

The poet, therefore, is also a doxophile, and is attacked precisely because he seems to favor, no less than the Presocratic *phusikoi* and some of the Sophists, the pseudoscience of Becoming, the slippery and uncertain world of appearance and the senses, where everything is in flux, where only the arbitrary, ceaseless play of physical forces reigns supreme, and where all knowledge and truth are relative. Socrates' quarrel, then, turns out to be a family quarrel as well, in which poetry serves again as a scapegoat.

Once Socrates gains the victory in his self-proclaimed contest with poetry, he shows himself magnanimous, allowing the possibility of the exile's return. But his conditions for this return clearly spell out the subordinate role that poetry must henceforth play in relation to philosophy as the science of Being. Poetry must find advocates "who are not poets but *lovers of poetry* [my emphasis] to plead her cause in prose without meter, and show that she is not only delightful but beneficial to orderly government and all the life of man. And we shall listen benevolently, for it will be clear gain for us if it can be shown that she bestows not only pleasure but benefit" (*Rep.* 10.607d6–e2). As in the *Ion* (532e–533c), Socrates alludes to the new profession of literary critic—a "lover of poetry" who under the direct supervision of (logo-rational) philosophy will establish, in prose and without meter, the guidelines for useful and serious literary production, rejecting the harmful kind as wasteful, childish play, not to be taken seriously.

■ *Excursus: Philosophy, Poetry, and Orality in the* Phaedrus

The Socratic substitution of philosophy for poetry in the *Republic* can also be seen as marking a shift from a predominantly oral to a predominantly literate culture in some Greek *poleis*, notably Athens. Yet one may misread the nature of the Socratic historical moment if one ignores the mentality of power underlying both orality and literacy. In predominantly literate cultures, power still determines all that is, but it no longer presents itself in unmediated, raw forms; rather, it disguises itself as "lost origin" and becomes transcendental. Consequently, the written remains dependent on the oral for its legitimation, precisely because the oral is a mode of manifestation of unmediated presence or power. Socrates is thus confronted with a problem in his contest with the poets: poetry is the oral par excellence, and if it is to be replaced by philosophy (which is abstract thinking and, therefore, the fictional and the literate par excellence) as cultural authority, then it must somehow be severed from orality, that is, from its main source of power. Socrates partly solves this problem in the *Republic* by turning poetry into "literature" (shifting its focus from utterance, rhythm, and meter to abstract thought or *dianoia*). But then he still has to establish philosophy's link to the oral or, even better, to legitimize it as the true orality. It is precisely this task that he attempts to accomplish in the last section of the *Phaedrus*, to which I shall briefly turn.[26]

In the *Phaedrus*, no less than in the *Republic*, Socrates opposes the *technē* of dialectic to the pseudo-*technai* of rhetoric and poetry. In this earlier dialogue, however, he not only elaborates the opposition between philosophy and rhetoric-poetry in terms of truth-saying versus truth-feigning, but also identifies dialectic with (live) speech and rhetoric-poetry with (dead) writing. Socrates accomplishes his task by establishing a link between myth and writing as opposed to philosophy-science, which he regards as the only possessor of true (self-)knowledge. But he establishes this link through one of his own logo-rational tales (compare the myth of Er at the end of book 10 of the *Republic*), thus revealing the essential complicity between philosophy-science and myth.

The myth that Socrates invents about the birth of writing is based on the Egyptian legend of Toth, who in the Socratic version becomes the

26. The studies looming in the background of the present excursus are Havelock's *Preface to Plato* and Jacques Derrida's "La pharmacie de Platon," in *La dissémination* (Paris, 1972). By confronting Havelock's views on orality and literacy with Derrida's views on grammatology, I hope to bring certain corrections to both, at least as far as these two thinkers' cultural historical interpretations of the Platonic moment are concerned. For a detailed examination of Derrida's essay, see Spariosu, "Mimesis and Contemporary French Theory," in M. Spariosu, ed., *Mimesis in Contemporary Theory: An Interdisciplinary Approach*, vol. 1, *The Literary and Philosophical Debate* (Philadelphia and Amsterdam, 1984).

resourceful god Theuth. Theuth is not only the inventor of all mathemati-
cal sciences or abstract thinking but also that of writing—itself a form of
abstraction. He presents his inventions to the king of Egypt, Thamus, for
approval and when it comes to writing, he recommends it as a "recipe for
memory and wisdom." But Thamus retorts:

> O man full of arts, to one it is given to create the things of art, and to
> another to judge what measure of harm and of profit they have for
> those that shall employ them. . . . If men learn this [writing], it will
> implant forgetfulness in their souls; they will cease to exercise
> memory because they rely on that which is written, calling things to
> remembrance no longer from within themselves, but by means of
> external marks. What you have discovered is a recipe not for
> memory, but for reminder. And it is not true wisdom that you offer
> your disciples, but only its semblance, for by telling them of many
> things without teaching them you will make them seem to know
> much, while for the most part they know nothing.[27]

Thamus' critique of writing parallels much of the Socratic critique of
poetry in the *Republic*. When the king claims that his *technē* is the ability to
discern between the morally good and bad, we realize that he is a
philosopher-king and are reminded of the division of the arts in book 10
of the *Politeia* (the art of the user, that of the maker, and that of the
imitator), which is also a hierarchy. It is proper for the artisan to present
his inventions, and proper for the philosopher-king to decide which one is
morally useful or harmful. The philosopher-king's verdict is that writing,
like poetry in the ideal state, is morally harmful because it belongs to the
art of the counterfeiter (who is both a simulator and a duplicator), and
therefore is a pseudo-*technē*: it produces a play of appearances under the
cover of which it attempts to pass as truth. Writing can only simulate
memory, knowledge, and truth, it is a bad form of play, and the man who
relies on it is no better than a Sophist.

Socrates also draws an analogy between writing and painting, reminiscent of his analogy between painting and poetry. Written words, like
painted images "seem to talk to you as though they were intelligent, but if
you ask them anything about what they say, from a desire to be in-
structed, they go on telling you just the same thing forever" (*Phaed.*
275d7–9). Writing, like painting (and poetry) is devoid of knowledge of

27. Plato, *Phaedrus*, 274e7–275b1, trans. R. Hackforth, in Hamilton and Cairns, *The
Collected Dialogues of Plato*.

Being, belonging to the realm of appearances. More dangerously, however, it defies reason because it resists philosophical questioning and interpretation; it has a tendency to get out of control, "to drift all over the place, getting into the hands not only of those who understand it, but equally of those who have no business with it; it does not know how to address the right people, and not address the wrong" (*Phaed.* 275e3–5). Like poetry, then, writing lacks *sōphrosunē* (moderation), it lacks all discipline.

Because writing, no less than poetry, is a form of mimesis, it is amphibolous by nature and therefore is not all bad. As Socrates observes, "there is nothing shameful in the mere writing of speeches" (*Phaed.* 258d1–2). Nevertheless, because writing *is* amphibolous, it needs the philosopher-hermeneutician to come to its aid, sifting the good from the bad and protecting it against itself and others. Just as there is good and bad mimesis, there is good and bad writing, and Socrates draws a distinction between written or recorded speech and live speech. The latter also proves to be a kind of writing, engraved on the speaker's soul, of which written speech is a sort of image or copy (*Phaed.* 276a5–7). Writing should at all times be guided by the oral, which in turn should be guided by the divine Forms imprinted on the righteous soul.[28]

Finally, by a Sophistic twist Socrates distinguishes between philosophers and writers on the same criteria that he distinguishes between philosophers and poets. Asking Phaedrus to deliver a message, first to Lysias and all composers of discourses (rhetoricians), second to Homer and all those "who have written poetry whether to be read or sung," and third to Solon and to authors of written laws, Socrates says that they ought not to be "designated by a name drawn from [their] writings but by one that indicates a serious pursuit" (*Phaed.* 278c8–d1). He thereby implies again that writing is not a serious, but a playful activity (note that Theuth, the inventor of writing, is also the inventor of games, such as "draughts and dice," *Phaed.* 274d1). Neither should all these authors be

---

28. The division of the soul into a noble and an inferior part that Socrates outlines in the first part of the *Phaedrus* anticipates a similar division in the *Republic*, and the Socratic myth of the journey of the soul toward, around, and away from Being has its close counterpart in the myth of Er. As in the *Republic*, true knowledge, no less than true love, depends on the relative distance of the soul from Being. The philosopher is the closest to this Being, whereas the tyrant is the farthest from it. The poet occupies the sixth place, before the artisan or the farmer, and before the sophist or the demagogue (*Phaed.* 248e); this order of rank is of course partly reversed in the *Republic*. Note also that in the *Phaedrus* Socrates defines poetry as a form of Dionysian madness or mimesis-play (245a1–8), but without the deprecating irony he displays in the *Ion*.

called *sophoi*, wise men, because "this epithet is only proper to a god" but rather *philosophoi*, lovers of wisdom. They deserve the latter name only if they carry out their work with a knowledge of the truth (the doctrine of Being), if they can defend their statements when challenged, and can orally prove the inferiority of their writings. In other words, the philosopher becomes oral man par excellence, whose authority derives not only from his proximity to Being, but also from his immediate presence, unobscured by writing. Note also the philosopher's agonistic nature as he must face the attacks of his opponents and defend his statements when challenged. "On the other hand," Socrates goes on, "one who has nothing to show of more value than the literary works on whose phrases he spends hours, twisting them this way and that, pasting them together and pulling them apart, will rightly . . . be called a poet or speech writer or law writer" (*Phaed.* 278d8–e2). Here, then, by a dexterous, ironic reversal the poet becomes the "man who writes," engaged in trivial play, whereas the philosopher becomes, like Socrates, the "man who does not write" (in Nietzsche's phrase), engaged in a serious pursuit. As in the *Republic*, moreover, the philosopher as truth-sayer becomes a *philosophous*, literally a poet's lover and guide.

The Socratic subordination of the written to the oral in the *Phaedrus* has been seen by Havelock as a futile, conservative attempt to revert the "literate revolution." Citing E. G. Turner, who says that in the *Phaedrus* Plato is "fighting a rearguard action," Havelock adds: "In fact his preference for oral methods is not only conservative but also illogical, since the Platonic *epistēmē* which was to supplant *doxa* was being nursed to birth by the literate revolution."[29] Havelock and Turner seem not only questionably to identify Plato with Socrates, but also to forget that, like all revolutions, the "literate revolution" is equally a return, that is, a reaffirmation of a mentality of power under new guises.[30] Writing itself has

29. Havelock, *Preface to Plato*, 56 n.17. My disagreement with Havelock does not, however, extend to his general thesis that Plato attacks the poets because he perceives them as the most powerful agents of Hellenic oral mentality. On the other hand, I attempt to explain why both Socrates and Plato must appropriate rather than reject orality. In this regard, I also modify Derrida's thesis according to which grammatology, at least in Plato, constitutes a sort of Achilles' heel for an ontology of presence. As I have already indicated, the problem of orality and literacy in Plato can best be understood in the context of a shift in cultural emphasis from archaic to median values in Hellenic thought. This problem certainly involves logic and philosophy (defined as the science of Being), but its nature is primarily historical, not philosophical or logical.

30. In all fairness to Havelock, I should point out that he corrects this impression in later essays, for example, in "The Orality of Socrates and the Literacy of Plato: With Some

often been viewed in our (and certainly in Hellenic) culture as a duplication of the oral, of the voice as unmediated authority. But Plato does not revert to oral structures or to an archaic mentality; rather, he theorizes a de facto situation in which writing is born as an aid to the oral, as its substitute and mediator (just as a median mentality often replaces immediate power with its abstract, representational counterparts). Hence the apparently contradictory steps that Socrates, the man who does not write (Plato—to state the often-neglected obvious—does write, despite his disclaimers in the seventh letter), is obliged to take. On the one hand, Socrates undermines the oral foundation of poetry's (and rhetoric's) claim to authority by transforming it into literature, or a mimesis of the oral; and on the other, he substitutes philosophy for poetry as the true *mousikē* (Havelock's formulation), the true oral authority.

■ Plato's Concept of Play: The Republic and the Laws

Of all ancient philosophers, perhaps with the exception of the Sophists, Plato is the most playful. His dialogues can be seen as *paignia*, as brilliant philosophical and literary essays (in the etymological sense of "weighing," "trying out," or "testing"), in which he stages various intellectual debates and explores conflicting doctrines, proposes new ethical values and turns the old ones upside down, puts on and casts off myriad personae and masks. Above all, they are dazzling displays or tours de force, through which Plato challenges his rivals, be it the poets, the Sophists, or the physiologists, to spirited verbal contests and, like Socrates, seeks to gain victory over them by fair and foul means alike. Nietzsche, for example, fully understands this playful, competitive Platonic spirit when he notes:

> That which . . . in Plato is of special artistic importance in his dialogues is usually the result of an emulation with the art of the orators, of the sophists, of the dramatists of his time, invented deliberately in order that at the end he could say: "Behold, I can also do what my great rivals can; yea I can do it even better than they. No Protagoras has composed such beautiful myths as I, no dramatist such a spirited and fascinating whole as the Symposium, no orator penned such an oration as I put up in the Gorgias—and now I reject

Reflections on the Historical Origins of Moral Philosophy in Europe," in E. Kelly, ed., *New Essays on Socrates* (Lanham, Md., 1984), 67–93.

all that together and condemn all imitative art! Only the contest made me a poet, a sophist, an orator!"[31]

But Plato, unlike some of his predecessors, is not unreservedly and uninhibitedly playful. He also shows a certain unhappy consciousness about play, which motivates him to reflect critically both on his own playfulness and on play in general. As a result, he develops an anthropology and a sociology of play, becoming the first play theorist in Western culture. I shall briefly review the various concepts of play with which Plato operates in the *Republic* and the *Laws*, and shall attempt to determine his own attitude toward these concepts, as well as their place in the larger context of Platonic thought. Needless to say, one cannot separate, in these dialogues, Plato's concept of play from his concept of mimetic poetry (which, as we have seen, he treats as a ludic form), and I shall constantly have to refer back to the issues discussed in the previous sections.

In the *Republic* we encounter all the play concepts examined in other thinkers, and we can properly begin with the Platonic notion of play as *agon*. The verbal contest between Thrasymachus and Socrates shows eristic as a form of agonistic play, of which Socrates is a consummate master. He excels the Sophists at their own game, and his pupil Adimantus points out the agonistic origins of the maieutic method. Those who are questioned by Socrates in accordance with this method, says Adimantus, may object that "owing to their inexperience in the game of question and answer they are at every question led astray a little bit by the argument, and when these bits are accumulated at the conclusion of the discussion mighty is their fall . . . and that just as by expert draughts players the unskilled are finally shut in and cannot make a move, so they are finally blocked and have their mouths stopped by this other game of draughts played not with counters but with words; yet the truth is not affected by that outcome" (*Rep.*, 6.487b3–c4).

31. Nietzsche, "Homer's Contest," in *Complete Works*, vol. 2, *Early Greek Philosophy and Other Essays*, 59–60. In addition to the critical studies already mentioned, here I have found particularly helpful G. J. de Vries, *Spel bij Plato* (Amsterdam, 1949); Glenn R. Morrow, *Plato's Cretan City: A Historical Interpretation of the Laws* (Princeton, N.J., 1960); Jerome Eckstein, *The Platonic Method: An Interpretation of the Dramatic-Philosophic Aspects of the Meno* (New York, 1968); Hans-Georg Gadamer, *Dialogue and Dialectic: Eight Hermeneutical Studies on Plato*, trans. P. C. Smith (New Haven, Conn., 1980); and Ludwig Marcuse, *Der Philosoph und der Diktator: Plato und Dionys. Geschichte einer Demokratie und einer Diktatur* (Zurich, 1984). Also, I should again like to single out Friedländer's *Platon*, which is perhaps the most important modern account of Plato as a philosopher-artist.

At the same time, Adimantus' objection that truth is not affected by the outcome of a verbal contest reveals Plato's own dissatisfaction (also frequently voiced by Socrates) with eristic, which ought to be replaced by dialectic.[32] On the other hand, dialectic as a method of arriving at the truth of Being inevitably implies another form of play, the *as if* approach to knowledge. The playful exchange between Socrates and Adimantus in *Rep.* 6.487e highlights not only the master's *mētis* or ability to wriggle out of any impasse in the debate, but also the indispensibility of the concept of play for the Platonic theory of knowledge. When Socrates, seeking a way out of the deadlock created by Adimantus' doubt about the logical necessity of philosophers-kings, attempts to employ a heuristic analogy or parable, his pupil derides him: "And you, of course, are not accustomed to speak in comparisons!" (*Rep.* 6.487e2). Nevertheless, after playfully complaining that Adimantus has added insult to injury by driving him into an impasse of argument and then making fun of him, Socrates proceeds with his analogy (*Rep.* 6.487e8–489a2). As both Socrates and Plato are well aware, analogies or heuristic fictions cannot be dispensed with as easily as eristic can, because they belong to the *as if* approach to knowledge that the logo-rational philosopher employs, as a rule, to solve particularly recalcitrant philosophical problems.

The ambiguous, double nature of the Socratic and Platonic attitude toward play is again perfectly illustrated, in book 7, by Socrates' definition of "true philosophy" (which draws the soul "away from the world of becoming to the world of being," *Rep.* 521d3–4): "So this, it seems, would not be the whirling of the shell in the children's game, but a conversion and turning about of the soul from a day whose light is darkness to the veritable day—that ascension to reality of our parable [of the cave] which we will affirm to be true philosophy" (*Rep.* 7.521c5–8).

Even as Socrates separates true philosophy from a child's game he invokes the parable of the cave (*Rep.* 7.514a1–518c2), which by his own account is a playful, heuristic fiction. Finally, the doctrine of Ideas itself is accessible only through the *as if* play of logo-rational thought:

> Understand then, said I [Socrates], that by the other section of the intelligible I mean that which reason itself lays hold of by the power

32. See, for example, Socrates' observation in book 5: "Many appear to me to fall into [logical contradiction] even against their wills, and to suppose that they are not wrangling but arguing, owing to their inability to apply the proper divisions and distinctions to the subject under consideration. They pursue purely verbal oppositions, practicing eristic, not dialectic on one another" (*Rep.* 5.454a4–9). Here Socrates implies that eristic is an agonistic form of play, whereas dialectic is not.

of dialectic, treating its assumptions not as absolute beginnings but literally as hypotheses, underpinnings, footings, and springboards so to speak, to enable it to rise to that which requires no assumption and is the starting point of all, and after attaining to that again taking hold of the first dependencies, so to proceed downward to the conclusion, making no use whatever of any object of sense but only of pure ideas moving on through ideas to ideas and ending with ideas. (*Rep.* 7.511b1–c2)

In view of the heavy epistemological burden that play must assume in the Socratic scheme of things, the light-hearted banter between Socrates and his pupils, where gravity is disguised as play and play as gravity, points to a difficult problem that confronts both Socrates and Plato. This problem concerning play as a whole is similar to that concerning poetry: Socrates and Plato must separate play from violent agon or contest and subordinate it to the tasks of philosophy as the science of Being, and, as we have seen, it is precisely this separation that Socrates effects through his trial of the poets. Plato is far from banishing play as such from his philosophy. What he wants to banish is, as in the case of poetry, its archaic forms, or its connection with violent, immmediate power. Socrates, therefore, retains the concept of play as agon in his ideal state, but in a logo-rational, nonviolent form reminiscent of Hesiod's good *eris.*[33]

Plato dramatizes the logo-rational transvaluation of the archaic notion of play as agon at the very beginning of the *Republic*, through Socrates' atttitude toward and handling of Thrasymachus in book 1. The Sophist not only espouses a violent doctrine (the right of the strong) but also behaves violently, as if in confirmation of his doctrine, arousing terror in Socrates. But Socrates, true to his own logo-rational doctrine, manages to control his fear and eventually tames the fierce Sophist with soothing, reasonable words. He thus reenacts, as it were, the "enlightened," median version of the history of Hellenic culture, according to which logo-

33. We have seen, for example, that both Socrates and Thrasymachus are engaged in a verbal contest. The agon metaphor, moreover, recurs throughout the dialogue. For example, in book 2 Glaucon's prerequisites for sharper distinctions between the just and the unjust man are jokingly compared by Socrates to the meticulous preparations for a wrestling match: "Bless me, my dear Glaucon, said I. How strenuously you polish off each of your two men for the competition for the prize as if it were a statue!" (*Rep.* 2.361d4–7). Socrates again takes up this metaphor in book 10 (for example, in *Rep.* 613b6–7), also using it in the closing speech of the dialogue, where he imagines the death of the righteous and wise soul as the aftermath of a competition, when prizes are awarded (*Rep.* 10.621c7–d1). We also recall that Socrates sees poetry and philosophy as engaged in a contest (*Rep.* 10.607b–608b), out of which the latter emerges victorious.

rational persuasion presumably replaces raw, physical violence as ruling instrument. Not unlike Dionysus in his mild guise at the beginning of the *Bacchae*, Socrates proves to outsophist the Sophist, by keeping a cool temper and beating his opponent at the latter's own game (eristic). On the other hand, Thrasymachus, like Pentheus, exemplifies the tyrannical type, who is both a "misologist and a stranger to the Muses." According to Socrates, such a man "no longer makes any use of persuasion by speech but achieves all his ends like a beast by violence and savagery, and in his brute ignorance and ineptitude lives a life of disharmony and gracelessness" (*Rep.* 3.411d8–e2).

As the reference to the Muses, disharmony, and gracelessness indicates, in *Rep.* 3.411 Socrates also redefines *mousikē* and gymnastics in terms of logo-rational play. A true "musician" is not the man who "brings the strings into unison with each other," but he who blends gymnastics with music, applying them most harmoniously to the soul (*Rep.* 3.412a4–7). Once Socrates purifies play of violent *eris* and relates it to *sōphrosunē*, defined as logo-rational harmony and order, he can reintroduce it as the chief instrument of education in his ideal state: "For why should one recite the list of the dances of such citizens [the guardians], their hunts and chases with hounds, their athletic contests and races? It is pretty plain that they must conform to these principles [median harmony and order, derived from a proper adjustment of the higher and the lower parts of the soul]" (*Rep.* 3.412b2–5).

Again, in book 4, Socrates explicitly calls *mousikē* a "form of play" which, although it is supposed to "work no harm," it can, as Adimantus observes, "by gradual infiltration . . . softly [overflow] upon the characters and pursuits of men and from these [it can issue] forth grown greater to attack their business dealings, and from these relations [it may proceed] against the laws and the constitution with wanton license . . . till finally it [can overthrow] all things public and private" (*Rep.* 4.424d7–e2). Consequently, Socrates chimes in, "our youth must join in a more law-abiding play, since, if play grows lawless and the children likewise, it is impossible that they should grow up to be men of serious temper and lawful spirit [*ennomous te kai spoudaios*]" (*Rep.* 4.424a5–425a1). Orderly play, stripped of arbitrariness and violence, can become a useful educational tool, because the children, who "in their earliest play are imbued with the spirit of law and order through their music [*mousikē*, also poetry and dance]," will continue in this spirit, later on, during their adult lives (*Rep.* 4.425a3–6).

In book 7, play resurfaces in relation to the teaching and practising of dialectic. In *Rep.* 7.536c1, Socrates suddenly reminds himself and Glaucon that they have all along conversed in a playful spirit (*epaizomen*) and that he should not have become overheated when speaking in defense of philosophy-dialectic.[34] Yet he has lost his playfulness for a good reason: "For, while speaking, I turned my eyes upon philosophy, and when I saw how she is undeservedly reviled, I was revolted, and, as if in anger, spoke too earnestly to those who are in fault" (*Rep.* 7.536c3–5). Glaucon replies that Socrates did not speak too earnestly for him as a hearer, thus stressing that philosophy-dialectic is no laughing matter; in other words, Plato draws a distinction between play and seriousness, dramatizing it through his characters' words and behavior. Socrates and his interlocutor resume their lighthearted, bantering manner once the philosopher-king is securely installed as the rightful ruler of the ideal state.

If dialectic itself is a serious matter, it must nevertheless be taught as if it were a game, and Socrates now establishes a correlation between play, education, and freedom. The principles of dialectic must be imparted to the children of free citizens not through compulsory instruction but through play: "A free soul ought not to pursue any study slavishly, for while bodily labors performed under constraint [*biai*, violence, force] do not harm the body, nothing that is learned under compulsion [*biai*] stays with the mind. . . . Do not, then, my friend, keep children [that are trained to be guardians] to their studies by compulsion [*biai*] but by play" (*Rep.* 7.536e1–537a1).

In this passage Socrates also contrasts *paidia* to *biai*, thus separating play from violence. But if the children of free men must not be treated with violence, they must learn how to use it against others, and Socrates relinks play and violence in his precepts of training children in warfare. In *Rep.* 7.536e6–537a2, he goes on to say that by observing children at play, the educator can also better "discern the natural capacities [dispositions] of each" and then he reminds Adimantus of their agreement that "they must conduct the children to war on horseback to be spectators, and wherever it may be safe, bring them to the front and give them a taste of blood as we do with whelps" (*Rep.* 7.537a4–7). The whelps will after all become watchdogs and must be trained to be ruthless toward the enemy. It is from among these watchdogs, moreover, that at a later stage the philosophers-kings will be selected (*Rep.* 7.537c9–d8). Socrates, then,

34. The reference is to book 2, in which Socrates proposes a game of educating the guardians in his ideal state: "Come, then, just as if we were telling stories or fables and had ample leisure, let us educate these men in our discourse" (*Rep.* 376d9–10). From the outset, then, Socrates claims that his discourse is playful rather than serious, in obvious imitation of the traditional *muthoi* or *logoi*.

makes it perfectly clear that he has no intention of excluding violence from an ideal citizen's education, but simply wishes to turn this violence, with the aid of play, to the community's benefit. He condones war abroad and rejects *stasis*, intestine strife, at home, where he advocates nonviolent forms of contest—a typical logo-rational position favored by median Western mentalities through the centuries.[35]

If Socrates favors median over archaic *agon*, he must also favor necessity over chance, attempting to eliminate the latter, as much as possible, from human affairs. A brief look at some of the passages in the *Republic* where necessity and chance are mentioned shows that this is indeed the case.[36] For example, among the "lies" that the poets tell about the gods (*Rep.* 2.379c9–d2), Socrates quotes *Iliad* 24.527, where Zeus is said to dispense good and bad lots arbitrarily and not according to merit. Socrates challenges the archaic notion of chance-necessity evident in Achilles' words of consolation to Priam, arguing instead for a logo-rational concept of causation and divine providence, which also implies a separation of necessity from chance. God is only the cause of the good and is associated with necessity, whereas what is evil is associated with chance and is caused by agents other than God. The "good" includes the various

35. It does not follow, however, that Socrates must necessarily favor democracy as a form of government that promotes median values. On the contrary, for him Athenian democracy promotes intestine, violent contest or *anarchy*. For example in book 8, in considering democracy as a potential paradigm for an ideal polity, Socrates sarcastically comments: "And the tolerance of democracy, its superiority to all our meticulous requirements, its disdain for all our solemn pronouncements made when we were founding our city, that except in the case of transcendent natural gifts no one could ever become a good man unless from childhood his play and all his pursuits were concerned with things fair and good—how superbly it [democracy] tramples underfoot all such ideals, caring nothing from what practices and way of life a man turns to politics, but honoring him if only he says that he loves the people! . . . These and qualities akin to these democracy would exhibit, and it would, it seems, be a delightful form of government, anarchic and motley, assigning a kind of equality indiscriminately to equals and unequals alike!" (*Rep.* 8.558b1–c6). Again, Socrates draws a distinction between the orderly play of his ideal polity and the "anarchic" (in the sense of chaotic) *stasis* within a democracy. Unlike Solon's *eunomia*, in Socrates' eyes democracy erases all class distinctions based on merit or excellence (*aretē*), whether this merit is defined in archaic terms as prowess or in median terms as moral virtue (*sōphrosunē*, moderation, sobriety). Finally, for Socrates democracy paradoxically breeds not only anarchy but also tyranny (*Rep.* 8.563d4–e4). Had he lived today, he would have probably invoked the various communist regimes around the world in support of his argument.
36. The Platonic dialogue in which necessity and chance are at the very core of the debate is, of course, *Timaeus*, but an examination of this dialogue must be reserved for another occasion.

punishments that God may mete out for feckless actions in order to reform the evil doer, and thus what appears as *tuchē*, chance or misfortune, may in the long run prove to be the effect of divine necessity (*Rep.* 2.379b–380c).

The notion of chance is again taken up in *Rep.* 10.604c5–7, previously quoted, where Socrates outlines a proto-game theory based on logical reasoning. In dealing with calamity we must not "chafe and repine because we cannot know what is really good and evil in such things," that is, what belongs to divine necessity and what belongs to chance. Instead of wailing like children about the unlucky numbers that turn up in the dice game of life, people ought to determine their next move in accordance with the precepts of reason, correcting the ill effects of a bad throw. In turn, Glaucon agrees that reasonable action "would be the best way to face misfortune [*tuchas*, chance] and deal with it" (*Rep.* 10.604d3–4).

That Socrates not only separates chance from but also subordinates it to necessity becomes quite obvious in the myth of Er at the end of book 10. Er, a young Pamphylian warrior who dies in battle, is sent back to life by the gods as a messenger to humans, to tell them what they are to expect after death. Socrates' myth is a logo-rational version of the heroic trip to Hades, challenging the traditional epic account of the underworld. Of particular interest is his description of the divine judgment by casting lots. After being duly purged of their past misdeeds, the souls of the dead come before the throne of Lachesis, one of the three Moirae (Fates), where they must choose a new life or lot. Lachesis, however, has a somewhat minor role, being the daughter of Ananke (Necessity). As in Parmenides, it is not Lachesis but Ananke who is at the center of the world-order, holding on her knees the entire celestial machinery. Socrates also pointedly distinguishes Lachesis from *tuchē*: he neither personifies *tuchē* as a goddess nor relates it to Ananke, as he does with Lachesis; rather, for Socrates *tuchē* is a bad lot or misfortune, either apparent if it comes from a god, or real if it comes from thoughtless human action.

Through his myth, then, Socrates attempts to show that cosmic events are ultimately determined not by chance-necessity or by an agonistic play of physical forces, but by a centralized, logo-rational power. Whereas this power is responsible for the distribution of lots, it is in no way responsible for the choice itself, which is left to the individual soul about to be reborn. Hence it is a prophet who takes the lots from Lachesis' knees and casts them among the souls, proclaiming: "No divinity [*daimōn*, guiding spirit] shall cast lots for you, but you shall choose your own deity [*daimōn*, guiding spirit]. Let him to whom falls the first lot first select a life to which he shall cleave of necessity. But virtue [*aretē*, excellence] has no master over her, and each shall have more or less of her as he honors her or does her despite. The blame is his who chooses. God is blameless" (*Rep.* 10.617e1–5).

Socrates seems to challenge not only the epic account of the distribution of good and bad portions by Zeus, but also the tragic mechanism itself. As Socrates observes later in regard to a soul that rashly chooses the fate of a tyrant without closely examining its consequences, such as "eating his own children and other horrors," this soul starts wailing and blaming for his woes "fortune [*tuchē*, chance] and the gods and anything except himself" (*Rep.* 10.619c5–6). Socrates' remark is reminiscent of Zeus' comment regarding Aegisthus in the *Odyssey* 1.32, although he rationalizes this comment so thoroughly that a hero can no longer claim *atē*, blindness or lack of foresight.[37] In the Socratic mythical version, the choice of a bad lot comes not from chance as a divine agency, but from an insufficiently examined life on the part of the chooser. In this regard, philosophy is precisely a remedy against chance as ill-fortune (*tuchē*), it is a mechanism through which *tuchē* is greatly reduced by philosophical *technē*, or ethical know-how. In turn, this ethical know-how is none other than the old wisdom of the Seven Sages. Although Socrates' account of the divine judgment seems partly based on the Pythagorean doctrine of metempsychosis, its message is unmistakably Hellenic, favoring the same median values that are advocated by the Delphic oracle. If men properly understand Er's divine message, then when they are confronted with choosing a new fate in the house of death, they will not be dazzled by "riches and similar trumpery" and will not "precipitate [themselves] into tyrannies and similar doings." On the contrary, they will always choose "the life that is seated in the mean and shun the excess in either direction, both in this world so far as may be and in all the life to come, for this [*sōphrosunē*, moderation] is the greatest happiness for man" (*Rep.* 10.619a5–b1).[38]

37. In this sense, Socrates no less than Euripides is fully aware that the tragic mechanism becomes inoperative in a predominantly median mentality (compare my comments at the end of chapter 3). As far as human affairs are concerned, Socrates seems to adopt Democritus' logo-rational opposition of *tuchē* and *technē*.

38. For a full analysis of the Hellenic notion of *sōphrosunē*, see Helen North, *Sophrosune: Self-Knowledge and Self-Restraint in Greek Literature* (Ithaca, N.Y., 1966). North traces the semantic development of the word beginning with the Homeric epic, where, in the case of heroic behavior, it is not tied with median morality, meaning mostly "prudence" in face of superior power, such as that of a god. On the other hand, in the case of Homeric women and (unheroic) children, *sōphrosunē* may mean "chastity, modesty, obedience, inconspicuous behavior." Although North does not say so explicitly, it is largely this

Sōphrosunē as sobriety or moderation is also designed to arrest the more drastic effects of competition and it is highly significant that Socrates has Odysseus, of all heroes, renounce his former heroic life and replace it with that of a commoner. Even though by chance (*kata tuchēn*) Odysseus receives the last lot and, therefore, must choose last, he skillfully offsets his disadvantage: "From memory of [his] former toils having flung away ambition [*philotimias*], [Odysseus's soul] went about for a long time in quest of the life of an ordinary citizen who minded his own business, and with difficulty found it lying in some corner disregarded by the others, and upon seeing it [Odysseus's soul] said that it would have done the same had it drawn the first lot, and chose it gladly" (*Rep.* 10.620c5–d2). By giving up *philotimia*, love of *timē*—the highest value of aristocratic contest—Odysseus manages to reverse his bad lot (*tuchē*), and thus Socrates shows not only the connection between *agōn* and *tuchē* in an archaic mentality, but also the way in which humans can offset their adverse effects through *sōphrosunē*, moderation or reason. As in the *Odyssey*, the hero exchanges the violent, archaic values of a Homeric *basileus* for the relatively quiet, median values of either a country gentleman or an upper middle-class citizen.

In the myth of Er one can also discern another reason why Socrates rejects eristic in favor of dialectic. Eristic is the intellectual equivalent of the heroic *philotimia*, belonging to the world of Becoming and the bad play of physical forces, that is, to a violent, archaic mentality. When Odysseus chooses his median but fully rewarding fate, he also implicitly replaces the bad play of eristic with the good play of dialectic, through which willful chance is tamed by logo-rational necessity.

Odysseus, then, becomes the first philosopher-king, and Socrates rewrites the trip to Hades in the *Odyssey* in order to illustrate the new kind of logo-rational fiction required for the education of children in his ideal state. The journey of the soul in the myth of Er corresponds not only to the spiritual journey of Odysseus but also to that of the participants in the Socratic debate at the house of Cephalus. The motif of the journey in the *Republic* converges with that of the contest, as Socrates reminds us at the end of the dialogue. In the beginning, Socrates goes to Piraeus in order to participate in a religious festival, that is, also to watch the games.

---

meaning that will later apply to praiseworthy human behavior in general. *Sōphrosunē* as moderation, in opposition to *koros* (excess) and *hubris* (overstepping of limits, miscalculation) is developed particularly by the Greek dramatists, Sophists, and philosophers, who associate it with the logo-rational, median ethics of "know thyself" and "nothing in excess."

It is precisely to these games that he alludes at the end, when he compares the journey of the soul through eternity to a heroic race, in which "we receive our reward [prize], as the victors in the games go about to gather in theirs" (Rep. 10.621c7–d1).[39] The crowned victor in the Socratic journey-race is the philosopher-king, who, as in Hesiod's race between Dike and Hubris (WD 217–18), starts out with a huge handicap but crosses the finishing line first. The narrative framework of the Republic thus evinces the same kind of ambiguities that we find in Plato's views on play. Not unlike Hesiod, Socrates rejects the archaic values embodied in the aristocratic contest in favor of the median values embodied in communal cooperation; yet he presents the incompatibility between the archaic and median values precisely in the form of a contest, thereby revealing the agonistic nature of both these sets of values.

By contrast, in the narrative framework of the Laws Plato seems, at least at first sight, to put agon behind him, preserving only the motif of the journey. Play, however, remains equally central to the later work, because here Plato closely interlaces the motif of the journey with a median form of play, the nonagonistic philosophical dialogue. The conversation between three old sages—an Athenian, a Cretan, and a Spartan who have embarked on a journey from Cnossus to Zeus' cave and shrine in the mountains nearby—is described as an entertaining game designed not only to shorten and lighten their trip but also to make it profitable (Laws 1.625c). The topic of the conversation is "politics and jurisprudence" and is proposed by the Athenian who, although unnamed, bears a strong resemblance to Socrates or, possibly, to Plato himself.

But even though the dialogue is conducted less in the form of a verbal contest than in the form of a collective search for truth, agon still looms large in its background.[40] Indeed, the main purpose of the Nomoi is to demonstrate that the spirit of the laws is guided not by war, but by peace and mutual goodwill. In this respect, the precept voiced at the beginning of the dialogue by Clinias the Cretan, according to which "Humanity is in a condition of public war of every man against every man, and private war of each man with himself," is an avatar not only of Thrasymachus' and

39. Compare Socrates' conclusion in book 10: "Such then are the prizes of victory which the gods bestow upon the just" (Rep. 613b6–7).
40. Note that Clinias the Cretan and Megillus the Spartan ultimately defer to the Athenian, who, not unlike Socrates, becomes the leader of the philosophical discussion. By having the Cretan and the Spartan recognize the Athenian's authority in philosophical matters, Plato indirectly affirms the cultural hegemony of Athens as the main disseminator of a logo-rational mode of thought among the Greek cities.

Callicles' doctrine of might makes right but also of Homer's and the Milesian physicists' principle of cosmic agon, whereas the Athenian's plea against intestine strife (*stasis*) and for cosmic, political, and psychic harmony is based on another version of Solonian and Socratic *eunomia*.[41] Hence, like Socrates', the Athenian's remarks on play scattered throughout the dialogue are designed to separate the ludic phenomenon from violent contest, associating it with peaceful activities such as education, the fine arts, religious and civic festivities, and philosophy itself. Many of these remarks appear, as in the *Republic*, in relation to *mousikē*, which is again censored for its close link to the world of the senses (especially pleasure and pain), appearance, and Becoming, or to the chaotic, arbitrary play of physical forces.

The discussion of the laws of Sparta and Crete begins with a consideration of the main civic virtues that these laws are meant to foster, which in turn raises the question of pleasure and pain, which then leads to the seemingly trivial issue of the symposium or convivial drinking, a familiar form of public entertainment, indeed of communal play, in ancient Greece. The Athenian observes that even though this custom may appear insignificant, its proper examination presupposes no less than a "true theory of music [*mousikē*]," which in turn involves a "theory of education at large" (*Laws* 1.642a5–6). This is not an implausible proposition because much Hellenic poetry, dancing, and music making took place in a sympotic context as well. The fact that Plato has the Athenian center his theory of *mousikē* and education around convivial drinking is, moreover, doubly significant. Dionysus is not only the "wine god" (*Laws* 1.643a7), the patron of this kind of entertainment (as well as the patron of drama and, with Apollo and the Muses, of all *mousikē*), but he is also the most influential carrier of archaic values in general. The Athenian is fully aware of Dionysus' power, and it is the god of many names that must ultimately be dealt with through a new theory of education based on new philosophical principles.

As in the *Republic*, the most effective instrument of education (*paideia*) is play (*paidia*), by which the Athenian understands children's games, gymnastics and athletic competitions, and *mousikē*. Therefore play must also be redefined and practised in accordance with new, logo-rational principles. The Athenian takes the first step toward this transvaluation of play when he stipulates that the random, unstructured games of children

41. See Plato, *Laws*, 1.625a4–b7, trans. A. E. Taylor, in Hamilton and Cairns, *The Collected Dialogues of Plato*.

must be given a direction, must be harnessed to utilitarian purposes: "If a boy is to be a good farmer, or again, a good builder, he should play, in the one case at building toy houses, in the other at farming, and both should be provided by their tutors with miniature tools on the pattern of real ones." Through play, children can be molded socially, and one "should seek to use games as a means of directing children's tastes and inclinations toward the station they are themselves to fill when adult." A boy destined to be a carpenter "should be taught by his play to use the rule and plumb line," and the one destined to be a soldier, "to sit a horse," and so forth (Laws 1.643b7–c6). This social compartmentalization of play is modeled on the hierarchical pattern of the three classes in the ideal state, and the goal of all education is "schooling from boyhood in goodness [aretē, excellence] which inspires the recipient with passionate and ardent desire to become a perfect citizen, knowing both how to wield and how to submit to righteous rule" (Laws 1.644b4–5). In other words, through play, the carpenter and the farmer are taught not only the mechanics of their profession but also how to be ruled, whereas the soldier and the philosopher-king are also taught how to rule. Although Taylor's translation might leave the impression that the same "goodness" is common to all, it is obvious that each station has its own aretē, some in ruling and others in being ruled (compare Homer, Hesiod, Solon, and other advocates of eunomia).

Gymnastics and mousikē are the other ludic forms through which education attains its goals, and the Athenian must again relate these ludic forms to logo-rational principles, such as moderation, discipline, and order. He acknowledges the archaic origins of both mousikē and gymnastics. For example, in book 2, he describes play as a vigorous, chaotic physical movement common to both humans and animals: "No young creature whatsoever . . . can keep its body or its voice still; all are perpetually trying to make movements and noises. They leap and bound, they dance and frolic, as it were with glee, and again, they utter cries of all sorts" (Laws 2.653d7–e3; see also Laws 2.665d9–e3). According to the Athenian, these chaotic cries and movements first give birth, through the mediation of Apollo, Dionysus, and the Muses, to mousikē, which is an orderly activity that distinguishes humans from beasts: "Now animals at large have no perception [aisthēsis] of the order or disorder in these motions, no sense of what we call rhythm and melody. But in our case the gods of whom we spoke [Apollo, Dionysus, and the Muses] as given us for companions in our revels have likewise given us the power to perceive and enjoy rhythm and melody" (Laws 2.653e3–654a3). The Athenian equally alludes to Socrates' notion of poetic performance as mimetic contagiousness in the *Ion*, when he says that the gods are our "choir leaders . . . string[ing] us together on a thread of song and dance, and have named our choirs [*chorous*] so after the delight [*para tēs charas*] they naturally afford" (*Laws* 2.654a3–5). The metaphor, however, is not that of the lodestone, but is ludic in nature, referring to the Athenian's previous contention that a human being is "a puppet made by gods, possibly as a plaything, or possibly with some more serious purpose [*spoudēi tini*]" (*Laws* 1.644d7–9). This puppet is pulled mainly by two strings, pleasure and pain, and in *mousikē* pleasure prevails.

Since no Greek would be willing to give up pleasure as a fundamental ethical principle, the Athenian's problem is to redefine it in logo-rational terms, which, as in the *Republic*, means separating it from the feeling of power and defusing its violent potential by subjecting it to a rigorous discipline (which, however, is only another form of power). Although in *Laws* 2.645 the Athenian says that it is the gods that pull the strings of the puppet, in the earlier passage, where the metaphor is first developed, the string puller is the law [*nomou*], a violent aid to nonviolent logos: "So a man must always cooperate with the noble drawing of law, for judgment [reasoning: *tou logismou kalou men ontos*] though a noble thing, is as gentle and free from violence as noble, whence its drawing needs supporters" (*Laws* 1.645a4–7). The willful, unpredictable violence of the gods, then, is replaced by the strictly regulated violence of the law, and the Athenian indirectly refers to this substitution when he says that the gods are not only our companions in revels, but have also given us order and harmony so that we can regulate our powerful feelings. The Athenian defines education as a "rightly disciplined state of pleasures and pains" (*Laws* 2.653b6–7).

Although the Athenian defers a detailed examination of gymnastics (the other half of a child's education) until book 7, in book 2 he traces its origins, as in the case of *mousikē*, in the frantic, random leaps of young beings at play, inspired by Apollo, Dionysus, and the Muses (*Laws* 2.672c8–673b8; see also *Laws* 2.673c9–d5). But here discipline is no less important, and the training of the body becomes true gymnastics only when the "dancing of creatures at play" culminates in physical excellence by "scientific bodily discipline" (*Laws* 2.673a3–5).

When, in book 7, the Athenian prescribes specific laws governing the play of children, gymnastics, and athletic games, he again emphasizes discipline, order, and utility. The children's games must constantly be surveyed and guided by adults (*Laws* 7.793d7–794d2), while gymnastics and competitive games must be practised for the "benefit of health and strength" rather than from "mere idle vainglory" (*Laws* 7.795d6–796e1). What the Athenian challenges here, again, is the archaic notion of competition, which values "vainglory" (the Platonic negative interpretation of heroic *timē*), or personal achievement based on violent agon over peaceful cooperation for the common good. He attempts to replace the Dionysian, ecstatic experience of power present in archaic play with the orderly, directed pleasure of utilitarian games. As Clinias points out, the object of the lawgiver in regulating play as well as all other social activities is "to avoid a life of untempered pain or pleasure, and steer a middle course in everything" (*Laws* 7.793a2–4; compare Socrates' similar principles for the foundation of his ideal republic).

Unlike Euripides, then, Plato emphasizes only the mild side of Dionysus, the god of ecstatic, violent play. The Athenian's efforts to gloss over the violent, irrational nature of the wine god are again obvious in his enlightened defense of drinking parties or symposia, to which he returns several times in the course of his argument. He challenges the traditional myth according to which Dionysus was "bereft of his wits by his stepmother Hera and . . . this is why he afflicts his victims with Bacchic possession and all its frenzied dancing, by way of revenge," which is the principal motive behind his gift of wine to men (*Laws* 2.672b2–7). The Athenian gives a logo-rational interpretation of the myth, which according to him is intended to explain the wild play of the young before they reach the sobriety of mature age: "So long as a creature has not yet attained its proper level of native sense [*oikeian phronēsin*, homegrown wisdom, common sense], it is quite mad, indulging in random cries, and, as soon as it has found its feet, in equally random leaps" (*Laws* 2.672c2–5). And here the Athenian also reminds his fellow travelers that they "pronounced these [random leaps] the source of both music and gymnastics," thus explicitly associating Dionysus with artistic and physical play. The Athenian proposes to replace the traditional myth with a median version, according to which wine is bestowed on men not out of vindictiveness, "to drive us frantic," but as a "medicine [*pharmakon*], to produce modesty of soul, and health and strength of body" (*Laws* 2.672d5–9). Earlier on, the Athenian had made the seemingly paradoxical suggestion that the choir of Dionysus be made up only of old men (*Laws* 2.665b4) and that full participation in symposia should be forbidden to men under forty (like many modern legislators, the Athenian completely prohibits drinking for those under eighteen years of age; *Laws* 2.666a1–c6), and one can readily see why: if not used properly, wine as medicine may turn into poison, and therefore wine drinking, like lying and the use of violence in the ideal republic, is the prerogative of a few initiates or old sages, who are also rulers. These sages are well prepared for the contest with the wine god, and by their sobriety will set an example for the young and inexperienced. (Socrates' moderate behavior at the end of Plato's *Symposium* is a prime example of what the Athenian has in mind here.)

Wine drinking is a form of play that highly gratifies the senses, and it is again the pleasure principle that is at issue here. The Athenian does not advocate the abolition of all pleasure, and therefore of all play, but rather its rational channeling through discipline.[42] Wine drinking, no less than children's games, can be given utilitarian value. For example, symposia may be used as a relatively inexpensive and safe way of testing (and, in some cases, correcting) a man's tendency toward anger, greed, lust, pride, cowardice, or toward whatever else "drives us frantic with the intoxication of pleasure," like wealth, beauty, and physical strength:

> What can we find more suitable than the sportive touchstone of the wine cup, provided only that it is employed with a little precaution? For do but consider. Which is the more dangerous course with a sullen and untamed temper—the source of so many crimes—to test it by entering into a business agreement, with the risk of its failure, or by association in a bacchanalian celebration? Or to put the soul of a slave of sex to the test by entrusting him with our own daughters, sons, and wives, and discover his character at the risk to our nearest and dearest? One might allege endless such illustrations without exhausting the advantages of a sportive [*paidias*, playful] method of inquiry involving no serious, painful cost. (*Laws* 1.649d8–650a7)

In his final comments on drinking, however, the Athenian makes it clear that his defense of the wine god is part of "the old men's game of legislation" (*Laws* 3.685a7) that he plays with his companions. If a city

42. This rational channeling of play and pleasure through discipline, which also involves the homeopathic principle of inoculating the patient with the feared virus in order to make him immune to the disease, is again presented in the form of a contest: "If a man can only attain mature courage by fighting the cowardice within himself and vanquishing it, whereas without experience and discipline in that contest [of such contest: *tou tō'outōn agōnōn*], no man will ever be half the champion he might be, is it credible he should come to fullness of self-command unless he fights a winning battle against the numerous pleasures and lusts which allure him to shamelessness and wrong, by the aid of precept, practice, and artifice, alike in his play and in his serious hours [*en spoudais*]?" (*Laws* 1.647c10–d7).

were to practise the custom seriously, it should do so only under the strict "control of law and rule, as a training in self-command, [allowing] a similar indulgence in other pleasures [only] as a means to mastery of them." On the other hand, the Athenian would emphatically withdraw his endorsement of this practice if it is to be treated "as mere play, and free license is to be given to any man to drink whenever he pleases, in what company he pleases, and when engaged in any undertaking he pleases" (Laws 2.673e8–674a2). Like Socrates, the Athenian dismisses play in favor of seriousness even as he goes on playing, and this apparent inconsistency becomes understandable if one realizes that he is forced to operate with two conflicting notions of play (archaic and logo-rational) and tries to replace one by the other.

Because education is the "rightly disciplined state of pleasures and pains," mousikē must also undergo disciplinarian action, and the Athenian revises the thesis, allegedly common in Plato's time, that "the standard of rightness in music [mousikē] is its pleasure-giving effect" (Laws 2.654e8–655d1). Unlike Socrates, the Athenian draws no distinction between mimesis and diegesis, nor does he compare poetry with painting. He nevertheless considers mousikē as mimesis on the example of "choric exhibitions" or drama, defined as a "mimic presentation of manners [mimēmata tropōn], with all variety of action and circumstance, enacted by performers who depend on characterization and impersonation" (Laws 2.655d5–7). As in the Republic, drama is condemned when it simulates reprehensible actions because in those cases "enjoyment and approbation are at variance" (Laws 2.655e4–5). The crucial issue is again whether a man is "the worse for enjoying degrading postures or melodies or . . . the better for getting his pleasure from the opposite quarter" (Laws 2.656a1–5). Like Socrates, the Athenian claims that through playful simulation or mimicry a man will inevitably "grow like whatever he enjoys, whether good or bad" (Laws 2.656b4–6) and therefore this "educative-playful function [paideian te kai paidian] of the Muse" should not be left to chance but strictly regulated by law (Laws 2.656c2–3). And again like Socrates, the Athenian gives the example of Egypt as a society that has wisely canonized melodies that "exhibit an intrinsic rightness permanently by law" (Laws 2.657a7–8).

The Athenian then examines another common argument, which claims that since during artistic performances we are "granted the liberty to play [paizein]," the poet who entertains us most should receive the highest reward (Laws 2.657e4). Although he does not deny that pleasure can be the supreme judge of mousikē, the Athenian redefines the notion of pleasure, attempting to relate it to the median *aretai*: "We may take it that the finest music is that which delights the best men, the properly educated, that, above all, which pleases the one man who is supreme in goodness and education" (*Laws* 2.658e8–659a1), and this man is undoubtedly the logo-rational philosopher.[43] In *Laws* 2.659, the Athenian also draws a distinction between high and low *mousikē* according to whether it produces high or low pleasure and he criticizes the popular taste that invariably favors the low pleasures connected with the inferior part of the soul.[44] He then reformulates this distinction in terms of seriousness versus play: poetic-dramatic performances are really "spells for souls, directed in all earnest to the production of the concord [between the psyche's superior and inferior parts] . . . but as the souls of young folk cannot bear earnestness, they are spoken of as 'play' and 'song,' and practiced as such" (*Laws* 2.659e1–5). In a properly run polity, the legislator will have the poet present, through his play, serious matters; the lawgiver will thus assume, in regard to *mousikē*, the role of the physician who makes tasteless but wholesome foods palatable to his patient, and the rich but unwholesome ones unpalatable. He "will persuade, or *if persuasion fails, will compel*, the man of poetic gifts to compose as he ought, to employ his noble and fine-filed phrases to represent by their rhythms the bearing, and by their melodies the strains, of men who are pure, valiant, and, in a word, good" (*Laws* 2.660a3–8, emphasis added).

The Athenian further develops his simile between the lawgiver and the physician when he considers art as a form of consumption. Like any food or drink, art has two components: "flavor" and "rightness and utility" (*Laws* 2.667b8–c1). The flavor is what makes it pleasurable, but this flavor

43. Compare *Laws* 2.662b1–e4, where the Athenian says he would "inflict a penalty little short of the capital," not only on the poets but on anyone who maintains, in keeping with common opinion, that the just life and the pleasant are not one and the same.

44. Compare *Laws* 3.700a4–701b3, where, like Socrates in the *Republic*, the Athenian relates the state of *mousikē*, corrupted by poets "possessed by a frantic and unhallowed lust for pleasure," to the state of democracy in his time: "As things are with us [i.e.,the assumption that in *mousikē* "there is no such thing as a right and a wrong, the right standard of judgment being the pleasure given to the hearer, be he high or low"], music has given occasion to a general conceit of universal knowledge and contempt for law, and liberty has followed in their train. Fear was cast out by confidence in supposed knowledge, and the loss of it gave birth to impudence. For to be unconcerned for the judgment of one's betters in the assurance which comes of a reckless excess of liberty is nothing in the world but reprehensible impudence." It is obvious, then, that the modern distinction between serious and pop art, as well as that between high and popular culture, is as old as Plato. For a fine discussion of this issue, see Alexander Nehamas, "Plato and the Mass Media," in *The Monist* 71 (1988): 214–34.

must be harmless and therefore must at all times be subordinated to utility. Suggesting that all *mousikē* is "capable of producing likenesses or representations [*eikastikēn te . . . kai mimētikēn*]" (*Laws* 2.668a6–7), the Athenian equates the representation with the flavor and the model represented with rightness and utility. Thus he naturally concludes that utility-truth must always take precedence over the representation: "A man's feeling of pleasure, or his erroneous belief, is never a proper standard by which to judge of any representation. . . . no, we should judge by the standard of truth, never, on any account, by any other" (*Laws* 2.667e10–668a4). It is also the harmless pleasure or flavor that the Athenian calls "play" (*paidia, Laws* 2.667e6), thus implying that not only *mousikē* but play in general must be judged in terms of utility. He equally implies that as the physician prescribes the right kind of diet for the body, so the lawgiver (or the logo-rational philosopher) prescribes what is right for the soul, separating the harmful pleasures from the harmless ones in both *mousikē* and all other forms of play.[45]

The Athenian, then, employs the opposition between play and utility in the same way that he has employed the opposition between play and seriousness. In effect, the two dichotomies are interchangeable, being equally subordinated to the standard of truth, that is, to the doctrine of Being. And what the Athenian ultimately hopes to accomplish through this doctrine is to separate not only *mousikē* but all education from excessive, potentially violent, sensual pleasure (that is, from an excessive feeling of power), harnessing it instead to the sober, intellectual pleasures of philosophy and thereby reshaping the whole Hellenic mentality in accordance with median ideals.[46]

45. Compare *Laws* 8.801b10–c1, where the Athenian follows Socrates and places the poets under state censorship because "they are not quite the most competent judges of good and evil."
46. Compare book 6, in which the Athenian considers the beginnings of mankind and explicitly outlines not only the disciplinary mission of the logos in its battle with the senses, but also the role assigned to fine art and play in this battle: "I observe that mankind are universally impelled by needs and desires, of three kinds, and that this impulsion results in virtue if men are well trained, in its contrary if they are ill trained. Their needs are, in the first place, food and drink, from the hour of their birth. All creatures have the instinctive appetite for gratification in that kind and are furiously defiant of the voice which says that one has any duty except to sate one's craving for pleasures from that source, and to avoid all discomfort of any kind; our third and most imperious need and fiercest passion arises later, but most of all fires men to all manner of frenzies—I mean lust of procreation with its blaze of wanton appetite. These three unwholesome appetites, then, *we must divert from the so-called pleasant toward the good; we must try to check them by the three supreme sanctions—fear, law, true discourse* [logo-rational

As in the *Republic*, in the *Laws* philosophy is the highest *mousikē* based on the pleasures of *dianoia* and thus it is also the highest form of play. At the beginning of the dialogue the Athenian proposes a game of legislation, and he periodically reminds his audience that his discourse must at all times be regarded only as a game (see, among other passages, *Laws* 3.685a7, 3.690d2, 4.712b2, 6.769a1, and 7.811d5–6). This game, however, is not one of competing young warriors but one of "sober, old men" (*peri nomōn paizontas paidian presbutikēn sōphrona, Laws* 3.685a7–8). Their play at law making is "sober" (*sōphron*), that is, moderate, reasonable, and ultimately serious (compare "our grave game of the aged," *Laws* 6.769a1). But the Athenian does not exclude competition from his game, even though he attempts to redefine it, in median, nonviolent terms (see *Laws* 1.647c7–d7 already discussed, as well as *Laws* 5.729c8–730a9 and 5.731a2–b3). In book 7, after dismissing both serious and playful poetry as an improper model of teaching *aretē* to the young, the Athenian playfully (but also earnestly) substitutes for it his own discourse as both the most appropriate educational model and the best kind of poetry: "As I look back on the discourse you and I have been holding together ever since daybreak until this moment . . . our converse has been, to my mind, just like a kind of poem. I dare say there is nothing surprising in my having felt this keen pleasure in reviewing this compact formation, as I may call it, of discourse [*logous . . . hoion hathroous*] of my own composition. The fact is that of all the many compositions I have met with or listened to, in verse or in plain prose, I find it the most satisfactory and the most suitable for the ears of the young" (*Laws* 7.811c6–d5). Note the military metaphor ("compact formation . . . of discourse") that the Athenian employs in describing his composition, which through its tightly ordered arguments can withstand any challenge from potential competitors—his power-oriented language is reminiscent of that in which Parmenides couches his notion of Being.[47] And shortly thereafter, when he explains why he will deny the dramatic poets a chorus in his ideal city, the Athenian explicitly acknowledges the rivalry between the poets and the philosophers: "Respected visitors [i.e.,

---

philosophy]—*not without the aid of the Muses and the gods of games*, and so to quench their growth and onrush" (*Laws* 6.782d10–783b, emphasis added). Note the passionate, agonistic, indeed *poetic* language in which the Athenian formulates the cultural historical mission of the logos.

47. Here, again, it is hard to decide whether Plato shares the Athenian's enthusiasm for his own logo-rational discourse or has an ironical attitude toward it. It is obvious that Plato realizes the problems raised by this kind of discourse but, perhaps, he employs it faute de mieux, seeing no viable alternative to it.

tragic poets] we are ourselves authors of a tragedy, and that the finest and best we know how to make. In fact our whole polity has been constructed as a dramatization [*mimēsis*, simulation] of a noble and perfect life; that is what *we* hold to be in truth the most real of tragedies. Thus you are poets, and we also are poets in the same style, rival artists and rival actors, and that in the finest of all dramas, one which indeed can be produced only by a code of true law" (*Laws* 7.817b1–8).

Like Socrates in the *Republic*, the Athenian fully acknowledges the poetic, fictional origin of philosophical discourse. He consciously appropriates certain poetic fictions and turns them into philosophical tools. Although Being is transcendental and therefore inaccessible, the philosopher-artist can build images of it in thought-speech. Hence the necessity of a playful, *as if* approach, and we have seen that both Socrates and the Athenian describe their discourse in terms of a game. That play, art, and an *as if* approach to knowledge-truth are one and the same for the Athenian (as they are for Socrates) is obvious when he proposes to Clinias that they build, in the imagination, an ideal state governed by ideal laws and then apply it to his city: "Suppose we apply the parable to your city and try to model its laws in imagination, like elderly men playing a boy's game" (*Laws* 4.712b1–2).

But the "parable" mentioned by the Athenian indicates that his legislative game is not pure philosophical fantasy; rather it seeks actualization and legitimation through powerful means, and here again we discern the close relationship between art, play, and power:

> O my friends never let yourselves be persuaded that there is any speedier or easier way to change the laws of a community than the personal guidance of those in authority; there is none today, and will be none hereafter. . . . We may say the same of power in all its forms. When supreme power is combined in one person with wisdom and temperance, then, and on no other conditions conceivable, nature gives birth to the best of constitutions with the best of laws. So you may take these oracular remarks as a parable embodying the proof that though in one way it is hard for a society to get good laws, in another, if things fall out as I say, it would be the quickest and easiest of all developments. (*Laws* 4.711c5–712a7)

What the Athenian implies is that the imaginative or poetic constructs of philosophy remain specious unless they are enacted, hence the need for a philosopher-king who has the power to imprint his vision upon a human community, molding it the way an artist molds a piece of clay or a stretch of language.[48] The most effective legislator is therefore the philosopher-king, who can devise beautiful fictions that are good for the community (rather than harmful, like those of the poets), and who can in turn persuade the community, by force if necessary, that these fictions are nothing but truths. The Athenian is no more relativistic than the Sophists, Socrates, and Euripides are: it is power that ultimately draws the line between truth and falsehood, between reality and fiction. The Athenian explicitly makes this point when, after he demonstrates that "an unjust life is not merely more dishonorable and despicable, but actually more truly unpleasant than a just and religious," he asks: "And even had it not been so . . . could a legislator of even moderate merits, supposing him to have ventured on any fiction for the sake of its good effect on the young, have devised a more useful fiction than this, or one more potent to induce us all to practice justice freely, and without compulsion?" (*Laws* 2.663d2–e2).

When Clinias objects that "truth is a glorious thing and an enduring thing, but it seems no easy matter to convince men of it," the Athenian reminds him of the mythological tales devised by the poets, some of which still enjoy, according to him, the status of truth. If people can believe that "teeth were once sown in the ground and armed men sprang up from them," then they can be made to believe anything. A lawgiver "need only tax his invention to discover what conviction would be most beneficial for the city, and then contrive all manner of devices to ensure that the whole of such community shall treat the topic in one single and selfsame lifelong tone, alike in song, in story, and in discourse" (*Laws* 2.663e2–664a7). Note that here the function of *mousikē* as play is again related to the political goals of the philosopher-legislator. It is precisely because the Athenian, like Socrates, is fully aware of the persuasive powers of poetry (which operates through pleasurable feelings) that he wants to enlist it in the service of his beautiful, logo-rational fictions.

One of these fictions is the Athenian's view of the gods as divine puppeteers, who have created humans, we recall, perhaps as playthings, or perhaps with a more serious (even though inscrutable) purpose in mind. Whereas in book 1 this view is mentioned in passing, in book 7 it is developed into a median *theologia ludens* that is designed to replace its Homeric, archaic counterpart. The issue of religion comes up again in relation to poetry and the need for its strict regulation (most poetic

48. In all likelihood, the Athenian's views here are also Plato's, especially if Plato's involvement with the tyrants of Syracuse is historical reality rather than edifying (logo-rational) legend. For a full discussion of Plato and Syracuse, see Marcuse, *Der Philosoph und der Diktator*.

performances took place in the context of religious festivals as well as symposia, which equally had a religious nature, being dedicated to the wine-god, and the Athenian naturally treats poetry and religion together). Recalling Egyptian practices, the Athenian proposes that poetic canons be permanently established for every festival and that poets be constrained not to depart from these canons on penalty of being tried for impiety: "No poet shall compose anything in contravention of the public standards of law and right, honor and good, nor shall he be at liberty to display any composition to any private citizen whatsoever until he has first submitted it to the appointed censors of such matters and the curators of law, and obtained their approval" (Laws 7.801c8–d4). Because the Athenian fears he might incur ridicule for imposing serious and stringent rules on a playful matter like poetry, he attempts to justify himself by reexamining the opposition between play and seriousness and showing that what men regard as serious is play and what they regard as play is serious.

The Athenian starts by observing that even though men's actions (pragmata) do not deserve to be taken seriously, men are forced by necessity (anankaion) to do so, and this is their lack of good chance (touto de ouk eutuches, Laws 7.803b3–5). Here necessity and chance are both opposite and complementary terms, and therefore the Athenian indirectly invokes the traditional concept of chance-necessity as well as the traditional, pessimistic image of man. According to archaic wisdom, man is far from being the "measure of all things" as Protagoras proudly declares, but only a puppet of the gods. At this point, however, the Athenian begins to challenge the Homeric, traditional view, which he uses only in order to place humans sub specie aeternitatis (he does not, any more than Socrates, share the archaic, anthropomorphic concept of divinity).[49] The fact that man "has been constructed as a toy for God" is the "finest thing about him" and is a cause for joy rather than for tragic lamentation. Even though humans may think that they have been dealt a bad hand, it is up to

49. When Megillus observes that the Athenian "must have but a poor estimate of our race," the latter says: "Do not be amazed at that, Megillus. Bear with me. It is because I had my eye fixed on God, and my spirit full of him that I said what I just said. However, if it pleases you, man shall be something not so insignificant but more serious [spoudēs]" (Laws 7.804b7–c1, trans. modified). In other words, the Athenian does not mean to belittle humanity, but only to put it in the proper perspective, which for him is that of a theologia ludens. If man views himself in relation to God then many things that before appeared important become insignificant and vice versa. Because God is the "goal of all beneficent serious endeavor [pasēs makairou spoudēs axion]," man should keep his "seriousness for serious things [to men spudaion spoudazein] and not waste it on [harmful] trifles" (Laws 7.803c2–6).

them to play it deftly (as ,Odysseus does in the myth of Er). "All of us, then, men and women alike must fall in with our role and spend our life in playing the most beautiful games [*kallistas paidias*]" (*Laws* 7.803c2–7, trans. modified).

But the Athenian's idea of what the most beautiful play is, as he himself points out, completely inverts the current belief which maintains that serious things like war are done for the sake of play: "But the truth is that war can never offer us either the reality or the promise of genuine play [*paidia pephukuia*], nor any education worth the name, and these are the things that I count supremely serious [*spoudaiotaton*] for such creatures as ourselves. Hence it is peace in which each of us should spend most of his life and spend it best [*ariston*, spend it nobly]. What, then, is our right course? We should live our lives playing, and playing those games which—like sacrifice, song and dance—would enable us both to gain the favor of the gods and to repel the attacks of our enemies, defeating them in combat" (*Laws* 7.803d5–e4, trans. modified).

In this apparently confusing passage, what the Athenian seems to challenge is again the archaic notion of play as violent agon. He argues that peace is more befitting for the best (that is, aristocratic) life than violent conflict, and that war for its own sake is not truly playful.[50] Rather, the only genuine play is the peaceful one, not least because it is beneficial or useful (whereas agonistic play is harmful or wasteful). The Athenian's pun on *paidia* and *paideia* (*Laws* 7.803d5–6) underscores the close relationship between play and education-culture in Plato's program of social reform: one is to be used as a means of accomplishing the other. Note again, however, that the Athenian is no more of a pacifist than Socrates is. War is acceptable as long as it is regarded not as a playful or gratuitous activity, but a serious or useful one, for example, in matters of self-defense.

Through his *theologia ludens*, the Athenian also raises the issue of play versus seriousness that stands at the very foundation of Plato's philosophical thought. Although Plato presents this thought in a dramatic, that is, playful form, he does so because he believes he has no other choice. For

50. Incidentally, the Athenian's argument can be regarded as indirect proof that an archaic, aristocratic mentality did consider war a form of play; otherwise, the Athenian's strenuous efforts to prove the contrary would be pointless. Modern readers may find this passage confusing because it argues for what in a rational culture has become a natural attitude: war is not pleasant play but painful work. Hence Taylor's translation: "our serious work should be done for the sake of play" (*Laws* 803d2–3). Of course, this attitude can occasionally be found in Homer as well, but only on the part of the defeated.

him no serious thinker will write in a serious manner about what most concerns him. He explains this paradox in his letter to the friends of Dion, in which he voices his doubts about Dionysius' ability to express in writing what Plato attempted to teach him in person. Developing a theory of knowledge of Being based on four elements (names, descriptions, bodily forms, and ethical concepts), Plato argues that a thinker can attain this knowledge only through a natural affinity with and long practice of the median virtues. The understanding of the doctrine of Being may at last come to him in a flash, when the mind, exerting "all its powers to the limit of human capacity, is flooded with light." Hence, "no serious man will ever think of writing about serious realities for the general public so as to make them a prey to envy and perplexity. In a word . . . when anyone sees anywhere the written work of anyone, whether that of a law-giver in his laws or whatever it may be in some other form, the subject treated cannot have been his most serious concern—that is, if he himself is a serious man."[51]

Plato is no doubt a serious man, but he needs play in order to remain serious. Through play he can have his cake and eat it too, for the dialogic form allows him to say what he cannot say. Hans-Georg Gadamer makes a similar point when he observes: "Precisely because of the seriousness of his purpose, Plato gives his mimesis the levity of jocular play. Insofar as his dialogues are to portray philosophizing in order to compel us to philosophize, they shroud all of what they say in the ambiguous twilight of irony. And in this way Plato is able to escape the trap of the ever so vulnerable written work, which cannot come to its own defense, and to create a truly

51. Plato, letter 7, 344b1–d2, trans. L. A. Post, in Hamilton and Cairns, *The Collected Dialogues of Plato*. Here Plato is probably influenced by the esoteric doctrine of Pythagoras, although, at least to us, there ought to be nothing "esoteric" about it: Pythagoras, like Plato, probably tries to inculcate a median mentality into the archaic mind by teaching the Greeks a mode of thought and behavior already largely available to them in the moral doctrines of the Seven Sages and the Delphic oracle. To a mentality of power, however, knowledge of this kind becomes more attractive if it is presented as the prerogative of a small select group. Despite Plato's (and probably Pythagoras') emphasis on "benevolent disputation by the use of question and answer without jealousy" (letter 7 344b5–6), any esoteric doctrine is necessarily based on a mimetic mechanism (in the Girardian sense) that recreates all the power-related ills that it purports to cure. One cannot agree more with both Pythagoras and Plato, however, that any ethical code is taught primarily by practice rather than exposition. Given Dionysius' subsequent behavior, it is clear that the tyrant of Syracuse learned nothing from Plato. But did Plato learn anything from Dionysius? Apparently not, if the Athenian's remark about the ability (or even willingness) of men in power to impose the virtuous life on everyone else is treated as Plato's own belief.

philosophical poetry which points beyond itself to what is of real consequence. His dialogues are nothing more than playful allusions which say
something only to him who finds meanings beyond what is expressly
stated in them and allows these meanings to take effect with him."⁵²

But what do the Platonic dialogues say to Gadamer himself? They say
that what is of "real consequence" for man is to reconcile his philosophical nature with "the violent drives in himself of self-preservation and the
will to power."⁵³ For Gadamer's Plato, philosophy is "what makes man as
a political being possible. Paideia, consequently, is not the cultivation of
some skill; rather it produces this *unity of power and the love of knowledge. It
only calms the inner strife which, though dangerous, is nonetheless essential to man.*
For although that strife will always prevent his pacification, it provides
the energy proper to each man individually and common to all. *Only a life
with this dynamic tension is a human life.*"⁵⁴ Gadamer thus gives a succinct
description of, as well as his seal of approval to, the Platonic, logo-rational
mode of thought which, far from giving up (immediate) power, seeks to
reconcile it to philosophical goals. But according to Gadamer's own
hermeneutical principle, Plato's dialogues, no less than Euripides' and
Aristophanes' plays, may allow other kinds of meanings to take effect with
their readers. Perhaps what they cannot say is not only what they do not
know how to say. It is also what can be neither thought nor intuited by
those who, like Gadamer, remain immersed in a mentality of power,
whether median or archaic.⁵⁵ Because of Plato's self-consciousness about
art, play, and philosophy, as well as his deep distrust of violent, arbitrary
power, his dialogues may point indirectly to a world outside and beside *all*
power, in which strife is nonessential to man and a human life does not
require dynamic tensions in order to be human.

52. Gadamer, "Plato and the Poets," in *Dialogue and Dialectic*, 70–71.
53. Ibid., 56.
54. Ibid., 57, emphasis added.
55. For a detailed examination of Gadamer's concept of play and power, see Spariosu,
Dionysus Reborn, pt. 1, sec. 3.2.

5 ■ Aristotle: Poetics, Politics, and Play ■

■ In contemporary Anglo-American scholarship it is widely assumed that Aristotle set out to restore the cultural prestige of poetry as *mimēsis*, bringing it, if not to what it had been before Plato, at least to an equal footing with philosophy. This assumption probably stems from a Neoplatonic reading of the *Poetics* and, in modern times, it is taken up by Lessing, Kant, Schiller, and Goethe and introduced in Anglo-American literary criticism by Coleridge and Shelley among others.[1] The reason for its largely unchallenged authority in our century, where Aristotelian *mimēsis* is mostly seen as an imitation not of the products but of the processes of Nature, can be sought in the Romantic emphasis on creativity and originality, which during the nineteenth century gradually replaced the Neoclassical emphasis on the conscious imitation of authoritative, cultural models.

The most influential Anglo-American proponents of Aristotle's theory of art as *mimēsis* in the sense of an imitation of natural process are Samuel

1. There is also a rhetorical tradition of the *Poetics*, which starts with Horace and which generally emphasizes the effects of poetry on its audience over its imitative nature, and which eventually leads to an emphasis of the *dulce* over the *utile*. For a discussion of this rhetorical tradition see Elder Olson's introduction to E. Olson, ed., *Aristotle's "Poetics" and English Literature* (Chicago, 1965); and Richard McKeon, "Rhetoric and Poetic in the Philosophy of Aristotle," in the same volume, 201–36. For a history of the Renaissance reception of the *Poetics*, see Bernard Weinberg, *History of Literary Criticism in the Italian Renaissance*, 2 vols. (Chicago, 1961). For Aristotle and the *Poetics* in Germany, see Max Kommerell, *Lessing und Aristoteles* (Frankfurt, 1940), and in France, Pierre Somville, *Essai sur la poétique d'Aristote* (Paris, 1975), chap. 4, "La postérité: quelques aspects," 133–73. For the Arab reception of the work in the Middle Ages, see especially Ismail M. Dahiyat, *Avicenna's Commentary on the Poetics of Aristotle* (Leiden, 1974).

H. Butcher, the Chicago neo-Aristotelians, and Gerald F. Else.[2] Although these scholars differ, sometimes considerably, in their reading of individual passages in the *Poetics*, I believe they all agree with Butcher's statement that " 'imitation' in the sense in which Aristotle applies the word to poetry is . . . equivalent to 'producing' or 'creating according to a true idea' which forms part of the definition of art in general."[3] Outside the Anglo-American tradition, especially in Germany, scholars usually discern a dramatic, performative function in Aristotelian *mimēsis*, in addition to its imitative or representational aspects. They often render Aristotelian *mimēsis* by terms like *Vorstellung* and *Darstellung* (presentation, performance, show) as opposed to *Nachahmung* (imitation) in order to convey the idea of bringing forth or presenting, which involves both process and performance. In English, "production," in the sense of both generating (images) and staging (a performance), is the closest approximation to the German notion of Aristotelian *mimēsis*.[4] The Anglo-American and the German

2. The most recent advocates of this position are John Boyd, *The Function of Mimesis and Its Decline* (Cambridge, Mass., 1968); Redfield, *Nature and Culture*; Wesley Trimpi, *Muses of One Mind: The Literary Analysis of Experience and Its Continuity* (Princeton, N.J., 1983); and Kathy Eden, *Poetic and Legal Fiction in the Aristotelian Tradition* (Princeton, N.J., 1986).

3. Samuel H. Butcher, *Aristotle's Theory of Poetry and Fine Art* (1894; rptd. 4th ed., New York, 1951), 153; hereafter cited as Butcher, *ATP*. There are also Anglo-American scholars who challenge this authoritative view from a Horatian rhetorical standpoint, arguing that Aristotle's theory of poetry emphasizes the *dulce* over the *utile*. See, for example, Allan H. Gilbert in the introduction and notes to his translation of the *Poetics*, in A. H. Gilbert, ed., *Literary Criticism: Plato to Dryden* (Detroit, 1977). This rhetorical view, however, also appears somewhat distorted: like Plato, Aristotle indeed regards poetry as pleasurable play, but then he redefines this play in logo-rational terms, enlisting it in the service of philosophy and thereby rendering it *utile*.

4. Among the most influential German theorists of *mimēsis* as production are Adorno and Horkheimer, *Dialektik der Aufklärung*; Walter Benjamin, "Über das mimetische Vermögen," in *Gesammelte Schriften* (Frankfurt, 1977), 2:210–13; Erich Auerbach, *Mimesis: Dargestellte Wirklichkeit in der Abendländischen Literatur* (Berne, 1946; trans. W. Trask [Princeton, N.J., 1953]); Koller, *Die Mimesis in der Antike*; Hans Blumenberg, " 'Nachahmung der Natur': Zur Vorgeschichte der Idee des schöpferischen Menschen," *Studium Generale* 5 (1957): 266–83; and Hans-Georg Gadamer, *Wahrheit und Methode: Grundzüge einer philosophischen Hermeneutik* (Tübingen, 1960). Auerbach's *Mimesis* constitutes a landmark in Anglo-American scholarship as well, although his concept of mimesis is often misunderstood, in part because of the misleading English translation of the subtitle of his book: "The Representation of Reality in Western Literature." Ironically, however, this misprision is probably also the main reason for the book's great popularity in Anglo-American criticism. From my point of view, Blumenberg's study is the most helpful because even though it adopts the usual German position regarding *mimēsis*, it places the term in a cultural historical perspective, showing how various ages have their own authoritative view of this Platonic-Aristotelian notion.

positions have recently been fused into a third, French position. In their widely acclaimed translation of the *Poetics*, Roselyne Dupont-Roc and Jean Lallot render *mimēsis* by "representation," taking advantage of the fact that the French term, like its German counterpart, can denote both artistic performance or production and representation or reproduction.[5]

Although all these interpretations of Aristotelian *mimēsis* contribute to the understanding of the *Poetics*, or rather to the understanding of its reception by Romantic and Modernist literary theory and criticism, here I should like to propose another view, which does not reject or necessarily invalidate the others but, rather, places them in a different light: Aristotle's notion of poetry as mimesis is a direct consequence of the temporary victory, through Plato, of the median values over their archaic counterparts in Hellenic thought. For Aristotle, as for Plato, poetry is a playful simulation of serious discourse (metaphysics, logic, ethics, politics, rhetoric, jurisprudence, and so forth), and its chief function is not cognition, but a special kind of entertainment or pleasure. At the same time, however, Aristotle no less than Plato is fully aware of the archaic, ecstatic nature of poetic play, which must be tamed before it can be turned into a useful philosophical tool.[6]

■ Poetica: *Art, Simulation, and Knowledge*

Although Aristotle, in contrast to Plato's Socrates, initially acknowledges the status of poetry as art, *technē*, he sets out in the *Poetics* to redefine the conditions of the possibility of this art along logo-rational, Platonic lines: poetry as *technē* must at all times take its cue from those arts that are more receptive to median conversion. To this end Aristotle turns, like Plato, to the notion of *mimēsis*, which to him seems the most effective way of subordinating poetic *technē* to those of metaphysics, ethics, and rhetoric.[7] For example, in a parenthesis at the beginning of his

5. Roselyne Dupont-Roc and Jean Lallot, *Aristote: La poétique* (Paris, 1980), Introduction, 17–22; hereafter cited as Dupont-Roc and Lallot, *ALP*.
6. Here I partially share Friedrich Solmsen's cultural historical evaluation of the *Poetics* in his brief but illuminating introduction to his edition of *The Rhetoric and Poetics of Aristotle*, trans. W. R. Roberts and I. Bywater (New York, 1954). What Solmsen implies and I should like to argue openly is that Aristotle writes the *Poetics* from a philosopher's point of view and, in his own quiet way (which has turned out to be more effective than the fiery passion of Plato), imposes on poetry logo-rational, philosophical values, thus setting the course for much of its subsequent historical development.
7. For *technē* and *mimēsis* in the *Poetics*, see especially Ada Neschke, *Die "Poetik" des Aristoteles: Textstruktur und Textbedeutung*, 2 vols. (Frankfurt, 1980), 1:76–110. Her view,

treatise, Aristotle takes great care to distinguish, on the basis of *mimēsis*, between poetic and other compositions in verse or prose. He opens this parenthesis in connection with a distinction among various mimetic arts according to the medium of imitation. He says that those mimetic arts whose medium of imitation is speech in prose or verse *without music* are at present nameless (*Poetics* 1447a28–b8). By claiming that these mimetic arts have so far been given no name, Aristotle attempts to separate poetry from *mousikē*. We have seen that for Plato *mousikē* often still involves an amalgam of what we understand today by music, poetry, and dance. The fact that Aristotle cannot take the modern distinction for granted seems to indicate that during the fourth century B.C. the archaic mythopoeic unity had still not entirely broken down into individual disciplines.[8]

Once Aristotle draws a distinction between poetry and other mimetic

however, is the traditional German hermeneutical one: Aristotelian poetic *mimēsis* is a special form of cognition. In addition to the studies mentioned so far (including those on Plato's theory of poetry in chapter 4), I have found especially helpful for my discussion of the *Poetics*: J. Vahlen, *Beiträge zu Aristoteles Poetik* (Leipzig, 1914); Lane Cooper, *The Poetics of Aristotle: Its Meaning and Influence* (Ithaca, N.Y., 1923); F. L. Lucas, *Tragedy: Serious Drama in Relation to Aristotle's Poetics* (London, 1927); K. Ulmer, *Wahrheit, Kunst, und Natur bei Aristoteles* (Tübingen, 1954); Ingemar Düring, *Aristoteles Protrepticus: An Attempt at Reconstruction* (Göteborg, 1961); Gerald F. Else, *Aristotle's Poetics: The Argument* (Cambridge, Mass., 1963) and *Plato and Aristotle on Poetry* (Chapel Hill, N.C., 1986); John Jones, *On Aristotle and Greek Tragedy* (London, 1962), esp. sec. 1, 11–62; Norbert Kaul, *Der Zufall und die Theorie des tragischen Handlungsbelaufes bei Aristoteles* (Reinheim, 1965); Eva Schaper, *Prelude to Aesthetics* (London, 1968); O. B. Hardison, *Aristotle's Poetics* (Englewood Cliffs, N.J., 1968); Edward M. Cope, *An Introduction to Aristotle's Rhetoric* (Hildesheim and New York, 1970); Eckart Schutrumpf, *Die Bedeutung des Wortes ethos in der Poetik des Aristoteles* (Munich, 1970); Norman Gulley, *Aristotle on the Purposes of Literature* (Cardiff, 1971); John P. Lynch, *Aristotle's School: A Study of a Greek Educational Institution* (Berkeley, 1972); Ingram Bywater, *Contributions to the Textual Criticism of Aristotle's Nichomachean Ethics* (New York, 1973); John A. Stewart, *Notes on the Nichomachean Ethics of Aristotle* (New York, 1973); J. L. Ackrill, *Aristotle on Eudaimonia* (London, 1975); Edwin Wallace, *Outlines of the Philosophy of Aristotle* (New York, 1976); André Dacier, *La poétique d'Aristote* (Hildesheim and New York, 1976); Richard Shute, *On the History of the Process by which the Aristotelian Writings Arrived at Their Present Form* (New York, 1976); Maria Ruth Ruegg, *Mimetology: Philosophy and/or Literature in the Platonic and Aristotelian Texts*, Ph.D. diss. Yale University, 1976; Richard Sorabji, *Necessity, Cause, and Blame: Perspectives on Aristotle's Theory* (Ithaca, N.Y., 1980); André Wartelle, *Lexique de la "Poétique" d'Aristote* (Paris, 1985); Viviana Cessi, *Erkennen und Handeln in der Theorie des Tragischen bei Aristoteles* (Frankfurt, 1987); and Michelle Gellrich, *Tragedy and Theory: The Problem of Conflict since Aristotle* (Princeton, N.J., 1988).

8. Compare Else, *Aristotle's Poetics: The Argument*, 37; hereafter cited as Else, *APA*. Else, however, does not sufficiently stress that Aristotle is unable to discard completely the archaic sense of *mousikē*, which he employs, for example, in the *Politics*.

arts, however, he is confronted with another problem: how to distinguish between various kinds of compositions in verse or prose without music. It is at this point that he introduces the parenthesis in which he establishes mimesis as a differential criterion for poetic compositions. There are compositions in verse and prose without music that must not be called poetic, because they are not *mimēseis*. Hence one must also draw a distinction between poets (*poiētai*) and science-writers (*phusiologoi*)— some of whom have equally composed in traditional verse—not according to whether they write in verse or not, but according to whether they "imitate" or not. Aristotle has visible difficulties with this argument because in his time, as he himself acknowledges, common usage of the word *poiētēs* does not differentiate poets from science-writers or philosophers: "Except people do link up poetic composition with verse and speak of 'elegiac poets,' 'epic poets,' *not treating them as poets by virtue of their imitation*, employing the term as a common apellation going along with the use of the verse. And in fact the name [*poiētēs*] is also applied to anyone who treats a medical or scientific topic in verses, yet *Homer and Empedocles actually have nothing in common except their verse*; hence the proper term for the one is 'poet,' for the other 'science-writer' [*phusiologos*] rather than poet."[9] Here Aristotle separates poetry not only from music but also from science-philosophy. Whereas in the *Republic* Socrates discriminates between poetic diegesis and mimesis (thus creating some logical confusion when he attempts to apply *mimēsis* to all *mousikē*), in the *Poetics* Aristotle subordinates diegesis to mimesis and turns poetry into a mimetic art par excellence.

The fact that Aristotle goes against common usage in his definition of the poet as *mimētēs* shows the importance he attaches to this definition. He introduces the word *mimēsis* in connection with the *poiētikē technē*, the art of poetic composition, in the second paragraph of his treatise, immediately after he says that "first things come first," thus indicating that

9. Aristotle, *Poetics* 1447b13–20. Because the numerous translations of Aristotle's treatise are primarily interpretive acts, I shall quote from those versions which come the closest to my own reading of a particular passage and, in some instances, shall propose my own translation. The above passage is cited from Gerald Else, *Aristotle: Poetics* (Ann Arbor, Mich., 1967). Other translations quoted in this chapter are by Samuel H. Butcher, in *ATP*; by Ingram Bywater, in F. Solmsen, ed., *The Rhetoric and Poetics of Aristotle*; and by A. H. Gilbert, in *Literary Criticism: Plato to Dryden*. I have used in parallel Rostagni's second edition of the Greek text (1954), reprinted in Else, *APA*, as well as A. Gudeman, *Aristoteles, Peri Poiētikēs* (Berlin, 1934); J. Vahlen, *Aristotelis de arte poetica liber* (Leipzig, 1885); and D. W. Lucas, *Aristotle: Poetics* (Oxford, 1968). The Greek text is cited from Aristoteles, *De Arte Poetica Liber*, ed. R. Kassel (Oxford, 1965).

mimesis is the fundamental principle of poetic art. Here he puts mimesis to uses different from those he does in other works. Outside the *Poetics*, Aristotle as a rule employs the term in order to reconcile the traditional dichotomy between *technē* and *phusis*. For example, in the *Physics*, Aristotle says that "in general, in some cases art [*technē*] completes what nature cannot carry to an end, in others, it imitates nature."[10] This statement is part of his demonstration that both *technē* and *phusis* "act for the sake of something," or are subject to a "final cause." Postulating that nature is both matter and form, he subordinates the first to the second, arguing that form is a final cause while matter exists for the sake of this cause. *Technē* "imitates" or acts like *phusis* at an early stage (when it still leaves things unfinished) and *phusis* acts like *technē* at a later stage: "Thus, if things done according to art are for the sake of something, clearly also those according to nature are done for the sake of something; for the later stages are similarly related to the earlier stages in those according to art and those according to nature" (*Physics* 2.199a13–15).

Employing a paralogism (ironically, he exposes this Sophistic device in the *Poetics* when he shows how poetry can tell lies skillfully), Aristotle redefines *phusis* on the model of *technē* rather than vice versa. The two become one because now both exist for the sake of an end. Note that thereby Aristotle also virtually eliminates chance from *phusis*, which seems to have been one of his chief objectives all along (compare his discussion of "proper" and "accidental causes" and, in this connection, his attack on the Presocratics, *Physics* 2.195a26–198b32). Like Socrates in the *Republic*, he directs his argument against the archaic notion of chance-necessity, attempting to both separate chance from and subordinate it to necessity. Poetry is not mentioned once, and there is no indication whatsoever that Aristotle deploys his arguments with poetry in mind. Rather, he refers to the traditional notion of *technē*, which, he implies, "imitates" *phusis* as much as the latter "imitates" it (he may even use *mimēsis* in a metaphorical sense here, invoking and at the same time revising the Platonic correlation between *mimēsis* and *technē*).[11] In any case, Aristotle's view of *technē* as

10. Aristotle, *Physics* 2.199a, trans. H. G. Apostle and L. P. Gerson, in Apostle and Gerson, eds., *Aristotle: Selected Works* (Grinnell, Iowa, 1982). Greek citations are from Aristoteles, *Physica*, ed. W. D. Ross (Oxford, 1950).

11. Aristotle seems to take up the question of *technē* as an imitation of nature for the first time in the *Protrepticus*. But the immediate context is again that of necessity and chance. Aristotle first separates both nature (*phusis*) and art (*technē*) from chance (*tuchē*) and relates them to necessity: "Of things that come into being some come from some kind of thought or art, e.g., a house or a ship . . . while others come into being through no art,

partial mimesis cannot affect his view of poetry as essential mimesis in the *Poetics*, where poetry is a curious kind of *technē* that "imitates" or acts like other *technai*, but must not be confused with them. Like music and painting, poetry explicitly falls under the special division of mimetic art, belonging to what we call "fine art," to be distinguished from the so-called useful arts, as well as from speculative art or philosophy.[12]

---

but by nature; nature is the cause of animals and plants, and all such things come into being according to nature. But some things, indeed, also come into being as a result of chance; for of most of the things that come into being neither by art nor by nature nor of necessity we say that they come into being by chance" (trans. Düring, in *Aristotle's Protrepticus: An Attempt at Reconstruction*, fragment B 11; further citations refer to this translation and employ Düring's numeration of the fragments). Aristotle next invokes the traditional dichotomy between *technē* and *tuchē*, arguing that in art everything comes into being for the sake of something or for a purpose and not by chance: "Everything therefore that is according to art comes into being for a purpose, and this is its best end [*telos*], but that which comes into being by chance comes into being without purpose; something good comes into being by chance, yet in respect of chance and in so far as it results from chance it is not good" (*Protrep.* B 12; compare B 30: "For the good man who lives according to reason never subordinates himself to chance, but more than any other man disengages himself from that which happens by chance"). Because Aristotle has already separated nature from chance, he assumes that he has also demonstrated that everything in nature comes into being for a purpose. Hence he concludes: "That which comes into being according to nature does so for an end, and is always constituted to better purpose than the product of art; for nature does not imitate art, but art nature, and art exists to fill up what nature leaves undone. For some things nature seems able to complete by herself without assistance, but others she does with difficulty or cannot do at all" (*Protrep.* B 13). That Aristotle's argument is tautological becomes obvious when he says: "If, then, art imitates nature, it is from nature that the arts have derived the characteristic that all their products come into being for an end. For we should assume that everything that comes into being rightly comes into being for an end . . . and everything that comes or has come into being, if the process is according to nature, it comes out beautifully, since that which is contrary to nature is bad and the opposite of that which is according to nature; natural coming into being, therefore, is for an end" (*Protrep.* B 14, trans. modified). As in the *Physics*, then, Aristotle employs a paralogism to demonstrate that art imitates nature in having a purpose, when in fact it is the other way around: insofar as it is ascribed a purpose, nature imitates art. Again, his main philosophical objective is to separate *phusis* from *tuchē* and link it to necessity and logos. Philosophy thereby also becomes the highest telos of nature.

12. Unfortunately, Aristotle never distinguishes explicitly between the mimetic and other arts in his earlier works, introducing this specific distinction only in the *Poetics*. Of course, there is no reason that he should have mentioned this distinction before, because the *Poetics* is his only (extant) treatise that specifically focuses on mimetic art. He nevertheless repeatedly emphasizes that all other arts must be subordinated to the speculative one (*philosophia, theoria*). In the *Protrepticus*, for example, he says: "Some kinds of knowledge produce the good things in life, others use this first kind: some are

Following Plato, therefore, Aristotle uses *mimēsis* in at least two senses in his work. In relation to the useful arts, *mimēsis* denotes a reproductive activity, conveying the idea of bringing something forth on the model of nature. In relation to fine art, *mimēsis* denotes a simulative activity, which conveys the idea of bringing something forth on the model of other arts. The crucial difference between useful art and fine art is that the first can be both reproductive and productive, that is, it can not only follow but also add to nature, whereas the second can be only reproductive, bringing into being nothing that has not already been produced through either useful art or nature.[13]

Both useful and mimetic or fine art are ultimately placed under the guidance of speculative art, but useful art is primarily related to knowledge and truth, whereas mimetic art is devoid of direct cognitive value and is primarily related to (logo-rational) pleasure. It must therefore be kept in mind that, for Aristotle, the specific difference between poetic and other *technai* is mimesis itself and not its end, object, or medium: these categories are employed by Aristotle not in order to fuse mimetic with nonmimetic art, but only in order to distinguish among various mimetic arts. In the *Poetics*, no less than in the *Republic*, the Greek term,

---

ancillary, others prescriptive; with these last, as being more authoritative, rests the true good. If then, only that kind of knowledge which entails correctness of judgment, that which uses reason and envisages good as a whole, that is to say, philosophy, can use all other kinds of knowledge and prescribe to them according to [principles of] nature, we ought to strive in every possible way to become philosophers, since philosophy alone comprises right judgment and unerring wisdom, commanding what ought to be done or not to be done" (*Protrep.* B 9). The mimetic arts, therefore, are equally subordinated to philosophy, which "uses reason [*logōi*] and envisages [*theorousa*] good [*tō agathon*] as a whole [*to holon*]."

13. In *Metaphysics* 6.1032a12–b14, Aristotle again invokes the opposition between *technē* and *phusis*, this time in order to distinguish between "generations by luck or chance," which he ascribes to nature, and "other generations," which he ascribes to "art," to "power," or to "thought" and which he calls "productions" (*poiēseis*). He observes that some "productions" can nevertheless also come about by chance and in this regard they "imitate" or "resemble" nature. This argument is the exact opposite of the one employed in the *Physics* and serves the purposes of a specific context (although even here physical matter is ultimately subordinated to form and chance to necessity). It cannot be inferred from it, however, that Aristotle considers fine art "productive" in the same sense that he does useful art, because he refers only to the latter (the art of medicine in particular). It is this double nature of useful art, productive and reproductive, that some modern commentators apply indiscriminately to fine art. But in the context of the *Poetics* fine art is clearly only reproductive, simulating the productions of other *technai*. In the case of fine art, *poiēsis* also acquires a special meaning, being inextricably linked with *mimēsis*.

when used in relation to fine art, largely denotes what I have called mimesis-imitation (without entirely losing its archaic connotations of mimesis-play) and can best be translated as "simulation."[14]

According to Aristotle, the poets simulate other *technai* and the success of their enterprise does not depend on how truthful they are (after all, imitation is by its very nature only a semblance, that is, an imperfect image of the model), but on how skillful they are in constructing their semblance of truth. Poetry does not speak the truth, it only speaks *like* the truth (in this respect, Defoe and the Neoclassicists knew their Aristotle well). One of the criteria of judging poetry is not truth, but plausibility, and Aristotle makes this point, for example, when he prefers a simulation that is logically impossible but appears probable over one that is probable but appears impossible:

> Now the wonderful is pleasing: as may be inferred from the fact that every one tells a story with some addition of his own, knowing that his hearers like it. *It is Homer who has chiefly taught other poets the art of telling lies skillfully. The secret of it lies in a* [logical] *fallacy*. For assuming that if one thing is or becomes, a second is or becomes, men imagine that, if the second is, the first likewise is or has become. . . . For the mind, knowing the second to be true, falsely infers the truth of the first. . . . Accordingly, the poet should prefer probable impos-

14. The modern epistemological rehabilitation of fine art in the *Poetics* depends precisely on a univocal interpretation of Aristotelian *mimēsis*, which is applied indiscriminately to both the useful and the mimetic arts. Thus McKeon: "Whereas for Plato the term 'imitation' may undergo an indefinite series of gradations of meaning . . . for Aristotle the term is restricted definitely to a single literal meaning" ("The Concept of Imitation in Antiquity," 130). Moreover, the fairly common practice of distinguishing between *technai* not according to the mimetic activity itself but according to its end facilitates fusing fine art with speculative art. On this view, for Aristotle poetry becomes a philosophical activity, because "its main aim for him was akin to wisdom" (Boyd, *Mimesis and Its Decline*, 32). Because by nature poetry is playful simulation it can certainly also be placed in the service of *sōphrosunē* (median wisdom, sobriety) and this is probably what Aristotle attempts to do in the *Poetics*. But even in this case, poetry can be made only to mime wisdom, without being itself the real thing, and therefore must be kept under constant philosophical surveillance. Finally, although Aristotle, like Plato, stresses the deceptive element of mimesis, he no longer openly attacks it on ethical grounds. Hence he appears to some as being more lenient toward poetry than Plato. It can be argued, however, that Aristotle sees no further need to do battle with poetry on philosophy's behalf because, in his eyes, this battle has already been won. He can afford to be magnanimous in victory (a magnanimity that, we recall, is also displayed by Socrates at the end of the *Republic*). Nevertheless, Aristotle essentially adopts Socrates' position on poetry when he considers fine art in a political context.

sibilities to improbable possibilities." (*Poetics* 1460a17–27, trans. Butcher, emphasis added)

Because the artist, like the Sophist, deals in appearances or simulacra, the success of an artwork is not measured by the amount of knowledge it imparts: a painter can represent a female deer as possessing horns without spoiling the artistic effect (*Poetics* 1460b29–32). Although it is advisable, in the interest of plausibility, that the artist follow the other *technai* as faithfully as possible, the critic must not demand "the same kind of correctness in poetry as in politics or indeed in any other art" (*Poetics* 1460b13–15, trans. Bywater). The poet should be judged poor only if he meant to "describe the thing correctly, and failed through lack of simulative power [*mimēsasthai ** adunamian*]" (*Poetics* 1460b17; trans. mine). On the other hand, he should not be condemned if he deliberately brings an error into his work, "one in a matter of, say, medicine or some other special science," because in that case the error "is not in the essentials of the poetic art" (*Poetics* 1460b20–21, trans. Bywater) but, on the contrary, may be demanded by this art. In principle, however, the poet must at all times keep before his eyes the scientific standard of truth: "If . . . the poetic end might have been as well or better attained without sacrifice of technical correctness in such matters, the impossibility is not to be justified, since the description should be, if it can, entirely free from error" (*Poetics* 1460b26–29, trans. Bywater).

In the background of Aristotle's view of art as simulation lies its Sophistic counterpart, related to *technē* as a whole. The author of *Dissoi logoi*, for example, says: "In the writing of tragedies and in painting, that man is best who best deceives us by making things appear like truth" (DK 3.10, trans. mine). He playfully reasons that since "lying" is acceptable in fine art, it should be acceptable in all fields. Like the *Dissoi logoi*, Gorgias' *Encomium on Helen* uses the case of fine art to prove that all reality is semblance or simulacrum which affects and shapes opinion (*doxa*) the same way that an artwork does (DK B 11.17–18). As Redfield remarks, Gorgias claims that "in creating a quasi-reality of appearance and imposing it on the world, [the artist] is doing nothing different from what everyone and everything does, since everything that is, appears, and is known to us as appearance. So Gorgias [unlike Plato] does not have to deny the poet the standing of teacher; rather he assimilates all teaching to poetry and makes all learning a *pathos* or passivity. Thus he can set science, rhetoric, and (sophistic) philosophy together."[15]

15. Redfield, *Nature and Culture*, 147. It is by no means clear, however, to what extent

Aristotle, however, writes after Plato, when science, rhetoric, and philosophy have already been separated from poetry and sophistic precisely on the criterion of mimesis. In the aftermath of Plato, the philosophical issue seems no longer to be how to keep poetry and truth together (for now it is philosophy that is married to the truth, and truth is no bigamist), but how to keep them apart. It is, therefore, difficult to see how in Aristotle's system poetry can have the major cognitive function that Redfield, in the wake of such influential hermeneuticians as Heidegger, Gadamer, and Ricoeur, attributes to it. This attribution seems possible only by erasing the Aristotelian tripartite division of the arts: poetry will then gain an epistemological value equal to that of all the other *technai*, partly "imitating" and partly completing *phusis*.

The view of poetry as a cognitive instrument, according to which poetic imitation leads to "the discovery of form in things,"[16] rests on two passages in the *Poetics* that are as a rule taken out of their immediate context. The first passage says that "the artist may imitate [simulate] things as they ought to be" (*Poetics* 1460b9–11). The second states that "poetry is more philosophical and a higher thing [*philosophōteron kai spoudaioteron*, more abstract and more serious] than history; for poetry tends to express [*legei*, select for expression] the universal, history the particular" (*Poetics* 1451b5–7, trans. Butcher). The immediate context of these passages, however, does not seem to warrant employing them in support of a theory of fine art as cognitive process. In the first case Aristotle lists possible ways of meeting critical objections about apparent lack of plausibility in poetry. In deciding whether poetry conforms to its mimetic nature, fulfilling its function as playful diversion, one has to look at what it purports simulating: historical events, common beliefs (*doxa*), or universal (philosophical or scientific) truths. As long as poetry skillfully simulates any of these objects, it ought to be considered successful *qua* fine art. The criterion of success in poetry is thus neither knowledge nor truth, but only plausibility.

The second passage is a parenthesis in which poetry is favorably compared to history from a philosophical point of view (on the other hand, it is possible, at least theoretically, that *philosophōteron* in *Poetics* 1451b5 is not even used in a strictly Platonic sense, but only to denote something like "spiritual" or "abstract"). Aristotle implicitly subordinates

Gorgias himself believes in this argument, since his oration is a *paignion*. Compare my discussion of the Sophists in chapter 2.
16. Redfield, *Nature and Culture*, 54. See also Trimpi, *Muses of One Mind*, 57–58; and Eden, *Poetic and Legal Fiction*, 48–50.

poetry to philosophy when he notes: " 'Universal' in this case is what kind of person is likely to do or say certain kinds of things, according to probability and necessity; that is what poetry aims at, although it gives its persons particular names afterward; while 'particular' is what Alcibiades did or what happened to him" (*Poetics* 1451b8–11, trans. Else). It now becomes apparent why Aristotle prefers (a certain type of) dramatic poetry to history: whereas dramatic plot, as Aristotle understands it, simulates logical process, Being, necessity, and order, historical narrative traces the chaotic course of historical events, subject to the vicissitudes of Becoming and arbitrary chance. In *Poetics* 1451b, however, Aristotle's emphasis is again on mimesis: although dramatic plausibility, like the Sophistic argument from probability, obeys the law of necessity, or that of cause and effect, it has only to simulate this law, through clever syllogisms rather than truly conform to it (compare Homer's artful lies, *Poetics* 1460a5–b2). Whether true or invented, a plot (*muthos*) will give the same pleasure, and it is pleasure, not cognition, that constitutes its telos. Aristotle implies this much when he observes that the comic poets build their plots on the basis of "general probabilities" and then assign fictitious names to their characters, whereas the tragic poets "still cling to the historically given names." The tragic poets presumably do so because "what is possible is persuasive; so what has not happened we are not ready to believe is possible, while what has happened is, we feel, obviously possible." But even in some tragedies the names are fictitious, such as in Agathon's *Antheus*, which "gives no less pleasure because of that." Therefore, "it is absurd to go searching for this kind of authentication, since even the familiar names are familiar to only a few in the audience and yet *give the same kind of pleasure to all*" (*Poetics* 1451b11–32, trans. Else, emphasis added).

But why is the *muthos* as plot the "first principle and soul" (*archē kai psuchē*, *Poetics* 1450a38) of tragedy, the most important of its six elements? Because, again, it is the one that most closely approximates (without being identical with) logic: "The structure of events is the goal [*telos*] of tragedy and *the goal is the greatest thing of all*" (*Poetics* 1450a22–23, trans. Else, emphasis added). For Aristotle, the *telos* is the ordering principle of reality, according to which nothing exists in the beginning that cannot be revealed, or accounted for, in the end. The *telos* creates organic form or the whole: " 'Whole' [*holon*] is that which has beginning, middle and end. 'Beginning' is that which does not necessarily follow on something else, but after it something else naturally is or happens; 'end,' the other way round, is that which naturally follows on something else, either necessarily or for the most part, but nothing else after it; and 'middle' that which naturally follows on something else and something else on it. So, then, well-constructed plots [*muthoi*] should neither begin nor end at any chance point but follow the guidelines just laid down" (*Poetics* 1450b26–34, trans. Else).

Aristotelian *muthos*, then, is a simulation of logical process itself, with its chains of causes and effects, premises and consequences, laws of necessity, possibility, and probability, and its exclusion of chance and the irrational (*alogon*). In fact, Aristotle's description of *muthos* as "whole" bears a certain family resemblance to parts of Parmenides' description of "what-is," or Being. Like Being and logic, Aristotelian plot is autotelic and self-referential, in other words, it is completely rational. If the act of telling and hearing stories for their own sake gives pleasure (*Poetics* 1460a17–18), *muthos* is the pleasure of order(ing) for its own sake, the beauty-producing play of reason. The beautiful itself is defined in logo-rational terms, for "beauty depends on size and order." Hence the plot, like a "living creature or anything that is composed of parts, should not only have these in a fixed order to one another but also possess a definite size which *does not depend on chance*." As neither a very tiny creature nor an excessively huge one can be beautiful—"for then it *cannot all be perceived at once and so its unity and wholeness are lost*"—beautiful plots must have length, but one that "can be taken in a single view" (*Poetics* 1450b34–1451a6, trans. Else, emphasis added).

The plot conforms to the aesthetic standards of a logo-rational taste, demanding that an artwork be "taken in a single view," that is, visualized so that the parts can then be related to the whole. The best method of composition is not sequential or temporal, as in epic song, but configurative or spatial. In this respect, "the argument [*logos*] of the play, whether previously made or in process of composition by itself, *should first be sketched out in abstract form* and only then expanded and other scenes ('episodes') added" (*Poetics* 1455a34–b2, trans. Else, emphasis added). It is also the plot that renders tragedy superior to epic, where length and loosely connected episodes allow for less visualization and therefore less unity: "The imitation [simulation] produced by the epic poets is less unified . . . so that if they do produce a unified plot it either, if briefly presented, seems curtailed or, if it follows the length of the norm, watery" (*Poetics* 1462b3–7, Else, trans. slightly modified). That tragedy allows for more unity is also proven by the fact that one epic simulation can be broken down into several tragedies (*Poetics* 1462b5), in which disconnected episodes become well-constructed plots. Conversely, the worst tragic plots are the "episodic" ones in which "there is no probability or necessity for the order in which episodes follow each other" (*Poetics* 1451b34–35, trans. Else).

Probability and necessity are invariably favored over chance. The complex plots are the best when recognition and peripeteia "grow out of the very structure of the plot itself, in such a way that on the basis of what has happened previously this particular outcome follows either by necessity or in accordance with probability" (*Poetics* 1452a18–20, trans. Else). Even what is unexpected will be more productive of wonder if it is logical rather than if it happens "merely at random, by chance—because even among chance occurrences the ones people consider most marvelous are those that seem to have come about as if on purpose." An example is Mitys' statue that during a religious festival fell on the man who caused Mitys' death, killing him in turn: "It stands to reason, people think, that such things don't happen by chance—so plots of that sort cannot fail to be artistically superior" (*Poetics* 1452a4–11, trans. Else).

Chance and the irrational shall find a place in the plot only if they can be tamed and recuperated, that is, if they can be made either plausible or charming:

> The plot must not be composed of irrational parts. Everything irrational should if possible be excluded; or at all events, it should lie outside the action of the play. . . . But once the irrational has been introduced and an air of likelihood imparted to it we must accept it in spite of the absurdity. Take even the irrational incidents in the *Odyssey*, where Odysseus is left upon the shore of Ithaca. How intolerable even these might have been would be apparent if an inferior poet were to treat the subject. As it is the absurdity is veiled by the poetic charm with which the poet invests it. (*Poetics* 1460a27–b2, trans. Butcher, modified)

This passage indicates that *muthos* in the sense of plot is like logic, not logic itself, and therefore simulates rather than imparts knowledge. It is because plot is only a simulation of a visual thought-pattern or a logo-rational thought-process that "absurdities" are tolerable, provided they are given an "air of likelihood." Aristotle often runs into examples of such "absurdities" in archaic poetry, where the principles of composition are an amalgam of archaic and logo-rational elements, and he invariably attempts to rationalize the archaic ones. *Muthos* itself is a good example of this attempt: Aristotle uses the term in several ways, including its archaic sense of "true narrative" and its logo-rational sense of well-constructed "plot," or mimesis of logical process.[17]

Aristotle's double employment of *muthos* is evident, for example, in his classification of the six elements of tragedy according to their poetic function. Two elements, diction or verbal expression (*lexis*) and the composition of songs (*melopoiia*), are a means of simulation; a third element, spectacle (*opsis*), is a manner of simulation; and the other three, story (*muthos*), character (*ta ēthē* or *ēthos*), and thought (*dianoia*), are objects of simulation (*Poetics* 1450a38–b20). Thus *muthos*, together with *ta ēthē* and *dianoia*, can be both the object and the product of mimesis. In this sense, it is confusing to translate *muthos* by "plot" throughout the *Poetics*, and here it should be translated by "true narrative" or that which becomes a plot as a consequence of aesthetic simulation according to logo-rational standards. To the archaic meaning of *muthos* as true narrative, Aristotle adds its recently acquired meaning of "invented story" or "lie" (see Herodotus and Thucydides, who oppose history as factual truth to myth as fantastic tale; it is also in this way that we still use the word "myth" in modern science or in everyday language); on these two common meanings, Aristotle then superimposes his own specialized sense of "plot," an invented story or an artificial structuring of events that simulates or appears like (logical) truth. This artificial ordering of events simulating logical process is also what distinguishes the poet from and renders him superior to the historian. It is perhaps in this sense that one can best understand Aristotle's somewhat garbled explanation as to why a poet simulating historical actions or events is still a poet-maker (*poiētēs*) and, as such, remains superior to the historian: "Even if it happens that he puts something that has actually taken place into poetry, he is none the less a poet; for there is nothing to prevent some of the things that have happened from being the things that can happen, and that is the sense in which he is their maker" (*Poetics* 1451b29–32, trans. Else). In other words, the poet simulates historical deeds according to philosophical principles (the law of necessity and probability) rather than historical contingency (compare Thucydides' view of history as chaotic Becoming governed by *tuchē*).

Like *muthos*, *ta ēthē* and *dianoia* are both objects of simulation and elements of tragedy. This double employment seems again to have misled

17. Wartelle lists the following meanings of *muthos* in the *Poetics*: "récit, conte, fable, mythe, sujet d'une pièce" (*Lexique de la "Poétique,"* 106). For the archaic notion of *muthos* as true "protonarrative," see Prier, *Thauma Idesthai*, 163–214.

commentators into believing that in the *Poetics* Aristotle attributes a major cognitive function to poetry. But Aristotle clearly implies that he uses *ta ēthē* and *dianoia* in both a poetic and a nonpoetic sense, for example when he defines these terms:

> Third in rank is thought. This is the ability to state the issues and appropriate points pertaining to a given topic, *an ability which springs from the arts of politics and rhetoric*; in fact the earlier poets made their characters talk 'politically,' the present day poets 'rhetorically.' But 'character' is that kind of utterance which clearly reveals the bent of a man's moral choice . . . while 'thought' is the passages in which they try to prove that something is so or not so, or state some general principle. (*Poetics* 1450b4–12, trans. Else, emphasis added)

This passage shows again that poetry has little to do with knowledge, being only a simulation thereof. In fact, a discussion of "thought" and "character" does not properly belong in the *Poetics*, and Aristotle refers the reader to his *Ethics*, *Rhetoric*, and *Politics*. Regarding *dianoia*, for example, Aristotle observes: "For a discussion of 'thought,' then, please consult our treatise on rhetoric, for the problem is particularly connected with that discipline" (*Poetics* 1456a33–35, Else).

Aristotle not only subordinates mimetic art to other *technai*, but he also polarizes aesthetic mimesis itself. As in Plato, fine art can be either good or bad mimesis, and the philosopher-critic is called upon to decide between the two on logo-rational criteria. Good aesthetic simulation is the one following the guidelines of logic; the bad is the one straying from these guidelines into the irrational and the aleatory.

■ Poetica: *The Pleasures of Mimesis*

Because in Aristotle aesthetic pleasure is inseparable from mimesis, it will appear equally polarized. For him, good aesthetic pleasure comes from the logo-rational play of the intellect (whose highest product is not mimetic art, but philosophical speculation), while the bad one comes from the violent or ecstatic play of the senses, present, for example, in archaic *mousikē*. Although Aristotle regards pleasure as the telos of poetry, his concept of aesthetic pleasure comes much closer to that of Plato than to that of the Sophists, who also viewed *mousikē* as pleasurable play.

Aristotle mentions aesthetic pleasure early in the *Poetics*, when he speculates on the origins and development of poetry. For him poetic pleasure seems to derive from two sources. The first source is the pleasure of imitating: "The habit of imitating is congenital to human beings from childhood (actually man differs from the other animals in that he is the most imitative and learns his first lessons through imitation), and so is the pleasure that all men take in works of imitation" (*Poetics* 1448b5–9, trans. Else, slightly modified). The second source of poetic pleasure is the pleasure of learning, which is related to the pleasure of imitation, because humans learn their first lessons by it. That humans take pleasure in the works of imitation is witnessed by the fact that although they are repelled at the sight of unpleasant animals and corpses, they nevertheless enjoy their *images*. This enjoyment is also traceable to the pleasure of learning, for learning "is eminently pleasurable not only to philosophers but to the rest of mankind in the same way." But there is a difference between the aesthetic pleasure of the philosopher and that of the common person insofar as the aesthetic pleasure of the latter is restricted by lack of knowledge: "The reason [nonphilosophers] take pleasure in the images is that in the process of viewing they find themselves learning, that is, reckoning what kind a given thing belongs to" (*Poetics* 1448b15–17, trans. Else). Because the common man learns by viewing, his pleasure cannot be properly called aesthetic, and it is for this reason that Aristotle finds it restricted. On the other hand, the philosopher already possesses the knowledge of the object presented, and therefore, presumably, he is free to enjoy it aesthetically, that is, *outside* the framework of learning.

Although *Poetics* 1448b is extremely condensed, telescoping various arguments that need to be sorted out and clarified, several points seem to emerge: Poetic mimesis originates in and is related to another kind of mimesis, through which humans acquire learning. This, perhaps, is the mimesis that Aristotle mentions in the *Physics* in connection with the general concept of *technē*, which, we recall, partly follows and partly completes *phusis* and which is productive of knowledge. As Else suggests, here Aristotle probably invokes, by way of analogy, a classroom situation in which pupils learn by looking at images of animals and bodies, or by what we call visual aids.[18] At the same time, however, Aristotle appears to make a tautological argument: pupils learn because they enjoy looking at the images and they enjoy looking at the images because they learn. But this tautology is mitigated if we realize that the pleasure of learning differs from artistic pleasure, being its "operative cause" (*aitia*). Aristotle does

18. Else, *APA*, 128. But Else does not discern two kinds of mimesis operating in this passage. Instead he believes that Aristotle polemicizes with Plato and attributes intellectual qualities to the experience of viewing an artwork.

not clearly spell out that he merely employs an analogy in order to explain the nature of poetic pleasure as deriving from the pleasure of learning, which is in turn related to the pleasure of imitating, and the clarity of his argument is hardly enhanced by the fact that in the same breath he attempts to distinguish among different kinds of pleasure on the basis of different kinds of mimesis.

The pleasurable experience of examining an object for didactic purposes and the pleasurable experience of viewing a work of art part ways, however, and Aristotle drops his analogy when he observes: "If the viewer happens not to have seen such an object before, the reproduction will not produce the pleasure *qua* reproduction but through its workmanship or color or something else of the sort" (*Poetics* 1447b17–19, trans. Else). It now appears that Aristotle not only invokes the pleasure that all men take in "works of imitation," that is, the second *aitia* of the development of poetry, but also distinguishes between two kinds of pleasure, corresponding to two kinds of mimesis: mimesis as learning and poetic mimesis. There is the pleasure of mimesis as cognition, employed in the process of learning and reserved for the useful arts and philosophy; and there is the pleasure of mimesis as recognition, which comes the closest to the pleasure of poetic mimesis. The first derives from learning about the model, the second from having previous knowledge about it.[19] The pleasure of recognition (which can also be part of aesthetic pleasure) is, moreover, directly subordinated to the pleasure of cognition, which, in its highest form, derived from intellectual speculation, is accessible only to the philosopher.[20]

19. Compare *Problemata*, 918a3–10: "Why do men take greater pleasure in listening to those who are singing such music as they already know than music which they do not know? Is it because, when they recognize what is being sung, it is more obvious that the singer is as it were achieving his aims, and this is pleasant to contemplate? Or is it because it is less pleasant to learn? And the reason of this is that in the one case there is acquisition of knowledge, in the other the use and recognition of it. Further, that which is familiar is always pleasanter than the unfamiliar" (in *The Works of Aristotle*, vol. 7, trans. E. S. Forster; line citations are from Aristoteles, *Opera*, 5 vols., ed., I. Bekker [Berlin, 1831–70]). Aristotle's reasoning seems again tautological. If the end (*telos*) of music is pleasure and if men derive more pleasure from a piece that they already know, then music best achieves its end not through cognition but recognition. In turn, the aesthetic pleasure of recognition is derived from "teleological" or philosophical pleasure (a pleasure of spatial visualization, *theoria*, rather than temporal succession): on hearing a musical piece again, one can recognize its end in the beginning, as it were. Conversely, learning produces less aesthetic pleasure, because it is cognition rather than recognition. 20. Gadamer, among other contemporary hermeneuticians, attempts to bridge the gap between fine art and knowledge precisely by fusing the notion of cognition with that of

Commentators seem justified in arguing that the Aristotelian concepts of *scholē* (leisure) and *diagōgē* (pastime, diversion) can range from the lowest to the highest kind of pleasurable activity, but they tend to forget the subordinate place of mimetic art within this hedonic order of rank. For example, Butcher fuses mimetic and speculative art (philosophy) on the basis of the wide range of *diagōgē*: "But [fine] art in its highest idea is one of the serious activities of the mind which constitutes the final well-being of man. Its end is pleasure, *but pleasure peculiar to that state of rational enjoyment in which perfect repose is united with perfect energy.*"[21]

Butcher's argument bears a marked resemblance to Gadamer's view of Platonic thought as "a unity of power and the love of knowledge" and of human life as "dynamic tension." Yet one should remember not only Aristotle's tripartite division of the arts (useful arts, mimetic arts, and philosophy—a division that Butcher himself acknowledges), but also the criterion by which Aristotle distinguishes the fine arts from the others. This criterion is, again, neither the object "imitated" nor the "end of imitation," but mimesis itself. Butcher argues that for Aristotle tragedy is a form of philosophy (although on the basis of *Poetics* 1451b5–7, previously cited, it could equally be argued that it is comedy, not tragedy, that is the most philosophical because of the comic poet's proper employment of general probabilities). But granted that for Aristotle tragedy is the highest pleasure available in the mimetic arts, it is so only because it simulates logo-rational, philosophical pleasure, being purged as much as possible of its sensuous, violent counterpart. It is hardly by chance that Aristotle ranks *melopoiia* and *opsis* last among the six elements of tragedy.

---

recognition, which he interprets as Platonic *anamnesis* (see *Wahrheit und Methode*, 102–4). Here Gadamer reacts to what appears to him as the post-Kantian, Romantic divorce between fine art as mimesis and knowledge. He advocates a "return" to Plato and Aristotle, not realizing that they themselves effect this divorce and that the modern history of literary theory has been little more than a series of attempts (including Kant's and Gadamer's own) to bring about a reconciliation. Typically, these attempts always presuppose a reappropriation of Plato and Aristotle. A recent example of this approach is Trimpi's *Muses of the Mind*, in which the rationalist reappropriation goes even beyond Greek philosophy, to Hesiod. From a contemporary perspective, Trimpi's rationalist "apology for poesie" as a synthesis of speculative, prudential, and productive activities appears as a brilliant but superfluous tour de force. The history of Western criticism seems oversaturated by rationalist apologies that reenact the Aristotelian subordination of poetry to metaphysics, rhetoric, and ethics. Perhaps what we now need is not a Sidneyan or Shelleyan reaffirmation of poetry and (serious) literature in general as cultural authority, but a thorough historical examination of the sources and grounds of any form of authority, including literature and literary criticism.

21. Butcher, *ATP*, 21, emphasis added.

These are the elements that are closest to the arbitrary play of the senses and to physical pleasure as ecstatic enhancement of the feeling of power. Consequently, Aristotle attempts to separate them from archaic, tragic pleasure and transform tragedy into the high entertainment of the Logos.

Aristotle deals with *melopoiia* and *opsis* in an ambiguous manner throughout the *Poetics*. For example, he contends that pity and fear should be aroused through the arrangement of events or plot rather than through spectacle: "to bring about this effect through spectacle [*opsis*] is less artistic and dependent on the attention given to staging. Those who by the means of spectacle seek to produce not the fearful but merely the monstrous have nothing in common with tragedy, for one should not seek every pleasure from tragedy but only that proper to it" (*Poetics* 1453b7–11, trans. Gilbert). Like Socrates, Aristotle rejects as inartistic the emotional impact that comes directly from the senses (image and sound) without being first sifted through the intellect. The events are selected and arranged in such a way that they bring about the tragic effect through logical reasoning rather than through performing.

Aristotle again stresses the pleasures of logo-rational plot over those of performance in his comparison of tragedy and epic. He indirectly rejects early tragedy, in which "the performers, as though they were appearing before a lot of stupid hearers, indulge in a great deal of action; bad flute-players, for instance, twist about when they have to represent [mime] discus-throwing and tug at the leader of the chorus when they are playing the music relating to Scylla" (*Poetics* 1461b29–32, trans. Gilbert). In his opinion, this kind of mimesis is addressed to a vulgar audience and has nothing to do with the poet, but with the performer, who panders to the lower tastes of the public (compare Socrates' somewhat similar argument against the art of the rhapsode in the *Ion*). Tragedy "may produce its effect without movement and action just as the epic does, for through reading we can find of what sort a play is" (*Poetics* 1462a11–13). This is in keeping with Aristotle's earlier statement, according to which "the song-composition [*melopoiia*] of the remaining parts [of tragedy] is the greatest of the sensuous attractions, and the visual adornment [*opsis*, spectacle] of the dramatic persons can have *a strong emotional effect but is the least artistic element, the least connected with the poetic art*" (*Poetics* 1450b16–18, trans. Else, emphasis added). Aristotle attempts to prove that these sensuous elements are unimportant by invoking a typically literate argument: "The force of tragedy can be felt even without the benefit of public performance and actors," that is, by reading alone. As to the production of the visual effect, *opsis*, the "property man's art [the art of the designer of scenery, trans. Gilbert] is even more decisive than that of the poets" (1450b18–20, trans. Else). In other words, tragedy can attain its full telos as philosophical pleasure without being performed.

Although Aristotle classifies *melopoiia* as being one of the two "means of imitation" in tragedy, he pays very little attention to it (he treats it somewhat more extensively in the *Politics*, but in relation to education, not to tragedy), focusing mainly on the other means, *lexis*. Even in regard to *lexis*, however, he ignores the impact of language as sound or utterance and mostly emphasizes its abstract or visual aspects. The ability to produce "metaphors" is the highest mark of good *poiēsis*: "By far the most important thing is to be good at metaphor. This is the only part of the job that cannot be learned from others; on the contrary it is a token of high native gifts, *for making good metaphors depends on perceiving the likeness in things*" (*Poetics* 1459a5–8, trans. Else, emphasis added). Scenic *opsis* is therefore replaced by the *opsis* of the mind, the visual ability of perceiving not movement and discontinuity, but continuity and sameness ("likeness" or identity) in things.

Aristotle's arguments in favor of plot against performance are perfectly understandable from a logo-rational viewpoint, given the fact that, as Plato points out in both the *Republic* and the *Laws*, tragic performance gives primacy to the emotions over the intellect. Like Plato, Aristotle is fully aware of the archaic power of sound and image, and he does not fail to invoke them when he argues the superiority of tragedy over epic: the first is more "dynamic" than the second, displaying the highest "vividness" (*enargestata*) through performance (*Poetics*, 1462a14–15). Tragedy is superior not only because it has a compact and consistent plot, but also because it has "in addition, as no trifling component, music and spectacle, in which the pleasure of tragedy to a great extent consists" (*Poetics* 1462a15–17, trans. Gilbert).[22] This argument flies in the face of everything that Aristotle has said about *opsis* and *melopoiia* up to this point. It appears more eristic than philosophical (as Vahlen points out), because it attempts to assert the superiority of tragedy by *all* (archaic and logo-rational) means. Else, for example, notes:

> Having just said that tragedy does not require performance, Aristotle ought not in decency to drag in its external trappings. Moreover the remark that "it can even use the (epic) verse" is a dubious one, after his demonstration that both tragedy . . . and the epic . . .

22. On the translation of this passage, which is hotly disputed, see Gilbert, *Literary Criticism*, 114 n.202.

had hit upon their respective meters as the only really suitable ones. We shall have to leave this as an unsolved minor puzzle.[23]

But this is a minor (or a major?) puzzle only from a rationalist standpoint, for the passage seems a perfect illustration of the double nature—archaic and logo-rational—of tragedy with which Aristotle had to contend and of which even he, despite his systematic attempts, could not entirely dispose.

Another archaic element that Aristotle attempts to rationalize is the tragic notion of catharsis, which seems to perform a volte-face in the *Poetics* when compared to its earlier version in the *Politics*. In the earlier work, most commentators agree that Aristotelian *katharsis*, when applied to *mousikē*, preserves its medical, homeopathic sense of curing the wound by the spear that inflicted it (as in Wagner's *Parsifal*), which is an ancient *mimetic* belief deeply rooted in the archaic mentality.[24] But what is most relevant to our discussion is the general context in which Aristotle employs the term: as in the *Republic* and the *Laws*, this context is education.

Aristotle first draws a distinction between three kinds of melodies: ethical, action-inspiring, and passionate or enthusiastic (in the archaic, mimetic, or ecstatic sense). Each of these has its proper place in the community, and Aristotle appears, at least at first sight, to be more tolerant than Plato's Socrates. *Mousikē* can be employed for the purpose of education, purgation (*katharsis*), and it "may also serve for the benefit of cultivation [*diagōgē*, also pastime, intellectual or otherwise], with which may be linked that of recreation and relaxation after exertion."[25] But even

23. Else, *APA*, 643.
24. For a detailed discussion of this concept, see Butcher, *ATP*, 246–73. I have trouble, however, with Butcher's reading of tragic *katharsis* as a moral concept through which the "spectator himself [is] lifted above the special case and brought face to face with universal law and the divine plan of the world" (271), even though I do believe that Aristotle attempts to rationalize the archaic notion. Butcher's view that in its beginnings Greek tragedy "was but a wild religious excitement, a bacchic ecstacy" whose aimlessness "was brought under artistic law" is nevertheless revealing: it is a rationalist, evolutionary version of the history of tragedy, to which Aristotle himself contributed a great deal, not least through his theory of catharsis.
25. *The Politics of Aristotle*, 8.1341b40, trans. E. Barker (Oxford, 1946). I have also used B. Jowett's translation, *The Works of Aristotle* (Oxford, 1921), ed. W. D. Ross, vol. 10, and have occasionally modified both Jowett and Barker in order to convey my sense of a certain passage. I have consulted two editions of the Greek text: the Guillaume Budé edition, *Aristote: Politique*, 3 vols. (Paris, 1968–86), established by Jean Aubonnet; and the Oxford edition, established by W. D. Ross (Oxford, 1957), from which I cite. I should

though all the modes are allowable, they should not be employed "in the same sort of way" (*Politics* 8.1342a1–2, trans. Barker), and it turns out that Aristotle's division of melodies is also a hierarchy: only the ethical melodies are appropriate in educating the young and, as such, are given priority over the others.

The specific difference between the ethical and the other two categories is that only the action-inspiring and the passionate or enthusiastic melodies lead to *katharsis*, purgation, a term that apparently remains unexplained because Aristotle adds, in a parenthesis: "the word 'purgation' we use at present without explanation, but when hereafter we speak of poetry, we will treat the subject with more precision" (*Politics* 8.1341b38–40, trans. Jowett). It seems fairly clear, however, that Aristotle employs the term in connection with archaic mimesis-play. For example, he observes that "feelings such as pity and fear, or, again, enthusiasm exist very strongly in some souls, and have more or less influence over all," and it is these feelings that the melodies of action and passion can both excite and soothe: "Some persons fall into a religious frenzy, whom we see as a result of the sacred melodies—when they have used the melodies that excite the soul to mystic frenzy—restored *as if* they had undergone medical treatment and purgation" (*Politics* 8.1342a4–11, trans. Jowett, modified and emphasis added). Following Socrates in the *Ion* and the *Republic*, Aristotle refers to Dionysiac frenzy—he mentions both this phrase and Socrates later in the argument (*Politics* 1342a32, 1342b4–5)—and describes mimesis-play in language similar to that of Euripides.

Through rhythmic chanting and dancing, a shaman, a soothsayer, a maenad or any other participant in an archaic religious ritual can bring himself to ecstatic frenzy, which will spend itself out either through (directed or random) violence or through sheer physical and emotional exhaustion. It is not unnatural to associate, on the analogy of homeopathy, the means through which the ecstatic frenzy is brought about with its "cure" (which, in this case, simply means self-exhaustion). Hence Aristotle, probably following accepted musical theory, attributes a "purging" or "purifying" effect to certain kinds of melodies, in both bacchic ritual and artistic performances:

A like sort of effect will also be produced [by certain melodies employed in artistic performances] on those who are specially

---

again emphasize that Aristotle's use of the term *mousikē* in the *Politics* fluctuates between its archaic and more recent meanings. For this reason I have left it in the original Greek, although both Barker and Jowett translate it as "music."

subject to feelings of pity and fear, or feelings of any kind; indeed it
will also be produced on the rest of us, in proportion as each is liable
to some degree of feeling; and the result will be that all will
experience a similar sort of purging and release of emotion, accompanied by pleasure. (*Politics* 8.1342a11–16, trans. Barker, modified)

Aristotle indicates thoughout this passage that he employs the medical
term only metaphorically, in order to describe the effect of a musical
performance on its audience. We have seen that the traditional singer of
tales can also bring his audience to a pitch of frenzy or an ecstatic feeling of
power, then gradually soothe its aroused emotions, and it is this mimetic
power of *mousikē* that Aristotle invokes. His emphasis, however, is on its
harmless, indeed beneficial (rather than potentially destructive) effect.
Hence his need for the medical analogy: the word *pharmakon*, with its
ambivalent connotations of both poison and medicine, would be an equally
appropriate metaphor in this context. Like the melodies of action, the
"purgative melodies give an innocent pleasure to mankind," and it is in this
innocent, harmless kind that "those who perform music at the theatre
should be invited to compete" (*Politics* 1342a14–18, trans. Jowett). Ultimately, then, by rationalizing his notion of catharsis Aristotle also
attempts to separate *mousikē* from its violent, agonistic context.[26]

In the *Poetics*, Aristotle modifies the traditional notion of catharsis even
further, in order to fit his logo-rational theory of tragedy. Since *melopoiia*
has now an unessential role among the six tragic elements and since
Aristotle must still explain the emotional impact of tragedy, he moves
catharsis from *mousikē* to plot and transforms it largely into an intellectual
or spiritual experience. Hence the puzzling character of the term in the
Poetics where, despite Aristotle's promise in the *Politics* to treat it extensively in connection with poetry, *katharsis* appears only once, in the
general definition of tragedy: "Tragedy, then, is an imitation [*mimēsis*,
simulation] of an action that is serious, complete, and of a certain
magnitude; in language embellished with each kind of artistic ornament,
the several kinds being found in separate parts of the play; in the form of
action, not of narrative; through pity and fear effecting the proper
purgation of these emotions" (*Poetics* 1449b24–28, trans. Butcher).[27]

26. It cannot be stressed enough, moreover, that the melodies conducive to *katharsis* are
not to be employed for educational purposes, but only for entertainment. See my
examination of Aristotle's notions of *mousikē*, play, and education in the next section.
27. It is possible, as Else and others think, that Aristotle did fulfill his promise and
treated tragic catharsis at length in one of the now lost sections of the *Poetics*, but that is
pure speculation and cannot essentially affect the present discussion.

Aristotle adds that by "language embellished" (*hedusmenos logos*, pleasurable, attractive speech) he means the one that includes rhythm (*ruthmos*), harmony (*harmonia*), and song (*melos*), that is, rhythmic speech with and without song. His explanation of *hedusmenos logos* is also a logo-rational interpretation, through which he implicitly both separates music from and subordinates it to (logo-rational) language: for him, the rhythmic speech of song is not *mousikē*, but an ornamental form of ordinary speech.

The phrase "through pity and fear effecting the proper purgation of these emotions" (*di' eleon kai phobou perainousa tēn ton toiouton pathēmaton katharsin*) has elicited countless interpretations reflected in various translations, and it is pointless to review all of them here.[28] Although my reading shares with some of the others the assumption that the *katharsis* of the *Poetics* is in some way connected to the one in the *Politics*, it places this connection in a different light: Aristotle attempts to turn the archaic notion into a logo-rational one by disconnecting catharsis from the powerful, ecstatic emotions aroused by *mousikē* in an archaic audience and reconnecting it to the moderate thrill aroused by a successful simulation of logical process (or what Aristotle calls "plot") in a classical audience. In this regard, Else's attempt to show how catharsis is related to other elements of the plot such as *hamartia* and *anagnorisis* seems to me fully justified. As Else points out, for Aristotle the pleasure of tragedy is "not automatic [as in *mousikē*, for example], it has to be *produced* by the poet

---

28. For a list of studies on Aristotelian *katharsis*, as well as for a useful summary of the controversy around the meaning of the term, which has been interpreted as either "purgation" or "purification" or both, see Else, *APA*, 225–27. Else concludes: "Since Bernays [in *Grundzüge der verlorenen Abhandlung des Aristoteles über die Wirkung der Tragödie* (Breslau, 1857) and *Zwei Abhandlungen über die aristotelische Theorie des Dramas* (Berlin, 1880)], there have been two main lines of interpretation of 'catharsis,' one holding to the medical sense (purgation or relief of the spirit *from* the emotions) and insisting on the 'autonomy' of art, the other explaining the word in various ways but tending towards an ethical concept (purification *of* the emotions). The latter view has been on the wane; but Rostagni, for example, though professing to accept the medical sense, combines it with the 'orgiastic' and arrives at an eclectic moral theory: catharsis is the reduction of the passions to measure and reason" (*APA*, 227). But Rostagni does not seem entirely wrong as far as the notion of catharsis in the *Poetics* goes. For recent discussions, some of them posterior to or not mentioned by Else, the reader can also consult: M. Pohlenz, "Furcht und Mitleid," *Hermes* 83 (1955): 49–74; W. Schadewaldt, "Furcht und Mitleid?," *Hermes* 83 (1955): 129–71; H. D. Goldstein, "Mimesis and Catharsis Reexamined," *Journal of Aesthetics and Art Criticism* 24, no. 4 (1966): 567–77; Schaper, *Prelude to Aesthetics*, 101–18; Krishna G. Srivastava, *Aristotle's Doctrine of Tragic Catharsis* (Allahabad, 1982); and Parker, *Miasma*, chap. 7, "Disease, Bewitchment and Purifiers," esp. 212–16.

through the arrangement of his work. . . . The poet's task of arousing the tragic emotions and the pleasure that springs from them [through catharsis] is a task of construction."[29] Since this construction is entirely logical, the emotion aroused in the audience and resolved into pleasure is "authorized and released by an intellectually conditioned structure of action."[30]

Else, however, sees his interpretation of Aristotelian catharsis in the *Poetics* threatened by Aristotle's employment of it in the *Politics* and takes great pains in refuting those who attempt to apply the medical metaphor to poetic catharsis. He is certainly justified in discussing poetic catharsis in the context of the *Poetics*, according to his principle that Aristotle's poetic notions should be examined in their immediate context and not referred to political, rhetorical, and ethical contexts (a sound principle that Else repeatedly emphasizes, but unfortunately does not always follow). Yet his rationalist standpoint prevents him from seeing that in the case of catharsis, as in the case of many other poetic elements, Aristotle deliberately transforms an archaic notion into a logo-rational one.

As to the concepts of pity (*eleos*) and fear (*phobos*), Else correctly perceives them as being brought by Aristotle into close relationship to the Logos and, like catharsis, made to serve the logo-rational goals of the plot.[31] But he does not consider that Aristotelian "pity" and "fear" may not be quite the same emotions (*pathēmata*) that are described, say, in the *Iliad* and the *Odyssey*, even though Aristotle himself is fully aware of the difference. For example, when Aristotle says that the tragic poet should not produce pity and fear through *opsis*, but through the logical arrangements of the incidents (*Poetics* 1453b1–3), he indirectly also attempts to redefine these emotions. In the *Iliad*, Achilles pities Priam not because of his compassionate nature in a Christian sense or because he identifies with the suffering of mankind in general, but because the old Trojan king reminds him of his father. The Aristotelian idea of pity still retains something of its archaic nature, for example in the *Rhetoric*. As Butcher points out, this work defines pity as that which "we would fear for ourselves if we were in a position of him who is the object of our pity." Hence the "tacit reference to self makes pity, as generally described in the *Rhetoric*, sensibly different from the pure instinct of compassion, the

29. Else, *APA*, 449–50.
30. Ibid., 449.
31. Ibid., 370–75 and 433–36.

unselfish sympathy with others' distress, which most modern writers understand by pity."[32]

It does not seem sufficient, however, to look at Aristotle's notions of pity and fear in a purely ethical or rhetorical context. Aristotle's correlation of pity and fear is not his own invention, being most likely of religious origin. An archaic suppliant would appeal to the aggressor's pity not only by exaggerating or making a spectacle of his own misery (that is, powerlessness) but also by invoking the greater power of Zeus, playing on the aggressor's fear of punishment: this is, for example, Odysseus' strategy while disguised as a beggar in the *Odyssey*. What seems relatively new is that Aristotle takes this correlation out of its religious context and generalizes it. By defining pity exclusively in relation to fear, and fear exclusively in relation to pity, he takes the first step toward a logo-rational redefinition of these concepts. Once this step is taken, the two concepts can again be separated.[33] An intermediary step in this process of separation is an emphasis on the emotions experienced toward close relatives, where pity and fear can be both correlated and independent of each other. It is for this reason that Aristotle recommends misfortune within a family as the best kind of tragic simulation, leading to pleasure by the catharsis of pity and fear (*Poetics* 1453b19–1454a10).

Else also takes Butcher to task for retaining the medical metaphor in his discussion of Aristotle's employment of *katharsis* in the *Poetics*.[34] But Butcher seems to me right when he points out that "Aristotle would probably admit that indirectly the drama has a moral influence in enabling the emotional system to throw off some perilous stuff, certain elements of feeling, which, if left to themselves, might develop dangerous energy and impede the free play of those vital functions on which the exercise of virtue depends."[35] Note, however, Butcher's equally rationalist, neo-Kantian view of what constitutes the "free play of vital functions," a free play that is explicitly divorced from "dangerous energy," or archaic, violent play. Butcher no less than Else gives a rationalist interpretation to the history of Greek tragedy when he concludes: "Greek tragedy in its beginnings was but a wild religious excitement, a bacchic ecstasy. This *aimless ecstasy was brought under artistic law*. It was ennobled by objects

32. Butcher, *ATP*, 257–58.
33. Butcher offers examples of this separation in Aristotle, *Rhetoric* 1389b8 and 1390a19, as well as in Euripides, *Electra* 294–95; see Butcher, *ATP*, 258 n.1.
34. Else, *APA*, 439. Butcher's discussion of catharsis is in *ATP*, 240–73.
35. Butcher, *ATP*, 269.

worthy of an ideal emotion. The poets found out how the transport of human pity and human fear might under the excitation of art, be dissolved in joy, and the pain escape in the purified tide of human sympathy." [36]

Butcher and Else appear to have adopted this interpretation from Aristotle himself, who also presents the history of Greek tragedy in logo-rational, evolutionary terms. For example, Aristotle describes tragedy as a "natural" development out of epic, or as a "necessary" entelechy of poetic form:

> As, in the serious style, Homer is pre-eminent among poets, for he alone combined dramatic form with excellence of imitation [simulation], so he too first laid down the main lines of Comedy, by dramatising the ludicrous instead of writing personal satire. His Margites bears the same relation to Comedy that the Iliad and Odyssey do to Tragedy. But when Tragedy and Comedy came to light, the two classes of poets still followed their natural bent: *the lampooners became writers of Comedy, and the Epic poets were succeeded by Tragedians, since drama was a larger and higher form of art.* (Poetics 1448b34–1449a6, trans. Butcher, emphasis added)

Furthermore, according to Aristotle, "tragedy advanced by slow degrees; each new element that showed itself was in turn developed. Having passed through many changes, *it found its natural form and there it stopped"* (Poetics 1449a14–15, trans. Butcher, emphasis added). The choral parts are slowly diminished in importance and the "speech of the protagonists" or the dialogue becomes predominant, which also means a gradual subordination of mousikē to logos. The point is not that tragedy did not undergo some of the changes mentioned by Aristotle (it probably did), but that Aristotle interprets these changes in logo-rational terms as a natural, inevitable development inherent in the poetic "form" as such, an interpretation that implies a teleological notion of history as orderly necessity, excluding arbitrariness and chance.

The examples above equally show that Aristotle's treatise on poetry is not ideologically innocent. Under the guise of systematic analysis and classification, this treatise completes the task begun by Plato of rationalizing poetry and turning it into a philosophical instrument. When rationalization proves impossible, then the archaic element is either judged inferior, as in the case of the mnemonic, aggregative narrative techniques

36. Ibid., 273, emphasis added.

of epic song, or it is largely minimized, as in the case of *melopoiia* and *opsis*, which, we have seen, Aristotle treats both cursorily and ambivalently. In this respect, what Aristotle does not speak about is at least as significant as what he does speak about, and lyrical poetry is another case in point.[37] He hardly mentions it in the *Poetics* and it is seldom that he speaks of traditional verse; when he does so, he either dismisses it as a minor appendage, for example when he identifies the poet *qua* poet by virtue of mimesis, or he subordinates it to the object simulated, for instance when he discusses what kind of meter is "natural" for what kind of mimesis (*Poetics* 1449a–31; compare Socrates' similar arguments about the "seemliness and unseemliness" of meter in *Republic* 3.400d–e). By minimizing the aural-oral and the performative aspects of poetry (rhythm, melody, and spectacle), Aristotle suppresses mimesis-play, or the side of poetry that has most to do with agon and power (note that in his eyes many of the shortcomings of individual tragedies are due to the fact that the poets composed them according to the demands of the poetic contest rather than those of logo-rational, structural unity). As Aristotle is well aware, this dark, Dionysian side points to the violent emotions, the irrational desires and the "sensuous attractions" that threaten the logo-rational order of both *psuchē* and *polis*. If encouraged they may lead to *dusnomia* and *adikia*, and eventually to moral and social disintegration. This is why archaic mimesis must be kept in check, controlled by the Logos, which purges it of arbitrariness, irrationality, and violence, imposing on it its own serene, "classical" rules of measure, order, beauty, and goodness (all of the latter being, as we have seen, interchangeable, median concepts). Aristotelian catharsis, then, can be seen not only as a purging of pity and fear by the arousal of these emotions, but also as the purification of tragedy itself, through the Logos, of any potentially threatening or unsettling elements.

37. On Aristotle's omission of lyrical poetry from the *Poetics*, see Dupont-Roc and Lallot, *ALP*, 21–22. The authors are fully aware of the rationalizing tendency present in the *Poetics*, but they account for this tendency largely in logical rather than historical terms. For example, they argue that Aristotle does not include lyrical poetry in the *Poetics* because it is not mimetic in a "dramatic" sense. It seems to me that Aristotle omits lyrical poetry from his treatise not because it is not "mimetic" but because it is too much so: lyrical poetry is the most stubborn and untameable vestige of *mousikē* or archaic mimesis-play, about which (rationalist) literary criticism has little to say. On the other hand, while largely excluding lyrical poetry from its theoretical discourse, literary criticism nevertheless regards it very highly, precisely because of its immediacy and imperviousness to critical analysis (Sartre's well-known essay "What is Literature?" is a perfect example of this rationalist attitude).

■ Politica, 7 *and* 8: *Aristotle's Politics of Art and Play*

Aristotle's view of art as playful simulation for a pleasurable end points to his logo-rational concept of play in general. In Aristotle we find the same polarization of the play concept that we find in Plato. Recreation and pastime are lower forms of pleasure, proper to poetic play. Intellectual diversion culminating in metaphysical speculation is the highest form of pleasure, proper to philosophy. Both seem to be ludic forms, but the lower form is strictly separated from and subordinated to the higher one. On the other hand, in contrast to Plato, Aristotle generally avoids calling the higher form *paidia*, and in his work the concept of play begins to lose its cultural and philosophical prestige not only in its archaic but also in its logo-rational aspect.

Aristotle discusses play particularly in books 7 and 8 of the *Politics*, in which he outlines his theory of education in response to (but also on the model of) that of Plato. Like his teacher, Aristotle considers education the most effective instrument of the rulers in attaining their political and cultural objectives. He equally acknowledges the importance of both physical games and mimetic art in shaping the mentality of the young and proposes legislation that would regulate these educational tools according to logo-rational principles. Unlike Plato, however, Aristotle seems, at least at first sight, to have a more tolerant attitude toward most forms of play and does not wish to exclude them from his ideal state. He nevertheless draws sharp distinctions among these play forms along social and moral lines, ultimately adopting, with minor variations, the same political and ethical program (behind which lies the same median concept of individual happiness as subordinated to communal well-being) that his teacher envisaged, particularly in the *Laws*.

Aristotle mentions play at the end of book 7, in connection with the education of infants up to the age of five. Although at this stage children should not be subjected to strenuous effort, they "need some movement to chase laziness [*argian*, also inactivity] from their body" (*Politics* 7.1336a26–27, trans. mine), and games are appropriate means to achieve this purpose. But these games must be neither disorderly (*aneimenas*) nor overexerting (*epiponous*), nor unbecoming for a free man (*Politics*, 7.1336a28–30). In a first stage, then, games appear as a prelude to gymnastics and are primarily connected to dynamic, physical movements that must, however, already be restrained and directed toward order and moderation.[38] But since these

---

38. No less than Socrates, Aristotle traces the origin of play as a whole (and *mousikē* in particular) to spontaneous movement that immediately becomes orderly. In the *Prob-*

games must also be worthy of free men, Aristotle clearly introduces a moral element in the play of infants, an element that will become increasingly important during later stages (for the education of *orexis* over and above that of the body, see *Politics* 1334b25–28, as well as *Nicomachean Ethics* 1128a16–22).

Fine art also has a role at this early stage, through the stories told to infants. As in Plato, the choice of these stories must not be left to the nurses (that is, to chance); rather, the *paidonomoi*, or the superintendents of education, must "determine the sort of tales and stories which children of this age ought to be told" (*Politics* 7.1336a30–31, trans. Barker). Although Aristotle does not specify what kind of fables the infants should be told (in Plato, we recall, these were beautiful, beneficial lies about the gods and heroes), he probably means stories conducive to military prowess and responsible citizenship. In any case, both games and stories must prepare the way for the infants' future occupations (and social status), and it is for this reason that, as in Plato, "infantile games should largely consist of simulations [*mimēseis*] of later serious tasks [*tōn husteron spoudazomenōn*]" (*Politics* 7.1336a33–34). The *paidonomoi* must constantly monitor the way in which the children amuse themselves, making sure that they spend as little time as possible in the company of slaves (*Politics* 7.1336a39–41). Significantly, Aristotle uses the word *diagōgē* in referring to the children's amusement or pastime. As a rule, *diagōgē* is translated as "cultivation of the mind" and indeed, in the *Politics*, the term usually refers to intellectual or cultural diversion (see, for instance, *Politics* 7.1339a25 and 29). In *Politics* 7.1336a40, however, *diagōgē* refers to infants and therefore must obviously be taken in a larger sense. The fact that Aristotle uses the term in relation to children seems to indicate that in everyday language *diagōgē* simply means "pastime" and is closely linked to play, amusement, despite Aristotle's later efforts to minimize this connotation in relation to the highest forms of cultural diversion (such as philosophical speculation; compare my discussion of the term in the *Poetics*). Aristotle seems again to give a common term a specialized, logo-rational or philosophical meaning, converting *diagōgē* from generic pastime into specific intellectual or cultural diversion.

---

lemata, for example, Aristotle says: "Why do all men delight in rhythm and melody and concords in general? Is it because we naturally rejoice in natural movements? This is shown by the fact that children rejoice in them as soon as they are born. Now we delight in the various types of melody for their moral character [*ethos*], but we delight in rhythm because it contains a familiar and ordered number and moves in a regular manner; *for ordered movement is naturally more akin to us than disordered, and is therefore more in accordance with nature*" (*Problemata*, 920b29–36, trans. E. S. Forster, emphasis added).

The *paidonomoi* must also see to it that children are not exposed to and do not practice "indecency" (*aneleutheria*, what is unworthy of a free man; compare *Republic* 3.395b8–e10), including shameful language (*aischrologia*). If the use of shameful language is to be forbidden, "it is obvious that we must do the same in the case of viewing [*theorein*] shameful pictures [*graphas*] and speech performances [*logous*]" (*Politics* 7.1336a13–14, trans. mine). The government should therefore prohibit the display of all shameful pictures and the performance of all shameful plays.[39] Aristotle nevertheless bows to common practice and relaxes these rules by allowing mature men, unaccompanied by their families, to attend certain religious and civic festivities, mostly connected with Dionysus, where "indecent" speech and acts were not unusual. The legislator should therefore forbid the viewing of mimes and comedies only to young persons "until they have reached the age when they are allowed to share with the older men in the right of reclining and taking wine at the common tables. By that time their education will have made them all immune from the evil effects of such performances" (*Politics* 7.1336b20–23, trans. Barker). Aristotle's position regarding archaic, Dionysian practices (of which the mime and old comedy seem to have been a part) is therefore not essentially different from that of Plato.[40]

39. In connection to "speech performances" (*logous*), Jean Aubonnet notes: "Il s'agit probablement de ces tirades indécentes que les acteurs mimaient et donnaient en spectacle aux auditeurs, telles qu'on en trouve dans la comédie et les iambes, dont Aristote parle à la 1.20. Au sujet de ces gens qui mêlent aux banquets de ces *paignia*, 'ludicra,' qui entremêlent propos scabreux et radotages frivoles, Plutarque (*Banquet* VII 8, 4 = *Mor.* 712 E) dit 'que la plupart font représenter, avec femmes et enfants impubères étendus à leur côté, des imitations d'actes ou de paroles qui agitent l'âme plus violemment que toute ivresse'" (*Aristote: Politique*, 3:325). Note Plutarch's (and Aubonnet's) logo-rational tone of disapproval of these archaic practices. Barker, on the other hand, notes: "Aristotle, beginning with the idea of protecting children from hearing bad language, allows himself to digress into the general problem of censorship, for old as well as for young. He takes censorship in his stride (as Plato had done before him), with little or no regard to our modern ideas of the artist's 'freedom' or to general 'freedom of thought'" (*Politics*, 330 n.1).

40. At the end of book 7, Aristotle again appears to invoke, in relation to education, the traditional argument that art partly completes nature. As in the case of the *Physics* and *Metaphysics*, however, the context in which Aristotle uses this argument does not seem to have anything to do with mimetic art, but with *technē* in general. He argues that "education, and art [in general], aim at filling up the deficiencies of nature" (*Politics* 7.1337a1). Note also that here he does not use the word *mimēsis*, which some translators arbitrarily supply from other contexts in which Aristotle describes *technē* as partial mimesis (compare *Physics* 8.199a15–17). Thus Barker writes: "The purpose of education, like that of art generally, is simply to copy nature by making her deficiencies good." By

In book 8 Aristotle raises the question of the four subjects that constitute the basis of education: reading and writing, drawing, physical training, and *mousikē*. The first two subjects are regarded as having practical utility, whereas physical education is generally thought to foster good health and military prowess. The object of training in *mousikē*, however, is "a matter of doubt and dispute." Although it is presently studied "as if its object were pleasure . . . the real reason which originally led to its being made a subject of education is something higher" (*Politics* 1337b27–32, trans. Barker). This something higher is the judicious employment of leisure, and here Aristotle draws a distinction between leisure (*scholē*), occupation (*ascholia*), and recreation (*anapausis*) or play (*paidia*). Leisure is the highest form of activity related to the speculative side of the logo-rational part of the soul and is pursued for its own sake.[41] Occupation is mostly related to the lower, practical side of the logo-rational part of the soul, being an activity that is pursued for the sake of something else (ultimately, for the sake of leisure). It is at this point that Aristotle departs from Plato, attempting to separate play (*paidia*) from leisure (*scholē*) by relating it to occupation:

> We can hardly fill our leisure with play. To do so would be to make play [*paidia*] the be-all and end-all of life [with due respect to Plato]. That is an impossibility. Play is a thing to be chiefly used in connexion with one side of life—the side of occupation. (A simple argument shows that this is the case. Occupation is the companion of work [*ponos*] and exertion: the worker needs relaxation [*anapausis*]: play is intended to provide relaxation.) We may therefore conclude that play and games should only be admitted into our state at the proper times and seasons, and should be applied as restoratives. (*Politics* 81337b36–41, trans. Barker)

bringing in the notion of mimesis, Barker needlessly garbles the meaning of the passage, which now seems to say that art "imitates" nature's way of making her deficiencies good—an obvious non sequitur. There is simply no good reason to believe that here Aristotle refers to the general concept of art as partial mimesis, let alone to mimetic art in particular.

41. Somewhat like Plato, Aristotle divides the soul into a lower and a higher part. The higher part is logo-rational, the lower part is not, but can obey the higher part. Whereas the lower part is associated with a violent life of war and contest, the higher part is associated with a life of peace and cooperation. The logo-rational part of the soul is in turn divided into a speculative and a practical one, the first being higher than the second (see *Politics*, 7.1333a16–b39). Like Plato, then, in his division of the soul Aristotle seemingly attempts again to subordinate the violent agonistic values of an archaic mentality to their median counterparts, and it is probably in this context that his discussion of *mousikē* in book 8 can best be understood.

As opposed to occupation, which needs the relaxation of play in order to attain pleasure, leisure is "intrinsic pleasure" and "intrinsic happiness" and hence it is pursued for its own sake. Its proper use involves the cultivation of the mind or intellectual diversion (*diagōgē*): *scholē* "is spent in *diagōgē*, and conversely *diagōgē* is pursued in and during *scholē*."[42]

It seems obvious, however, that for Aristotle pleasure is the common element of *paidia*, *scholē*, and *diagōgē*. He acknowledges this much when he says in relation to *mousikē*: "Amusement [*paidia*, play] is intended to produce relaxation; and relaxation which is in its nature a remedy for the pain produced in exertion, must necessarily contain the element of pleasure. Similarly, again, cultivation of the mind [*diagōgēn*, intellectual diversion, but also pastime] is generally agreed to have an element of pleasure as well as an element of nobility [*to kalon*, goodness]; and the spirit of true felicity [*eudaimonein*] is a spirit composed of both these elements" (*Politics* 8.1339b15–19, trans. Barker). In *mousikē*, play is that which both unites and separates occupation and leisure. By arguing that occupation exists for the sake of play and play for the sake of occupation, both existing for the sake of leisure, Aristotle moves in circles. This circularity becomes especially evident when Aristotle lists the benefits of *mousikē* as *paideia*, education, *katharsis*, release of emotion, and *diagōgē*, intellectual diversion, and then adds that the last benefit "may be linked with that of recreation and relaxation after exertion" (*Politics* 8.1341b41, trans. Barker, modified), that is, with play. Since *diagōgē* can also denote pastime in general, it is probably this common meaning that Aristotle has in mind here, a meaning that is, moreover, naturally related to *paidia*. Aristotle's argument thereby ends up in hopeless tautology.

Aristotle's tripartite division of leisure, play, and occupation may be

42. See Barker, *Politics*, 324. One should nevertheless remember that here Aristotle possibly uses *diagōgē* in a specialized, logo-rational sense (see my discussion of book 7 above). Barker also quotes Newman in connection with *scholē*, which is "employment in work desirable for its own sake—the hearing of noble music and no doubt noble poetry; intercourse with friends chosen for their worth; and *above all the exercise, in company or otherwise, of the speculative faculty*" (Newman's Greek edition of *The Politics* [Oxford, 1887–1902], 3:442; emphasis added). Like Aristotle, Newman avoids the word "play" in defining *scholē*, but unlike Aristotle and in true Victorian fashion, he introduces the idea of "work" into this definition. Newman also acknowledges that even though Aristotle regards the highest kind of music and the highest kind of poetry as worthy leisurely pursuits, he places the exercise of the speculative faculty (rational philosophy) above all such pursuits. For helpful discussions of the notion of leisure in Western thought see, among others, Josef Pieper, *Leisure: The Basis of Culture* (New York, 1952); Sebastian de Grazia, *Of Time, Work, and Leisure* (New York, 1962), which also briefly discusses Aristotle's *Politics* (11–21); and Joffre Dumazedier, *Le loisir et la ville* (Paris, 1962).

tautological but it is certainly not gratuitous: he attempts, like Plato, to redefine the Hellenic notion of pleasure in logo-rational, median terms. For example, Aristotle observes: "It is true that all are not equally agreed about the nature of the pleasure which accompanies felicity. Different persons estimate its nature differently, according to their own personality and disposition. But the highest pleasure, derived from the noblest sources, will be that of the man of greatest goodness" (*Politics* 1338a7–9; the key terms here are *aristos* and *ta kalista*, obviously interpreted in a logo-rational sense). Like Plato, then, Aristotle attempts to dissociate the highest pleasure from the lower part of the soul related to the world of violent contest and to associate it primarily with *sōphrosunē* and *dikaiosunē*, the virtues of the soul's highest logo-rational part. But in contrast to Plato, for Aristotle this separation also seems to involve the removal of play (*paidia*) from the highest region of the soul and its relegation to the lower regions, probably because play in general has been connected too long with the world of sensuous pleasures (including the pleasure of violent agon). The fact that here Aristotle does depart from Plato indicates not that his logo-rational goals are different from his teacher's but, on the contrary, that he probably finds the recent Platonic marriage between play and philosophy too precarious and wishes to put as much distance between the two as possible within a mentality where pleasure reigns supreme.

As long as both *diagōgē* and *scholē* remain inseparable from pleasure, however, they also remain inseparable from play. Only a modern mentality that strongly favors work over play, such as that of a predominantly Protestant, middle-class community, will be able to separate *diagōgē*, in the sense of intellectual diversion, from *paidia* and link it up with *ponos*, work, transforming *scholē*, leisure, into the hard labor of scholarship. In the wake of Aristotle this mentality will look upon play in utilitarian terms as a form of relaxation or the opposite of work, but it will also attach to play an element of shame or guilt that is certainly not present in Aristotle. Indeed, because Aristotle still lives in a predominantly aristocratic cultural environment, what he manages to accomplish is again not that different from Plato. Even though he no longer designates the highest activity of the mind (philosophical speculation) as *paidia*, in effect he nevertheless distinguishes between a higher, serious play of the logos and a lower, frivolous play of the senses, associating the first with the upper classes and the second with the commoners.[43]

43. The same distinctions reappear in German idealism once philosophical speculation is reconnected with play. For instance, Kant reintroduces the play concept in philosophical

Aristotle's ambivalent view of *mousikē* in the *Politics* again reveals both his unsuccessful attempt to divorce *paidia* from *diagōgē* and *scholē* and his tendency to transform his distinctions into hierarchies. In relation to *mousikē*, as we have seen, he seems initially to propose two separate distinctions: one according to its "effects" and one according to its "benefits." These distinctions shift around, however, and at times become interchangeable. For example, in book 8 Aristotle says that *mousikē* can serve the purposes of amusement and relaxation (*paidia*), of moral training, and of intellectual diversion (*Politics* 8.1339a11–1340b19). Later in the same book, he fuses *paidia* and *diagōgē*, adding *katharsis*, and seems to say that *mousikē* serves the purpose of both intellectual diversion and play, as well as catharsis, and moral training (*Politics* 8.1341a39–1342b26). The reason for this shift is obvious: play can now be subordinated to the proper use of *scholē* in intellectual diversion, and Aristotle's distinction becomes a hierarchy, with *katharsis* and *paidia* at the bottom, moral training in the middle, and intellectual diversion at the top of the scale.

This order of rank is also evident in Aristotle's classification of the various kinds of melodies. As we recall, he classifies them into ethical, action-inspiring, and passionate or enthusiastic. But he plainly ranks the ethical melodies above those of action and passion. It is only the ethical melodies that can be used for educational purposes. Aristotle emphasizes twice that only "those modes and melodies should be employed [for education] which are ethical, such as the Dorian . . . though we may include any others [that is, other *ethical* modes, not other modes in general, such as the action-inspiring or the purgative ones] which are approved by philosophers who have had a musical education" (*Politics* 8.1342a28–32, trans. Jowett; compare *Politics* 8.1342a1–7). Aristotle prefers the Dorian mode not only because it is the "gravest and manliest," but also, most importantly, because it is "a mean" between the other modes. Since "the extremes are to be avoided and the mean followed . . . it is evident that our youth should be taught the Dorian music" (*Politics* 8.1342b14–17, trans. Jowett).

On the other hand, Aristotle believes that certain melodies as well as "certain methods of teaching and learning music do really have a degrading effect" (*Politics* 8.1341a4–5, trans. Jowett), and predictably, it is the

speculation but stops short of openly calling this speculation *Spiel*, thus remaining close to Aristotle. On the other hand, Schiller "returns" to the Platonic view of play as the noblest and the most serious activity of reason. Finally, Nietzsche revives the notion of aristocratic *otium* (versus middle-class *negotium*) as the most important producer of high culture. See Spariosu, *Dionysus Reborn*, pt. 1, secs. 1 and 2.

action-inspiring and the enthusiastic melodies that turn out to have this effect. Aristotle even criticizes Plato for the "error of selecting the Phrygian mode as the only one to be kept along with the Dorian [for educational purposes]." He finds Plato's error all the more striking since the latter previously rejected the use of the flute, and justifiably so, because the effect of the flute, like that of the Phrygian mode, is "religious excitement and general emotion." This is exemplified in poetry, especially in the dithyramb, where "Dionysiac frenzy and all such agitations of the mind, are more naturally expressed by an accompaniment on the flute than by one on any other instrument" (*Politics* 8.1342b2–5, trans. Barker, slightly modified).

Both the flute and the Phrygian mode properly belong not to the ethical melodies but to those of action and passion, and now we begin to understand why in the *Poetics* Aristotle attempts to separate catharsis from *melopoiia* and link it to *muthos* as plot: he steers tragedy away from the dithyramb and from its violent, Dionysian aspects in general, attempting to associate it with median values instead. In mythical terms, he replaces Dionysus as the patron of tragedy (and *mousikē*) with a logo-rational Athena. At the end of the *Politics* he recounts, in the manner of Socrates, an appropriate myth about the invention of the flute, giving it a logo-rational interpretation: "There is a meaning also in the myth of the ancients which tells how Athene invented the flute and then threw it away. It was not a bad idea of theirs, that the Goddess disliked the instrument because it made the face ugly; but with still more reason may we say that she rejected it because the acquirement of flute-playing contributes nothing to the mind, since to Athene we ascribe both knowledge and art" (*Politics* 8.1341b3–8, trans. Jowett).

Aristotle rejects the flute as a useful tool in (logo-rational) education because it tends to induce religious frenzy, because it is not "expressive of moral character" (*Politics* 8.1341a21) and, above all, because "the impediment which the flute presents to the use of the voice detracts from its educational value" (*Politics* 8.1341a21–25, Jowett); in other words, the flute excludes the voice, that is, language as the only means of transmitting logical concepts.

Whereas ethical music serves the higher purposes of education or intellectual diversion, action-inspiring and enthusiastic music is reserved for the purpose of vulgar pleasure, and Aristotle draws a distinction between highbrow and lowbrow entertainment, which is the same as his distinction between serious and frivolous play. Significantly, he associates lowbrow entertainment with "professional instruments and the professional mode of education" in *mousikē*, and by "professional" he means "that which is adopted in contests." In contests "the performer practises the art, not for the sake of his own improvement, but in order to give pleasure, and that of a vulgar sort, to his hearers. For this reason the execution of such music is not the part of a free man but of a paid performer and the result is that the performers are vulgarized, for the end at which they aim is bad" (*Politics* 8.1341b10–15, trans. Jowett; see Aristotle's similar complaints about tragic contests in the *Poetics*; see also, Plato, *Republic* 3.399a1–e7 and *Laws* 3.700a7–d2). As opposed to competitive performances, educational ones must aim at achieving the "right measure," rather than excessive feats of execution merely for the sake of excelling (that is, merely for the sake of *aretē* in the archaic, agonistic sense). They should be carried to the point where the students "are able to feel delight in noble [*kalois*, also good] melodies and rhythm, and not merely in that common part of music in which every slave or child and even some animals find pleasure" (*Politics* 8.1341a13–17, trans. Jowett). Again, then, Aristotle sharply separates the higher pleasures of the intellect from the lower pleasures of the senses, including the pleasure of agon.[44]

44. Aristotle's attitude toward contests in general, however, is by no means free of contradictions. For example in the *Problemata*, he says regarding literary disputations: "Why are contentious disputations useful as a mental exercise? Is it because they involve frequent victories and defeats? They therefore quickly instil a spirit of rivalry; for, when men are victorious, they are induced by their joy to contend yet more, and, when they are defeated, they continue the struggle in hopes of turning defeat into victory. Those engaged in struggles of other kinds act in the same way, and so when fighting and getting the worst of it often refuse to come to terms" (*Problemata* 916b20–25, trans. Forster). The ambiguous, logo-rational vocabulary of Forster's translation reflects to some extent Aristotle's own, although here Aristotle seems ultimately to accept both literary and other kinds of contests as a "fact of life." Later, Aristotle again brings up the notion of competition when he attempts to distinguish between men of action and artists in terms of *mētis*: "Why do we talk of an orator, or a general, or a business man as being shrewd, but not use the term of a musician or of an actor? Is it because the powers of the two last are exercised apart from any desire of gaining an advantage (for their aim is pleasure), whereas the first three aim at some advantage? For a good orator or general or business man is one who can gain some advantage, and shrewdness consists mainly in getting the better of someone else" (*Problemata* 916b36–917a2). Here, again, Forster's translation gives the impression that Aristotle favors the actor and the musician over the man of action because they aim at pleasing rather than at obtaining an advantage. But it seems that Aristotle conducts his argument from the point of view of archaic *mētis*, of which he grudgingly approves. Like Socrates, however, he disapproves of contests in the domain

Aristotle operates, moreover, with a distinction between two kinds of audiences, one "free and educated, and the other a vulgar crowd composed of mechanics, laborers and the like" (*Politics* 8.1342a19–21, trans. Jowett). One derives pleasure from the lower world of the senses entangled in agon and excessive, irrational feelings, the other derives pleasure from intellectual diversion and median emotion. In contrast to Plato, Aristotle will allow both the lower and the higher kinds of entertainment in his ideal state, but on condition that they be segregated according to social class: "There ought to be contests and exhibitions instituted for the relaxation of the second class also. And the music [*mousikē*] will correspond to their minds; for as their minds are perverted from the natural state, so there are perverted modes and highly strung and unnaturally colored melodies. A man receives pleasure from what is natural to him, and therefore professional musicians may be allowed to practise this lower sort of music before an audience of a lower type" (*Politics* 8.1342a21–25).

Aristotle implicitly envisages a good (median) kind of contest versus a bad kind and, more generally, a good kind of play versus a bad kind. By allowing each audience its own kind of performance in principle, Aristotle can appear liberal and also circumvent the problems that arise from the agonistic context of *mousikē* and that Plato met head on. In practice, however, as long as artistic performances remain inextricably tied up to competition (during the religious festivals), only the lower kind of entertainment will be available in the theaters, as Aristotle himself often complains. Aristotle's problem thus does not go away: how can one bring *mousikē* up to logo-rational standards and at the same time preserve its competitive framework? Aristotle shows himself aware of this problem when he repeatedly stresses, in the *Poetics*, that tragedies can achieve their end through reading as well as performance, and one has the feeling that he would almost prefer doing away with performance altogether. Short of this radical solution, however, he can only envisage an intellectual kind of drama that would appeal to the superior (logo-rational) taste of the educated and that would presumably employ, in a right measure, the same melodies that are appropriate in education. This kind of drama is not readily available in his time, but may arise in the future through the education of the young according to median ideals ("the mean, the

---

of philosophy and science (see, for instance, *De caelo* 294b6–13), an attitude that may in turn have determined his position toward poetic contests in the *Poetics* and *Politics*.

possible, and the proper," the three cornerstones of Aristotelian poetics, which are also the last words of the *Politics*, 8.1342b34: *to te meson kai to dunaton kai to prepon*), or through the fruitful employment of leisure in intellectual diversion. It is the conditions of the possibility of logo-rational drama that Aristotle specifies in the *Poetics* under the guise of a descriptive, historical treatise on poetry.

Our brief examination of Aristotle's concept of play in the *Politics*, then, has led to the same conclusions that we have reached in our examination of Aristotle's concept of poetry in the *Poetics*. Aristotle, no less than Plato, favors the median forms of play over their archaic counterparts, which he rejects as culturally inferior and harmful. Moreover, Aristotle continues Plato's attempts to redefine archaic *mousikē* in logo-rational terms, thereby further contributing to its division into various disciplines. Some of these disciplines he classifies as "mimetic arts," separating them from the others on both epistemological and ethical grounds. Hence for Aristotle, as for Plato, poetry is an ambivalent form of play, resulting not in production but reproduction; not in true knowledge, but simulation thereof; not in a higher, philosophical pleasure, but mostly in a lower, sensuous kind. Under certain conditions, when it is purged of mimesis-play and placed under the guidance of the philosopher-critic, poetry may become the good play of the Logos. In the *Poetics*, this play assumes a peculiar, Aristotelian form of tragedy and epic, in which *muthos* becomes *logos*, participating in the logo-rational enjoyment or the higher pleasures of the ordering and classifying will. Play in general, however, loses a great deal of its cultural prestige in Aristotle, who is perhaps the first Western thinker who seeks to separate it from and oppose it to serious philosophical activity.

Finally, there certainly are considerable differences between Plato's and Aristotle's epistemological approaches, but these differences hardly affect the inferior cognitive value accorded to poetry by both philosophers. Granted that Aristotle does not exclude *mousikē* from his ideal state, he nevertheless censors and controls it as strictly, if more quietly, than Plato does. And like Plato, he subordinates it, through good and bad mimesis (and good and bad play in general) to logo-rational philosophy as the master *technē*. Plato still feels the need to prove that poetry tells lies, but Aristotle takes this proposition for granted and builds an entire poetics on it. He goes even farther than Plato, because in his scheme of things it is only poetic discourse that turns out to be a useful lie or fiction, while philosophy-science achieves the status of universal truth. Ironically, it will be only in Neoplatonism, during the Hellenistic period and after, that mimetic art will fuse with speculative thought, but still under the sign of Platonic mimesis. The poor cousin of rhetoric will become the little sister of philosophy, as the nearest sensuous embodiment of the Idea. But like the vengeful ghost of Hamlet's slain father, poetry as archaic play will return to haunt philosophy, from the Church fathers to the German idealists, and from Nietzsche to Heidegger to the contemporary artist-metaphysicians.

Index

About the Author
Mihai Spariosu is Professor of Comparative Literature at the University of Georgia at Athens. His books include *Dionysus Reborn: Play and the Aesthetic Dimension in Modern Philosophical and Scientific Discourse* and *Literature, Mimesis, and Play: Essays in Literary Theory*. He has published many essays and articles on philosophy and literary theory and is director of *The Margins of Literature* series and coeditor of the *Cultura ludens* series.

Library of Congress Cataloging-in-Publication Data
Spariosu, Mihai.
God of many names : play, poetry, and power in Hellenic thought from Homer to Aristotle / Mihai I. Spariosu.
Includes bibliographical references and index.
ISBN 0–8223–1127–5 (cloth).—ISBN 0-8223-1146-1 (paper)
1. Play (Philosophy)—History. 2. Power (Philosophy)—History. 3. Philosophy, Ancient. 4. Poetics. 5. Greek literature—History and criticism. I. Title
B187.P55S62   1991
128—dc20   90–46298 CIP